EUROSTUDIA
Vol. 7, No. 1-2 (2011)

Editors
Mathieu Denis
Ulrich Ufer

L'Allemagne et l'Europe: frontières et passeurs
Deutschland und Europa: Grenzen und Grenzgänge(r)
Germany and Europe: Borders, and how to cross them

Études présentées lors de la Conférence interdisciplinaire des Centres d'études allemandes et européennes de l'Office Allemand d'Échanges Universitaires (DAAD), tenue à Berlin en 2010

Ausgewählte Beiträge der interdisziplinären Konferenz der DAAD-Zentren für Deutschland- und Europastudien 2010 in Berlin

Selected contributions from the Berlin 2010 interdisciplinary Conference of the Centers for German and European Studies of the German Academic Exchange Service (DAAD)

DAAD

WZB

Centre canadien d'études
allemandes et européennes

SHAKER
VERLAG

Bibliographic information published by the Deutsche Nationalbibliothek
The Deutsche Nationalbibliothek lists this publication in the Deutsche Nationalbibliografie; detailed bibliographic data are available in the Internet at http://dnb.d-nb.de.

Printed in Germany.

ISBN 978-3-8440-0223-2
ISSN 1718-8946

Shaker Verlag GmbH • P.O. BOX 101818 • D-52018 Aachen
Phone: 0049/2407/9596-0 • Telefax: 0049/2407/9596-9
Internet: www.shaker.de • e-mail: info@shaker.de

Table des matières / Inhalt / Contents

Eurostudia, Vol. 7, No. 1-2 (2011)

Deutschland und Europa: Grenzen und Grenzgänge(r).
Ausgewählte Beiträge der interdisziplinären Konferenz der DAAD-Zentren für Deutschland- und Europastudien 2010 in Berlin

Editors: Mathieu Denis and Ulrich Ufer

Avant-Propos / Begleitwort / Preface

Il nous fait grand plaisir de vous inviter à lire ce numéro spécial de la revue *Eurostudia.* Il s'agit en effet d'un numéro tout à fait exceptionnel, soit le premier à paraître sous forme imprimée. Fondée en 2004 par Dietmar Köveker, qui était à l'époque professeur invité du DAAD au Centre canadien d'études allemandes et européennes à l'Université de Montréal, *Eurostudia* est une revue électronique avec comité de lecture qui publie des articles en français, anglais et allemand. Elle se distingue par ses perspectives pluri- et interdisciplinaires sur les études européennes comprises dans leur sens le plus large ; la revue a réussi à attirer des contributions de jeunes chercheurs, d'universitaires établis et de personnalités publiques bien connues des deux côtés de l'Atlantique.

La publication d'une sélection des textes présentés au colloque « Deutschland und Europa : Grenzen und Grenzgänge(r) », qui a réuni, en mai 2010 au Centre Scientifique de Berlin pour la Recherche en Sciences Sociales (WZB), des chercheurs du réseau mondial des Centres d'études allemandes et européennes soutenus par le DAAD ainsi que d'autres experts internationaux de l'Allemagne et de l'Europe, offre à *Eurostudia* l'occasion de se relancer et de se faire mieux connaître à l'échelle mondiale. Jusqu'à maintenant accessible par le biais de la plateforme électronique *Érudit,* qui lui assure une vaste distribution au sein de la francophonie, *Eurostudia* est désormais disponible en accès libre : www.cceae.umontreal.ca/-revue-Eurostudia-.

Avant de vous souhaiter bonne lecture, nous tenons à remercier le Dr. Mathieu Denis et le professeur invité du DAAD Ulrich Ufer d'avoir dirigé ce numéro.

Es freut uns sehr, den Lesern diesen Sonderband der Zeitschrift *Eurostudia* präsentieren zu können, der um so mehr als Sonderband gelten darf, als er der erste in Buchform veröffentlichte Band von *Eurostudia* ist. Der ehemalige DAAD-Gastprofessor am Kanadischen Zentrum für Deutschland- und Europastudien an der Universität von Montreal, Dietmar Köveker, gründete *Eurostudia* 2004 als online-Zeitschrift mit peer-review Prozess, in der Artikel auf Englisch, Französisch und Deutsch veröffentlicht werden. Die Zeitschrift ist seither bekannt für ihre multi- und interdisziplinären Beiträge zu den Europastudien. Unter den Beiträgern finden sich sowohl renommierte Wissenschaftler wie auch Nachwuchsforscher und bekannte Vertreter des öffentlichen Lebens von beiden Seiten des Atlantiks.

Dieser Sonderband beinhaltet eine Auswahl von Texten, die im Mai 2010 auf der Konferenz „Deutschland und Europa: Grenzen und Grenzgänge(r)" am Wissenschaftszentrum Berlin für Sozialforschung (WZB) von Wissenschaftlern aus dem weltweiten Netzwerk der durch den DAAD geförderten Zentren für Deutschland- und Europastudien und weiteren internationalen Deutschland- und

Europaforschern als Vorträge präsentiert wurden. Wir hoffen, mit diesen Beiträgen das Interesse eines noch breiteren, internationalen Publikums anzuziehen. Die bisher hauptsächlich in der frankophonen Wissenschaftswelt über die elektronische Plattform *Érudit* zugängliche Gesamtausgabe von Eurostudia ist nun auch komplett und kostenfrei über folgende Adresse zugänglich: http://www.cceae.umontreal.ca/-revue-Eurostudia-.

Wir wünschen allen Lesern dieser und weiterer Ausgaben von *Eurostudia* eine inspirierende Lektüre. Wir bedanken uns auch bei Dr. Mathieu Denis und DAAD-Gastprofessor Ulrich Ufer, die dieses Sonderheft herausgegeben haben.

We are pleased to invite you to read this special issue of the journal *Eurostudia*. It is indeed a very special issue, namely the first to be published in paper format. Founded in 2004 by Dietmar Köveker, at the time DAAD Visiting Professor at the Canadian Centre for German and European Studies at Université de Montréal, *Eurostudia* is an on-line peer-reviewed journal that publishes articles in English, French, and German. The journal has made a name for itself thanks to its multi- and interdisciplinary approach to European studies in their broadest sense; it has succeeded in attracting contributions from younger scholars, established academics, and public figures well-known on both sides of the Atlantic.

With the publication in this special issue of a selection of texts presented at the "Deutschland und Europa: Grenzen und Grenzgänge(r)" conference, which brought together, in May 2010 at the Social Science Research Center Berlin (WZB), scholars from the world-wide network of Centres for German and European Studies supported by the DAAD and other experts on Germany and Europe, *Eurostudia* wishes to take advantage of the occasion to relaunch the journal and to reach out to an even broader international readership. Until now available through the electronic platform *Érudit*, with outstanding visibility in the francophone world, the entire contents of *Eurostudia* is now available in full and free access http://www.cceae.umontreal.ca/-revue-Eurostudia-.

Before wishing you much pleasure in your reading, we would like to thank Dr. Mathieu Denis and DAAD Visiting Professor Ulrich Ufer for having edited this issue.

Laurence McFalls
Directeur
Centre canadien d'études allemandes et européennes
Université de Montréal

Annette Julius
Leiterin der Programmabteilung Nord/
Director Northern Hemisphere Department
Deutscher akademischer Austauschdienst/
German Academic Exchange Service
Bonn

VORWORT DES WISSENSCHAFTLICHEN KONFERENZBEIRATES

Yuichi Morii
Zentrum für Deutschland- und Europastudien, Universität Tokyo, Komaba (DESK)

Barbara Thériault
Centre canadien d'études allemandes et européennes (CCEAE), Université de Montréal

Michael Werner
Centre interdisciplinaire d'études et de recherches sur l'Allemagne (CIERA) / EHESS

Die Beiträge des vorliegenden Bandes gehen aus der Konferenz „Deutschland und Europa: Grenzen und Grenzgänge(r)" hervor, die der Deutsche Akademische Austauschdienst (DAAD) in Kooperation mit dem Wissenschaftszentrum Berlin für Sozialforschung (WZB) im Mai 2010 in Berlin veranstaltete.

Die Konferenz stellt ein Novum dar: Erstmals tauschten sich die Forscher an den zwanzig interdisziplinären Zentren für Deutschland- und Europastudien, die der DAAD seit 1991 in elf Ländern auf drei Kontinenten initiierte und fördert(e), über ein Querschnittsthema der Deutschland- und Europastudien fachlich aus. Angesprochen wurden mit der Ausschreibung der „Grenzen- und Grenzgänge(r)"-Konferenz (Nachwuchs-)Wissenschaftlerinnen und Wissenschaftler an den DAAD-Zentren in den USA, Kanada, Großbritannien, Frankreich, den Niederlanden, Polen, Bulgarien, der Russischen Föderation, China, Japan und Israel, darüber hinaus aber auch weitere Kreise in- und ausländischer Deutschlandexpertinnen und -experten aus unterschiedlichen Disziplinen der Geistes-, Kultur- und Sozialwissenschaften, um den vielstimmigen und – wie sich in Berlin zeigte: höchst lebendigen – Dialog über dieses Kernthema aktueller Deutschland- und Europastudien auch in diesem Sinne „über die Grenzen hinweg" zu führen. Ein zentrales Anliegen der Konferenz war es also, bezogen auf die Leitthematik, in und mit diesem Teilnehmer- und Referentenkreis eine Kombination der Blicke von außen und von innen auf Deutschland und Europa herzustellen und die in den vom DAAD geförderten Zentren gesammelten Ressourcen in einen fruchtbaren Austausch mit deutschen und internationalen Wissenschaftlerinnen und Wissenschaftlern zu bringen. Die Zusammenarbeit mit dem WZB als einer der führenden interdisziplinären und internationalen Forschungseinrichtungen in Deutschland bildete dabei eine ideale Partnerschaft. Es erschien uns zudem besonders wichtig, junge Forscherinnen und Forscher aktiv in das Berliner Forum einzubeziehen: Die Impulse, die wir aus den

Interessen und Zugängen der Nachwuchswissenschaftlerinnen und Nachwuchswissenschaftler beziehen können, sind für die Produktivität und die kontinuierliche Weiterentwicklung unserer *academic community* unverzichtbar; umgekehrt ist der Austausch für junge Wissenschaftlerinnen und Wissenschaftler im internationalen Umfeld der Deutschland- und Europastudien ein wesentlicher Schritt in die akademische Zukunft. Gleichzeitig spiegelte sich in der Begegnung erfahrener und junger Forscherinnen und Forscher auf der Berliner Konferenz ein verbindendes Element aller DAAD-Zentren wider: Sie bündeln in ihren jeweiligen Ländern nicht nur die wissenschaftliche Beschäftigung mit Deutschland und Europa und vermitteln diese oft auch an eine breitere Öffentlichkeit, sie alle engagieren sich darüber hinaus mit innovativen, interdisziplinären Master- und Doktoratsstudiengängen für die Ausbildung einer jungen Expertengeneration.

Die von uns für die Konferenz formulierte Leitthematik „Grenzen und Grenzgänge(r)" zielte darauf, neue Forschungen in diesem in den vergangenen zwei Jahrzehnten viel bearbeiteten und für Deutschland und Europa besonders relevanten Themenfeld zur Diskussion zu stellen und verschiedene disziplinäre Zugangsweisen zu verknüpfen. Die Diskussion um Grenzziehung, Grenzräume, Überwindung von und Umgang mit Grenzen wurde und wird in den einzelnen Fächern der Sozial- und Kulturwissenschaften unterschiedlich geführt. Die wissenschaftlichen Disziplinen haben verschiedene Perspektiven entwickelt, die bislang nur unzureichend miteinander kommunizieren. Die gegenseitige Kenntnis umeinander und den Austausch über unterschiedliche Zugänge zu fördern, bildete daher ein weiteres Hauptanliegen der Konferenz, von dem die hier publizierten, ausgewählten Beiträge ein beredtes Zeugnis ablegen. Mit den Stichworten „Grenzgänge" und „Grenzgänger" rückten sowohl das gesellschaftliche, politische und kulturelle Handeln an und mit Grenzen als auch dessen Akteure in den Mittelpunkt des Interesses.

Die Diskussion des übergreifenden Konferenzthemas wurde in Berlin in sieben Themenfelder aufgefächert, die keinen disziplinspezifischen Vorgaben folgten, wenngleich manche das eine oder andere Fach mehr angesprochen haben mögen. Im Themenfeld „Grenzen und Grenzräume" konzentrierte sich die Debatte auf binneneuropäische Grenzräume als Aktionszusammenhänge und die Auswirkungen grenzübergreifender Kontakte auf Identitäts- und Gruppenbildungsprozesse sowie auf die Hinterfragung des politischen Umgangs mit Grenzräumen (siehe die Beiträge von Leslie/Clunan und Opiłowska). Darüber hinaus wurde die Leitthematik auf das dynamische Konzept der „kulturellen Räume" bezogen, das die Vorstellung geschlossener Kulturräume ablöst, und insbesondere in Hinblick auf Berlin seit 1989 untersucht wurde (siehe die Beiträge von Thijs und Sheffi). Einen weiteren Schwerpunkt bildete die Beschäftigung mit „literarischen Grenzgänge(r)n" in Deutschland und Europa, deren Hintergründe, Entwicklungen und Auswirkungen untersucht wurden (siehe die Beiträge von Colvin, Ma, Simo und Wolff). Grenze und Grenzgänger bilden darüber hinaus klassische Gegenstände der

Migrationsforschung, einem anderen Themenschwerpunkt der Konferenz, bei dem Eigenheiten im Verhältnis von Minderheiten und Mehrheiten in Deutschland und Europa herausgearbeitet wurden (siehe den Beitrag von Akiyama). Die damit verbundenen unterschiedlichen Aspekte „transnationaler Identitäten" wurden ebenfalls in den Blick genommen (siehe die Beiträge von Jürgens und v. Mering), etwa – aber nicht nur – mit der Frage, welche Effekte nationale Integrationspolitiken auf die Entstehung oder Abwesenheit „transnationaler Identitäten" in modernen europäischen Gesellschaften zeitigen (siehe den Beitrag von Williams). Der Blick auf die „Grenzen Europas" erlaubte die Auseinandersetzung u. a. mit den neuen Außengrenzen der EU (siehe den Beitrag von Tomaszewska). Beiträge zur „Transformation von Staatlichkeit" untersuchten Natur und Ausmaß der Veränderungen, die der Nationalstaat im Europa der letzten Jahrzehnte erfahren hat, und beleuchteten Perspektiven für das 21. Jahrhundert (siehe die Beiträge von Escach und Wissel).

Wir freuen uns, dass es gelungen ist, eine repräsentative Auswahl der Konferenzbeiträge im vorliegenden Sonderheft von *Eurostudia* einem breiteren Publikum zugänglich zu machen. Wir sind sicher, dass sich daraus zahlreiche Anregungen für die weitere, interdisziplinäre Beschäftigung mit Deutschland und Europa ergeben.

Tokyo, Montréal, Paris, im März 2011

VOICES FROM THE BORDERLANDS
Women Writing from Prison in Germany and Beyond

Sarah Colvin
Institute for German Studies, University of Birmingham

> *The born female criminal is, so to speak, doubly exceptional, first as a woman and then as a criminal. This is because criminals are exceptions among civilized people, and women are exceptions among criminals. [...] As a double exception, then, the criminal woman is a true monster.*[1]

Prisons tend to be invisible, on the margins of the community and, if not entirely out of sight, largely out of mind. Prisons are border zones in the sense that they are liminal spaces between the community and, in some times and places, banishment or death. When immigrants or asylum seekers are expelled then those whom the community has rejected are literally shifted across borders. Where capital punishment is legal, prison can be the border between life and death.

I am not the first to suggest that women in prison can be read as doubly marginalized.[2] Angela Davies wrote of the "hyperinvisibility" of women prisoners,[3] who disappear, as Diana Medlicott explains, even inside the invisible system: "Concealed within the hidden institution of the prison is the women's prison population, an even more shadowy phenomenon that has generally been [...] subsumed, in terms of policy needs, into the male prison population."[4] Yet criminal women, particularly the small minority who commit violent crimes, seem doubly visible in the cultural imagination. The contemporary media still reproduce Lombroso's and Ferrero's notion that criminal women are monstrous;[5] in Ann Lloyd's words, they are "doubly deviant" and "doubly damned."[6]

---

[1] Cesare Lombroso and Gugliemo Ferrero, *Criminal Woman, the Prostitute, and the Normal Woman (1893)*, trans. by Nicole Hahn Rafter and Mary Gibson (Durham: Duke University Press, 2004), 185.
[2] See e.g. Judith Scheffler, *Wall Tappings: An International Anthology of Women's Prison Writings, 200 to the Present*, 2nd edn. (New York: The Feminist Press at the City University of New York, 2002), xxii.
[3] Angela Davies, foreword in Michael Jacobson Harvey, *Behind the Razor Wire: Portrait of a Contemporary American Prison System* (New York: New York UP, 1999), xi.
[4] Diana Medlicott, "Women in Prison," in *Handbook on Prisons*, ed. Yvonne Jewkes (Cullompton: Willan, 2007), 246.
[5] Compare Yvonne Jewkes, *Media and Crime* (London: Sage, 2004), 107-138.
[6] Ann Lloyd, *Doubly Deviant, Doubly Damned: Society's Treatment of Violent Women* (London: Penguin, 1995).

EUROSTUDIA — REVUE TRANSATLANTIQUE DE RECHERCHE SUR L'EUROPE
Vol. 7, No.1-2 (2011): 1-11

In this essay I will engage with the study of women prisoners as overlooked objects,[7] to set that research alongside the cultural fetishization of female criminality (rarely mentioned in reports that focus on hard data), and finally to address the subjective responses of women prisoners to their situation in "the marginal texts too often lost in the marginal literature of the prison."[8] Like some others I will suggest that women's experience of prison and of themselves as prisoners needs to be understood as an experience simultaneously of the real (the conditions of their imprisonment) and the ideal (sociocultural constructions of womanhood, motherhood, violence, and crime);[9] but I am also asking: how do women in prison negotiate their experience of marginalization and stigma, as writers?

1. WOMEN AND PRISON

In the ten years between 1992 and 2002 the male prison population in the UK increased by 50% while the female prison population increased by 173%.[10] In Cyprus the population of women prisoners increased by 410% over the same period.[11] Nonetheless, a report for the European Parliament in 2008 noted that women in Europe still constitute an average of only 4.5% to 5.0% of the total prison population (from 2.9% in Poland to 7.8% in Spain),[12] and find themselves "confined in a system essentially designed, built and run by men for men."[13] Prisons are micro-communities that reflect and intensify the structures and practices of the societies they border on,[14] and women in prison, like women almost everywhere, are measured against a masculine norm. Female prisoners are held to be a lower security risk

---

[7] See e.g. Holly Dustin (ed.), *Women and the Criminal Justice System: A Report of the Fawcett Society's Commission on Women and the Criminal Justice System* (London: Fawcett Society, 2004); Frieder Dünkel, Claudia Kestermann and Juliane Zolondek (eds.), *Reader: International Study on Women's Imprisonment. Current Situation, Demand Analysis and "Best Practice"* (University of Greifswald, 2005); Quaker Council for European Affairs, *Women in Prison: A Review of the Conditions in Member States of the Council of Europe* (Brussels: QCEA, February 2007); Marie Panayotopoulos-Cassidou, *Report on the Situation of Women in Prison and the Impact of the Imprisonment of Parents on Social and Family Life*. Committee on Women's Rights and Gender Equality (Brussels: European Parliament, 2008); Kings College London International Centre for Prison Studies, *International Profile of Women's Prisons* (London, April 2008); Sharon Smee (ed.), *Engendering Justice – from Policy to Practice: Final Report of the Commission on Women and the Criminal Justice System* (London: Fawcett Society, 2009).

[8] Scheffler, *Wall Tappings*, xv.

[9] Compare Medlicott, "Women in Prison," 246.

[10] Dustin (ed.), *Women and the Criminal Justice System*, 5.

[11] Quaker Council, *Women in Prison*, 5.

[12] www.europarl.europa.eu/oeil/FindByProcnum.do?lang=en&procnum=INI/2007/2116. The report is drawing on figures cited in 2005 by Dünkel, Kestermann, and Zolondek (eds) in their *International Study on Women's Imprisonment*, 3.

[13] Panayotopoulos-Cassiotou, *Report on the Situation of Women in Prison*, 4.

[14] Compare James Thompson, "Introduction," in *Prison Theatre: Perspectives and Practices*, ed. James Thompson (London: Jessica Kingsley, 1998), 9.

and less aggressive than their male counterparts,[15] although given the high levels of self-harming among women prisoners[16] we should perhaps not be denying the existence of aggression so much as asking questions about where aggression is being directed. Women are also overrepresented as drug users in the prison population, where drug use in prisons is already significantly higher than in the population at large. Menstruation is still perceived as an oddity for which "special" hygiene arrangements must be put in place;[17] but the clearest indication that prison is conceived and designed as a space to contain men is the system's helplessness in the face of pregnancy, birth, and childcare. The average age of imprisoned women in Europe is between 20 and 40 and in 2008 a half of all women in European prisons were mothers, many of whom had sole responsibility for their children as lone parents prior to their arrest.[18] The small number of women prisoners overall means a small number of single-sex prisons and this situation increases the likelihood of women being held at some distance from their families.[19] When Marie Panayotopoulos-Cassiotou presented her report (on behalf of the Committee for Women's Rights and Gender Equality) on the situation of women in European prisons to the European Parliament, responding MEPs showed particular concern on the reproductive issue: how are prisons to accommodate pregnant and breastfeeding women, and the growing children of mothers who offend?[20] Without question there are practical issues associated with imprisonment, pregnancy and childcare that need to be addressed. That the reproductive question was the burning issue in the minds of European parliamentarians reflects (I would suggest) the *ideal* as well as the real; effective parenting ensures the future of the species but specifically *maternal* nurturing is the ideological pillar of "safe" family structures that are the discursive microcosms of a "safe" society. The single most positive role ascribed to women across Europe and the world is childcare, and factors around dependants are more likely to affect the sentencing of women than any other factor.[21]

---

[15] Katherine van Wormer, *Working with Female Offenders: A Gender-Sensitive Approach* (Hoboken, NJ: Wiley, 2010), 4.

[16] "Outside prison men are more likely to commit suicide than women but the position is reversed inside prison, and self-harm in prison is a huge problem and more prevalent among women in prison." Quaker Women in Prison Project Group, *Women in Prison and the Children of Imprisoned Mothers: A Briefing for Friends* (London, August 2007), 9.

[17] Dünkel, Kestermann, and Zolondek, *International Study on Women's Imprisonment*, 12.

[18] Panayotopoulos-Cassiotou, *Report on the Situation of Women in Prison*, 13, 15. In the UK in 2004, 66% of imprisoned women were mothers, at least one-third of those lone parents; see Medlicott, "Women in Prison," 255.

[19] See the Quaker Women in Prison Project Group, *Women in Prison*.

[20] "The preservation of family ties and the necessity to create adequate infrastructures for women and their children in conformity with national legislation constituted the common denominator of the interventions of MEPs." mariepanayotopouloscassiotouen.blogspot.com/2008_04_01_archive.html, accessed 6 January 2011.

[21] Medlicott, "Women in Prison," 252; C. Hedderman and L. Gelsthorpe, *Understanding the Sentencing of Women: Home Office Research Study* (London: Home Office, 1997), 170.

2. Bad Mothers: The Subjects of Guilt and Shame

The idea of the bad mother is, then, both an existential and a social threat, and it attracts particular attention, even revulsion. Describing a project with women in German prisons in the late 1970s, researchers Uta Klein and Gertrud Hardtmann highlight the theme of guilt ("die Schuldfrage") that characterized women's self-perception.[22] Indeed, guilt is a remarkably consistent theme in the self-perception of women prisoners over time and across national boundaries, and this sense of guilt often centers on the issue of maternal failure. "Le sentiment de culpabité est très présent chez l'ensemble des mères" (the sense of culpability is very present among the mothers) reports Juliette Laganier, who observed women inmates of France's Fleury-Mérogis prison in the early 2000s.[23] "Mütter im Knast: "Ich habe schwere Schuld auf mich geladen"" (Mothers in Prison: "I'm weighed down with guilt"), the northern German *Hamburger Abendblatt* titled an article in 2009 about Germany's progressive mother-and-baby units,[24] while a similar article called "Doing time with Mum" a few months later in the UK's *Guardian* newspaper opens: "Kelly Bendall feels appallingly guilty that her baby daughter started life in prison."[25] Research completed for the EU Directorate-General in 2005 observes that

> motherhood featured as a topic of foundational importance in many of the interviewed women's narratives about their lives, and especially, in their discussions about the pains of imprisonment. The feeling of failure as mother, and guilt feeling were especially strong, as evidenced by all national reports. [...] Fears that children would turn away from their criminal mother were also discussed in some cases.

Imprisonment, the authors concluded, "causes serious ruptures in the life of women due to separation from their children, which becomes a key source of everyday stress, guilt feelings, worrying and experience of failure."[26] Concern for their children is cited by women in custody as one of the most influential factors in depression, anxiety, and self-harm.[27]

Women prisoners write a great deal about the experience of both guilt and shame. In the mid 1980s, in a poem with the title "Meine Gedanken" (My Thoughts), the imprisoned Irene Dreier wrote the following poem to a child:

---

[22] Gertrud Hardtmann, "Straftäter müßte man sein," in *Frauen im Gefängnis*, ed. Marlis Dürkop and Gertrud Hardtmann (Frankfurt a.M.: Suhrkamp, 1978), 167.

[23] Juliette Laganier, "La maternité en milieu carcéral," *Lettre de Genepi* 64 (2003).

[24] Hanna-Lotte Mikuteit, "Mütter im Knast: 'Ich habe schwere Schuld auf mich geladen,'" *Hamburger Abendblatt*, 9 May 2009.

[25] Beth Gardiner, "Doing Time with Mum," *The Guardian*, 19 December 2009.

[26] Marta Cruells and Noelia Igareda, *Women, Integration and Prison: An Analysis of the Processes of Sociolabour Integration of Women Prisoners in Europe* (EU Directorate-General for Research, September 2005), 40.

[27] Panayotopoulos-Cassiotou, *Report on the Situation of Women in Prison*, 16.

> Meine Gedanken
> drehen sich
> um Dich –
> mein Kind!
> Durch meine Haft
> nahm ich dir
> ein Stück
> von Deinem Leben
> Ich bitte Dich
> versuch
> mir zu verzeihen.[28]
> (My thoughts revolve around you, my child! When I went to prison I took away a piece of your life. I ask you to try to forgive me).

Even a political prisoner like the Argentinian Alicia Partnoy, whose criminal "guilt," like that of all political prisoners, is relative to the view of the regime that incarcerated her, feels a need to explain herself, in poetic "letters" to her eighteen-month-old daughter from prison:

> Dear gentle heart, new eyes.
> Listen: [...]
> The reason is so very simple:
> I could not
> keep from fighting for the happiness
> of those who are our brothers and sisters.[29]

But the pressure is external as well as internal: "Ich weiß, viele werden mich als *Rabenmutter* bezeichnen" (I know lots of people will call me a wicked mother) worries Patricia, a 27-year-old mother in prison whose son was in the care of his grandparents at the time of her interview in the early 2000s.[30]

In psychology, guilt is often grouped among the "self-conscious" family of emotions, alongside shame, embarrassment, and pride, whereby guilt and shame are particularly closely related emotions (often to the extent of being confused with one another).[31] Research suggests that subjects who describe shame focus on others' evaluations of the self, where guilty experiences are focused on the respondents' effect on others. Shame involves

> a negative evaluation of the global self; guilt involves a negative evaluation of a particular behavior. [...] this differential emphasis on self ("*I* did that horrible thing")

[28] Irene Dreier, "Meine Gedanken," in *Laßt mich leben: Frauen im Knast*, ed. Luise Rinser (Hagen: Padligur, 1987), 114.

[29] Alicia Partnoy, "To My Daughter (Letters from Prison)," in *Wall Tappings*, ed. Scheffler, 195.

[30] Patricia, "Links ein Teufel, rechts ein Engel," in *Die schlimmsten Gitter sitzen innen: Geschichten aus dem Frauenknast*, ed. Katrin Panier (Berlin: Schwarzkopf & Schwarzkopf, 2004), 154.

[31] See e.g. June Price Tangney and Kurt W. Fischer (eds.), *Self-Conscious Emotions: The Psychology of Shame, Guilt, Embarrassment, and Pride* (New York: Guildford Press, 2007).

> versus behavior ("I *did* that horrible thing") sets the stage for very different emotional experiences.[32]

The emotional experience of shame is considered more painful even than guilt,

> because one's core self – not simply one's behavior – is at stake. Feelings of shame are typically accompanied by a sense of shrinking or of "being small" and by a sense of worthlessness or powerlessness. Shamed people also feel exposed [...] there is often the imagery of how one's defective self would appear to others.[33]

Shame and guilt are of course often experienced in parallel. In a recent collection of biographical prisoner narratives from Germany, nineteen-year-old Stefanie recalls feeling torn between two possible paths of action, one of which is guilt-driven, the other shame-driven:

> Oft stand ich vor der Polizeiwache. Ich wollte hineingehen und sagen: "Nehmt mich fest! Ich hab ihn umgebracht." Aber ich konnte nicht hineingehen. Es ging nicht! Ich dachte an die Familie – an meinen Bruder, an meine Mutter. [34]
> (I often went and stood in front of the police station. I wanted to go inside and say "arrest me! I killed him." But I couldn't go in. I just couldn't! I thought of my family – of my brother, my mother.)

In this account, guilt drives Stefanie to the police; but shame, projected on to her family, prevents her from confessing (she focuses on their, rather than her own, experience of other people's reactions if her crime becomes known). Her eventual sentencing addresses her guilt but not her shame: "Ich habe mich so geschämt" (I was so ashamed) is her recollection of her feelings on going to prison.

Social pressure on women and girls to "be good" means that women offenders bear a particular burden of shame. Interviews with, and biographical texts by, women in prison often describe a consciousness of being publicly shamed through criminalization. A poem called "Patchwork" anticipates its author's release; but release into the mainstream social context is coded as an experience of shame:

> irgendwann werde ich vor den toren stehen
> rufe mir ein taxi
> nehme mir ein zimmer im hotel
> und maskiere mein gesicht
> daß niemand die spuren darin liest[35]
> (one day I'll stand in front of the gates, call a taxi, take a room in a hotel, and cover my face, so that no-one can read the telltale signs)

---

[32] June Price Tangney, Jeff Stuewig and Debra J. Mashek, "Moral Emotions and Moral Behavior," *Annual Review of Psychology* 58 (2007): 349.

[33] Ibid.

[34] "Stefanie, 19 Jahre," in *Knast: Eine Dokumentation*, ed. Brigitte and Dieter Kübbeler (Oldenburg, 2003), 97, 102.

[35] Barbara W., "Patchwork," in *Rückkehr in die Freiheit: Ängste und Hoffnungen. Gefangene schreiben*, ed. Hans Jürgen Lehmann (Bonn: Bundeszusammenschluß für Straffälligenhilfe, 1981), 46.

3. Bad Girls

In the late nineteenth century, the new science of criminology developed alongside the now-discredited "science" of sexology. Cross-fertilization occurred, and a long line of criminological writings posited an essential divide between male and female criminality, where the latter depends more heavily on biology and sexuality.[36] But even from the fifteenth century the peculiarly feminine crime of witchcraft was constructed with reference to peculiarly feminine sexual perversity. The Dominican authors of the notorious *Malleus Malleficarum* or *Hexenhammer* (Hammer of Witches) of 1487 point out that Eve seduced Adam in collaboration with the devil, making all womankind the enemy of (masculine) humanity.[37] The discourse of witchcraft (which echoes through the "confessions" of accused witches) describes non-reproductive intercourse with the devil and the murder of newborns; as the polar opposite of the (Marian) ideal of maternal nurturing, the idea of the witch anticipates modern notions of criminal bad mothers in thrall, perhaps, to a violent (devilish) male.

During the six weeks from 8 March to 16 April 2010, a theater project for women prisoners ran in Her Majesty's Prison Greenock, on the west coast of Scotland. HMP Greenock was built as a facility for male offenders in the first decade of the twentieth century. From 1955 it was repurposed as a women's prison for twenty years, but after a specialist women's facility in Scotland was completed at Cornton Vale in 1975, Greenock reverted to its original function. In March 2009, however, women prisoners were re-introduced into one of the prison's three halls (Darroch Hall), and Greenock is now in the unusual situation for the UK of being a mixed prison. The theater project, called *A Woman's Place*, was designed and delivered by Glasgow's Citizens Theatre.[38] As part of the project, the women prisoners wrote song texts that were set to music by Scottish singer-songwriter Carol Laula. One song was called "Bad Girls," and the lyrics betray ambivalence about that stigma: "They punish us because we're bad girls, but we're not; we just like our fun and thrills, because we're bad girls."[39] We are but we aren't, the song says, and that contradiction or confusion mirrors a widespread cultural confusion about the desirability of "badness" in women. Because female deviance is primarily understood to be sexual, "bad girls" are both particularly interesting (because they are constructed as sexually available) and particularly objectionable (because they are constructed as sexually available). When the final show was performed for a mixed prison audience, the men's reaction to this song was vigorous, and, in the view of some of the women performers, disrespectful.

---

[36] See e.g. Alfred Springer, "Kriminalanthropologie und Kriminalitätspsychopathologie des weiblichen Geschlechts: Eine ideologiekritische Studie," *Kriminalsoziologische Bibliografie* 6 (1979): 67-100.

[37] Jakob Sprenger and Heinrich Institutoris, *Der Hexenhammer*, trans. by J. W. R. Schmidt (Munich: Artemis & Winkler, 1993) [1982], I/105.

[38] In the context of a wider project called *Inspiring Change*, led by Motherwell College and funded by the Scottish Arts Council.

[39] Text kindly provided by Carol Laula.

Conceivably the cat-calling members of the male audience were primarily looking to support their own gender identity. Prison is a space that feminizes men (in that it subjects them to kinds of constraints and objectification more normally associated with women's position in society); the male prisoner, if we believe Gresham Sykes, is "figuratively castrated."[40] In the context of the song that was so enthusiastically received, it is worth noting that cultural clichés suggest women turn "bad" when the men around them are insufficiently masculine. Ulrike Meinhof, Myra Hindley, and Rose West were all constructed in the tabloids as women who dominated weak men (even a German government report asserted that Meinhof became a terrorist and a lesbian because her husband was unable to satisfy her will to be dominated).[41] As an imaginary phenomenon, criminal women are exotic and in need of strong rule. Rather like the imaginary Orient they invite objectification and voyeurism, as successful television series such as Germany's *Hinter Gittern* and its English-language counterpart *Bad Girls* demonstrate. The films of the so-called WiP (Women in Prison) genre are an extreme variant, offering the viewer the spectacle of sexual violence against imprisoned women. In the sadistic imagination of the viewer these women clearly "deserve" violence, and the sexual nature of the "punishment" might be imagined as a hair-of-the-dog remedy for the sexualized nature of female crime (a particularly inappropriate fantasy given the high percentage of women prisoners who have been the victim of real sexual violence).[42]

In rare cases we find women prisoners "writing back" in the face of their sexual objectification. A collection edited in the late 1980s by former German political prisoner Luise Rinser (who was incarcerated under the Nazis) contains a couple of such exceptional cases, written in the context of what is probably the apex of the second women's movement and its (since discredited[43]) project to reclaim or create a new language for women. One contributor celebrates her own sexuality with a provocative reference to witchcraft:

> wild und unbändig
> ist die versuchung
> die gier nach dir [...]
> maulhexe

---

[40] Gresham M. Sykes, *The Society of Captives: A Study of a Maximum Security Prison* (Princeton: Princeton U.P., 2007) [1958], 70.

[41] *Der Baader-Meinhof-Report: Dokumente – Analysen – Zusammenhänge. Aus den Akten des Bundeskriminalamtes, der "Sonderkommission Bonn" und dem Bundesamt für Verfassungsschutz* (Mainz: Hase & Koehler, 1972), 34.

[42] Between 40% and 48% across various countries; see Dünkel, Kestermann, and Zolondek, *Reader: International Study on Women's Imprisonment*, 24. The Quaker Women in Prison Project Group notes that "women prisoners as a group are more likely than other women generally and/or male prisoners to have experienced sexual assault:" Quaker Women in Prison Project Group, *Women in Prison*, 10.

[43] By the late 1980s, feminist linguists already doubted that this project was realisable: words cannot simply mean what we wish them to mean. See e.g. Sally McConnell-Ginet, "The Sexual Reproduction of Meaning: A Discourse-Based Theory," [1989] in *The Feminist Critique of Language: A Reader*, ed. Deborah Cameron, 2nd edn. (London: Routledge, 1998), 198-210.

> gierig und sündig
> verfressen und versoffen.[44]
> (the temptation of you and my greed for your are wild, untamed [...] a witch, greedy and sinful, gluttonous and drunk.)

Another insists on her intellectual integrity, even in the context of corporeal constraint:

> Dir hat man nun die Hände gebunden,
> und man fühlt sich sicher vor dir. [...]
> Es gibt keine starke Fessel [...]
> die Gedanken halten kann.
> Meinen Körper lasse ich sie
> nur für eine begrenzte Weile lang kennen.
> Doch eines gelingt ihnen nie:
> die Fähigkeit, meine Gedanken zu nennen[45]
> (Your hands have been bound and they feel safe from you. [...] There are no bonds powerful enough to contain thoughts [...]. I will let them know my body just for a limited time. But there is one thing they will never manage to do, and that is to say what my thoughts are.)

4. Writing back from the margins?

The best known names in prison writing are men's. Isidore Abramowitz in his *First Anthology of Literature Written in Prison* (1946) includes twenty-eight men and five women (Joan of Arc, Anne Hutchinson, Madame Roland, Constance Markievicz, Rosa Luxemburg).[46] All are "political" prisoners, in the sense that theirs are crimes of conscience (politics, religion, sexuality). This is the acceptable face of prison writing, where the incarcerated writer figures not as a shameful and marginal figure but as a heroic outsider. But valorizing this type of outsider status, Elissa Gelfand has argued, is the luxury of those who are not already marginalized.[47] Women prisoners who are classed or classify themselves as "political" do regularly characterize themselves as virtuous outsiders - Mme Roland, Rosa Luxemburg, and Luise Rinser, for example.[48] In most cases, however, the focus is on virtue rather than on heroism:[49] women political prisoners are keen to cast themselves as the exception to the sexually deviant rule embodied by the common female offender. We might read this as resistance to stigma. But does the literary production of non-political women prisoners indicate

---

[44] Gaby Krücken, "ich kann nicht ewig alles hochziehen," in *Laßt mich leben*, ed. Rinser, 120.

[45] Petra Schulz, "Handschellen," in *Laßt mich leben*, ed. Rinser, 74.

[46] Isidore Abramowitz, *The Great Prisoners: The First Anthology of Literature Written in Prison* (New York: E.P. Dutton, 1946).

[47] See Elissa Gelfand, "Imprisoned Women: Toward a Socio-Literary Feminist Analysis," *Yale French Studies* 62 (1981): 185-203.

[48] See Kim Richmond, "Re-capturing the Self: Narratives of Self and Captivity by Women Political Prisoners in Germany, 1915-1991," (Ph.D thesis, U. of Edinburgh, 2010).

[49] Ulrike Meinhof is a striking counterexample here. See e.g. Sarah Colvin, *Ulrike Meinhof and West German Terrorism: Language, Violence and Identity* (Rochester, NY: Camden House, 2009).

that they have accepted their shaming as bad girls, wicked mothers, and lascivious witches; or can they, too, find in writing a means of resisting?

Gert-Peter Merk called the work done by a group of women in Frankfurt's Preungesheim prison "Geschichten schreiben gegen das Anderssein" (writing stories to counter otherness).[50] The women who participated in the Greenock theater project wrote a collective letter envisaging a future self emphatically *within* social boundaries:

> Dear Future Me,
> When I imagine you, you are content, sober, homely and settled. Determined and driven with a career ahead of you, you are independent but also motherly and wise. You spend time with your children and family, also working and travelling [...]. Compared to how I am now I see you as more lady-like, well dressed and slimmer with good teeth and a nice smile. You make the best of yourself. Comfortable in your own skin, you are a lot stronger, more ambitious, happier, satisfied and smoke free! Your life is settled, stable, comfy, cosy. [...] You are loved. My advice for the future is to keep your head down and put family first.[51]

This is no celebration of edginess, of liminality. But in the context of powerfully controlling and long-lived discourses around criminality and femininity, we might consider how remarkable it is for these women to imagine themselves visible: not as monsters or perverts or the objects of sexual torture, but in a mundane and comfortable way.

5. Conclusions

> The prison is not an autonomous system of power; rather, it is an instrument of the State, shaped by its social environment, and [...] reacts to and is acted upon by the free community.[52]

Prisons are a mirror and a microcosm of the societies that create them. Like the societies that create them they are largely designed for and dominated by men; and the "figurative castration" of incarceration may well—as the metaphor suggests—be felt more keenly by male than by female inmates, for whom constraint, disempowerment and social invisibility are familiar from life outside. When women are visible in the prison context, then (like in society outside) in their sexual and reproductive function: issues around motherhood and childcare attract attention where adequate education and professional training for women prisoners (for example) do not.

---

[50] Gert-Peter Merk, "Geschichten schreiben gegen das Anderssein. Eine Schreibgruppe im Frauengefängnis Preungesheim," in *Gefangenenliteratur: Sprechen Schreiben Lesen in deutschen Gefängnissen,* ed. Ute Klein and Helmut H. Koch (Hagen: Padligur, 1988), 140-145.

[51] Text kindly provided by Lynda Radley, playwright-facilitator for the Citizens project in HMP Greenock

[52] Sykes, *The Society of Captives*, 8.

Many women's experience of being imprisoned is colored by the experience of shame and guilt in a sexual and reproductive context: the experience of being perceived and of perceiving themselves as stigmatized "bad girls" and bad mothers. Stigma always brings with it a sense of existential danger. No wonder, then, that contemporary women's prison writing tends to express a will to insiderdom, as the writers seek to reinscribe themselves in the discourse of good motherhood, sexual continence, honor, domesticity and sobriety that seems to promise safety and comfort in society outside. This kind of prison writing may well represent normalization within a patriarchal system "designed to produce greater conformity in [...] women;"[53] but it also represents resistance to stigma and a will to survive.

Sarah Colvin
s.colvin@bham.ac.uk

[53] Madlicott, "Women in Prison," 251-252.

ARCHITECTURE AND PLANNING AS A MENDING TOOL
The Spatial and Morphological Consolidation of Berlin

Nofar Sheffi
Centre for German Studies, Hebrew University of Jerusalem

Urban planning has often been defined as a public policy aimed at regulating land use in urban space through the orderly disposition of land, resources, facilities and services. From this point of view, planners and planning authorities regulate the distribution of different land uses by drawing administrative "borders" to distinguish between the functions of different areas.

In contemporary theoretical discourse, however, urban processes and spatial dynamics are perceived as tangible realities shaped by, and in turn shaping, wider political discourses.[1] Indeed, recent research acknowledges the constraints of social structures and the power of interest groups in shaping the information-based infrastructure within which planning outcomes are often determined.[2] The process of planning, though commonly represented as "technocratic" or "neutral," is thus more properly understood as a central tool with which dominant economic, social or ethnic groups work to preserve their dominance of urban space.[3] In these ongoing struggles over exclusion and inclusion, planning and zoning enable the creation and preservation of economic or social partitions along the involuntary lines of status and power.[4]

Tensions between place and nation or between distinct economic interests are, of course, most visible along the external frontiers of the polity. Yet social, ethnic and economic partitions can also coincide with regional, municipal, urban and communal frontiers. Such internal frontiers, like external ones, are generally created on the basis of competing locational, regional or ideological demands for spatial control.[5] In other words, the marking of internal urban frontiers enables the state apparatus to establish within the city a desired pattern of economic, social and political relations, to optimize conditions for economic growth and capital accumulation and to benefit powerful groups.

---

[1] O. Yiftachel and H. Yacobi, "Urban Ethnocracy: Ethnicization and the production of space in an Israeli Mixed city," *Environment and Planning: Society and Space* 21 (2003): 673-693.

[2] M. Huxley and O. Yiftachel "New Paradigm or Old Myopia? Unsettling the Communicative Turn in Planning Theory," *Journal of Planning Education & Research* 19, 4 (2000): 102-103.

[3] Lefebvre defines planning as "the production of social space by political power in the service of economic goals." See: H. Lefebvre, *The Production of Space* (Cambridge, MA: Blackwell, 1991), 151-152.

[4] Yiftachel and Yacobi, "Urban Ethnocracy;" P. Marcuse and R. Van Kempen (eds.), *Of States and Cities: the Partitioning of Urban Space* (New York: Oxford University Press, 2002), 3-10.

[5] O. Yiftachel, "The Internal Frontier: Territorial Control and Ethnic Relations in Israel," *Regional Studies* 30, 5 (1996): 496.

EUROSTUDIA — REVUE TRANSATLANTIQUE DE RECHERCHE SUR L'EUROPE
Vol. 7, No.1-2 (2011): 13-28

In this article I will offer a "reverse" perspective on planning policies by approaching planning not only as a tool in the construction of social or economic partitions but also as a mending tool in the diffusion of communities and the deconstruction of such partitions. From this perspective, planning policies should also be understood (both during the planning process itself and within the framework of ex-post examination) as a valuable tool for removing social or economic partitions. In order to examine the validity of this basic argument and its constraints, I will explore the spatial and morphological development of post-*Wende* Berlin, focusing on the planning policies formulated after reunification. Whereas the existing theoretical discourse on the social role of spatial policies presents German unification in terms of absorption (of East into West) rather than merger, portraying the East-West relationship as an asymmetrical one in which West Germans are the dominant economic and social group, I will show how Land and Federal authorities attempted to utilize planning policies as part of a more general effort to shape a single, consolidated urban identity and to break down existing physical and mental partitions between the two communities. Because these same planning policies were themselves shaped by the aforementioned wider political discourses, post-*Wende* Berlin can serve as an interesting study case: its planners strove for physical and mental consolidation not only through architectural iconography but also by remaking the complex and dynamic mosaic of urban life through everyday encounters, opening the door to a discussion about the role of urban planning and other spatial dynamics in the remaking of this urban mosaic.[6]

1. The spatial consolidation of Berlin: between past and future

In the social imaginary, the reunification of Germany is epitomized by the fall of the Berlin Wall, at which point a heretofore external frontier between East and West became an internal frontier within the newly unified Germany. Yet despite its historical centrality, the taking down of the Wall in itself removed neither the physical nor the psychological barriers between the two parts of this divided city.

In many senses, Berlin remained physically divided: first, parts of the Wall outside the city center remained intact for years; second, the two suddenly-united polities had completely different urban atmospheres, cultural characteristics and physical forms; third, the spontaneous tearing down of the physical wall in the city center left the city with a stretch of neglected wasteland, a physical void in the city center; finally, the historic center, market and cultural forces continued to pull both East and West in the directions of their previous urban centers. Furthermore, the tearing down of the Wall did not bring down the mental "wall" between the two communities (the so called "Mauer im Kopf"), but rather exposed a myriad of other, equally obstinate psychological, economic and social barriers. In fact, the post-*Wende* era emphasized the cultural and

[6] M. Hebbert, "The Street as Locus of Collective Memory," *Environment and Planning: Society and Space* 23 (2005): 583.

economic chasm between Easterners and Westerners. The now invisible Wall became the symbol of Germany's identity crisis.[7]

One way in which this unresolved identity of Berlin was negotiated was in terms of its spatial development; the form of its newly unified space. The accepted wisdom is that two basic strategies for using spatial policies as an identity-building tool dominated the discourse, coined the "Architectural Debate" or "the Berlin architecture controversy."[8] In aesthetic terms the debate has centered on two approaches to design and architecture,[9] each of which presented a different strategy for the spatial weaving of the urban fabric. The champions of urban planning along traditional lines embodied in the "Critical Reconstruction"[10] approach called for the creation of a city modeled after the pre-modern prototype.[11] Advocates of this approach did not seek to invent a new identity but to restore an urban identity lost over decades of wars and division: the nostalgic memories of a common past would form a fertile ground upon which a unified identity could be shaped.[12] Critical Reconstruction promotes a return to traditional urban forms enriched by and utilizing contemporary building techniques and materials. In Berlin, the Critical Reconstructionists aimed to bring Berlin back to the architectural principles (with regard to building materials and scale) and the urban ground planning of its late nineteenth- and early twentieth-century golden age.

One can identify four main criticisms of Critical Reconstruction. The first concerns the symbolism of choosing a past-oriented approach to design. Promoting the idea of a common national past may mask anti-liberal and nationalistic tendencies with potentially dangerous implications. The second criticism concerns the politics of memory. The seemingly arbitrary choice of one specific period of time is read as a conscious or unconscious decision not to deal with, or even to erase, other periods of the city's history. In the case of Berlin, some critics have interpreted the architectural return to pre-war urban forms as an attempt to gloss over the memories and injustices carried out during the Second World War and the years of separation. The third, more conservative criticism, concerns Critical Reconstruction's dialogic approach to urban renewal. While Critical Reconstructionists apply traditional planning and design

---

[7] B. Ladd, *The Ghosts of Berlin: Confronting German History in the Urban Landscape* (Chicago: University of Chicago Press, 1997), 32-33.

[8] E. Strom, *Building the New Berlin: the Politics of Urban Development in Germany's Capital City* (Oxford: Lexington Books, 2001), 139-145; G. Kähler, "As the Steam Began to Rise…," in *City of Architecture of the City: Berlin 1900-2000,* ed. T. Scheer, J.-P. Kleihues, and P. Kahlfeldt (Berlin: Nicolaische Verlagsbuchhandlung, 2000), 139-145.

[9] Strom, *Building the New Berlin,* 381-387.

[10] Critical Reconstruction was developed by a group of young West Berlin architects like Josef Paul Kleihues and Wolf Jobst Siedler in the late 1960s and the 1970s. See: K. von Beyme, "Ideas for a Capital City in East and West," in *City of Architecture of the City: Berlin 1900-2000,* ed. T. Scheer, J.-P. Kleihues, and P. Kahlfeldt (Berlin: Nicolaische Verlagsbuchhandlung, 2000), 247.

[11] J. Giovannini, "Berlin's new walls," *Architecture* 87, 9 (1998).

[12] Ladd, *The Ghosts of Berlin,* 231.

principles within the framework of modern-day construction in order to to resurrect the feeling of the time, this conservative approach favors a radical reconstruction of the city center through the literal reproduction of historical symbols (of which the most prominent example is the *Stadtschloss*).

The fourth criticism, and the one most relevant to our discussion, is concerned more with the aesthetic and architectural principles of Critical Reconstruction than with their symbolic meanings. In aesthetic terms, the future-oriented critics were less concerned with the general planning policy of inner Berlin and more case-specific, favoring the large-scale projects of glass and steel built in the International Style. In this way, the fourth criticism is more concerned with economic calculus: the increase of professional prestige (of the international architects involved in the projects), the maximization of the usable floor-space, the minimization of land-acquisition and building costs and the increase of the international marketability of the design.[13] The primary opposition to Critical Reconstruction also stems from this fourth criticism. The champions of the International Style chose to focus on creating a prosperous urban future. In order to attract global firms, they favoured large blocks designed by world-renowned architects and called for the adaptation of planning and zoning laws according to the nature and scale of contemporary commerce.

The hyper-modern visions and computer-generated designs of the International Style supposedly provide a stark contrast to the historically-rooted vision of Critical Reconstruction. However, according to Andreas Huyssen, the boundaries between these two styles have blurred over time, producing what he has described as a "palimpsest," a complex web of historical markers that point to the continuing heterogeneous life of a vital city ambivalent about its past and future.[14] A similar notion to Huyssen's palimpsest concept is what Rolf Goebel terms "architectural citations."[15] According to Goebel, "citational" projects — such as the *Reichstag*'s combination of a historic facade with a postmodern glass dome and new interior — inscribe contemporary architectural styles with allusive reinventions of previous cultural manifestations and discourses, incorporate actual remnants of older edifices or use partial reconstruction for new social purposes.[16]

The production of the mosaic of old and new, which both Huyssen and Goebel discuss, was not, however, "harmonious." Whereas most criticism of the resulting appearance of Berlin was directed at the Critical Reconstructionists, this appearance was intensely influenced by these conflicting strategies and must be seen as a mix of the two styles. The lack of a comprehensive spatial policy with regard to the desired future of the urban realm left champions of the two styles to tussle over each and

---

[13] Strom, *Building the New Berlin*, 140-144.

[14] A. Huyssen, "After the War: Berlin as Palimpsest," *Harvard Design Magazine* 10 (2000): 3-5.

[15] R. J. Goebel, "Berlin's Architectural Citations: Reconstruction, Simulation, and the Problem of Historical Authenticity," *PMLA* 118, 5 (2003), 1268-1289.

[16] Goebel, "Berlin's Architectural Citations," 1268-1269.

every area, project and building. What resulted was a unique amalgamation of Critical Reconstruction and International Style in each. Each physical object constructed in post-*Wende* inner Berlin can therefore be situated differently on a continuum ranging from the Critical Reconstruction archetype to that of the International Style. The specific interplay between the champions of each style will be examined with regard to several projects, providing a new perspective on both the final mixture composing each tile of the urban mosaic and of the pattern of the mosaic as a whole.

2. PLANNING THE URBAN FABRIC OF POST-*WENDE* BERLIN

Institutionally, the general planning guidelines for a unified Berlin were shaped by a joint decision-making body (*Gemeinsamer Ausschuss*) consisting of equal representation for federal and municipal authorities.[17] This served both to marginalize the powers of the district authorities (the *Bezirk*),[18] traditionally given the right of final approval for all building plans,[19] and to make the planning process more efficient.[20]

The Berlin Ministry of Urban Development and Environmental Protection, headed by Hans Stimmann (the city's Building Director from 1991 to 1996 and later State Secretary for Urban Development) proposed a design that would mend the once-divided city through the resurrection of a history common to both West and East – the vivid pre-1914 Berlin etched in the social imaginary as the city's golden age.[21] Inspired by the design concept of Critical Reconstruction, Stimmann and his counterparts called for the resurrection of the historic urban fabric of the city center. They understood the historic city center as a void at the city's heart, the absence of which precluded a harmonious whole. The planning authorities of unified Berlin thus diagnosed the city as lacking a central organ to pump blood through its vessels, rather than as suffering from a more general identity disorder. Consequently, their efforts were mostly directed at the inner city and not at the city as a whole.[22]

---

[17] Strom, *Building the New Berlin*, 164-165.

[18] Ibid., 30-32; "Unless specifically removed from its jurisdiction, as was done in this case, all building plans must be submitted for the *Bezirk*'s approval. Moreover, as *Bezirk* officials are considered to be the representatives of those interests, they are included in the drawing of citywide plans and invited to sit on the juries of architectural competitions or topical commissions" (Ibid.).

[19] Ibid., 32, 165.

[20] Ibid., 165. As a direct result of these changes the public's ability to influence the planning process was diluted in three senses: the *Bezirke*, which are considered to be the representatives of the local interests, were taken out of the process; the public's ability to bring their objections before the planning institutions was revoked; only half of the last-instance decision-making body is now consisted of elected representatives.

[21] W. J. V. Neill, *Urban planning and cultural identity* (London: Routledge, 2004), 93; Strom, *Building the New Berlin*, 109-110.

[22] Unlike the heated and intense debate waged over the future development of the historic core, the development of the rest of the city was not the subject of any real discussion. The fall of the Wall meant that the heretofore self-contained (subdivided) city suddenly acquired some breathing room;

As Building Director, the "nostalgic" Stimmann hired several planning experts and urban historians sympathetic to his agenda to draft a set of design guidelines for the inner city, especially the historic district of *Friedrichstadt*. Though not legally binding these guidelines were enforced through informal leverage on developers and architects.[23] After his 1995 appointment as State Secretary for Urban Development, Stimmann began pushing for the approval of a legally-binding plan. The proposed plan tackled many obstacles which had hindered the Critical Reconstructionists' efforts to that point; for example, traffic policies and the effective enforcement of aesthetic requirements.[24] *Planwerk Innenstadt* (the Inner City Building Plan) was ratified by the Berlin senate and the Berlin House of Representatives in 1999.[25]

Planwerk Innenstadt drafters and promoters aspired to "take down the real and invisible borders that were dividing the city" and to promote a dialog with the city's prewar past.[26] The planning authorities' vision for the historic city center was best articulated by Stimmann himself in 1995:

> ... the fundamental question was: what should the new construction relate to – the fragments of the historical city, or the high-rises around *Leipziger Straße* and *Friedrichstraße Station*? The answer came loud and clear in the form of a "critical reconstruction" of the ground plan of the city. Following years of failed urban experiments, the prevailing wish was not for an entirely new city, but for a return to traditional urbanism. There was a desire for East and West to grow together across the strip where the Wall used to stand, and for a common future expressed in a re-defined city center."[27]

---

tens of thousands of middle-class residents from both East and West moved to the urban hinterlands: the newly-built cottages in the Brandenburg periphery and residential areas within Berlin's municipal boundaries (W. Kil, "Berlin: Without Boundaries," in *City of Architecture of the City: Berlin 1900-2000*, ed. T. Scheer, J.-P. Kleihues, and P. Kahlfeldt (Berlin: Nicolaische Verlagsbuchhandlung, 2000), 374). Thus, in addition to the creation of a new center-periphery tension within Berlin itself, the accelerating process of residential suburbanization has further created a new tension between the new city-state and the surrounding *Land* of Brandenburg. In architectural and design terms, the planning of the new residential periphery was drawn not in structural but merely in aesthetic terms, resulting in residential estates, isolated in the urban periphery and struggling to create an urban identity (Ibid., 376). The new *Speckgürtel* (literally, "belt of fat") surrounding Berlin consisted of numerous subsidized retail centers, hypermarkets, industrial plants and golf courses, and exacerbated the center-periphery competition between Berlin and Brandenburg (Ibid., 375; Allan Cochrane and Andrew Jonas, "Reimagining Berlin: world city, national capital or ordinary place?," *European Urban and Regional Studies* 6, 2 (1999): 155-156).

[23] Strom, *Building the New Berlin*, 109, 140.

[24] Ibid., 110. The speedy allocation of entire blocks forced the planning authorities to, as Stimmann puts it, "collaborate with" owners of large parcels to "develop a mix of independent buildings" through different manners of informal leverage: H. Stimmann, "Urban Design and Architecture after the Wall," in *World Cities: Berlin*, ed. A. Balfour (London: Academy Editions, 1995), 51-52. The approval of the binding plan enabled them, for example, to require the developers of block-size parcels to build with varied façade.

[25] Neill, *Urban Planning*, 96.

[26] See the website of the Berlin Senate Department for Urban Development – goals of *Planwerk Innenstadt*: http://www.stadtentwicklung.berlin.de/planen/

[27] Stimmann, "Urban Design and Architecture after the Wall," 51.

The plan, like the design guidelines that preceded it, was based on Critical Reconstruction's five primary rules: the reconstruction of, or respect for, historical street patterns and building lines; the limitation of building height in accordance with local tradition (a maximum of 22 meters eaves-height and 30 meters ridge-height);[28] the designation of approximately 20 percent of the overall floor space for residential accommodation in keeping with the traditional mix of residential and commercial uses; the maintaining of a building density of around five structures; the enforcement of a maximum permitted lot size of one urban block.[29] In addition, the plan attempted to minimize the demolition of traditional buildings and encourage the use of such pre-war architectural elements as the inner courtyard and the stone-glass facade.[30]

For the Critical Reconstuctionists Berlin's heart was to be resurrected from the remains of the pre-war city; for the advocates of International Style it was to be made up of a wholly new, global city.[31] The resulting fusion, a resurrected/transplanted heart, has four chambers: the Government Quarter, *Potsdamer Platz*, *Alexanderplatz* and *Friedrichstraße*.[32] Each of these developments are situated differently on the continuum ranging between the Critical Reconstruction archetype to that of the International Style. The Government Quarter consists of Norman Forster's redesigned *Reichstag* (see above building and the "Federal Band" (the *Band des Bundes*), a half-mile East-West corridor of federal buildings (a contrast to Albert Speer's notorious north-south axis) designed by architects Axel Schultes and Charlotte Frank. The band runs north of the iconic *Reichstag* building, with Schultes' and Frank's Federal Chancellery at its Western end and Stephan Braunfels' *Marie Elisabeth Lüders Haus* (the Bundestag's Library) at its other.[33] Apart from Foster's "citational" *Reichstag*

---

[28] According to the Berlin Building Code of 1929, the maximum building height could not exceed 27 feet. In addition, the planning authorities re-enforced some of the other articles of the Code, such as the option of stepping the upper stories back (an architectural element creating the illusion of a traditional slanted roof) and the designation of the districts of *Friedrichstadt* and *Dorotheenstadt* as commercial areas (Stimmann, "Urban Design and Architecture after the Wall," 52; Ladd, *The Ghosts of Berlin*, 109).

[29] Stimmann, "Urban Design and Architecture after the Wall," 51. Reunification was followed by a massive re-privatization of property. This process opened a debate about the size of the parcels put up for sale. While the "nostalgic" city planners favored the division of blocks into modest-sized parcels (10-20 per block), city government favored the sale of entire city blocks to large, established developers (Ladd, *The Ghosts of Berlin*, 232; Hebbert, "The Street as Locus of Collective Memory," 591; Strom, *Building the New Berlin*, 201-206).

[30] Hebbert, "The Street as Locus of Collective Memory," 591; A. Huyssen, "The Voids of Berlin," *Critical Inquiry* 24, 1 (1997): 68; Goebel, "Berlin's Architectural Citations," 1270.

[31] S. Sassen, *The Global City: New York, London, Tokyo* (Princeton, NJ: Princeton University Press, 1991).

[32] In this inner city system, the East-West axis of *Unter den Linden* allows the circulation of traffic between the Government Quarter, *Friedrichstraße* and *Alexanderplatz*. An additional urban center, located outside the historic core, is of course the district of the *Kurfürstendamm*, the former center of West Berlin.

[33] For an extended discussion on the Government Quarter, see: M. Z. Wise, *Capital Dilemma: Germany's Search for a New Architecture of Democracy* (New York: Princeton Architectural Press, 1998), 57-64.

project, with its ornamental historic façades, entirely new interior and new glass dome, all buildings in the Government Quarter are modern in appearance and use transparent building techniques conveying a message of openness, transparency and democracy.

Even more than the *Band des Bundes*, the *Potsdamer Platz* complex is marked by the dominance of the International Style architecture and scale with its skyscraper agglomerations, where a once barren wasteland has been transformed into a powerful showpiece of global capitalism and international architecture. The complex is centered on two skyscrapers – Renzo Piano's and Christoph Kohlbecker's twenty-one-storey stone-glass Debis Tower (the heart of the DaimlerChrysler Areal nineteen-building complex) and Helmut Jahn's twenty-six-storey glass DB Building, part of the Sony Center complex centered on an ultra-modern glass-steel plaza with a striking glass roof. The site of DaimlerChrysler Areal was sold to Daimler-Benz InterServices around the time of the fall of the Wall in 1989 that of the Sony Center in spring 1991.[34] While the initial vision of the planning authorities saw the redevelopment of *Potsdamer Platz* as a chance to recreate the old city fabric of traditional street blocks lined by low-rise buildings, members of the futuristic camp and investing companies preferred a more modern statement on Berlin's future as a competitive global-city. And so, whilst the overall urban design for the site (designed by Heinz Himler and Christoph Sattler), had conceptualized the planning authorities' past-oriented vision, the detailed planning of specific projects adhered to the vision of future-oriented developers and largely abandoned the principles of the general site plan.[35] Indeed, though some elements of Critical Reconstruction — the traditional mix of residential and commercial uses, the stone-glass façades of the Debis Tower and the incorporation of few prewar remnants (the *Weinhaus Huth* and the *Grand Hotel Esplanade*) — are evident in the complex,[36] as a whole it is nevertheless much closer to the International Style end of the continuum.

In the case of *Alexanderplatz*, the post-*Wende* planning process began in 1992, at which point the surrounding land had already been sold to developers without any pre-arranged planning requirements. Thus diminished, the city's leverage was further hampered by the unprecedented incorporation of private investors in the jury competition issued for the area – the investors had representatives in the jury and even selected a number of the architects invited to submit designs. The competition's guidelines did require, for example, the preservation of the two historic Behrens buildings and the incorporation of mixed-use planning (only 30% offices), but the winning design was decidedly future-oriented. Hans Kollhoff's futurist proposal calling for 12 high-rise towers of over forty stories won, but drew extensive public criticism both during and after the competition. Public criticism was likewise di-

---

[34] Strom, *Building the New Berlin*, 188, 190. The exact date of the sale to Daimler-Benz InterServices is unknown. The company claims the agreement was reached before the reunification took place.

[35] Ibid., 192-198.

[36] Goebel, "Berlin's Architectural Citations," 1276.

rected at the selection process, rejecting the architects' and developers' skyscraper vision and the highly competitive capitalist real estate market which influenced the choice. Following the public uproar and the slowdown of the Berlin real estate market in the late 1990s, many of the approved building plans did not reach the building height and density originally envisioned in Kollhoff's design. The developers' decision not to exhaust the maximal limits laid out in the plan for *Alexanderplatz* cannot, however, be attributed to the successful leverage of the planning authorities, but rather to the persistent public pressure and the bursting of the Berlin real estate bubble.

Ownership, time, and public involvement play a part in locating any development on the Critical Reconstruction-International Style continuum. The past-oriented approaches had the upper hand among planning authorities, making the champions of forward-facing approaches the extra-institutional opposition. Thus the ability of the futurists to influence the outcome of the planning processes was dependent on the amount of leverage they were able to exercise on decision-making bodies. Purchasing land before planning processes had begun was an important factor in increasing negotiating leverage, as suggested by the example of *Potsdamer Platz* and *Alexanderplatz*. Another factor is time: the more quickly the land is purchased, the greater leverage yielded by the investors. Also, and because of the longer time it took the planning authorities to adjust to the new reality and the even longer time it took the general public to get involved, the faster the planning process began the bigger the investors' ability to influence its outcome was. In the case of *Alexanderplatz*, for example, despite an unprecedented incorporation of the private investors in the planning process (the surrounding land was already sold when the process began) the public controversy was nevertheless a prominent factor in the failure of the developers to realize their ultimate goals.

The development of the fourth chamber of Berlin's old/new heart will now be discussed in greater length. I focus on *Friedrichstraße* for two reasons: first, the path of the historic north-south axis was, in part, the path of the physical partition between the two Berlins; second, the boulevard's development is located closer to the Critical Reconstruction end of the continuum.

3. THE (CRITICAL) RECONSTRUCTION OF *FRIEDRICHSTRAßE*

Friedrichstadt district, of which *Friedrichstraße* served as the main north-south axis, was built in the eighteenth century to the south of the medieval *Nikolaiviertel* (Nikolai Quarter), by the King of Prussia Friedrich Wilhelm. The new residential district was developed on a grid plan of wide streets and rectangular blocks of two- or three-storey stone houses.[37] After the 1871 unification of Germany and the rapid industrialization of the city, *Friedrichstadt* gradually transformed from a residential neighborhood into a bustling commercial district. The baroque residential houses

[37] T. H. Elkins, *Berlin: the Spatial Structure of a Divided City* (New York: Methuen & Co, 1988).

were replaced by ornate five-storey buildings with courtyards housing mostly offices and shops.[38] Together with *Potsdamer Platz* and *Unter den Linden*, *Friedrichstraße* became the cultural and economic center of the blossoming metropolis.

Friedrichstraße was almost completely destroyed during the Second World War, and the division of Berlin reinforced its decay. The street was divided in two: a large northern portion, from *Checkpoint Charlie* to *Torstrasse* belonged to East Berlin and a smaller southern portion, from *Checkpoint Charlie* to the *Hallesches Tor U-Bahn* in the *Kreuzberg* district to West Berlin. Far from its previous centrality, the boulevard was now relegated to a peripheral position and turned into a half-neglected wasteland. The commercial center of East Berlin was now concentrated around *Stalinallee* and *Alexanderplatz* while government buildings were located on the northern part of the *Friedrichstadt*, around *Marx-Engels-Platz*, the former site of the Prussian *Stadtschloss* demolished in 1952. The commercial activity of the Western part of the city was concentrated around the shopping and entertainment district of *Kurfürstendamm*, between *Ernst-Reuter-Platz* and *Wittenbergplatz*.

The new social and political developments of the late 1960s brought new hope to southern *Friedrichstadt*. Frustrated with the lack of urban substance and the profit-orientated functionalism of post-war modernism, many young West German architects and urban planners began to challenge the hegemony of modernist architecture and adopted a more historically-oriented approach to design. This new approach was articulated in a series of historically-aware urban renewal projects across the "Western" part of *Friedrichstadt* leading up to the 1987 IBA (*Internationale Bauausstellung*).[39]

The past-oriented design trends in the West were mirrored by parallel developments in the East. Until the late 1960s the GDR had favored new construction, but soon it began to revisit its existing housing policies to emphasize renovation of existing urban structures, investing increasing funds in the refurbishment and enhancement of the existing urban fabric.[40] Beginning in the 1970s and leading up to Berlin's 750th anniversary in 1987, neo-historical forms were increasingly used in Eastern showcase projects (for example, *Nikolaiviertel* and the *Platz der Akademie*). *Friedrichstraße*'s proximity to the Wall, once the reason for it being overlooked, was now perceived as one of its *fortes*: the East justifiably understood *Friedrichstraße*'s appearance as its outward image to the West.[41]

---

[38] Ladd, *The Ghosts of Berlin*, 109; Elkins, *Berlin: the Spatial Structure of a Divided City*, 163.

[39] Strom, *Building the New Berlin*, 139.

[40] S. Hain, "Between Arkonaplatz and the Nikolaiviertel. The City as a Social Form Versus the City as Mise-en-scène. Conflicts Raised by the Return to the City," in *City of Architecture of the City: Berlin 1900-2000*, ed. T. Scheer, J.-P. Kleihues, and P. Kahlfeldt (Berlin: Nicolaische Verlagsbuchhandlung, 2000), 337-339.

[41] Elkins, *Berlin: the Spatial Structure*, 209. The book was published in the West in 1989 and provides a vivid description of the building project on the GDR side.

Between *Französische Straße* and *Mohrenstraße* (*Friedrichstraße* 66-78), the Ministry of Construction planned a glamorous Art Nouveau and Art Deco shopping center (*Friedrichstadt Passagen*), to consist of 105 shops, 4 department stores, 44 restaurants and luxurious apartments. The neighboring *Block 204* was to include a bar and discothèque while a *House of Entertainment* was planned for the opposite side of the boulevard as well as the 1987 *Grand Hotel* (today's Westin Grand Berlin) and the 1985 *Spreeterrassen*. [42] All of these projects were to feature ornamental historical references and to remain compatible with the existing pre-war buildings in terms of both scale and design. Over the course of the 1980s, the project's budget was repeatedly cut, so that it remained largely a work-in-progress when the Wall was torn down in 1989. The unfinished shells left behind by the GDR, including the uncompleted *Friedrichstadt Passagen*, were themselves symbolically taken down only to be "critically reconstructed" several years later.

After reunification, *Friedrichstraße*, along with *Potsdamer Platz*, found itself at the heart of public polemic over the city's architectural future. The boulevard's rich and colorful history and its location at the beating heart of pre-war Berlin made its reconstruction a crucial goal of the nostalgic camp's strategy and among the most desirable piece of property in the city.[43]

At the exact location of *Friedrichstadt Passagen*, three luxurious shopping arcades were erected. The project, *Friedrichstadt Passagen*, consists of three block-sized buildings: Mathias Ungers's *Quartier 205* (*Friedrichstraße* 66-70); Pei Cobb Freed & Partners' *Quartier 206* (*Friedrichstraße* 71-74); and Jean Nouvel's *Quartier 207* (*Friedrichstraße* 76-78) of the latter housing the French department store *Galeries Lafayette*. The arcades are connected by an underground passage spanning the length of the complex, allowing traffic to move freely at street level. The underlying concept links contemporary shopping pleasure with the Berlin urban shopping tradition, dating back to the nineteenth century.[44]

In accordance with the principles of Critical Reconstruction, all three arcades are multi-functional (they comprise a retail space, offices and residential apartments) and correspond with the traditional height limitation. All three buildings include references to the traditional "courtyard," using different architectural techniques (an atria, a glass-roofed central area, or a light-cone). Mathias Ungers and Pei Cobb Freed & Partners both used architectural techniques which create an illusion of a traditional slanted roof.[45] *Quartier 205* and *Quartier 206* are made up of building materials which correspond to the principles of Critical Reconstruction, the façades are covered with

---

[42] F. Urban, "Friedrichstraße, 1987: Neo-Historical Urban Design in the German Democratic Republic," *Planning Perspectives* 23 (2008): 4.

[43] Strom, *Building the New Berlin*, 200-201.

[44] Goebel, "Berlin's Architectural Citations," 1979-1981; Urban, "Friedrichstraße, 1987," 6.

[45] *Quartier 205*'s upper floors are gradually withdrawn creating the illusion of a traditional slanted roof. *Quartier 206*'s upper floors are tilted back at an angle and are differentiated from the lower ones by darker building material and less stone.

neutral-color sandstone. *Quartier* 206 corresponds most fully with the principles of Critical Reconstruction: its façades are decorated with triangular stone elements and horizontally oriented windows which, from street-level, recall the plaster ornaments of nineteenth-century buildings. Its black-and-white checker motif interior also recalls early twentieth-century design trends. *Quartier 207*, with its all-glass, translucent façade, corresponds less fully with the principles of Critical Reconstruction.[46]

Although the Passages and the rest of the new buildings along *Friedrichstraße* follow the approach of Critical Reconstruction in their general orientation towards traditional Berlin city forms,[47] they also exemplify the tensions between past- (Critical Reconstruction) and future-oriented (International Style) approaches to design. As with the overall planning level, specific projects and buildings can be placed on a continuum ranging from the Critical Reconstruction archetype to that of the International Style.

Several factors determined the final location of specific projects on this continuum. Importantly, most sites along *Friedrichstraße* had been allocated and were near completion long before Stimmann's guidelines were formulated, as events moved too quickly to allow the newly formed planning entities to develop and enforce a planning strategy for the area.[48] As a result, many of the buildings along the boulevard have not been subjected to the planning authorities' guidelines, prominently the *Galeries Lafayette* and its all-glass façade, approved before the formulation of Stimmann's guidelines.

One of the main bones of contention on this issue, were the plot sizes allocated to developers. As in other parts of the city, the city gave in to pressure and hastily allocated large-block parcels to developers in an attempt to lure international developers.[49] The nostalgic camp's vision for *Friedrichstraße* found itself at odds with the contemporary scale of commerce. Whereas the pre-war subdivided city blocks were celebrated for creating a mix of functions along the grand boulevards, the consolidation of entire blocks for development by a single owner and a single architect, some suggest, had created a form of homogeneity.

The interplay between the two approaches is evident, for example, in these buildings' "courtyards." The nostalgic vision attempted to bring back the small courtyards within long, narrow parcels, ideal for a variety of small-scale trade. This

---

[46] A. Balfour (ed.), *World Cities: Berlin*, 256-257.

[47] Goebel, "Berlin's Architectural Citations," 1279.

[48] Strom, *Building the New Berlin*, 201-206. The responsibility to choose a developer for each city-center site was placed in the hands of an *ad hoc* steering committee, the Coordinating Committee for Inner City Investment (KOAI). The committee met regularly from February 1991 through September 1993, when most of the contested development sites, including sixteen on *Friedrichstraße*, had already been sold. See Strom, *Building the New Berlin*, 107-108.

[49] Ladd, *The Ghosts of Berlin*, 232; Hebbert, "The Street as Locus of Collective Memory," 591; Strom, *Building the New Berlin*, 201-206.

vision of informal and intimate trade found itself at odds with the enclosed nature of contemporary commerce, sealed off as it is from the rest of the public realm by tight security, various physical obstacles, and its maximization of floor space. In today's reality, informal, small-scale trade is not permitted, and courtyards, insofar as they exist, are intended only for rent-paying private use. In reality, then, most of *Friedrichstraße*'s commercial buildings are not centered on truly public courtyards but on inaccessible light wells such as Nouvel's glass cones or otherwise void spaces. Of the three *Passagen*, for example, only *Quartier 205* is centered on non-commercial open-air courtyards.

A third example of these same interplays is the branding of *Friedrichstraße* and the definition of its target market. The boulevard's high visibility and the high cost of properties along it have attracted big international investors and high-end brands that concentrate their efforts on higher social classes and wealthy tourists. *Friedrichstraße*'s new luxurious image presents a stark contrast to the romantic image of the boulevard at the center of the artistic and commercial culture of the 1920s. In the environment of contemporary capitalism, the revival of such a vivid urban atmosphere was virtually precluded.

The fourth example of these interplays between the two approaches to design can be found in the exteriors of the *Passagen* and the rest of the new buildings along *Friedrichstraße*.[50] Whilst Critical Reconstruction attempted to promote a dialog with the past and recreate the urban fabric by bringing back the ornamental use of such traditional architectural elements as slanted roofs and a fixed ratio of stone to glass, the champions of the International Style favored the use of clean lines and modern materials. The architectural elements that contributed to the success of the iconographic palimpsest/citational projects, like the *Reichstag*, were not as effectively incorporated into the commercial construction along *Friedrichstraße* and the neighboring streets. The buildings' height and materials might echo those of pre-World War II buildings, but their overall geometric feel and grayness make them visually similar to other contemporary commercial buildings across the world. Despite the promotional rhetoric used by the *Friedrichstadt Passagen*'s planners and developers, the buildings themselves can be easily imagined as an integral part of a contemporary development project anywhere else in the worldwide.[51]

4. Conclusion

Urban planning can be understood as a tool in the partitioning of public space along involuntary lines of status and power. This process of marking internal urban frontiers enables state authorities to shape patterns of economic, social and political relations. In this context, post-reunification spatial policies in Berlin can be analyzed as a tool for reinforcing the existing frontier between East and West and as an instrument

[50] Goebel, "Berlin's Architectural Citations," 1285.

[51] Idem.

to further (Western-led) governmental goals. However, I have offered here an alternative perspective on planning policies. By focusing on the development of inner Berlin, I suggest that planning can also serve as a mending tool in the consolidation of communities and the removal of social partitions.

Though in and of itself not necessarily successful, the Berlin experiment can teach six valuable lessons on the power of planning mechanisms to remove social and economic partitions. First, planning policies cannot stand on their own, but are part of a larger formation of spatial policies. The state apparatus for the production of social space consists not only of planning mechanisms but also of other instruments intended to further governmental goals regarding the use, control and development of land. In the case of Berlin the tension between planning and land policies is particularly apparent. Most land in the inner city had been allocated before the planning authorities established any organized planning strategy, a fact which later diminished the leverage of the planning authorities to approve or enforce official planning regulations. It is not my assertion that land policies should serve planning policies (that is, that planning policies are necessarily prerequisites for land allocation); but that the two, along with other spatial policies, should be enacted in tandem so as to achieve the desired social space.

Second, the process of planning must be understood and discussed separately from architectural discourse and work: though planning and architecture clearly have many commonalities and interfaces, they shape distinct planes of social space. The planning process aims at producing a structural and analytical strategy for the planned area as a whole: by regulating land use, incorporating the planned area into its surroundings, taking into account long-term development goals, regulating internal dynamics and functioning and by shaping its general aesthetic characteristics. The architect, meanwhile, is expected to work within the constraints set down by planning mechanisms on a specific lot and to produce a functional (and aesthetic) building. An architectural criticism on the specific constraints in which the architect is forced to work and the more general criticism of the structural (dis)function of the wider social space must therefore be distinguished. These two critiques are intertwined, but not identical. In the case of Berlin, both architects and planners overreached their roles, interfering excessively in the work of the other. This rhetorical and functional confusion resulted not only in a struggle to find a common vocabulary, but in some cases the town planners and architects even presented contradictory messages.

Third, public involvement is generally understood to be a basic principle of the planning process, certainly when there is an explicit aspiration to shape social reality and wider political discourse. In the case of Berlin, despite publicly declaring such intentions, the planning authorities actively worked to neutralize the public's ability to take part in the process and to influence its outcomes. The neutralizing of public involvement in the planning process was achieved by the removal of the *Bezirk*, whose officials are considered to be the representatives of the public interest, from the planning process and by the overriding of the standard planning process through which the public is given the opportunity to voice its concerns. It is therefore not surprising that the post-*Wende* planning process has enjoyed little to no public legitimacy and failed to meld together the city and its public, intentionally and demonstratively excluded from the process.

Fourth, communities are not mended solely by the removal of partitions but also by the further uniting of the two parts into one whole. Attention must therefore be drawn not only to the area where the barrier is understood to stand but to the entire space to be united. I therefore see focusing on Berlin's historic core – rather than on the city as a whole – as a crucially problematic element of post-reunification planning policies. To return to a previous metaphor, unified Berlin seems to have been misdiagnosed as suffering from a heart problem as opposed to a wide-ranging dissociative identity disorder. The re-development of the historic core should have been part of an overarching spatial-development policy for the city as a whole. The creation of a new identity for the center of the city, while its residents left for the suburbs and its residents had no say in the process, was unlikely to create a new holistic identity for the city.

Fifth, the commonly understood interplay between past- and future-oriented approaches to design may not in fact be the true conflict behind Berlin's post-*Wende* spatial development: it is not clear which partition was to be deconstructed and which entities integrated. In many senses, the new core of Berlin is more appealing to foreign investors and international tourists than to its own residents, becoming a global enclave of tourists and international firms devoid of the unique characteristics of Berlin. Was the targeted social and economic partition the one which separated the two sides of the city or the one which separated Berlin (and Germany) from the rest of the Western world? Was the aim to unite the two Berlins or to unite Berlin with London, New York and Tokyo? The real point of contention was perhaps not how to unify the two parts of Berlin (by adopting past- or future-oriented approaches to design) but how to unite Berlin with the rest of Europe and the Western world. Which image to sell to the global market: the awakening sleeping beauty or the showy newcomer? In the end, the city's spatial and morphological future may not have been an interplay between Critical Reconstruction and the International Style at all, but a response to answers of each actor to the above questions.

Finally, the "positive" role of planning – that is, its ability to take down social and economic partitions – cannot be isolated from its "negative" role: its tendency to mark or reinforce internal urban frontiers. From the experience of Berlin we should learn that social and economic partitions do not simply disappear but shift. The role of the planning authorities, therefore, is not only to identify existing social/economic partitions but also to decide where to move them. In the case of Berlin it is not only unclear which partition was targeted for deconstruction (my fifth point), but also to where it was intended to be moved. Berlin's new urban frontiers did not correspond to the municipal borders of the unified city, as may have been expected, but rather along the boundaries of its historic core. Thus was a wholly new and wholly internal social and economic partition between center and periphery (my fourth point) formed.

Nofar Sheffi
nofar.sheffi@mail.huji.ac.il

ENTFERNTER ERFAHRUNGSRAUM
Überlegungen zu West-Berlin und 1989

Krijn Thijs
Duitsland Instituut Amsterdam, Universiteit van Amsterdam

„Die Mauer ist offen."
„Ach du Scheiße."
Kneipengespräch, *Herr Lehmann*[1]

Zwanzig Jahre danach – wer die fachhistorischen Publikationen der beiden deutschen Jubiläumsjahre 2009 und 2010 zu überblicken versucht, wird feststellen, dass darin der zentrale Ort des Geschehens, nämlich die Grenz- und Mauerstadt Berlin, nur sehr einseitig präsent ist. Es ist Ost-Berlin, auf das unser Blick im Regelfall fokussiert, und vom anliegenden West-Berlin erfährt man wenig. Das ist kaum verwunderlich. Das Ende des sozialistischen Zukunftsprojekts, die Auflösung der SED-Macht, der Zettel von Schabowski, der Ansturm auf die Mauer – alles das fand in der DDR statt, in ihrer implodierenden Hauptstadt und teilweise mehr noch in der heruntergewirtschafteten Provinz. Die große Geschichte wurde an anderen Orten gemacht – zunächst in Gdansk, Moskau, Ungarn, Leipzig, Prag, Ost-Berlin und Dresden. Im Herbst 1989 fand West-Berlin kaum statt.

Auch unsere Erzählungen über den anschließenden Prozess der deutschen Vereinigung im Jahr 1990 führen uns an viele Orte der sich auflösenden bipolaren Welt, nur nicht nach West-Berlin: Verhandlungen und Gipfeldiplomatie in Bonn, Moskau, Washington, Paris, London, Warschau, Ost-Berlin und dem Kaukasus. Was war nun mit der „freien" Insel im „roten" Meer, der ehemaligen „Frontstadt," dem „Schaufenster des Westens," das doch als Pfand der Einheit und als Hebel einer Wiedervereinigung vom Westen immer beibehalten worden war? Im *moment suprême*, so scheint es, wehte der Mantel der Geschichte an West-Berlin vorbei.

Oder doch nicht? Denn schließlich war die ummauerte Insel des Westens das erste Ziel aller ostdeutschen Ausreisenden. Als Objekt der Begierde wurde das kleine West-Berlin von Ostdeutschen überschwemmt, nachdem diese die Mauer eingedrückt hatten. Am ersten Wochenende kamen etwa zwei Millionen Menschen in

[1] Sven Regener, *Herr Lehmann: Ein Roman* (München: Goldmann, 2003) [2001], 280. Dieser Artikel entstand im Rahmen des von NWO unterstützten Forschungsprojekt „The literary construction of German cultural Identity after the Wende" (Universität Leiden). Ich danke Stefanie Eisenhuth, Joes Segal und Angelika Wendland für Ihre Kommentare. Die Arbeit von Stefanie Eisenhuth, „West-Berlin und der Umbruch in der DDR: Grenzübergreifende Wahrnehmungen und Verhandlungen 1989" (Magisterarbeit, Humboldt-Universität zu Berlin, 2010), die sich das hier umrissene Thema in vielversprechender Weise vornimmt, wurde mir erst nach Abschluss dieses Artikels zugänglich.

die Stadt – eine glatte Verdoppelung der West-Berliner Einwohnerzahl. Die dramatischen Szenen der „flutenden Massen" an zwischenstädtischen Grenzübergangsstellen führten zum finalen Legitimitätsverlust des DDR-Staates. Ohne West-Berlin hätte es diese Szenen so nicht gegeben – denn die Wiesen und Wälder der innerdeutschen Grenze luden nicht wie der Kurfürstendamm zum freudetaumelnden und mit Sekt besprühten Trabbi-Korso ein. Also: ohne West-Berlin kein 9. November 1989.

Und dennoch. Auch in dieser Erzählform findet West-Berlin kaum statt. Die „Insel" bleibt passiver Zielort in einer aus ostdeutscher Perspektive erzählten Geschichte des Mauerfalls. West-Berlin ist bloß Bühne und Dekor, es gibt den Ku'damm und das klatschende Publikum für die ostdeutsche Selbstbefreiung her. Später liefert es in Form seines Regierenden Bürgermeisters auch den Gastgeber für die symbolischen Grenzüberschreitungen namhafter Bundespolitiker und am Ende der Erzählung noch den Reichstag als Kulisse der Einheitsfeier.

Dementsprechend fehlen in der neueren Literatur zum Mauerfall und zum Einheitsprozess West-Berliner Handlungen und Perspektiven in auffälliger Weise. So fehlt in Klaus-Dietmar Henkes breit angelegtem Sammelband bezeichnenderweise ein Beitrag zu West-Berlin.[2] Jüngere Gesamtdarstellungen verlegen oft ihren Blick von der West-Berliner Freudennacht schleunigst wieder zurück auf Ost-Berlin und dann auf Bonn.[3] Sogar in der bislang einzigen Gesamtgeschichte West-Berlins, letztes Jahr von Wilfried Rott vorgelegt, werden die ansonsten konsequent verfolgten West-Berliner Erfahrungsräume ab November 1989 auf einmal durch die auf den 3. Oktober ausgerichtete Meistererzählung der nationalen Wiedervereinigung kolonisiert.[4] Das Eigenleben im Biotop scheint plötzlich nicht mehr interessant: Aus West-Berliner Warte bleibt diese Geschichte größtenteils unerzählt.[5]

Auffällig ist dies insofern, als das mitten in der DDR liegende West-Berlin über eine einmalige westliche Nahsicht auf die turbulenten Ereignisse im ostdeutschen Umbruchsgebiet verfügte. Dazu gehörten auch die kürzesten Verbindungen zu allerlei Geschehnissen und Akteuren des ostdeutschen „Endspiels" (Kowalczuk). Bis tief in den Herbst 1989 hinein fanden hier abtastende Begegnungen zwischen den

---

[2] Klaus-Dietmar Henke (Hg.), *Revolution und Vereinigung 1989/90. Als in Deutschland die Realität die Phantasie überholte* (München: DTV, 2009).

[3] Vgl. v.a. Andreas Rödder, *Deutschland einig Vaterland. Die Geschichte der Wiedervereinigung* (München: C. H. Beck, 2009); Ilko-Sascha Kowalczuk, *Endspiel. Die Revolution von 1989 in der DDR* (München: C. H. Beck, 2009); Wolfgang Schuller, *Die deutsche Revolution 1989* (Berlin: Rowolt, 2009). Einzig als Erinnerungsort der DDR ist „Westberlin" in der jüngeren Literatur verzeichnet: David E. Barclay, „Westberlin," in *Erinnerungsorte der DDR*, hg. Martin Sabrow (München: C. H. Beck, 2009), 431-440. Nur als von außen wahrgenommenes Biotop und in ihrer „objektiven" Rolle in der ostdeutschen Revolution scheint die ummauerte Halbstadt bislang historiografische Relevanz gewinnen zu können.

[4] Wilfried Rott, *Die Insel. Geschichte West-Berlins 1948-1990* (München: C. H. Beck, 2009).

[5] Vgl. aber Wilfried Rott, „Abschied von West-Berlin," *Aus Politik und Zeitgeschichte* 11/2010: 41-46 sowie Eisenhuth, „West-Berlin."

noch getrennten Blockwelten statt. Hier musste die liberaldemokratische Gesellschaftsordnung in kürzester Distanz auf die Veränderungen im Osten reagieren; hier mussten westliche Politiker den plötzlichen Erdrutsch sowohl praktisch als auch theoretisch im engsten Zeitrahmen bewältigen, und hier mussten dann die epochemachenden Veränderungen durch den Mauerfall auch in die alltäglichen Lebenswelten der eben noch abgeschirmten Stadtkommune eingeordnet und entschärft werden.

Zur Verführungskraft des nahezu unerforschten West-Berliner Blicks gehört überdies die Vermutung, dass die Haltungen und Erfahrungen der West-Berliner sich in erheblichem Maße von denen der Westdeutschen unterschieden haben dürften. Denn die politische Kultur der Insel hatte sich im Laufe der 1970er und 1980er Jahre erheblich von der ihres bundesdeutschen Festlandes emanzipiert. Gerade die Wochen der unerwarteten Grenzöffnung und Neuorientierung versprechen somit nähere Aufschlüsse über den politisch-kulturellen Raum West-Berlins und damit über eine eigenständige Deutungswelt mit ihren eigenen Handlungszwängen und -logiken: an sehr prominenter Stelle asymmetrisch angesiedelt zwischen Ost und West, gedanklich-politisch näher an der Bundesrepublik, geographisch-perspektivisch näher an Ost-Berlin. Umso unbegreiflicher scheint es daher, dass die Frage nach West-Berlin in der reichen historischen Forschung zum „deutschen Jahr 1989" (Wirsching) bislang so noch kaum gestellt wurde. Nur West-Berliner Nostalgiker beklagen seit einiger Zeit das „Vergessen" der Inselstadt in der gesamtdeutschen Erinnerungslandschaft und produzieren entweder verklärend-romantische Titel des Genres „Westalgie" oder anekdotenhafte Merkwürdigkeiten der Sorte Spiegel-Einestages.[6]

Im diesem Aufsatz werde ich anhand der bisher veröffentlichten Literatur die West-Berliner Blicke auf das Jahr 1989 verfolgen. Konform mit vielen Selbst- und Fremdzuschreibungen, zeitgenössischen wie rückblickenden, werde ich West-Berlin dabei als eigenständigen Erfahrungsraum und als hybriden Grenzraum zwischen Ost- und West-Deutschland konzipieren und versuchen, Aspekte von Entfernung, Reise und Begegnung besonders herauszustellen. Zugleich hoffe ich, bei der Verfolgung dieses Ansatzes einige mögliche Erklärungen für den Verlust der West-Berliner Perspektive sammeln zu können.

1. Wohin mit West-Berlin?

West-Berliner Politiker haben, anders als die in Bonn, keine eigenen Spuren in die Geschichte des Mauerfalls und der Vereinigung ziehen können. Die Stadt samt

---

[6] Olaf Leitner, *West-Berlin! Westberlin! Berlin (West)! Die Kultur – die Szene – die Politik. Erinnerungen an eine Teilstadt der 70er und 80er Jahre* (Berlin: Schwarzkopf & Schwarzkopf, 2002); Kerstin Schilling, *Insel der Glücklichen. Generation West Berlin* (Berlin: Parthas, 2005); D. Holland-Moritz und Gabriela Wachter (Hg.), *War jewesen. West-Berlin 1961-1989* (Berlin: Parthas, 2009). Vgl. „Kalter Krieg bizarr," 26. Juni 2008 und „West-Berlin und der Mauerfall," 9. November 2009, www.einestages.spiegel.de.

ihrer Führung war schwach, und vor 1989 war der Eindruck weit verbreitet, dass die historische Rolle der einstigen Frontstadt ausgespielt war. West-Berlin sei das „Abfallprodukt einer gescheiterten Politik," schrieb Peter Bender 1987 lakonisch, „ein zweckloses Gebilde."[7] In der Tat war seit der Stabilisierung seiner merkwürdigen geografischen Lage durch die Verträge der frühen 1970er Jahre in West-Berlin eine zunehmende Normalisierung eingetreten, die auf Dauer die Rationalität und Zweckmäßigkeit seiner vorgeschobenen Position mitten im sozialistischen Osten radikal in Frage stellte. Sinn und Zweck des einstigen Schaufensters[8] waren mit der Befestigung der Teilung fragwürdig geworden, und das Selbstverständnis der Enklave war von immer mehr Fragezeichen umgeben.

Zunehmend schrumpften die zur Schau gestellte Zukunftsfähigkeit und Leistungskraft des westlichen Gesellschaftsmodells gerade in der vermeintlichen Vorzeigekommune aufs Schmerzlichste. Politische, wirtschaftliche und gesellschaftliche Skandale und Affären lädierten nachhaltig die öffentliche Kultur und den Ruf Berlins. Selbst in der von vielen als „golden"empfundenen kurzen Ära des Regierenden Bürgermeisters Richard von Weizsäcker (1981-1984) war die politische und kulturelle Provinzialisierung mit Händen zu greifen. Vollständig abhängig von bundesdeutschen Subventionen, veranschaulichte das einstige Aushängeschild eher das Stagnationspotenzial als die etwaige Innovationskraft liberaldemokratischer Gesellschaftsordnungen. Wirtschaftskraft und Bevölkerungszahl sanken kontinuierlich, und nur der aufgeblähte öffentliche Dienst garantierte ein gewisses Maß an Beschäftigung. Skeptiker erkannten im einstigen Schaufenster nunmehr selbst „sozialistische, staatswirtschaftliche Züge."[9]

Auch deutschlandpolitisch hatte sich die Position West-Berlins seit den Deutschlandverträgen geschwächt, wenn nicht gar erübrigt. Zur großen Verärgerung der West-Berliner Eliten fanden westdeutsche Politiker den Weg in die DDR in zunehmendem Maße an West-Berlin vorbei. In den 1980er Jahren reisten Landespräsidenten nunmehr ohne West-Berliner Zwischenstopp nach Ost-Berlin. Damit wurde der Insel der letzte identifikatorische Strohhalm – ihre erhoffte Brückenfunktion – schmerzhaft entrissen. Stattdessen schienen künftige Legitimationsressourcen nur noch in freistädtischen Leitbildern zu liegen – wären da nicht realpolitisch unüberwindbare Hindernisse gewesen wie die totale Subventionsgebundenheit an West-Deutschland und die überaltert wirkende, aber dennoch peinlich genau gehandhabte Alliiertenhoheit der Franzosen, Briten und Amerikaner. Dennoch spielte man in Bonner Zukunftsszenarien für die Insel

[7] Peter Bender, *Wenn es West-Berlin nicht gäbe* (Berlin: Corso bei Siedler, 1987), 15.
[8] Michael Lemke (Hg.), *Schaufenster der Systemkonkurrenz. Die Region Berlin-Brandenburg im Kalten Krieg* (Köln: Böhlau, 2006).
[9] Rott, *Insel*, 318.

inzwischen offen mit der Idee einer „allmählichen Assimilierung mit ihrem sozialistischen *Umland*."[10]

Anders als am Anfang der deutschen Teilung, wo Luftbrücke und Kennedybesuch symbolhistorische Weichenstellungen waren, spielte West-Berlin bei ihrem Ende kaum eine aktive Rolle. Richard von Weizsäckers Besuch in Ost-Berlin wurde 1983 noch als bedeutendes Signal gewertet – doch dies vor allem, weil man Weizsäcker hier als avisierten Bundespräsidenten und weniger als West-Berliner Regierenden beobachtete. Honeckers Gegenbesuch fand drei Jahre später, trotz vieler Bemühungen des Senats, in Bonn und nicht in West-Berlin statt.[11] Für die bundesdeutsche Regierung war die überteuerte und von drei Fremdsouveränen kontrollierte Insel längst ein „störender Annex" (Rott) geworden, der mit seinen komplizierten Statusfragen jeden Entspannungsversuch und jeden deutsch-deutschen Vertragstext zu sprengen drohte. Auch symbolisch zehrte die Insel Ende der 1980er von Legenden. Die 750-Jahr-Feier lief auf eine krampfhafte Identitätssuche hinaus, die im urbanen Mythos der „Goldenen Zwanziger" neues Symbolkapital jenseits deutsch-deutscher Kategorien fand.[12] Reagans Worte an der Mauer („Mr. Gorbatschow, tear down this wall!") appellierten 1987 hauptsächlich an vergangenes Pathos aus Kennedy-Zeiten, und ansonsten beschränkten sich West-Berlins aktive Eingriffe in die große Geschichte des sinkenden Staatssozialismus auf die Veranstaltung von Rockkonzerten, deren Klänge über die Mauer wehten.[13] Die ummauerte Stadt, Zentrum des geteilten Deutschlands, lag im deutschlandpolitischen Abseits.

Dennoch entwickelte sich West-Berlin jenseits des skizzierten politisch-diplomatischen Bedeutungsverlustes in den späten 1980er Jahren zu einem hybriden Grenzraum der sich verschiebenden Fronten. Denn als sich die Krise der sozialistischen Welt zuzuspitzen begann, bekam die Insel dies sofort zu spüren. Mit der langsamen Lockerung der staatssozialistischen Grenzregime des Warschauer Paktes gab es überall in West-Berlin Flüchtlinge aus anderen Welten. Die

---

[10] „Sofern nicht die weltpolitischen Veränderungen (…) der Teilstadt tatsächlich eine neue Perspektive eröffnen, scheint die Zukunft des freien Teils der Stadt unausweichlich in der allmählichen Assimilierung mit ihrem sozialistischen *Umland* zu liegen." Ralf-Georg Reuth, „Berlin-Bonn. Eine Konkurrenzsituation?," in *40 Jahre Bundeshauptstadt Bonn 1949-1989,* hg. Bundesminister für Raumordnung, Bauwesen und Städtebau (Karlsruhe: C. F. Müller, 1989), 40.

[11] Die noch für die beteiligten Zeitgenossen so aufregende „Politik der kleinen Schritte," mit der der Diepgen-Senat in den späten 1980er Jahren Ost-Berlin zu zähmen versuchte, sieht im Lichte des Erdrutschs von 1989 natürlich etwas blass aus. Zur Berlin-Diplomatie in diesen Jahren: Eberhard Diepgen, *Zwischen den Mächten: Von der besetzten Stadt zur Hauptstadt* (Berlin: Bebra, 2004), Detlev Stronk, *Berlin in den achtziger Jahren: Im Brennpunkt der deutsch-deutschen Geschichte* (Berlin: Berlin Story, 2009); Hans Otto Bräutigam, *Ständige Vertretung: Meine Jahre in Ost-Berlin* (Hamburg: Hoffmann und Campe, 2009) sowie Krijn Thijs, *Drei Geschichten, eine Stadt: Berlin und die Stadtjubiläen von 1937 und 1987* (Köln: Böhlau, 2008).

[12] Zur 750-Jahr-Feier in Ost und West: Thijs, *Drei Geschichten.*

[13] Stefan Wolle, *Heile Welt der Diktatur. Alltag und Herrschaft in der DDR 1971-1989* (München: Econ&List, 1999) [1998], 114-116; Kowalczuk, *Endspiel*, 162-168.

Auffanglager waren überfüllt, und die Stadt wurde eine beliebte Anlaufstelle für osteuropäische Abenteurer, Grenzgänger und Schwarzhändler. Der hartnäckig wandernde „Polenmarkt" beispielsweise forderte die öffentliche Ordnung West-Berlins unmittelbar heraus: Hatte man ihn am ehemaligen, peripheren Potsdamer Platz aufgelöst, so wuchs er am Rande des Tiergartens wieder nach usw. Das einstige Schaufenster des Westens verwandelte sich in ein Tor zum Osten, und auch dieses Thema ist bis heute nahezu unerforscht geblieben.[14]

Vieles weist darauf hin, dass für einen Großteil der West-Berliner die „Veränderungen im Osten" sich bis dahin in einem separaten Paralleluniversum abspielten, das in der eigenen Erfahrungswelt, wenn überhaupt, nur wenig Bedeutung gewann. Auf der „Insel" tickten die Uhren nun einmal anders. Schon Kohls „geistig-moralische Wende" war in West-Berlin kaum durchsetzbar gewesen, wo linke Bürgerinitiativen die großen Museumspläne sabotierten und stattdessen NS-Gedenkstätten initiierten. Die Bonner Rhetorik über die alte Reichshauptstadt und das Zentrum der Nation, die Berlin in der Rolle als Nationalgarten der deutschen Vergangenheit zurückzulassen schien, missfiel längst nicht nur den Bürgerbewegten, Hausbesetzern und Autonomen. Bis in die regierende CDU hinein distanzierte sich so mancher Politiker, wie zum Beispiel Kohls Parteifreund Senator Volker Hassemer, vom Pathos des Kanzlers, während die Identitätsdebatten hier schon vor 1989 eher im Bereich der Stadterneuerung und der Erinnerungsorte geführt wurden, ebenso wie nach 1990 auch.[15] Die Stadt atmete in den innenstädtischen Bezirken den Geist der schwer subventionierten Off-Szene: Seit den 1970er Jahren war es in zunehmendem Maße – und ungeplanterweise – die neue Aufgabe Berlins geworden, im bundesdeutschen Rahmen „die neuen alternativen Kulturen zu integrieren, sie nicht nur als Unruheelemente, sondern als Belebung zu sehen."[16] Viele Berliner lebten auf ihrer Insel leicht überheblich in einer gefühlten Äquidistanz sowohl zum weit entfernten Westdeutschland mit seinen kleingeistigen Berlinbesuchern und seinem provinziellen Kanzler, als auch zur unbeliebten DDR, der man hauptsächlich in Form der sächselnden Grenzbeamten und der langen Wartezeiten im gespenstischen Transitverkehr begegnete. West-Berlin war eben „etwas anderes," und nationale Identität, Wiedervereinigungsgebot und Hauptstadtaspirationen waren für weite Teile der „Generation West-Berlin" topographisch wie temporal Begriffe aus anderen Welten.[17]

---

[14] Rott, *Insel*, 405.

[15] Zum Scheitern der ersten DHM-Pläne in West-Berlin: Thijs, *Drei Geschichten*, 101-116; Moritz Mälzer, *Ausstellungsstück Nation: Die Debatte um die Gründung des Deutschen Historischen Museums in Berlin* (Bonn: Friedrich Ebert Stiftung, 2005). Zur Kontinuität im (West)Berliner Geschichtsdiskurs: Krijn Thijs, „...um den Besitz der deutschen Geschichte. Städtebau und Geschichtsdebatten im spätgeteilten Berlin," in *Auf dem Weg zur Friedlichen Revolution? Ost-Berlin in den Jahren 1987/1988*, hg. Martin Gutzeit (Berlin: Landesbeauftragte für die Unterlagen des Staatssicherheitsdienstes, 2008), 35-60.

[16] Rott, *Insel*, 331.

[17] Kerstin Schilling, *Insel der Glücklichen: Generation West-Berlin* (Berlin: Parthas, 2005).

Hier dürfte ein erster Grund für den Verlust der West-Berliner Perspektive in der historischen Forschungslandschaft nach 1990 liegen. Die Inselstadt hatte politisch wie gesellschaftlich eine Eigenkultur entwickelt, die in den späten 1980er Jahren stark ausgeprägt war, dann aber in kürzester Zeit als solche verschwand bzw. rasch im vereinten „Neuen Berlin" aufging. West-Berlin existierte somit nicht, wie die neuen Bundesländer, mit erkennbarer Identität in der Nachwendezeit fort; es hatte keine Stimme in der gesamtdeutschen Erinnerungslandschaft, wurde weder angeklagt noch verteidigt. Die Merkwürdigkeiten etwa des Transitverkehrs oder der Kreuzberger Szene reichten für das Raritätenkabinett des geteilten Deutschlands, nicht aber für eine fortlebende Vertretung in den Geschichtsdebatten nach 1990. Der eigenartige Beobachtungsstandpunkt „West-Berlin" ging nach 1990 verloren, auch in der Historiographie.

2. West-Berlin und 1989

Die Verortung des späteren West-Berlins ist in der deutschen Nachkriegsgeschichte von Fachhistorikern also bislang weitgehend undiskutiert geblieben.[18] Wie öfter in solchen Fällen bietet die Literatur Abhilfe: Das explosive Potenzial des Themas, gerade im Hinblick auf den November 1989, veranschaulicht zum Beispiel Sven Regeners Erfolgsroman *Herr Lehmann*, dessen West-Berliner Protagonist den Fall der Mauer nur im Vorbeigehen registriert. („Was soll das überhaupt heißen, die Mauer ist offen."[19]) Die West-Berliner Nischenwelt sollte nach dem November 1989 durch die unvermeidbaren Veränderungen einem umfassenden Praxistest ausgesetzt werden, der politisch vielleicht noch am ehesten an dem Schicksal der übrigens zu dieser Zeit regierungsverantwortlichen Alternativen Liste (AL) zu studieren wäre. Weil aber für eine solche West-Berliner Erfahrungsgeschichte des 9. November bislang kaum historische Vorstudien vorhanden sind, beschränke ich mich im Folgenden auf die besser dokumentierte politische Bühne West-Berlins und versuche, den Ertrag eines Perspektivenwechsels mithilfe eines bekannten Beispiels auszuloten: der Schöneberger Katerstimmung am Tag danach.

Im unbewussten Anlauf zum historischen November verstärkte sich diese Isolation noch um ein Vielfaches, als in West-Berlin ausgerechnet im April 1989 ein experimenteller rot-grüner Senat antrat, der nun auch offiziell vorhatte, die überholten statusrechtlichen und an „Einheitsfantasien" orientierten Grundlagen West-Berlins endlich den postnationalen Realitäten der Gegenwart anzupassen. Deutschlandpolitisch setzte der bundesweit zunächst eher unbekannte SPD-Politiker Walter Momper in seiner Regierungserklärung (13. April 1989) auf die Anerkennung der Teilung:

---

[18] Krijn Thijs, Rezension zu Wilfried Rott, *Die Insel: Eine Geschichte West-Berlins 1948-1990* (München: C. H. Beck, 2009), H-Soz-u-Kult, 30.03.2010, http://hsozkult.geschichte.hu-berlin.de/rezensionen/2010-1-241.

[19] Regener, *Herr Lehmann*, 281.

> Eine europäische Friedensordnung wird es in überschaubarer Zeit nur mit zwei gleichberechtigten und miteinander kooperierenden deutschen Staaten geben können, die ihre Existenz nicht gegenseitig in Frage stellen. Es gilt, bei fortdauernder Zweistaatlichkeit soviel an Zusammenarbeit wie möglich zu schaffen. Wir wollen den bestehenden Grenzen ihren trennenden Charakter nehmen.[20]

Mit dieser Denkhaltung konnte Momper sich der Unterstützung weiter Teile der West-Berliner Gesellschaft sicher sein, denn gerade in der einstigen Frontstadt waren die Einheitsideale erheblich verblasst. So schrieb – stellvertretend für viele andere – ein ehemaliger Chefredakteur beim Sender Freies Berlin noch Anfang des Jahres 1988 einen vernichtenden Essay über die armselige Suche nach einer „Rolle" für West-Berlin, die er sich höchstens „als Ort eines politikvorbereitenden gesamteuropäischen Dialogs" vorstellen konnte.

> Und was ist mit der deutschen Frage? Die ist offen wie alle Geschichte – aber nicht nach rückwärts. (…) Berlin kann deshalb nicht Hauptstadt im Wartestand sein. Es ist Zeit, dass wir ehrlich werden und die alten Träume begraben. Die deutsche Nation wird fortbestehen, aber für alle politisch planbare Zukunft in zwei Staaten. Die Mauer quer durch Berlin kann dennoch keinen Bestand haben. Aber sie wird nicht verschwinden, weil der andere deutsche Staat sich irgendwann selbst aufgibt, sondern an dem Tage, an dem die DDR sich eine offene Grenze zum Westen leisten kann.[21]

In diesem Geiste war Anfang 1989 auch Mompers Senat angetreten, und dass seine Regierungserklärung keine leeren Worte enthielt, bewies zwei Monate später eine stellvertretende Parlamentspräsidentin aus den Reihen der Alternativen Liste, Mompers grüner Koalitionspartner. Ihr Gewissen erlaubte es ihr am 25. Mai 1989 nicht, die traditionellen „Mahnworte" auszusprechen, mit denen das Abgeordnetenhaus seit 1955 seine Sitzungen eröffnete und die den „unbeugsamen Willen" bekundeten, dass Deutschland mit Berlin als Hauptstadt wiedervereinigt werde. Die Sprecherin sah hierin ein Relikt des Kalten Krieges, verweigerte sich nunmehr demonstrativ dem politischen Ritual (nachdem AL und SPD schon länger durch Lachsalven und Sitzenbleiben daran gekratzt hatten[22]). Die Folge war ein handfester Skandal. Das Exempel traf den antiquierten Kern des politischen Selbstverständnisses West-Berlins.[23] Auch die Berliner SPD geriet in die Kritik. Momper hatte, wie so mancher in der SPD, seine Hoffnungen auf Reformern innerhalb der SED gesetzt und hielt auch in der finalen Krise der DDR an Kontakten zur Staatsführung fest. Das Verhältnis zu ostdeutschen Oppositionellen war schwierig und ungeklärt.

---

[20] „Regierungserklärung Momper," 13.04.1989.

[21] Joachim Braun, "Berlin ist keine Hauptstadt," *Der Spiegel* 52/1987, 32-33.

[22] So z. B. bei der Konstituierung des neu gewählten Abgeordnetenhauses am 2. März 1989, als das „feierliche Bekenntnis zur Wiedervereinigung" laut Protokoll zunächst „Lachen bei der SPD und der AL" hervorrief, dann zu einem nur „zögernd[en]" Erheben führte und schließlich in „anhaltende[r] allgemeine[r] Unruhe" endete (*Plenarprotokolle des Abgeordnetenhauses von Berlin* [PP], 1/11, 02.03.1989, S. 3A-B.).

[23] Rott, *Insel*, 406.

Unter der politischen Leitung dieses Senats verspielte West-Berlin zumindest aus Bonner Sicht seinen letzten Rest deutsch-deutscher Politikfähigkeit. Ohnehin sanken die Beziehungen zwischen der konservativen Regierung Kohl und dem linken Senat Momper rasch auf den Tiefpunkt. Schon bei den rot-grünen Koalitionsverhandlungen ließ FDP-Chef Lambsdorff verlauten, dass Bonn nicht „jeden Unfug" an der Spree mitfinanzieren werde.[24] Momper und Kohl verband eine persönliche Feindschaft, die im Vorfeld der ostdeutschen Herbstrevolution eher zunahm als abebbte. Die Ironie war, dass West-Berlin ausgerechnet unter dieser einheitsskeptischen Führung auf den 9. November 1989 und anschließend auf den Weg zur nationalen Einheit zusteuerte.

Denn als sich die Krise der DDR im Herbst verschärfte, musste sich die West-Berliner Stadtverwaltung kurzfristig auf die Folgen einer möglichen Grenzöffnung vorbereiten. Berlin nahm nun seine vergessene Stellung unter ganz anderen Vorzeichen wieder ein: Nicht vom Westen, sondern vom Osten her wurden nun die alten Brückenfunktionsideale wieder aktuell. Die Senatsverwaltung erwartete einen Zustrom von ostdeutschen Besuchern an jenem „Tag X," an dem die DDR ihre rigide Grenzpolitik lockern würde. Zugleich sorgte man sich um die Stabilität des sozialistischen Umlands, von dem die isolierte Metropole in jeglicher Hinsicht abhängig war: vom geregelten Zugang über die Transitstrecke und die Wasserwege über die Müllabfuhr bis hin zur Stromversorgung etwa der S-Bahn sowie von U-Bahn-Tunneln unter DDR-Territorium. Vor diesem Hintergrund praktischer Sorgen und Vorbereitungen erhielten auch die Differenzen mit der Bonner Regierung neue Nahrung, denn die Inselstadt verlangte in diesen Umbruchszeiten zusätzliche Unterstützung. Doch „wie üblich" stieß Momper mit seinen Hilferufen in Bonn "auf taube Ohren und Unverständnis,"[25] und sein Senatskanzleichef notierte später, dass „aus Westdeutschland nur ziemlich von der realen Lage abgehobene Ratschläge zu erwarten waren."[26] Während das Meer unruhig wurde und die Insulaner improvisieren mussten, gab man sich zu Mompers Verzweiflung am trockenen Bonner Ufer unbeeindruckt der „überflüssige[n], in die Sackgasse führende[n] Wiedervereinigungsdiskussion" hin.[27] Der Berliner Senat beanspruchte aus seiner geografischen Nähe heraus Erfahrungswissen über die Veränderungen in der DDR und brachte gegenüber dem entfernten Bonn unter der Hand seine spezifische Lesart der „Wende" als vom Westen zu unterstützende DDR-Reform ins Spiel. Überflüssig anzumerken, dass sich Kohls Regierung darauf nicht einließ. Im Herbst 1989 spielte West-Berlin für sie keine Rolle, schon gar nicht Mompers rot-grüner Senat.

---

[24] Zit. n. "Revolutionäre Geduld," *Der Spiegel* 12/1989, 27.

[25] Walter Momper, *Grenzfall: Berlin im Brennpunkt deutscher Geschichte* (München: Bertelsmann, 1991), 22.

[26] Dieter Schröder, *Von Politik und dummen Fragen: Beobachtungen in Deutschland* (Rostock: Konrad Reich, 2002), 144.

[27] So erinnert jedenfalls Kohl Mompers Vorwürfe, vgl. Helmut Kohl, *Erinnerungen 1982-1990* (München: Droemer, 2005), 951.

Hier liegt ein zweiter Grund für die verlorene West-Berliner Geschichte: Mompers im Rückblick verfehlte und wenig einflussreiche deutschlandpolitische Position trug wenig zum gesamten Gang der Entwicklungen bei – hin zur Deutschen Einheit. Darauf komme ich noch zurück.

Die ungleiche Deutungskonkurrenz zwischen Bonn und West-Berlin entlud sich auf gewaltige Weise im Chaos um den unerwarteten Fall der Mauer. Neben aller Freude über die plötzliche Grenzöffnung und über den bis dahin friedlichen Verlauf der Umwälzung lagen binnen kürzester Zeit alle politischen Nerven blank. Große Nervosität gab es bezüglich der Haltung der Sowjetarmee und der Reaktionen von Menschen in Ost und West. Der Kanzler war im Ausland, und Berlins Regierender Bürgermeister feierte seine Deutungshoheit über die spektakulären Ereignisse in der eben noch ausrangierten Stadt Berlin. Die ungeklärte Lage führte am „Tag danach" zu offenen Verstimmungen, die bis weit in den späteren Verlauf der Vereinigung hinein ihre Spuren hinterlassen sollten.

3. Der Tag danach

Am Abend und in der Nacht des 9. November fand Geschichte statt, das war jedem Zeugen klar. Die zufällig tagenden Bundestagsmitglieder im fernen Bonn erhoben sich um 21.10 Uhr plötzlich von ihren Sitzen und stimmten die Nationalhymne an. Nachts folgte das Unvorstellbare: Ost-Berlin öffnete tatsächlich die Mauer. Ab dem nächsten Morgen sollte diese Geschichte erzählt werden – interpretiert, erklärt, gedeutet und gefeiert. Nur: Wie, wo und von wem? Was bedeuteten eigentlich die zweifellos „historischen" Ereignisse der Grenzöffnung, der langen Berliner Nacht der Freude, des Trabikorsos am Ku'damm, der Freudentränen an der Bornholmer Brücke?

Auch „the morning after" wurde ein Tag von vielerlei Grenzüberschreitungen. Helmut Kohl war am Nachmittag des 9. November gerade nach Polen abgereist, zu einem schwierigen Staatsbesuch in Warschau. Noch in der Nacht des 9. November beschloss er, den Besuch am nächsten Tag zu unterbrechen und nach West-Berlin zu fliegen. Walter Momper aber wurde am Freitag, dem 10. November, für einen wichtigen Termin ausgerechnet in Bonn erwartet. Nach zehn Jahren war Berlin ab dem 1. November 1989 turnusgemäß wieder an der Reihe, der bundesdeutschen Länderversammlung vorzusitzen. Im Falle des gar nicht offiziellen Bundeslandes Berlin war dies ohnehin eine sensible Angelegenheit, und nun stand die erste Sitzung in Bonn zufällig auch noch für Freitag, den 10. November 1989 auf dem Plan. Beide Reisen „am Tag danach," die von Momper und die von Kohl, wurden memorable Expeditionen in fremde Welten.

Mompers Besuch in Bonn folgte auf eine sensationelle Nacht, in der West-Berlins Regierender Bürgermeister den festgefahrenen Verkehr zwischen Ost- und West-Berlin an der Grenzübergangsstelle Invalidenstraße mit einem Megafon geregelt hatte – einer der wenigen ikonischen Momente des West-Berliner Bürgermeisters im

November 1989. Morgens um sieben flog er nach Bonn, und zwar mit einem ihm persönlich zur Verfügung gestellten militärischen Transportflugzeug der US-Amerikaner, damit er „nicht länger als unbedingt nötig" abwesend sein würde. „In Bonn war von der fundamentalen Veränderung, die heute Nacht durch Deutschland gegangen war, nichts zu spüren," notierte er später hämisch. „Keine Trabis, keine jubelnden Massen, normaler Alltag. Fast unwirklich. Das Regierungsviertel war so früh am Morgen ruhig und leer."[28] Seine erste Rede als Vorsitzender des Bundesrates musste er mit einem „ungewöhnlichen Geständnis" eröffnen: „Ich habe heute Nacht nicht geschlafen." Dann sprach er, schon morgens in Bonn, seine geflügelten Worte: „Gestern Nacht war das deutsche Volk das glücklichste auf der Welt."[29] Nach einer Reihe improvisierter Festreden und gegenseitiger Glückwünsche der westdeutschen Landesoberhäupter und nach der in Windeseile erledigten Arbeit (Abstimmung über immerhin fünfzig Gesetzesentwürfe) flog Momper am Mittag sofort wieder zurück nach West-Berlin, wo riesige Menschenmassen unterwegs waren. Am 10. November 1989 war Bonn die falsche Adresse.

Noch nachdrücklicher dokumentierte Helmut Kohls hastiger Besuch in West-Berlin das Aufeinanderprallen zweier Politikkulturen. Der Kanzler hatte mit einigen Mitarbeitern seinen polnischen Staatsbesuch unter dem Protest seiner Gastgeber unterbrochen und war aus Warschau abgereist. Er wollte die Situation selbst begutachten und ahnte die Gelegenheit für eine historische Rede. Seine Motivation entstand teilweise *ex negativo*: 1961 war Adenauer auffällig abwesend geblieben, als die Mauer errichtet wurde. Kohl wollte diesen Fehler bei ihrem Fall um keinen Preis wiederholen. Doch auch für seine Reisegruppe war es schwierig, die soeben „entmauerte" Stadt zu erreichen: Aufgrund von Statusfragen durfte die spontane Reise nicht über DDR-Territorium führen, sondern verlief über die Ostsee, Schweden, Hamburg und dann über den Luftkorridor nach West-Berlin, die letzte Etappe ebenfalls mit einer amerikanischen Militärmaschine. Kohl war spät. Bei seiner Ankunft hatte die West-Berliner Politik ihren stümperhaften Ruf schon bestätigt: Zu des Kanzlers großem Ärger hatte man sich vor Ort nicht auf *eine* Veranstaltung verständigen können, sondern es gab derer zwei. Neben dem „offiziellen" Programm des Abgeordnetenhauses in Schöneberg hatte die Berliner CDU an einer eigenen Bühne an der Gedächtniskirche festgehalten. Hausgemachte Konkurrenz also, und Kohl sollte im Eiltempo an beide Adressen geführt werden.[30]

Es sollte nicht bei diesem einen Ärgernis bleiben. Die westdeutsche Prominenz traf im Laufe des Tages in der tobenden Inselstadt ein und versammelte sich im

---

[28] Momper, *Grenzfall*, 154.

[29] Bundesrat, „Plenarprotokoll 606," 10.11.1989, 453 (A).

[30] Vgl. die Darstellungen bei Klaus Dreher, *Helmut Kohl: Leben mit der Macht* (Stuttgart: DVA, 1996), 452-457; Eberhard Diepgen, *Zwischen den Mächten: Von der besetzten Stadt zur Hauptstadt* (Berlin: Bebra, 2004), 118-122; Horst Teltschik, *329 Tage: Innenansichten der Einigung* (Berlin: Siedler, 1991), 16-24; Kohl, *Erinnerungen*, 964-973; Eduard Ackermann, *Mit feinem Gehör: Vierzig Jahre in der Bonner Politik* (Köln: Gustav Lübbe, 1994), 310-312; Rott, *Insel*, 412-419.

Abgeordnetenhaus, im Rathaus Schöneberg. Dort hielt die West-Berliner Volksvertretung gerade eine Sondersitzung ab, die in der Nacht der Nächte von den Regierungsfraktionen beantragt worden war. Ziel war es, gemeinsam eine Resolution zu den historischen Ereignissen abzugeben.[31] Die Debatte wurde mit Lautsprechern live auf den Platz vor dem Rathaus übertragen, wo eine wachsende Menge auf die anschließende Kundgebung mit Genscher, Kohl und Brandt wartete. Während die bundesdeutschen Politpromis, teilweise aus dem Westen, teilweise aus Polen kommend, im West-Berliner Parlament eintrafen und in der für sie reservierten ersten Reihe Platz nahmen, lief die feierliche Debatte unter den West-Berliner Abgeordneten langsam aus dem Ruder. CDU-Fraktionschef Eberhard Diepgen, ehemaliger Regierender Bürgermeister, hatte sofort den „Tag der nationalen Einheit" ausgerufen und rhetorisch alle Register gezogen: „Deshalb rufe ich Herrn Krenz zu: Öffnen Sie dieses Brandenburger Tor!"[32] Die SPD reagierte irritiert auf Diepgens Nationalpathos. Die Alternative Liste weigerte sich daraufhin, einer Resolution zuzustimmen, in der das Wort „Einheit" vorkäme. Die Party entgleiste nun völlig und das Publikum draußen hielt sich mit Unmutsbekundungen nicht zurück. Zu allem Überfluss setzte ein Vertreter der Republikaner am Rednerpult zum Deutschlandlied an; bei der vierten Zeile wurde er „unter tumultartige[r] Unruhe" im Parlament vom Ordnungsdienst entfernt.[33] Die Resolution, die nach vielen Zänkereien und gegen die Stimmen der CDU und der Republikaner schließlich verabschiedet wurde, war ein haarsträubender Kompromiss zwischen AL und SPD. Die Senatsparteien hatten eine von der CDU vorgeschlagene Formulierung aus Willy Brandts Brief zur deutschen Einheit (1972) förmlich vergewaltigt, indem sie gerade den Begriff der „Einheit" durch einen unlesbaren Brei ersetzt hatten.[34] Mit großem Staunen verfolgte die Bonner Politikelite, darunter Altbürgermeister und Ehrenbürger Brandt selbst, das klägliche Schauspiel des politischen West-Berlin. Berlins Parlamentspräsident Jürgen Wohlrabe (CDU) erklomm später den Gipfel der Absurdität, indem er draußen auf dem Platz schlichtweg Brandts ursprünglichen Text vortrug, als hätte die ganze Debatte nicht stattgefunden.[35]

Damit noch immer nicht genug. Nach dem misslungenen Auftritt des Abgeordnetenhauses erschienen die führenden Politiker am späten Nachmittag im Portal des Schöneberger Rathauses. Oben an der Freitreppe war eine kleine Bühne

---

[31] Momper, *Grenzfall*, 154.

[32] PP 11/17, 10.11.1989, 780C.

[33] Ebenda, 784B.

[34] Der ursprüngliche, an Brandt angelehnte Text lautete: „Das Abgeordnetenhaus von Berlin hält fest an dem Ziel, auf einen Zustand des Friedens und der Einheit Europas hinzuwirken, in dem auch das deutsche Volk in freier Selbstbestimmung *seine Einheit erlangen kann.*" Nach langem Ringen hinter den Kulissen wurde daraus: „Das Abgeordnetenhaus von Berlin hält fest an dem Ziel, auf einen Zustand des Friedens und der Einheit Europas hinzuwirken, in dem auch das deutsche Volk in freier Selbstbestimmung *zu der Gestaltung seines Zusammenlebens gelangen kann, für die es sich in Ausübung seines Selbstbestimmungsrechtes entscheidet.*" (PP 11/17, 787C und D).

[35] Momper, *Grenzfall*, 164.

improvisiert worden. Die Stimmung war angespannt. Die Alternative Liste – immerhin West-Berliner Senatspartei – hatte gleich ganz auf Vertretung verzichtet; für sie war jede Form von Wiedervereinigung ein „reaktionäres Projekt," und zum Mauerfall hatte sie dementsprechend wenig zu sagen.[36] Die Redner waren, in dieser Reihenfolge, Momper, Wohlrabe, Genscher, Brandt und Kohl. Sie mussten in einem Eiertanz versuchen, die unberechenbare Lage am Tag nach dem Mauerfall zu beschwören und missverständliche Signale an die Innen- wie die Außenwelt zu vermeiden. Noch während der Reden auf der Schöneberger Treppe trafen laufend neue Nachrichten aus Ost-Berlin und aus Moskau bei den Spitzenpolitikern ein. Und vor ihren Füßen versammelte sich das aktivistische West-Berlin der späten 1980er Jahre.

Das Publikum empfing Wohlrabe und vor allem den unpopulären Kanzler sofort mit einem Pfeifkonzert. Momper sprach als Erster und sagte demonstrativ: „Gestern war nicht der Tag der Wiedervereinigung, sondern der Tag des Wiedersehens in unserer Stadt!" Während er dem „Volk der DDR" zu seiner gelungenen Revolution gratulierte, zischte Kohl hinter ihm: „Volk der DDR – unglaublich, unglaublich." Momper wagte sich noch weiter vor: „Die demokratische Kultur der Bürger der DDR ist unverbraucht. Sie zeugt von sozialer Verantwortung und der Abneigung gegen die Ellenbogengesellschaft. Davon werden sich bei uns manche eine Scheibe abschneiden können." Jubel in West-Berlin, aber hinter ihm, so berichtet Momper, kochte Kohl vor Wut: „Lenin spricht, Lenin spricht."[37] Nach Momper wurden Genscher und der in West-Berlin populäre Brandt vom Publikum enthusiastisch begrüßt.[38] Als Kohl schließlich an die Reihe kam, stiegen schrille Pfeifkonzerte aus der Menschenmenge empor. Seine Rede ging im Geschrei und Gepfeife unter. Abschließend zeigte sich Wohlrabe so taktlos, spontan zum Deutschlandlied anzusetzen. Kohl, Brandt, Genscher und Momper hatten keine Wahl und stimmten ein. Live in alle Welt übertragen, sang die bundesdeutsche Repräsentanz eine schiefe Nationalhymne, falsch, viel zu tief, auch noch schlecht beleuchtet und vor allem begleitet von gellenden Pfeifkonzerten. Die *taz* legte die denkwürdige Aufnahme triumphierend ihrer Ausgabe des nächsten Tages bei.[39] Das war West-Berlin am 10. November 1989.

Die gespenstische Szene am Schöneberger Rathaus bedeutete für die Delegation aus Bonn, bei aller Freude über die Öffnung der DDR, eine harte Landung im vergessenen Berlin. Wutentbrannt verließ Kohl nach Abschluss der Kundgebung die

---

[36] Zit. n. Rott, *Insel*, 417.

[37] Momper, *Grenzfall*, 166.

[38] Brandt vergaß während der Rede im Übrigen seinen Satz „Jetzt wächst zusammen, was zusammengehört" – der wurde vom Altmeister später zum Manuskript hinzugefügt… Vgl. Bernd Rother, „Gilt das gesprochene Wort? Wann und wo sagte Willy Brandt: "Jetzt wächst zusammen, was zusammengehört"?," *Deutschland Archiv* 1/2000: 90-93.

[39] Wolfgang Jäger, *Die Überwindung der Teilung: Der innerdeutsche Prozeß der Vereinigung 1989/90* (Geschichte der deutschen Einheit, Bd. 3) (Stuttgart: DVA, 1998), 46. Vgl. Kowalczuk, *Endspiel*, 460-464.

Szene. Dem Kanzler war der West-Berliner Senat, der bei den akuten und „existentiellen Schwierigkeiten" des immensen Besucherzustroms händeringend warmherzigen Zuspruch und harte Finanzmittel aus West-Deutschland brauchte, keinen Blick wert. Dass er kurz darauf bei der CDU-Kundgebung am Breitscheidplatz nach eigenen Angaben von einer großen Menge Berliner jubelnd empfangen wurde, registrierten die Medien nicht mehr, und nur aus Notizen seines Umfeldes erfahren wir von seinem spontanen Besuch am nunmehr weit geöffneten Checkpoint Charlie, wo ihm von vielen Ostberlinern energisch zugejubelt worden sei.[40]

Und so lieferte am 10. November das Schöneberger Publikum einen dritten Grund für West-Berlins Absenz in unseren Erzählungen von 1989 und 1990. Die peinliche Treppenszene fällt bis heute in jeder Fernsehdokumentation oder DVD aus der Reihe: Die Insel hatte sich danebenbenommen. Viele Bonner Gäste waren zutiefst enttäuscht und beleidigt, vor allem im konservativen Umfeld Helmut Kohls. West-Berlin erwies sich endgültig sich als ein schwieriges, undankbares Pflaster, als eine eigene Erfahrungswelt. Der Affront sollte bei vielen Westdeutschen die Berlinskepsis bis tief in die Hauptstadtdebatte von 1991 nähren und diente den Freunden Bonns als Beweis dafür, dass man inmitten dieses Straßenmobs doch wohl nicht in Ruhe regieren könne. Aus München ertönte mit Verweis auf den 10. November die Warnung vor einer „Hauptstadt Kreuzberg."[41] Der Erfahrungsraum West-Berlin schien dem ganzen Geschehen im besten Falle ambivalent gegenüberzustehen, und genau das gilt seit 1990 scheinbar eher als Argument gegen als für eine nähere Erforschung.

4. Harte Landung und die Verführungen der Teleologie

Der Schöneberger Kater dokumentierte in hoher Dichte die Orientierungskrise, die der Mauerfall zunächst für die alte Bundesrepublik bedeutete. Der Historiker Andreas Wirsching spricht in diesem Sinne von einer „tiefgründigen Symbolik" der verkorksten Veranstaltung, weil sie „ziemlich genau die deutschlandpolitischen Positionsunterschiede der alten Bundesrepublik wider(spiegelte)."[42] Jetzt kam es darauf an, diese alten Positionen in das noch zu vermessende neue Zeitalter hinein zu übersetzen. Dabei war kurz nach dem Mauerfall noch lange nicht klar, dass es Helmut Kohl sein würde, dessen Person und Politik die nachfolgenden Monate ebenso dominieren sollte wie die spätere Geschichtsschreibung. Denn die auf den 3. Oktober 1990 ausgerichtete Teleologie stellt bis heute die alternativen zeitgenössischen Deutungen des 9. November 1989 in den Schatten. Dazu gehören nicht nur, wie Martin Sabrow jüngst veranschaulichte, die unterschiedlichen von

[40] Teltschik, *Tage*, 21.

[41] Vgl. Alois Rumel (Hg.), *Bonn. Sinnbild deutscher Demokratie: Zur Debatte um Hauptstadt und Regierungssitz* (Bonn: Bouvier, 1990).

[42] Andreas Wirsching, *Abschied vom Provisorium. Geschichte der Bundesrepublik Deutschland 1982-1990* (München: DVA, 2006), 647.

DDR-Oppositionellen bis weit ins Jahr 1990 getragenen Vorstellungen eines „Dritten Weges" einer eigenständigen DDR,[43] sondern ebenso die einheitsskeptischen Haltungen vieler Westdeutscher.

Auch die West-Berliner Pfeifkonzerte am Rathaus Schöneberg können samt protokollarischer Protesthaltung der regierenden AL diesen alternativen, vom weiteren Verlauf des Einheitsjahres 1990 gleichsam widerlegten, zeitgenössischen Deutungen des Mauerfalls zugerechnet werden. Sie bargen nicht zuletzt auch eine geographische Dimension in sich, denn die „tiefgründige Symbolik" der Schöneberger Treppenszene lag nicht nur in den „deutschlandpolitischen Positionsunterschieden," sondern auch in der topo-kulturellen Verschiebung innerhalb der „alten" Bundesrepublik. Auf einmal hatten die Bonner von weither kommen müssen, um „dabei" zu sein. Und im Gejohle an diesem West-Berliner 10. November wurde auch die (Macht)Frage verhandelt, wie sich die verunsicherte, gerade von einem abenteuerlichen Linkssenat geführte Symbolkommune eigentlich verstand und wem sie gehörte. Die Runde am Schöneberger Rathaus entschieden die Linken für sich, am Breitscheidplatz sammelte sich der CDU-Überlieferung nach dann Kohls Klientel, während der mysteriöse Abstecher zum Checkpoint Charlie bereits einen Vorgeschmack auf Kohls immense Popularität bei den baldigen Neubundesbürgern gab.[44]

Bis dahin demonstrierte aber der Kater von Schöneberg vor allem, wie sehr die Stadt Berlin in der alten Bundesrepublik symbolisch überfrachtet worden war und wie tief der Graben zur West-Berliner Realität der 1980er Jahre klaffte. Die Veranstaltung am Rathaus suchte in Pathos, Form und Ort Anschluss an die Tradition der legendären Jahre 1948 und 1963, der großen Berlin-Reden von Reuter und Kennedy. Doch das versammelte West-Berlin war im November 1989 nicht mehr das heroische Volk, das der bundesdeutschen Mythologie nach tapfer viele Krisen bestanden, die von Stalin und Ulbricht bedrohte Demokratie verteidigt und der gebeutelten Stadt in aussichtsloser Lage immer die Treue gehalten hatte. Seit den späten 1960er Jahren war ein neues, oft aus West-Deutschland zugewandertes, junges und kritisches West-Berlin hinzugekommen, und diese Polarität prägte jetzt den Erfahrungsraum West-Berlin.[45] Die ernüchternde Realität am John-F.-Kennedy-Platz 1989 war eine von Linken, Autonomen und Bürgerbewegten dominierte neue Generation, deren Hauptanliegen der Protest gegen Kohl, seine Wendepolitik und

---

[43] Martin Sabrow, „Der vergessene "Dritte Weg"," *Aus Politik und Zeitgeschichte* 11/2010, 6-13.

[44] Teltschik, *Tage*, 21, berichtet: „Kaum werden die Menschen seiner gewahr, ertönen Helmut-Helmut-Rufe. Hände strecken sich ihm entgegen, Tränen fließen. Dem Kanzler gibt das Bad in der Menge sichtlich Kraft." Der Besuch am Checkpoint Charlie ist auffälligerweise kaum dokumentiert. Abends, zurück in Bonn, erzählte Kohl in Telefongesprächen der britischen Premierministerin Thatcher und dem US-amerikanischen Präsidenten Bush davon. Vgl. Hanns Jürgen Küsters und Daniel Hoffmann (Hg.), *Dokumente zur Deutschlandpolitik: Deutsche Einheit. Sonderedition aus den Akten des Bundeskanzlers 1989/1990* (München: Oldenbourg, 1998) [DD Sonderedition], Dokumente 81 und 82.

[45] Hierzu ausführlicher: Eisenhuth, „West-Berlin."

seine Wiedervereinigungsträume war. Berlins CDU-Chef Diepgen sprach rückblickend von einem „Pöbel" und von der örtlichen „Fundamentalopposition," die den Platz „strategisch besetzt" und eine „aggressive" Stimmung verbreitet habe (und rechtfertigte mit diesem Hinweis auf das ungeeignete Publikum nebenbei sein Festhalten an einer eigenen CDU-Veranstaltung). Alles das sei West-Berlins „demonstrationserprobte politische Szene" gewesen.[46] Sogar Walter Momper gab sich nachher überrascht, dass so viele „junge Leute in Jeans und Lederjacke" gekommen waren und nicht mehr „ältere Berliner," „Leute mit Kerzen in der Hand, die sich noch an den Mauerbau und John F. Kennedys legendären Auftritt 1963 erinnerten."[47] Helmut Kohl brachte den Realitätsschock mit zugehöriger Empirieverweigerung abends deutlich zum Ausdruck: „Das war nicht das wirkliche Berlin."[48]

So entlarvten die Ereignisse in und um das Schöneberger Rathaus auch das imaginäre Berlin als die „versprochene Stadt" von schier mythologischem Ausmaß. Natürlich wäre die „historische" Nacht des 9. November ohne die direkte Nähe von West-Berlin undenkbar gewesen. Und sicher hat sich deshalb Berlins Rolle als „Pfand" oder „Hebel" der Einheit rückblickend glänzend bewährt. Doch diese von ihrem Ende her komponierte Sicht auf die „Insel" verkennt das eigenartige West-Berlin der 1980er Jahre. Denn wie journalistische Kommentare, politische Debatten und eben die Pfiffe in Schöneberg zeigen, war gerade in weiten Teilen der West-Berliner Normalität das politische Ideal einer nationalen Einheit tief weggesunken.

Vor diesem Hintergrund legt die politische Realität (oder auch: Irrealität) im letzten Jahr des alten West-Berlins die Umrisse einer politischen Stadtkultur bloß, die in die bundesdeutsche Meistererzählung des Mauerfalls nicht hineinpassen will. Mit ihrer von Kohls 10-Punkte-Programm geleiteten und auf die deutsche Einheit vom 3. Oktober 1990 ausgerichteten Teleologie verweist dieses Narrativ die Stimmen, Vorstellungen und Praxen West-Berlins in ein historisch ungültiges, weil vom „Lauf der Geschichte" widerlegtes Universum. „In einer rauschhaften Nacht, mit überschäumender Freude und Begeisterung," schreibt beispielsweise Wirsching zum 9. November 1989, „feierten die Menschen der geteilten ehemaligen Reichshauptstadt ihre Wiedervereinigung."[49] Abgesehen davon, dass sie durch den Bezug auf die Zeit vor 1945 einen ganz spezifischen Bedeutungszusammenhang anbietet, speist die Formulierung einen offenkundigen Anachronismus. Sie überträgt die Perspektive der späteren staatlichen Einheit auf die soeben erlebte Maueröffnung und schließt somit die erfahrene Offenheit der chaotischen Novembertage. Die vielfach anderen zeitgenössischen Lesarten degenerieren aus dieser auf den 3. Oktober fixierten Nach-Sicht zu postnationalen Spinnereien einer unbedeutenden Minderheit. Wer wie Wirsching vorgeht, verschließt sich auch dem Zugang zum

---

[46] Diepgen, *Mächten*, 118-121.
[47] Momper, *Grenzfall*, 165.
[48] DD Sonderedition, Dok. 82, 508; Kohl, *Erinnerungen*, 972.
[49] Wirsching, *Abschied*, 646.

eigenartigen, auf jeden Fall einmaligen West-Berliner Erfahrungsraum, der in den hektischen Novembertagen die erste und prominenteste Bühne für die epochemachenden Veränderungen in Deutschland hergab. Die Träger dieses kulturellen Erfahrungsraumes griffen, auch wenn sie wie Regeners Herr Lehmann gar nichts taten, vielfach in die unmittelbare Nach- und Interpretationsgeschichte des Mauerfalls ein. So geben auch und gerade die verkaterten Kopfschmerzen der Schöneberger Treppenszene „am Tag danach" Aufschluss über diese Primärerfahrungen und damit über die Kanalisierung historischer Kontingenz in westlichen Gesellschaften. Darin beschlossen lag auch die schockartige Adaption dreier so verschiedener kultureller Räume wie der Bundesrepublik, der DDR und eben West-Berlins.

Postskriptum

Eine letzte, leicht paradoxe Erklärung der auffälligen West-Berlin-Blindheit der historischen Forschung dürfte in den zunächst unvermuteten, dann aber ins Auge springenden kulturellen Kontinuitäten zur Hauptstadt der neuen „Berliner" Republik liegen. Denn die zunächst offenkundige Feststellung, dass West-Berlin Ende 1990 im Gegensatz zur DDR sang- und klanglos unterging, täuscht auf den zweiten Blick gewaltig – denn sie bezeugt vor allem, dass vieles aus West-Berlin eben gerade nicht verschwand, sondern nahtlos in das „neue Berlin" überging. Dies betrifft neben der Politik, der Justiz und der Verwaltung auch zahllose stadtplanerische, gedächtniskulturelle und symbolpolitische Strukturen und umfasst überraschenderweise viele prominente Projekte des „Neuen Berlins," wie etwa die Renovierung des Reichstags (diskutiert seit 1985), die Neubebauung des Spreebogens (seit 1982), die Erschließung des Potsdamer Platzes (seit 1988), die „kritische Rekonstruktion" (seit 1984) und die Errichtung eines Holocaust-Denkmals (seit 1988). Trotz der gewaltigen kontextuellen Veränderungen, die solche Projekte ideell teilweise in ihr Gegenteil verkehren ließen, verliefen personell, topographisch und diskursiv unzählige Linien vom alten West-Berlin in die neue Bundeshauptstadt. Die Vermutung liegt nahe, dass es bei aller Entfremdung gerade auch die perspektivische und oft biografische Nähe ist, die einer Distanzierung, und somit einer Historisierung des späten West-Berlins bis heute im Wege steht.

Krijn Thijs
k.thijs@uva.nl

Grenzgang als zögernde Wieder-Annäherung

Die deutsche Staatsbürgerschaft und der jüdisch-deutsche Dialog

Sabine von Mering
Center for German and European Studies, Brandeis University

„Ich bleibe Emigrant"
George L. Mosse

Wer von Juden und dem heutigen Deutschland spricht, spricht in der Regel von den Juden, die selbst oder deren Eltern in den letzten zwanzig Jahren aus der ehemaligen Sowjetunion im Rahmen des „Kontingentflüchtlingsgesetzes" nach Deutschland gekommen sind. Über 190.000 russische Juden sind laut Jeffrey Peck zwischen 1989 und 2005 nach Deutschland emigriert, und die wirkliche Zahl mag noch höher liegen, denn viele wurden nicht Mitglied in der offiziellen jüdischen Gemeinde und blieben daher ungezählt. Schätzungen liegen bei 200.000 bis 250.000. Diese jüngste russisch-jüdische Immigration nach Deutschland ist bereits vielfach untersucht worden. Eine Reihe von Veröffentlichungen z. B. des Moses-Mendelssohn-Zentrums in Potsdam und des Kollegiums für Jüdische Studien an der Humboldt-Universität beschäftigen sich mit den soziologischen, politischen und religiösen Hintergründen dieser transnationalen Gruppierung. Auch diese Grenzgänger mögen ihren Schritt zunächst zögerlich nach Deutschland gewandt haben. Doch handelte es sich bei ihrem Grenzgang nicht um eine Rückkehr. Sie trugen keine Erinnerungen an ein früheres Deutschland mit sich und mussten nicht nachweisen, dass ihnen ihre deutsche Staatsbürgerschaft im Dritten Reich aberkannt worden war.[1] Eine deutsche Abstammung war nicht Bedingung für die Einwanderung. Jeffrey Peck schreibt über die Immigranten sie seien „proud Russians as well as Jews," von denen viele ihre Loyalität zum alten *Heimatland* mit den militärischen Auszeichnungen demonstrieren, die sie als Rotarmisten im Kampf gegen die Wehrmacht erwarben. Dass sie aus der ehemaligen Sowjetunion nach Deutschland und nicht nach Israel oder Amerika auswanderten, müssen sie vor Israelis und Amerikanern oft rechtfertigen — wie ein Interviewpartner Peck erklärt: „They [American Jews] keep asking me why I want to live here, but Germany does not mean fascism for me and America is not so great."[2]

[1] Sie bekommen auch nicht automatisch die deutsche Staatsbürgerschaft, sondern müssen sich nach 6-7 Jahren darum bewerben. Dabei können sie diese auch verlieren, wenn sie z. B. noch immer von staatlichen Unterstützungsleistungen abhängig sind.

[2] Jeffrey Peck, *Being Jewish in the New Germany* (New Brunswick, NJ and London: Rutgers University Press, 2006), 42.

Sie begründen ihre Einwanderung nach Deutschland u. a. mit dem Hinweis darauf, dass Deutschland ihnen einfach geographisch und vielleicht auch ideologisch näher liegt. Peck: „Many choose to live in Germany, sometimes selecting it over Israel or the United States, because in Eastern Europe Germany is seen as a major economic powerhouse and a land of economic opportunity. Some like its proximity to Russia and its familiar European heritage and others prefer Germany because it is presumed safer and more secure than Israel."[3]

1. Juden in Deutschland

Im Gegensatz zu den neuen Einwanderern aus der ehemaligen Sowjetunion ist das Verhältnis amerikanischer Juden zu Deutschland nach wie vor stark von der Erfahrung der Verfolgung geprägt. Dennoch beginnt sich auch in jüdischen Kreisen in den USA ein neues Verhältnis zu Deutschland zu entwickeln. Die „zögernden Grenzgänger," deren Verhalten im Folgenden beleuchtet wird, sind amerikanische Juden deutscher Herkunft, die sich in jüngster Zeit häufiger entscheiden, nach Deutschland zu reisen und in einigen Fällen sogar die deutsche Staatsbürgerschaft wieder anzunehmen. Was motiviert sie, diesen Schritt zu tun? Wie verhandeln die Familien untereinander ihre Beziehung zu Deutschland? Was beeinflusst ihre Entscheidungen?

Um einige Antworten vorwegzunehmen: Die Generationenunterschiede liegen auf der Hand. Während die Überlebenden selbst nach wie vor mit dem Trauma der Verfolgung kämpfen und in den seltensten Fällen eine Rückkehr nach Deutschland ernsthaft in Erwägung ziehen, sehen die von der Wirtschaftskrise in den USA besonders hart getroffenen Jüngsten der Enkelgeneration das vereinigte Deutschland im vereinten Europa, mit EU-Reisepass und Arbeitserlaubnis, ähnlich wie ihre Religionsgenossen aus St. Petersburg oder Tel Aviv als attraktive potentielle Alternative. Sie sehen in Deutschland und Europa vor allem hohe Lebensqualität. Dazu zählen die meist guten öffentlichen Verkehrsmittel, ein reiches Kultur- und Sozialleben, angenehm geringe Distanzen (im Gegensatz zu den USA) zwischen vielen interessanten Städten und Ländern in Europa. Auch wenn sie als kleinste Minorität in den USA oft selbst Erfahrung mit Antisemitismus gemacht haben, ist ihr Deutschlandbild nicht in erster Linie vom Antisemitismus geprägt. Deutsche Organisationen wie die Goethe-Institute, die Konsulate, der DAAD, auch deutsche Wirtschaftsunternehmen in den USA und natürlich auch Deutschprogramme an Schulen und Universitäten sind bestrebt, ein modernes Bild von Deutschland zu zeichnen, das der Vergangenheit Rechnung trägt und zugleich Eindrücke jüngster Entwicklungen vermittelt – die von der deutschen Botschaft unterstützten Campuswochen zum 20. Jahrestag des Mauerfalls zum Beispiel, denen im Herbst 2010 eine Aktion zum Klimawandel folgte und 2011 ein Besinnen auf die deutsche Sprache folgen wird, tragen dieser Aufgabe Rechnung. Sehr wichtig ist auch die

[3] Ibid.

Arbeit von Organisationen wie *Facing History and Ourselves*, die viele US-Amerikaner bereits im Mittelschulalter von 8-10 Jahren im Geschichtsunterricht kennenlernen, und die bestrebt ist, die Erfahrung von Diskriminierung und Verfolgung im Zweiten Weltkrieg in größere historische Zusammenhänge einzubetten. Auch das Internet hilft über anfängliche Berührungsängste hinweg. Ein kurzer Aufenthalt in Berlin, München oder Frankfurt während einer Europareise oder ein Schüleraustausch bilden oft den nächsten Schritt zur weiteren Auseinandersetzung mit dem Land, das ihre Großeltern vertrieb.

Das Deutschlandbild der Jungen erscheint den Älteren dagegen oft naiv und ahistorisch. Die Überlebenden selbst stehen der jüngsten Entwicklung eher skeptisch gegenüber — hier gibt es kaum Unterschiede zwischen Israelis und Amerikanern. Nur wenige entscheiden sich selbst zu einem Besuch in Deutschland. Für die meisten überwiegt der Schmerz des erfahrenen Verlustes — und dies, obwohl und oft gerade weil die emotionale Beziehung zu Deutschland als Heimatland durchaus nach wie vor sehr stark ist.

2. Hintergrund: Deutsche Staatsangehörigkeit

Im neunzehnten Jahrhundert kämpften Juden in Deutschland jahrzehntelang vergebens um ihre bürgerlichen Rechte. Geringe Fortschritte (wie im Zuge der Napoleonischen Eroberungen) wechselten wiederholt mit Enttäuschungen ab. Erst die Reichsverfassung von 1871 machte alle in Deutschland lebenden Juden de jure zu gleichberechtigten Staatsbürgern; de facto gab es nach wie vor viele Einschränkungen. Doch auch Staatsbürger blieben sie keine 65 Jahre. Als Teil der „Nürnberger Gesetze" machte das „Reichsbürgergesetz" die Juden in Deutschland im November 1935 explizit zu Bürgern zweiter Klasse. Im November 1941 wurde deportierten deutschen Juden durch die 11. Verordnung des Reichsbürgergesetzes „mit dem Grenzübertritt ins Ausland" automatisch die Staatsbürgerschaft entzogen. Als Volks- und Staatsfeinde gebrandmarkt, hatte das Gros der Überlebenden keine Ambitionen, die deutsche Staatsbürgerschaft nach 1945 zurückzufordern. Auch von den ca. 250.000 aus Konzentrationslagern in Deutschland befreiten Juden (die Mehrheit aus Polen stammend), die in den ersten Nachkriegsjahren in DP Camps untergebracht waren, und von denen Tausende in den Wochen nach Kriegsende an den Folgen von Unterernährung und Folter starben, verließen mehr als 90% Deutschland noch in den ersten Nachkriegsjahren.[4]

Nur um die 20.000 blieben (wie z. B. Victor Klemperer) im Lande — zumeist, wie Klemperer, wegen ihrer „arischen" Ehepartner und Familien — oder kehrten, wie der 2010 verstorbene Publizist Ernst Cramer oder der Vater der Autorin Stefanie Zweig (bekannt durch Caroline Links Verfilmung ihres Buches *Nirgendwo in Afrika*[5])

---

[4] Siehe Atina Grossmann, *Jews, Germans, and Allies: Close Encounters in Occupied Germany* (Princeton and Oxford: Princeton Univrsity Press, 2006), 1.

[5] Stefanie Zweig, *Nirgendwo in Afrika* (München: Langen-Müller, 1995).

aus Sehnsucht zu Sprache und Kultur in die deutsche Heimat zurück, wo sie, das beschreibt Zweig sehr eindrücklich im Folgeroman *Irgendwo in Deutschland*, und Atina Grossmann hat dies in ihrer Studie *Jews, Germans, and Allies. Close Encounters in Occupied Germany* (2006) bestätigt, durchaus nicht immer herzlich willkommen geheißen wurden. Andere kamen auch in die DDR, mit dem Traum, beim Aufbau eines anderen, antifaschistischen Deutschlands zu helfen.[6] Doch die Rückkehrer wurden oft bitter enttäuscht: Antisemitismus war auch im Nachkriegsdeutschland weit verbreitet:

> ...there should be no doubt that the philosemitism or shamed silence that tabooized anti-Jewish acts or utterances — attitudes often attributed to postwar Germany — not only coexisted with, but were often overwhelmed by, a strong and entirely acceptable antisemitism.[7]

Im Kampf gegen Antisemitismus fanden sich auch nach dem Krieg in der restlichen Bevölkerung keine Verbündeten. Grossmann beschreibt z. B. eine Demonstration von über 1.000 Juden gegen antisemitische Gewalt und Polizeiaktionen in München 1949, an der offensichtlich keine Nicht-Juden teilnahmen.

Seit 1950 ermöglicht Artikel 116 des Grundgesetzes ehemaligen Verfolgten des Nazi-Regimes sowie deren „Abkömmlingen" die Wiedererlangung ihrer deutschen Staatsbürgerschaft. Jahrzehntelang machten von dieser Möglichkeit nur wenige Gebrauch — und dies, obwohl für emigrierte deutsche Juden die Möglichkeit der doppelten Staatsbürgerschaft sofort bestand, die erst im Jahre 2000 allgemein durchgesetzt wurde. Die Wiederannahme der deutschen Staatsbürgerschaft zwang sie also nicht, die Staatsbürgerschaft des Landes, in das sie geflohen waren, aufzugeben. Doch obwohl viele unter der Exilerfahrung zeitlebens litten, waren die Erfahrungen mit Nazi-Deutschland zu schmerzhaft, als dass sie eine Rückkehr in Erwägung ziehen wollten. Selbst eine Besuchsreise war für die meisten ausgeschlossen.

Unter dem Eindruck des Traumas der Eltern und aus Respekt vor ihnen kehrten auch die Kinder der Überlebenden sich nur selten nach Deutschland zurück. Die wenigen, die es dennoch tun/taten, müssen/mussten sich oft vor ihren Familien und Gemeinden rechtfertigen. Sue Stern, die lange Jahre als (in England geborene) Lektorin an der Universität Frankfurt tätig war, sprach auf Vortragsreisen durch die USA oft von Begegnungen mit amerkanischen Juden, die Sterns Entscheidung, in Deutschland zu leben, als Verrat empfanden. Sie trat dem entschieden entgegen: 1996 veröffentlichte sie ein Buch zum Thema — *Speaking Out: Jewish Voices from United Germany*.[8] Darin vermittelte sie amerikanischen Juden Deutschland so, wie sie es kannte, mit dem Ziel, auf beiden Seiten Vorurteile abzubauen.

---

[6] Grossmann, *Jews, Germans, and Allies: Close Encounters in Occupied Germany*, 92.
[7] Ibid, 258.
[8] Sue Stern (ed.), *Speaking Out: Jewish Voices from United Germany* (Carol Stream, IL: edition Q, 1995).

3. Perspektive auf Deutschland: Israel vs USA

Das Verhältnis amerikanischer Juden zu Deutschland unterscheidet sich nicht nur von demjenigen der Juden aus der ehemaligen Sowjetunion. Auch im Vergleich mit Israelis besteht ein Unterschied, den es ausführlicher zu untersuchen gilt. Die online-Zeitschrift *Israel Heute* berichtete am 10. September 2007, dass im Jahre 2006 über 4.000 Israelis die deutsche Staatsbürgerschaft beantragten, was einen 50%igen Anstieg gegenüber dem Vorjahr bedeutete.[9] Schon 2003 beschrieb das Magazin *hagalil* den dramatischen Anstieg der Anträge seit 2000, und zitierte einen Antragsteller: „Ich habe die deutsche Staatsbürgerschaft als eine zukünftige Versicherungspolice ausstellen lassen. In Stuttgart ist die Verzweiflung bequemer."[10] Laut Wikipedia lebten im Jahre 2005 60.000 Juden mit deutschem Pass in Israel. Diese Zahl mag, wenn man Wikipedia Glauben schenkt und der Trend anhielt, heute fast doppelt so hoch liegen.[11] Die politischen Unsicherheiten in Israel sind sicherlich der Hauptgrund für den hohen Anstieg. Andere Erklärungen für die Differenzen zwischen Israel und den USA können in der unterschiedlichen politischen Ausrichtung derer zu finden sein, die in den 1930er Jahren aus Deutschland nach Israel bzw. in die USA gingen. Auch wird die Tatsache, dass das Engagement deutscher Nachkriegsregierungen sich auf Israel konzentrierte (von Reparationszahlungen bis zur Etablierung von Städtepartnerschaften, von gemeinsamen wirtschaftlichen und militärischen Projekten bis zur Arbeit der christlich-jüdischen Gesellschaft etc.) mit eine Rolle spielen sowie natürlich die geographische Nähe Israels zu Europa. Tatsache ist aber auch, dass in den USA heute noch immer mindestens ebenso viele Juden leben wie in Israel[12] und dass man die besonderen Bedingungen des amerikanischen Exils berücksichtigen muss, wenn man das Verhältnis von Juden zu Deutschland heute untersuchen oder verbessern möchte.

Auch in den USA wird inzwischen eine Zunahme des Interesses an der deutschen Staatsbürgerschaft verzeichnet. Das Generalkonsulat für Neuengland in Boston bearbeitet inzwischen jährlich ca. 100 Anträge auf Staatsbürgerschaft von ehemals deutschen Juden, von denen 99% positiv beschieden werden. Die Mehrheit der Antragsteller sind Enkel von Überlebenden. Die deutsche Staatsbürgerschaft wird ihnen nicht einfach ausgehändigt. Es muss ein Antrag gestellt werden und mit diesem Antrag der Nachweis erbracht werden, dass jemand tatsächlich Deutsche/Deutscher war und Deutschland aus politischen, religiösen oder rassischen Gründen verlassen musste. Die deutschen Behörden sind dabei aber grundsätzlich recht großzügig. Im Gegensatz zu anderen Verfahren helfen sie z. B. bei der Ermittlung, stellen Suchanträge an Archive usw. Alles, was irgendwie relevant ist,

[9] http://www.israelheute.com/default.aspx?tabid=116&view=item&idx=1540.

[10] http://www.nahost-politik.de/deutschland/staatsangehoerigkeit.htm.

[11] Alex Weingrod und André Levy, "Social Thought and Commentary: Paradoxes of Homecoming: The Jews and Their Diasporas," in *Anthropological Quarterly* 79 (1999): 691.

[12] http://www.hagalil.com/01/de/Israel.php?itemid=1669.

wird für die Dokumentation akzeptiert. Sind die Antragsteller Kinder, Enkel oder Urenkel von Verfolgten, müssen sie darüber hinaus die Abstammung von den Verfolgten nachweisen, also durch die Geburtsurkunde sowie Heiratsurkunde der Eltern. Je weiter es in der Abstammungslinie heruntergeht, desto mehr Dokumente müssen vorgelegt werden.

Das Gesetz hat eine kuriose Ausnahme, die Kinder von deutschen Frauen betrifft. Abgelehnt werden Anträge von Kindern in den Fällen, in denen die verfolgte Person weiblich war/ist und ihr Kind vor 1953 geboren ist. In diesem Fall hat nur die Mutter, nicht aber das Kind ein Recht auf die deutsche Staatsbürgerschaft. Diese Ausnahme hängt mit dem deutschen Staatsangehörigkeitsrecht zusammen, nach dem man erst ab 1975 die deutsche Staatsangehörigkeit durch eine deutsche Mutter erwerben konnte. (Interessanterweise sind uneheliche Kinder, bei denen Gefahr bestünde, dass sie staatenlos würden, von dieser Regelung ausgeschlossen.) Diese Ungleichbehandlung betrifft alle Kinder (egal ob jüdisch oder nicht-jüdisch), die vor 1975 geboren wurden und nur eine deutsche Mutter, aber keinen deutschen Vater hatten. Es gab von 1975 bis 1978 eine dreijährige Übergangsfrist, während derer Betroffene die deutsche Staatsbürgerschaft beantragen konnten. Nach Ablauf der Frist war dieser Anspruch jedoch verjährt. Nur für Wiedergutmachungsfälle wird diese Frist bis 1953 zurückverlegt. Das Jahr 1953 wurde deshalb als Frist festgesetzt, weil das 1949 verabschiedete Grundgesetz die Bestimmung enthielt, dass Frauen und Männer gleichberechtigt sind. Den Verfassungsgebern war jedoch klar, dass es viele Gesetze gab, die gegen diesen Grundsatz verstießen. Da 1949 nicht alle alten Gesetze sofort außer Kraft gesetzt wurden, wurde festgelegt, dass alle gegen diesen Grundsatz verstoßenden Gesetze reformiert oder außer Kraft gesetzt werden sollten. Für den Fall, dass dies nicht gelänge, wurde die Frist 1953 gesetzt. Alle Gesetze, die zu diesem Zeitpunkt noch gegen den Gleichheitsgrundsatz verstießen, wurden automatisch ungültig. Das Problem dieser Regelung ist natürlich, dass jüdische Frauen, die durch die Nazis gezwungen worden waren, Deutschland zu verlassen, gezwungen waren, Nicht-Deutsche zu heiraten. Dementsprechend sollte auch ihren Kindern die deutsche Staatsbürgerschaft bewilligt werden. Gegen diese Ungleichbehandlung wurde aber bereits durch mehrere Instanzen hindurch erfolglos geklagt.

4. Generationenwandel: Zurück nach Deutschland, ja oder nein?

Um die deutsche Staatsbürgerschaft bewerben dürfen sich sowohl die Überlebenden selbst, als auch ihre Kinder oder Enkel. Jede Kombination ist möglich. Die Mehrzahl der Anträge in Neuengland wird von Enkelkindern gestellt. Wenige Überlebende selbst wollen diesen Schritt tun. Befragt, was sie zu diesem Schritt bewegt, geben die meisten pragmatische Gründe an — den Erwerb des EU-Passes. Emotionale Gründe werden eher von den wenigen Überlebenden gegeben, die selbst den Antrag stellen. Das Konsulat verzeichnet eine Zunahme der Anträge in den vergangenen Jahren. Aufgrund von Gesprächen mit den übrigen neun Konsulaten in den USA konnte Konsulin Kirsten Hardt bestätigen, dass die grundsätzlichen Aspekte sich ähneln — die Anzahl der Ablehnungen, die Anforderungen, Motive usw.

Natalie Tauchner kann die Einschätzung des Bostoner Konsulats ebenfalls bestätigen. Sie betreut in ihrer Anwaltskanzlei in New York inzwischen Dutzende von Anträgen im Jahr. Im Monat erreichen sie ca. dreißig Anfragen, von denen im Endeffekt fünf den eigentlichen Antrag stellen. Allerdings werden aus diesen fünf dann in der Regel fünfzehn bis zwanzig, denn die Anträge werden zumeist von ganzen Familien gestellt. Viele, die Interesse bekunden, so Tauchner, erweisen sich bei genauerem Hinsehen nicht als berechtigt. Laut Tauchner verfolgen 80% derer, die berechtigt sind, den ganzen Prozess bis zu Ende. Auch sie bestätigt, dass die Anträge in der Regel von Enkeln von Holocaust-Überlebenden gestellt werden, die es insbesondere ins kosmopolitische Berlin — und natürlich nach Europa insgesamt — zu ziehen scheint.

Nicht nur die Frage der Staatsbürgerschaft, auch die Entscheidung, nur nach Deutschland zu reisen, wird von den Generationen unterschiedlich gehandhabt. Während die Enkelgeneration pragmatisch denkt und ihre transnationale Identität im Wesentlichen als Möglichkeit betrachtet, Neugier zu befriedigen und berufliche Aussichten zu erweitern, sind die Kinder von Emigranten oft eher emotional motiviert, auf der Suche nach den eigenen Wurzeln.

So beschreibt es z. B. Karen Frank, die Tochter von Lore und Gustav Frank in Sybille Tiedemanns Dokumentarfilm *Briefe aus Chicago* (2008), dem Folgeprojekt, das zehn Jahre nach ihrem Dokumentarfilm *Kinderland ist abgebrannt* (1998) entstand, für den sie 1998 mit dem deutschen Filmpreis ausgezeichnet wurde. In *Briefe aus Chicago* zeigt die Filmemacherin, wie Gustav Frank, der bis zu seinem Lebensende fließend schwäbelte, sich nicht von seinen Fotos aus Ulmer Kindertagen trennen mochte, während seine Frau Lore den Kontakt nach Deutschland nach wie vor vehement ablehnte – in *Kinderland ist abgebrannt* war sie die einzige der zwölf ehemaligen Schulkameradinnen, die sich bis zum Schluss weigerte, am Klassentreffen in Ulm teilzunehmen. Nur zur Filmpremiere entschied sie sich, nach Deutschland zu reisen. Erst nach Gustavs Tod und ihrer Übersiedelung in ein Altersheim dekoriert sie ihre Wände mit Szenen aus der alten Ulmer Heimat. Die Tatsache, dass sie dies unter dem Einfluss der Alzheimer-Krankheit tut, mag die traumatischen Hintergründe verwischen. Die deutsche Sprache haben Lore und Gustav ihrer Tochter bewusst nicht beigebracht. Karen erinnert sich, dass die Eltern während ihrer Kindheit zwar untereinander Deutsch sprachen, mit ihr jedoch grundsätzlich auf Englisch bestanden.

Als sie zur Uraufführung des Films dann doch gemeinsam nach Deutschland kamen, war es die Tochter, die von der starken emotionalen Berührung sprach, die die Begegnung mit der Heimat der Eltern und der Besuch des ehemaligen Elternhauses für sie bedeutete.

5. Jüdisch-Deutscher Dialog

Bei einer Besprechung des Films im jüdisch-deutschen Dialogkreis in Brandeis wurde deutlich, wie sehr diejenigen, die selbst als Kinder von Überlebenden in den USA aufwuchsen, sich mit Karen Frank identifizieren können. Genau so sei das bei ihnen zuhause gewesen — Kaffeekränzchen am Sonntagnachmittag, Bilder von deutschen Landschaften an den Wänden — aber Deutsch lernen, das Land selbst besuchen — ausgeschlossen. Ihr Deutschsein empfindet die Generation der Kinder von Überlebenden oft als Belastung, die einer Art Phantomschmerz gleichkommt, denn sie haben keine wirkliche Erinnerung an den Verlust und sind doch geprägt von den schmerzhaften Erinnerungen der Eltern. Uta Larkey vom Goucher College in Baltimore bestätigt dies in ihrem Projekt *Past Forward: the Holocaust in Family Memory*, das die Beziehung zu Holocaust und Erinnerung zwischen den Generationen untersucht und das demnächst in Buchform erscheinen wird. Arbeiten wie die von Sybille Tiedemann und die Arbeit der Organisation *One-by-One* ermöglichen einen Einblick in die Generationenkonflikte dieser besonderen „transnationalen" Immigranten-Gruppe und helfen, die Konflikte einer breiteren Öffentlichkeit in beiden Ländern verständlich zu machen.

Der von Gershom Scholem totgesagte deutsch-jüdische Dialog kann in der Tat im Schatten des Holocaust nur weiterexistieren, wenn man den historischen Hintergrund in die Gegenwartsdiskussionen mit einbezieht. Auch Klaus Berghahn hat dies in seiner Einleitung zum Symposium für George L. Mosse *The Jewish-German Dialogue Reconsidered* schon 1996 festgehalten. Dennoch hält Berghahn die Weiterführung des Dialogs im Sinne Mosses für unabdingbar: „Whereas Scholem is insterested in the question of how much German Jews had to sacrifice in order to become part of the German *Bildungselite*, Mosse points out how much they contributed to the German ideal of *Bildung*."[13] Mosse, so Berghahn, sah auch nach dem Holocaust die Möglichkeit für einen Neuanfang. Der deutsch-jüdische Dialog muss keine Flucht in „post-memory" sein. Positive Ansätze zur Weiterführung des Dialogs gibt es viele: Man kann sie sowohl in der Ausweitung jüdischer Studien an deutschen Universitäten, als auch in den Publikationen der German Studies in den USA finden.

Die Brandeis University war in gewisser Hinsicht schon immer Teil dieses Dialogs. Als einzige nicht konfessionell gebundene amerikanische Privatuniversität in jüdischer Trägerschaft wurde die Universität 1948 von Immigranten gegründet, motiviert durch den bestehenden numerus clausus für jüdische Studenten an amerikanischen Eliteuniversitäten und durch das Bedürfnis der jüdischen Religionsgemeinschaft, es den übrigen Religionen gleichzutun und dem Land eine Universität anzubieten, wie der Historiker und Gründungspräsident Abraham L. Sachar es in seinem Buch *A Host At Last* formulierte.[14] In den ersten Jahrzehnten war

---

[13] Klaus L. Berghahn (ed.), *The German-Jewish Dialogue Reconsidered. A Symposium in Honor of George L.Mosse* (New York: Peter Lang, 1996), 3.

[14] Abraham Sachar, *A Host at Last* (Boston: Little Brown, 1976).

Deutsch an der Universität eine Art inoffizielle lingua franca, denn die Mehrzahl der Professoren kam aus Europa, viele, wie z. B. Herbert Marcuse, aus Deutschland selbst. Die Eltern von Louis Dembitz Brandeis, dem ersten jüdischen Richter am Obersten Gerichtshof, nach dem die Brandeis University benannt wurde, gehörten zu denen, die Deutschland nach der vergeblichen Revolution von 1848 enttäuscht verlassen hatten. Brandeis selbst kehrte als Jugendlicher noch einmal nach Deutschland zurück, um an der Annen-Realschule in Dresden seinen Schulabschluss zu machen — er sprach fließend Deutsch, und viele seiner späteren Bildungskonzepte wurden von dieser Erfahrung stark beeinflusst. Auch er ist also ein frühes Beispiel transnationaler Identität.

Deutsch war von Anfang an Unterrichtsfach an der Universität, über vier Jahrzehnte hinweg gelehrt von Professor Harry Zohn (von 1951-1996), der sich u. a. mit Übersetzungen von Walter Benjamin, Martin Buber und Gershon Scholem einen Namen machte. 1994 gründeten Fakultätsmitglieder den Jewish-German Dialogue mit Unterstützung durch den Rabbiner Albert Axelrad und Gisela Schwing, der Ehefrau eines Mitarbeiters am Deutschen Konsulat, durch deren Initiative noch drei weitere solcher Gruppen im Bostoner Raum entstanden. Im Gegensatz zu einigen der anderen Gruppen, die sich in privaten Wohnzimmern treffen, finden die Dialogtreffen an der Universität statt. Themen reichen vom Einfluss der russischen Zuwanderer auf die jüdischen Gemeinden in Deutschland über Wibke Bruhns' Biographie ihres Vaters bis hin zur US-Premiere der Musik des von den Nazis in Litauen ermordeten Komponisten Edwin Geist. Die Teilnehmer an den ca. 6-8 Veranstaltungen im Jahr rekrutieren sich aus mehreren Generationen: Holocaust-Überlebende, Kinder und Enkel von Überlebenden, jüdische und nicht-jüdische deutsche Fakultätsmitglieder ebenso wie (sowohl jüdische als auch nicht-jüdische) deutsche Studentinnen und Studenten.

6. Deutschlandreise

Über zehn Jahr lang reiste eine kleine Zahl der jüdischen Mitglieder der Bostoner Gruppen auf Einladung der Bundesregierung jeweils im August zu einem 10-tägigen Seminar nach Berlin, das von Dr. Jaroslav Szonka in der Europäischen Akademie betreut wurde. Anschließend berichteten die Reisenden in einem gemeinsamen Treffen von ihren Erfahrungen, und auch von den Alpträumen, die der Reise vorausgingen. Das Reiseprogramm umfasste sowohl Besuche bei Konzentrationslager-Gedenkstätten, als auch Treffen mit Politikern und anderen, z. B. mit Lehrern, die das Thema Holocaust im Unterricht behandelten.

Das sehr intensive 10-tägige Seminar bot den Besuchern einen Einblick in die Arbeit, die in Deutschland zum Gedenken an den Holocaust geleistet wird — und machte zugleich aufmerksam auf die besonderen Herausforderungen der Wiedervereinigung und z. B. auf die Arbeit zur Integration von Minderheiten. Auch Treffen mit Vertretern der jüdischen Gemeinden waren Teil des Besuchsprogramms.

Bei der Auswahl derer, die an den Seminaren teilnahmen (in der Regel war die Reisegruppe auf sechs Personen beschränkt), wurde darauf geachtet, den Teilnehmern die Möglichkeit zu einem die Generationen übergreifenden Dialog zu bieten. Beim letzten Bericht-Treffen derer, die im August 2009 nach Berlin gereist waren, erschien dies besonders gelungen. Deutlich wurden die Unterschiede in der Wahrnehmung Deutschlands: Während die Studenten relativ unbefangen Vergleiche anstellten, z. B. zwischen dem, was in Deutschland in Sachen Holocaust im Schulunterricht getan wird, und dem, was sie selbst in ihrer Schulzeit erfahren hatten, stand für die älteren Teilnehmer nach wie vor die Frage im Vordergrund: Wie konnte dieses Land derartige Massenverbrechen begehen? Larry Loewenthal, lange Jahre Vorsitzender des *American-Jewish Committee* in Boston, brachte die Gefühle der älteren Reisenden auf den Punkt: Als Jude sei er trotz aller Gastfreundschaft und Herzlichkeit der Gastgeber in Deutschland immer auf der Hut. Er könne nicht umhin, ständig die Verbrechen der Nazis an seinen Familienmitgliedern vor Augen zu haben, und er frage sich permanent: Wie konnte das geschehen? Hier, in diesem zivilisierten, hochkultivierten Land? Loewenthal sprach im Anschluss an seine Reise vor einer Reihe von jüdischen Gemeinden über seine Erfahrungen. Bei seinen Vorträgen erfuhr er, was Sue Stern schon vor fünfzehn Jahren erlebte: Viele seiner Zuhörer sahen es noch heute als Verrat an den Ermordeten an, dass er überhaupt nach Deutschland gereist war.

Dennoch zeichnet sich in der Haltung zu Deutschland deutlich eine Veränderung ab. Während es vor zehn Jahren noch häufiger passierte, dass Studentinnen hinter vorgehaltener Hand erzählten, sie könnten ihren Großeltern gegenüber nicht erwähnen, dass sie Deutsch lernten, kommen inzwischen mehr und mehr Studierende schon aus der High School, die auf einer Europareise auch in Berlin oder München Station gemacht haben — oft war dies ausschlaggebend für ihre Entscheidung, Deutsch studieren zu wollen — eine Sprache, die leider zunehmend aus den Lehrplänen der amerikanischen High Schools und inzwischen auch aus Colleges und Universitäten zu verschwinden droht.

Die Veränderung bietet sowohl Herausforderungen als auch Chancen: Die Jüngeren gehen mit weniger Vorbehalten auf Deutschland zu. Sie kommen zudem aus einer Generation, die an kulturelle Vielfalt gewöhnt ist — auch Brandeis ist stolz auf seine ausgeprägte *diversity* unter den Studierenden. So gibt es z. B. deutlich steigende Zahlen von Studierenden mit asiatischem Hintergrund. Zehn bis fünfzehn Prozent eines Jahrgangs kommen aus anderen Ländern. Die Jüngeren kennen Deutschland aus den Medien als Land des Fortschritts, des Umweltschutzes, als Land von Wissenschaft, Literatur und Musik. Zugleich ist der Generationenwechsel auch ein Verlust: Mit dem herannahenden Ende der Generation der Holocaust-Überlebenden muss die Darstellung ihrer Erinnerungen zunehmend durch historische Dokumente, Filme und Berichte aus zweiter Hand ersetzt werden.

Dies erschwert den direkten Zugang zum Verständnis der Erfahrung von Verfolgung und Exil und erhöht das Risiko der Verharmlosung und des Vergessens. In den nächsten Jahren werden neue Konzepte erforderlich werden, die den verantwortungsvollen Umgang mit der Vergangenheit für die Zukunft sicherstellen.

Sabine von Mering
vonmering@brandeis.edu

Yoko Akiyama
Zentrum für Deutschland- und Europastudien, Universität Tokyo, Komaba (DESK)

Obwohl die Religionsfreiheit ein Grund- und Menschenrecht darstellt, wird die Ausübung religiöser Praktiken aus verschiedenen Gründen häufig beschränkt oder verboten. Damit wird eine Grenze zwischen der religiösen Mehrheit und der religiösen Minderheit in einer Gesellschaft gezogen, welche soziale Exklusionslinien markiert und legitimiert. Da in demokratisch verfassten Staaten Religionsfreiheit im Allgemeinen als persönliches Grundrecht garantiert wird, lassen sich die Ausübung und Beachtung religiöser Gebräuche nicht ohne weiteres verbieten. Um die Einschränkung dieses Grundrechts dennoch legitimieren zu können, spielt das Kriterium «Kultur» eine entscheidende Rolle. Mit dem Argument des kulturellen Unterschieds werden die religiösen Gebräuche, welche die Mehrheit einer Gesellschaft nicht akzeptieren kann, abgelehnt. Solch eine kulturelle Grenzziehung kommt nicht nur in undemokratischen Ländern, sondern, wie die Ereignisse in der Schweiz zeigen, auch in demokratischen Ländern vor.

Im November 2009 sprach die Mehrheit der Schweizer sich in einer Volksabstimmung gegen den Bau von Minaretten aus.[1] Das Resultat, dass die Mehrheit der Schweizer der Volksinitiative «Gegen den Bau von Minaretten» gegen den Willen des Bundesrates und des Parlaments zustimmte, wird von der internationalen Gemeinschaft als überraschend und problematisch wahrgenommen.[2] Die Antragsteller der Abstimmung verteidigen sich gegen den Vorwurf der Diskriminierung mit dem Argument, dass die Anti-Minarett-Initiative sich nicht gegen den Islam als Religion richte, sondern der Abwehr eines «religiös-politischen Macht- und Herrschaftsanspruches» diene. Die Diskussion um das Verbot, seine Ursachen und möglichen Auswirkungen hält bis heute an. Die Argumente für und wider das Verbot beziehen sich dabei in der aktuellen Diskussion fast ausschließlich auf die Gegenwart der Schweiz und das historisch relativ neuartige Phänomen einer vermeintlichen oder tatsächlichen Bedrohung durch den Islam. Die historische

[1] Ein Minarett ist ein Turm für den Gebetsrufer bei oder an einer Moschee.

[2] 57,5% der Schweizer Stimmbürger stimmten dem Minarett-Verbot zu. Nur vier Kantone waren dagegen. Diese Initiative wurde von der rechtskonservativen Schweizerischen Volkspartei und der Eidgenössisch-Demokratischen Union lanciert. Aber der Bundesrat ist der Auffassung, dass diese Initiative gegen international garantierte Menschenrechte verstößt und im Widerspruch zu zentralen Werten der schweizerischen Bundesverfassung steht. *Schweizerisches Bundesblatt*, Botschaft zur Volksinitiative «Gegen den Bau von Minaretten» vom 27. August 2008, *Schweizerisches Bundesblatt*, Bundesbeschluss über die Volksinitiative «Gegen den Bau von Minaretten» vom 12. Juni 2009.

EUROSTUDIA — REVUE TRANSATLANTIQUE DE RECHERCHE SUR L'EUROPE
Vol. 7, No.1-2 (2011): 59-71

Perspektive wird dabei meist nicht berücksichtigt. Die Dynamik der Diskussion und ihr Verlauf lassen sich jedoch nicht verstehen, ohne den historischen Kontext einzubeziehen.

Wenn man auf die Geschichte der Schweiz zurückblickt, stößt man auf ein vergleichbares Ereignis, nämlich das Schächtverbot von 1893. Im ausgehenden 19. Jahrhundert war die Judenemanzipation – vor allem in rechtlicher Hinsicht – weit vorangeschritten. Glaubens- und Gewissensfreiheit sowie das Recht auf die freie Ausübung gottesdienstlicher Handlungen waren durch die Artikel 49 und 50 der Bundesverfassung von 1874 gewährleistet. In den gleichen Zeitraum fällt die hier zu behandelnde Volksabstimmung über das Schächten. Das Schächten, die jüdische Schlachtmethode, wurde als Ergebnis dieser Volksabstimmung verboten und das Schächtverbot in der Bundesverfassung verankert.[3] Seitdem ist das Schächten in der Schweiz verboten und dieses Verbot gilt heute noch.

Die Entscheidung in der Schächtfrage führte von Beginn an zu Konflikten zwischen den Juden in der Schweiz und der nichtjüdischen Schweizer Bevölkerung. Welchen Stellenwert die schweizerischen Juden der Schächtfrage beimaßen, zeigt sich beispielsweise in der Gründung des Schweizerischen Israelitischen Gemeindebunds (SIG) im Jahr 1904. Dieser Bund wurde mit dem ausdrücklichen Ziel, gemeinsam auf der Bundesebene gegen das Schächtverbot zu kämpfen, gegründet. Demgegenüber lehnt die Mehrheit der nichtjüdischen Schweizer Bevölkerung die Praxis des Schächtens bis heute als grausam und nicht tolerierbar ab. Deutlich wurde diese Haltung im Jahr 2001/2002, als der politische Versuch der Bundesregierung das Schächtverbot aufzuheben am Widerstand der Bevölkerung scheiterte.

In der vorliegenden Abhandlung beschäftige ich mich mit den folgenden zwei Fragen. Erstens beschreibe ich den Verlauf der Debatte um das Schächtverbot in der Schweiz aus historischer Perspektive. Dabei geht es mir vor allem darum, herauszuarbeiten, inwiefern das Schächten (als religiöse Praxis) in der schweizerischen Gesellschaft problematisiert wurde und wird und wie stark die schweizerische Gesellschaft gegen diese Kultur einer Minderheit eine Abneigung hegte und immer noch hegt. Zweitens beschäftige ich mich mit der Frage, warum das Schächten im ausgehenden 19. Jahrhundert in der Schweiz verboten wurde. Abschließend möchte ich als Schlussfolgerung aus dem Fall des Schächtverbots zwei Thesen in Bezug auf die kulturelle Grenzziehung vorschlagen.

---

[3] In der Verfassung stand das Wort „Schächtverbot" nicht in dieser Form, sondern es wurde durch folgende Formulierung angedeutet: „Das Schlachten der Tiere ohne vorherige Betäubung vor dem Blutentzug ist bei jeder Schlachtart und Viehgattung ausnahmslos untersagt" (Art. 25bis). Da beim Schächten die vorherige Betäubung der Tiere nicht gestattet ist, entsprach der Artikel praktisch dem Schächtverbot.

1. Das Schächtverbot in der Schweiz

Das Schächten

Das Schächten[4] ist eine rituelle Schlachtmethode der Juden, die in der Thora, der Heiligen Schrift des Judentums, vorgeschrieben ist.[5] Beim Schächten werden Tiere durch ununterbrochenen Halsschnitt durch alle weichen Teile des Halses bis zur Wirbelsäule geschlachtet. Dabei ist die vorherige Betäubung nicht erlaubt, weil das Töten allein durch den Schnitt vollzogen werden muss und der Tod nur durch die Bewegung des Tieres nach dem Schlachten kontrolliert werden kann.[6] Das Schächten darf ausschließlich durch qualifizierte Personen, Schochet (Schächter), durchgeführt werden, nicht zuletzt um durch unsachgemäßes Schächten die Qualen des Tieres nicht unnötig zu verstärken.[7] Dem Halsschnitt folgt das möglichst rückstandslose Ausbluten des Tieres, da der Genuss von Blut im Judentum verboten ist.[8]

Die Vorgeschichte des Schächtverbots

Die Ansicht, dass das Schächten Tierquälerei sei, und der Versuch der Einführung eines Schächtverbots haben eine lange Geschichte in der Schweiz. Im Hintergrund standen verschiedene Faktoren, z. B. der Tierschutzgedanke, die Humanisierung der Schlachtmethoden und die Industrialisierung des Schlachtens. Betrachtet man die Schächtfrage vor dem Hintergrund der Geschichte der Juden in der Schweiz, lassen sich für die zweite Hälfte des 19. Jahrhunderts zwei Phasen des Konfliktes benennen.

In der ersten Phase zeigt sich ein Zusammenhang zwischen dem Bemühen um ein Verbot des Schächtens und der vorangegangenen Judenemanzipation. Die Polemik gegen das Schächten lässt sich in dieser Phase auf eine allgemeine Ablehnung der Judenemanzipation zurückführen. Diese ersten Versuche das Schächten zu verbieten waren vereinzelt und nicht organisiert. In der zweiten Phase ging die Initiative für ein Verbot des Schächtens vorwiegend von den

---

[4] In dieser Abhandlung bezieht sich das Wort „Schächten" ausschließlich auf die jüdische Art des Schlachtens, weil es im ausgehenden 19. Jahrhundert nur um das Schächten nach jüdischer Art ging. Aber in neuester Zeit bezeichnet der Begriff „Schächten" auch das Schlachten nach islamischem Ritus. Pascal Krauthammer, „Schächten nach islamischer Tradition und dessen Verbot im schweizerischen Recht," in *Muslime und schweizerische Rechtsordnung,* Hg. René Pahud de Mortanges und Erwin Tanner (Freiburg: Universitätsverlag, 2002), 289.

[5] Nach der Tradition des Judentums besteht die Thora aus der mündlichen und schriftlichen Thora, die Moses am Berge Sinai übergeben wurden. Für die religiösen Grundlagen des Schächtens siehe Israel Meir Levinger, „Die Jüdische Schlachtmethode – das Schächten," in *Schächten. Religionsfreiheit und Tierschutz,* Hg. Richard Potz, Brigitte Schinkele, Wolfgang Wieshaider (Freistadt: Roman Kovar, 2001), 1-3.

[6] Ebenda, 4.

[7] Es gibt eine Reihe von Tierschutzgesetzen im Judentum. Der Tierschutz zeigt sich z. B. in den strengen Vorschriften des Schächtens. Ebenda, 3.

[8] Genesis 9:4, Levitikus 3:17. Die gute und schnelle Ausblutung des Tieres hat auch eine Bedeutung für die Fleischhygiene. Ebenda, 8.

Tierschutzvereinen aus. Die Vereine organisierten den Protest gegen das Schächten und bereiteten damit letztlich die Volksabstimmung vor.

Seit den 1850er Jahren wurde in einigen Kantonen versucht, das Schächten gesetzlich zu verbieten. Im Kanton Aargau, in dem damals die schweizerischen Juden wohnen durften, wurde zwar 1854 das Schächten auf eine indirekte Weise gesetzlich verboten.[9] Wegen einer Petition von Juden wurde das Schächten aber in Oberendingen und Lengnau, in den sogenannten jüdischen Dorfghettos, ausnahmsweise erlaubt.[10]

Als die Israelitische Gemeinde 1859 in Baden gegründet wurde, wurde die Schächtfrage erneut aktuell. Die dortigen Juden wollten auch in Baden das Schächten legalisieren. Diese Bemühungen um eine Zulassung des Schächtens führten zu einer neuen Debatte. Im Vordergrund stand dabei die Frage, ob das Schächten Tierquälerei sei oder nicht. Nach einer Besichtigung des Schächtens in Endingen kamen zwei Sachverständige, die der aargauische Polizeidirektor mit der Untersuchung des tierschützerischen Aspekts des Schächtens beauftragt hatte, zu dem Schluss, dass das Schächten nicht schmerzhafter und grausamer sei als das Töten des Tieres durch einen Schlag auf den Kopf.[11] Obwohl die Regierung aufgrund dieser Ergebnisse dem Großen Rat im Oktober 1861 einen Gesetzesvorschlag zur Abänderung des Gesetzes über die Tierquälerei überwies, wurde die Behandlung dieses Gesetzesvorschlags wegen der aufkommenden Emanzipationswirren bis 1866 nicht in Angriff genommen.[12]

Der Kanton Aargau war der einzige Kanton, der die Judenemanzipation als Innenpolitik behandeln musste, weil die meisten schweizerischen Juden im Kanton Aargau lebten. In den 1850ern und 1860ern waren die Emanzipationsgegner in der Mehrheit und unter dem Einfluss der anti-emanzipatorischen Stimmung wurde versucht, das Schächten zu verbieten.

Vor dem gleichen Hintergrund wurde das Schächtverbot im Kanton St. Gallen durchgesetzt. Offiziell und nach außen hin wurde als Grund für das Verbot der Aspekt der Tierquälerei angeführt. Ausschlaggebend für die Begründung des Schächtverbots war der Tierschutzgedanke. Allerdings lässt sich das Verbot wahrscheinlich nicht allein auf den Aspekt der Tierquälerei zurückführen, sondern muss vielmehr in engem Zusammenhang mit der 1866 neu gegründeten israelitischen Gemeinde in St. Gallen, mit der Angst vor einer Zunahme der Juden

---

[9] Das aargauische Gesetz vom 23. Wintermonat 1854 über Tierquälerei bestimmte, dass großes und kleines Schlachtvieh sowie Pferde durch einen Schlag auf den Kopf getötet werden mussten. Schweizerisches Bundesblatt, 1890, Band I, Heft 12, 640.

[10] Das Gesetz vom 13. Wintermonat 1855. Ebenda, 640.

[11] Pascal Krauthammer, *Das Schächtverbot in der Schweiz 1854-2000: Die Schächtfrage zwischen Tierschutz, Politik und Fremdenfeindlichkeit* (Zürich: Schulthess, 2000), 29.

[12] Ebenda, 30.

und der damit verbundenen Angst vor einer wirtschaftlichen Konkurrenz durch die Juden gesehen werden.[13]

1866 forderte ein Obmann (Metzger von Beruf) ein Verbot des Schächtens mit der Begründung, dass diese Praxis tierquälerisch sei. Der Gemeinderat sprach daraufhin im Sommer 1866 kurzerhand ein Verbot des Schächtens aus.[14] Dieses Verbot wurde jedoch bereits ein Jahr später aufgrund jüdischer Einwände wieder aufgehoben.[15]

1874 wurde in St. Gallen erneut versucht, ein Verbot des Schächtens durchzusetzen, indem der Gebrauch der Schussmaske von Bouterole beim Schlachten zur Pflicht gemacht wurde.[16] In der öffentlichen Debatte um das Verbot des Schächtens beriefen sich die Gegner des Schächtens nun immer öfter auch auf die «Sittlichkeit und Wahrung der öffentlichen Ordnung» – hier wird sichtbar, dass der Gedanke des Tierschutzes nicht den einzigen Grund für die Vorbehalte gegen die Praxis des Schächtens bildete.[17] Dieser Vorstoß, auf indirektem Wege das Schächten zu verbieten, scheiterte an der Intervention des Bundes.[18]

Die neue Bundesverfassung von 1874 brachte zwei Änderungen bezüglich der Schächtfrage mit sich. Zum einen sollte das Schächten als religiöse Handlung erlaubt werden, weil die Bundesverfassung von 1874 den Juden die Gewissens- und Kultusfreiheit gewährleistete. Die Schächtgegner brachten daraufhin neue Argumente für ein Verbot des Schächtens in die Diskussion ein. Neben dem Aspekt der Tierquälerei betonten sie, dass es sich nicht um eine religiöse Praxis handele und das Schächten aus ihrer Sicht zugleich der öffentlichen Ordnung und Moral widerspreche.

Die Schweizer Juden konnten sich nun ihrerseits unter Bezug auf die Religionsfreiheit beim Bundesrat über die Schächtverbote in einzelnen Kantonen beschweren und diese anfechten. Umgekehrt konnte der Bund sich seinerseits in die kantonale Schächtfrage einmischen. Die Schächtfrage wurde dadurch zu einer bundesstaatlichen Angelegenheit. Damit verlagerte sich auch der Konflikt um das Schächten auf die Ebene des Bundes. Die Gegner des Schächtens mussten sich national organisieren, um ihr Ziel zu erreichen.

---

[13] Sabine Schreiber, *Hirschfeld, Strauss, Malinsky, Jüdisches Leben in St. Gallen 1803 bis 1933* (Zürich: Chronos, 2006), 205; Krauthammer, *Das Schächtverbot in der Schweiz*, 30.

[14] Lothar Rothschild, *Im Strom der Zeit, Jubiläumsschrift zum hundertjährigen Bestehen der Israelitischen Gemeinde St. Gallen* (St. Gallen: Buchdruckerei Volkstimme, 1963), 77.

[15] Ebenda, 78.

[16] Ebenda, 79.

[17] Schreiber, *Hirschfeld*, 205.

[18] Rothschild, *Im Strom der Zeit*, 79.

Die Tierschutzvereine und das Schächtverbot von 1893

Bei der Einführung des Schächtverbots von 1893 waren die Tierschutzbewegung und die deutsch-schweizerischen Tierschutzvereine eine treibende Kraft. Für die Tierschutzvereine war die Ächtung des Schächtens als Tierquälerei seit ihrer Gründung eines ihrer zentralen Anliegen. Vor allem seit den 1880er Jahren widmeten sie sich der Schächtfrage mit voller Kraft. Im April 1886 richtete der Centralvorstand der Schweizerischen Tierschutzvereine eine diesbezügliche Eingabe an das Departement des Inneren. Sie verlangten, dass das Töten der Schlachttiere in den öffentlichen Schlachthäusern und den Privatschlachtereien ohne vorgängige Betäubung der Schlachttiere durch Schlag oder Schuss im ganzen Gebiet der Eidgenossenschaft verboten werden solle.[19] Sie waren fest überzeugt, dass das Schächten an sich mit seinen Vorbereitungen und Ausführungen eine arge und große Tierquälerei in sich schließe und dass es in keiner Weise ein unerlässliches Requisit der mosaischen Religion sei.[20] In der Petition beriefen sich die Gegner auf die Artikel 50 und 4 der Bundesverfassung im Namen der Moral und der öffentlichen Ordnung sowie im Namen der Gleichheit aller Bürger vor dem Gesetz. Der Bundesrat forderte als Reaktion auf diese Petition einen Beweis dafür, dass das Schächten tatsächlich eine Tierquälerei sei und dass durch deren Anwendung die öffentliche Ordnung und Sittlichkeit beeinträchtigt werde.[21]

Inzwischen wurden von den Tierschutzvereinen Versuche zur Einführung des Schächtverbots auf der Kantonalebene unternommen. Besonders aktiv waren sie in den Kantonen Aargau und Bern. In Baden (Kanton Aargau) wurden drei jüdische Metzger wegen Verletzung des Tierquälereigesetzes von 1854 und des Gesetzes von 1855, welches das Schächten ausnahmsweise nur in Oberendingen und Lengnau gestattete, vom Tierschutzverein in Aargau angeklagt und schließlich als schuldig verurteilt.[22] In Bern wurde eine Verordnung des bernischen Regierungsrates über das Schlachten von Vieh und über den Fleischverkauf vom 14. August 1889 erlassen, Artikel 13 dieser Verordnung legte ein allgemeines Schächtverbot fest.[23]

Die jüdischen Gemeinden der jeweiligen Kantone legten sofort beim Bundesrat Beschwerde ein. Die beiden Beschlüsse wurden durch den Entscheid des Bundesrates vom 17. März 1890 zurückgewiesen.[24] Nach einer langen Untersuchung beschloss der Bundesrat schließlich, dass das Schächten als eine gottesdienstliche Handlung der Israeliten anzuerkennen sei und dass das Schächten aufgrund des Artikels 50, der die freie Ausübung gottesdienstlicher Handlung innerhalb der

---

[19] „Eingabe des Centralvorstandes der Schweiz. Thierschutzvereine betreffend das Schächten an das Eidgen," Department des Innern in Bern, Aarau, April 1886.

[20] „Summarischer Bericht über die Tätigkeit des Central-Vorstandes der deutsch-schweizerischen Thierschutzvereine, Juni 1885 bis 31. Dezember 1890," Zürich: [s. n.], 1891, S. 11.

[21] Krauthammer, *Das Schächtverbot in der Schweiz*, 38.

[22] Ebenda, 38.

[23] Ebenda, 45-46.

[24] *Schweizerisches Bundesblatt*, 1890, Band I, Heft 12, 639-663.

Schranken der Sittlichkeit und der öffentlichen Ordnung gewährleistete, erlaubt werden dürfe. Auch sei das Schächten keine Tierquälerei, wenn es durch bestimmte Fachleute durchgeführt werde. Gegen diesen Beschluss des Bundesrates erhoben die Kantone Bern und Aargau einen Rekurs im Februar 1891.[25] Aber dieser wurde nach der Verhandlung im Nationalrat zurückgewiesen.[26]

1892 lancierten die Tierschutzvereine eine Volksinitiative zur Partialrevision der Bundesverfassung, um das Schächten auf der gesamten eidgenössischen Ebene zu verbieten. Sie sammelten die nötigen Unterschriften und die Volksabstimmung kam zustande.[27] Drei Viertel der Unterschriften stammten allein aus Bern, Aargau und Zürich, wo die Tierschutzvereine besonders aktiv waren. In der Volksabstimmung vom 20. August 1893 erreichte die Initiative der Tierschutzvereine gegen den Willen des Bundesrates mit 191.527 Ja- gegen 127.101 Nein-Stimmen problemlos die Volksmehrheit und mit elfeinhalb Ja- gegen zehneinhalb Nein-Stimmen knapp die Mehrheit in den Ständen.[28] Trotz des großen Interesses der schweizerischen Bürger an der Volksabstimmung zum Schächtverbot war die Stimmbeteiligung, die bei rund 47% lag, niedrig.[29] Die gesamten französischsprachigen und italienischsprachigen Kantone verwarfen die Initiative, während die vorwiegend protestantischen Kantone der Deutschschweiz, allen voran Aargau, Bern und Zürich, in denen die Tierschutzvereine ihre Kampagne besonders engagiert führten, ihr mit absoluter Mehrheit zustimmten.[30]

Die Nachgeschichte des Schächtverbots

Die Aufnahme des Schächtverbots in die Bundesverfassung brachte die Diskussion über das Schächten jedoch nicht zu Ende. Anfang des 20. Jahrhunderts wurde versucht, das Schächtverbot auch auf Geflügel auszudehnen. Das Bundesgericht war aber der Auffassung, dass das Schächten von Geflügel nicht unter das Schächtverbot falle. Dieses Urteil bedeutete, dass das Wort «Viehgattung», das in der Bundesverfassung stand, nicht für Geflügel galt.

Ende der 1960er und Anfang der 70er Jahre wurde die Aufhebung des Schächtverbots neben der Aufhebung des Jesuitenverbots und des Klosterartikels diskutiert. Die Aufhebung des Schächtverbots fand aber nicht statt und die Diskussion ging vielmehr zunehmend in die Richtung einer Ersetzung des

---

[25] „Rekursbegründung der Regierungen der Kantone Bern und Aargau gegen den Entscheid des Bundesrathes vom 17. März 1890 betreffend das Schächten der Schlachtthiere an die Bundesversammlungen der Schweizerischen Eidgenossenschaft vom 10. Februar 1891."

[26] Krauthammer, *Das Schächten in der Schweiz*, 50-52.

[27] Der Zentralvorstand der deutsch-schweizerischen Tierschutzvereine setzte erhebliche Geldmittel ein und zahlte den Sammlern für jede Unterschrift eine Prämie. Beatrix Mesmer, „Das Schächtverbot von 1893," in *Antisemitismus in der Schweiz, 1848-1960*, Hg. Aram Mattioli (Zürich: Orell Füssli, 1998), 232.

[28] *Schweizerisches Bundesblatt*, 1893, Band 4, Heft 44, 401.

[29] Dany Rothschild, *Das Schächtverbot der Schweizerischen Bundesverfassung* (Zürich: Buchdruckerei Moritz Lande, 1955), 58.

[30] *Schweizerisches Bundesblatt*, 1893, Band 4, Heft 44, 401.

Verfassungsartikels durch eine entsprechende Vorschrift in einem zu schaffenden schweizerischen Tierschutzgesetz.[31] Mit der Zustimmung des Volkes bei den zwei Volksabstimmungen (1973 und 1978) wurde das schweizerische Tierschutzgesetz (TschG) angenommen und das Tierschutzgesetz sowie die Tierschutzverordnung traten am 1. Juli 1981 in Kraft.[32] Zwar verschwand das Schächtverbot aus der Bundesverfassung, aber das Schächtverbot ist weiterhin im Art. 20 im 7. Abschnitt des Tierschutzgesetzes enthalten.[33]

1997 gab es einen erneuten Versuch, wie schon während der Jahrhundertwende, das Schächtverbot auch auf Geflügel auszudehnen, aber der Versuch scheiterte am Protest des SIG.

Als jüngster Vorgang bezüglich des Schächtverbots lässt sich der Versuch zur Aufhebung des Schächtverbots vom Bundesrat 2001/02 durch die Revision des Tierschutzgesetzes nennen. Der Bundesrat vertrat den Standpunkt, dass das betäubungslose Schlachten für Juden und Muslime eine wichtige Kulthandlung darstelle und die Verhältnismäßigkeit des Schächtverbots nicht gegeben sei.[34] Dieses Vorhaben des Bundesrates stieß jedoch auf heftigen Widerstand von Bürgern, besonders Tierschützern, infolgedessen musste er die Aufhebung des Schächtverbots aufgeben.

2. Gründe und Hintergründe des Schächtverbots

Die Schächtfrage führt bis heute immer wieder zu Diskussionen und Konflikten zwischen Schweizer Juden und nichtjüdischen Schweizern und belastet darum bis heute das Verhältnis beider Gruppen. Nicht zuletzt kann die Schächtfrage immer wieder zu einer Erneuerung und Aktualisierung von allgemeinen Vorbehalten gegenüber Juden führen.

In der bisherigen Forschung herrscht ein weitgehender Konsens darüber, dass der Versuch zur Einführung des Schächtverbots und die Annahme des

---

[31] Linz Herbert Kalb, „Rituelles Schlachten in der Schweiz," in *Schächten. Religionsfreiheit und Tierschutz*, Hg. Richard Potz, Brigitte Schinkele, Wolfgang Wieshaider (Freistadt: Roman Kovar, 2001), 162.

[32] In der Volksabstimmung im Jahr 1973 wurde nach der Ersetzung des Schächtartikels der Bundesverfassung (Art. 25bis) durch ein Tierschutzgesetz gefragt und in der Volksabstimmung im Jahr 1978 nach dem neuen Tierschutzgesetz.

[33] Artikel 20 Absatz 1 des Tierschutzgesetzes vom 9. März 1978 lautet: „Das Schlachten von Säugetieren ohne Betäubung vor dem Blutentzug ist verboten." Inzwischen wurde das Tierschutzgesetz revidiert und Artikel 21 Absatz 1 des Tierschutzgesetzes vom 16. Dezember 2005 lautet: „Säugetiere dürfen nur geschlachtet werden, wenn sie vor Beginn des Blutentzugs betäubt worden sind." Die beiden Gesetzestexte erwähnen das Schächten nicht direkt, aber sie verpflichten zu einer vorherigen Betäubung beim Schlachten.

[34] Sibylle Horanyi, *Das Schächtverbot zwischen Tierschutz und Religionsfreiheit, Eine Güterabwägung und interdisziplinäre Darstellung von Lösungsansätzen* (Basel, Genf, München: Helbing & Lichtenhahn, 2004), 20.

Schächtverbots als Verfassungsartikel durch die Volksabstimmung vom 20. August 1893 vom Antisemitismus beeinflusste Ereignisse in der zweiten Hälfte des 19. Jahrhunderts darstellen.[35] In der Forschung findet sich häufig der Hinweis, dass die Annahme des Schächtverbots auf den damals im deutschen Sprachraum verbreiteten Antisemitismus zurückgeführt werden könne. Der Tierschutzgedanke lässt sich so als eine verdeckte und latente Form des Antisemitismus verstehen.[36] Als Indiz hierfür lässt sich das Ergebnis der Volksabstimmung heranziehen, aus der klar hervorgeht, dass sich die deutschsprachigen Kantone überwiegend für ein Verbot des Schächtens aussprachen, wohingegen die französisch- und italienischsprachigen Kantone es ablehnten. Der Zusammenhang zwischen Schächtverbot und Antisemitismus lässt sich vielfach belegen. Dieses Argument kann jedoch eine weitere Frage nicht beantworten: Warum wurde die Schächtfrage im Unterschied zu den anderen deutschsprachigen Ländern seit der Judenemanzipation gerade in der schweizerischen Gesellschaft heftig diskutiert und dort schließlich zum Kristallisationspunkt einer breiten staatsrechtlichen Debatte?[37]

Im 19. Jahrhundert änderte sich langsam die grundsätzliche Einstellung zu Tieren und der moderne Tierschutzgedanke entstand. Die Auseinandersetzung um das betäubungslose Schlachten nahm in den beiden letzten Jahrzehnten des 19. Jahrhunderts stark zu und neue Schlachtmethoden wurden entwickelt. Vor diesem Hintergrund wurde das Schächten in vielen europäischen Ländern infrage gestellt und es wurde darüber diskutiert, ob das Schächten Tierquälerei sei oder nicht.[38]

In den deutschsprachigen Ländern war die Schächtfrage neben dem Aktionsgegenstand der Tierschützer auch das antisemitische Aktionsgebiet. Aber die Bedeutung, welche der Schächtfrage beigemessen wurde, war in den jeweiligen Ländern unterschiedlich. Im Deutschen Reich, in dem offensichtlich antisemitische Parteien und Zeitungen die Judenemanzipation wieder infrage stellten, war die Schächtfrage ein marginales Thema.[39] Im Reichstag wurde die Schächtfrage aufgrund

---

[35] Sibylle Horanyi vertritt aber die Ansicht, dass mit der Statuierung einer bedingungslosen Betäubungspflicht für Säugetiere in Art. 20 Abs. 1 des Tierschutzgesetzes, dem sogenannten Schächtverbot, kein unverhältnismäßiger Eingriff in die Religionsfreiheit vorliegt. Horanyi, *Das Schächtverbot*, 293.

[36] Friedrich Traugott Külling, *Antisemitismus bei uns überall?* (Zürich: Auslieferung Schweizerischer Israelitischer Gemeindebund, 1977), 383, 386. Külling weist auch darauf hin, dass sich die Annahme des Schächtverbots bei näherer Betrachtung direkt mit der deutschen Sprache in Verbindung bringen lässt, dass aber das Schächtverbot besonders populär in solchen Gebieten war, welche von judenfeindlichen Zeitungsschreibern verseucht waren, was hauptsächlich die zum Deutschen Reich hin geöffneten Kantone betrifft, hier S. 373 und S. 383; Krauthammer, *Das Schächtverbot*, 90-94.

[37] Mesmer, „Das Schächtverbot," 215.

[38] Richard Potz, „Tierschutz und religiöse Schlachtbestimmungen – Eine historische Einleitung," in *Schächten. Religionsfreiheit und Tierschutz*, Hg. Richard Potz, Brigitte Schinkele, Wolfgang Wieshaider (Freistadt: Roman Kovar, 2001), 34-35.

[39] Mesmer, „Das Schächtverbot," 215. Mesmer weist darauf hin, dass dieser Gewichtungsunterschied sich auch im Forschungsstand niederschlug. Während in der Antisemitismusforschung Deutschlands die Schächtfrage kaum thematisiert wurde, gibt es hingegen eine ganze Reihe von juristischen und

der Petition vom Vorstand des Verbandes deutscher Tierschutzvereine, die Blutentziehung ohne vorherige Betäubung beim Schlachten zu verbieten, in der Session 1885/86 verhandelt, aber die Agitation gegen das Schächten blieb erfolglos.[40] Trotz der mehrfachen Einwirkung der Tierschutzvereine wurde das Schächten nach der Verhandlung 1887 im Reichstag aufgrund eines vom Reichstag eingeholten Sachverständigengutachtens nicht zur Tierquälerei erklärt.[41] Eine Ausnahme war das Königreich Sachsen, in dem ein Jahr früher als in der Schweiz das Schächten verboten wurde.[42]

Auch in Österreich wurde die Diskussion über das Verbot des betäubungslosen Schlachtens unter dem Einfluss der Tierschutzbewegung geführt und das Schächten wurde als problematisch angesehen. Besonders in Wien, wo der Anteil der Juden hoch war, war eine Konfrontation mit Tierschützern unvermeidlich.[43] Die Ablehnung des Schächtens durch die Tierschützer manifestierte sich im elften internationalen Tierschutzkongress 1883 in Wien.[44] Das Verbot des betäubungslosen Schlachtens wurde im Rahmen einzelner Schlachthofordnungen eingeführt, aber diese wurden entsprechend der Auffassung des österreichischen Verwaltungsgerichtshofes aufgehoben.[45] In der zweiten Hälfte des 19. Jahrhunderts herrschte auch in Österreich eine antisemitische Stimmung. Die Schächtfrage betraf nicht nur den bloßen Tierschutzgedanken, sondern wurde vielfach als Vehikel tagespolitischer und antisemitischer Auseinandersetzungen benutzt.[46]

Der in den beiden letzten Jahrzehnten des 19. Jahrhunderts verbreitete Antisemitismus steht offenbar in enger Beziehung zur Schächtfrage. Aber die unterschiedliche Gewichtung der Schächtfrage in den verschiedenen Ländern lässt sich nicht nur mit diesem Argument erklären. Antisemitische Phänomene entstehen nicht nur aus dem «ewigen Antisemitismus,»[47] sondern hängen immer mit historischen und zeitlichen Konstellationen zusammen. Daher ist es umso wichtiger, die jeweils eigene Bedeutung des Antisemitismus in den jeweiligen Ländern zu verstehen.

In der Schweiz entstanden keine Parteien und Zeitungen, die einen offenen Antisemitismus bekundeten, und abgesehen von wenigen Ausnahmen gab es keine

historischen Studien über die Schächtfrage in der Schweiz.

[40] Potz, „Tierschutz," 35.

[41] Ebenda, 35.

[42] Auf dem Wege eines gesetzlichen Betäubungszwanges wurde das Schächten zwischen 1892 und 1900 verboten, Roman Merth, „Das Schächten im kommunalen Schlachthaus und der Vollzug des Tierschutzrechts," in *Schächten. Religionsfreiheit und Tierschutz*, Hg. Richard Potz, Brigitte Schinkele, Wolfgang Wieshaider (Freistadt: Roman Kovar, 2001), 112.

[43] Ebenda, 110.

[44] Ebenda, 110.

[45] Ebenda, 112.

[46] Ebenda, 110.

[47] Hannah Arendt, *The Origins of Totalitarianism* (New York: Harcourt, Brace & World, 1968), 7.

radauantisemitische Bewegung und kein vergleichbares Ereignis wie die Dreyfusaffäre in Frankreich.[48] Die Zahl der Juden war im Vergleich zu den Nachbarländern gering und ihre Rolle in der schweizerischen Gesellschaft war begrenzt.[49] Trotzdem lassen sich Formen des Antisemitismus historisch auch in der Schweiz nachweisen. Dabei handelt es sich – von wenigen Ausnahmen abgesehen – insgesamt um einen latenten Antisemitismus. Der Antisemitismus verband sich in der Schweiz im ausgehenden 19. Jahrhundert besonders mit dem Rückgriff auf Traditionen und mit der Verstärkung des inneren Zusammenhalts sowie einem integralen Nationalismus.[50]

In dieser Zeit gab es eine Änderung in der politischen Welt: In der zweiten Hälfte der 1880er Jahre begannen die Freisinnig-Liberalen und die Katholisch-Konservativen, sich einander anzunähern. Im Jahr 1891 trat Josef Zemp aus Luzern als erster Vertreter der Katholisch-Konservativen (der späteren Katholisch-Konservativen Volkspartei und heutigen Christlichdemokratischen Volkspartei, CVP) in den Bundesrat ein. Dieser politische Prozess bedeutete die Versöhnung zwischen den Freisinnig-Liberalen und den Katholisch-Konservativen, weil sich die Katholisch-Konservativen nach der Niederlage des Sonderbundskriegs am Rand der politischen Welt befanden.

Aus der Sicht von Beatrix Mesmer stellt das Schächtverbot ein Zeichen für das Ende des pragmatischen Liberalismus dar, eine Zeit, die durch den Rückgriff auf traditionelle Werte charakterisiert war. Mesmer beschreibt eine Tendenz, «echte Schweizerart» und «helvetische Normen» zu redefinieren. Bei dieser Redefinition der nationalen Identität habe das Schächtverbot die Funktion gehabt, sowohl die einheimischen, als auch die ausländischen Juden auszugrenzen.[51]

Angesichts dieser sozialen Tendenz kann man das Schächtverbot nicht nur als antijüdisches und antisemitisches Ereignis betrachten, sondern zugleich auch als einen hiermit in engem Zusammenhang stehenden Faktor der inneren Nationsbildung. Vor diesem Hintergrund lässt sich die bundesweite Initiative der Tierschutzvereine als eine Bewegung zur Stärkung des inneren Zusammenhalts der Schweizer Nation verstehen. Es lassen sich also drei Faktoren benennen, die sich hierbei wechselseitig überlagern und durchdringen: der Tierschutzgedanke, der latente Antisemitismus und die innere Nationsbildung. Diese drei Faktoren lassen

---

[48] Aram Mattioli, „Antisemitismus in der Geschichte der modernen Schweiz – Begriffsklärungen und Thesen," in *Antisemitismus in der Schweiz, 1848-1960*, Hg. Aram Mattioli (Zürich: Orell Füssli 1998), 14.

[49] Die Zahl der Juden betrug 8.069 Personen im Jahr 1888 (Anteil an Gesamtbevölkerung: 0,3%). Sie wuchs im Jahr 1900 auf 12.264 (0,4%). Heiner Ritzmann-Blickenstorfer (Hg.), *Historische Statistik der Schweiz* (Zürich: Chronos, 1996), 155.

[50] Jakob Tanner, „Diskurse der Diskriminierung, Antisemitismus, Sozialdarwinismus und Rassismus in den schweizerischen Bildungseliten," in *Krisenwahrnehmungen im Fin de Siècle, jüdische und katholische Bildungseliten in Deutschland und der Schweiz*, Hg. Michael Graetz, Aram Mattioli (Zürich: Chronos, 1997), 329.

[51] Mesmer, „Das Schächtverbot," 234.

sich nicht isoliert voneinander betrachten, sondern müssen als Einheit gesehen werden.

Dieser Zusammenhang spiegelt sich auch in der Argumentation der Tierschützer wider. Die Argumentationsführung gegen das Schächten hatte sich wegen der Veränderung der gesellschaftlichen Konstellation verändert. Am Anfang ging es ausschließlich um «Tierquälerei», dann wurde das Argument, dass das Schächten «kein religiöses Ritual» sei, hinzugefügt und schließlich ging es um die kulturelle Frage und kulturelle Normen: Das Schächten widerspreche der schweizerischen Kultur und der öffentlichen Ordnung.

Die Tierschutzvereine hielten das aus ihrer Sicht brutale Verfahren des Schächtens per se für Tierquälerei. Das Niederlegen der Tiere, der in einem Zug durchgeführte Halsschnitt und der völlige Blutauszug waren für sie nicht zu akzeptieren.[52] Diese Betrachtung lässt sich als anthropozentrischer im Gegensatz zu einem zoozentrischen Tierschutz verstehen – im Vordergrund stand das Gefühl der bedrohten Sittlichkeit.

Der eifrigste Schächtgegner in den Tierschutzvereinen war Keller-Jäggi, der Präsident des Tierschutzvereins des Kantons Aargau. Er war die treibende Kraft der Initiative gegen das Schächten und er propagierte die Wichtigkeit des Schächtverbots, indem er viele Vorträge hielt und viele Publikationen über die Schächtfrage veröffentlichte. Er argumentierte, dass das Schächten der öffentlichen Ordnung und der Moral widerspreche.[53] Er behauptete, dass eine Ausnahmegenehmigung für das Schächten im Kanton Aargau nur gelten könne, solange die Juden Bürger zweiter Klasse seien. Aber nach der Emanzipation müssten Christen und Juden vor dem Gesetz gleich sein. Wenn die Israeliten auf alle Rechte aargauischer und schweizerischer Bürger Anspruch erheben würden, hätten sie «auch die sittlichen Anschauungen des Schweizervolkes, dem sie nunmehr in allen rechtlichen Beziehungen angehören, zu respektieren.»[54] Mit dieser Argumentation ging er davon aus, dass das Ausnahmegesetz für das Schächten abzuschaffen sei und das Schächten in der ganzen Schweiz verboten werden müsse. Für ihn bedeutete die Emanzipation keineswegs die Anerkennung der anderen Kultur oder die Toleranz gegenüber der anderen Kultur, sondern eine völlige Assimilation mit schweizerischen Anschauungen und schweizerischer Kultur.

Bei der Schächtfrage ging es nicht nur um Tierquälerei, sondern auch um die Beseitigung der fremdartigen Kultur, die das Schächten zum Gegenstand hatte. Immer wenn die Tierschützer des Antisemitismus bezichtigt wurden, leugneten sie

---

[52] Die Tierschützer behaupteten, dass die Gelehrten, die verkündeten, das Schächten sei keine Tierquälerei, nie einem Schächtakt beigewohnt haben. „Einundzwanzigster Jahresbericht des Aargauschen Thierschutzvereins vom 1. Juli 1890 bis 30. Juni 1891," Aarau: [s. n.] 1891, 1-2.

[53] Siebzehnter Jahresbericht des Aargauischen Thierschutzvereins vom 1. Juli 1886 bis 30. Juni 1887, Aarau: [s. n.] 1887, 25.

[54] Ebenda, 26.

antisemitische Motivationen. Vieles spricht dafür, dass sich die Bewegung für ein Verbot des Schächtens mit antisemitischen Vorbehalten vermischte und es den Gegnern des Schächtens auch darum ging, eine kulturelle Assimilation der Schweizer Juden zu erzwingen. Die Vorbehalte richteten sich daher nachweislich nicht nur gegen die vermeintliche Tierquälerei, sondern ebenso gegen kulturelle Praktiken, die von der Mehrheit der Schweizer als Bedrohung ihrer nationalen Identität wahrgenommen wurden. Der «Kampf» um das Schächtverbot lässt sich – wie gezeigt wurde – daher auch als ein «Kampf» für die Bewahrung der «schweizerischen Kultur» verstehen.

Aus dem Fall des oben dargestellten Schächtverbots lässt sich ableiten, dass die Bewahrung der eigenen Kultur die Ausschließung der fremdartigen Kultur zur Folge hatte. In vielen Gesellschaften zeigen sich Abgrenzungen/Exklusionsprozesse von sozialen Gruppen, welche die gesellschaftliche Mehrheit repräsentieren, gegenüber Gruppen, die als Minderheiten wahrgenommen werden. Die Gründe dafür sind vielfältig und sie hängen von der gesellschaftlichen Konstellation ab. Bei der Schächtfrage wurde das Schächten des jüdischen religiösen Rituals (der jüdischen Kultur) aus der schweizerischen Gesellschaft ausgeschlossen, um, so die zeitgenössische Lesart, die «schweizerische Kultur» bewahren zu können. Diese kulturelle Grenzziehung wurde von der Mehrheit (nichtjüdischen Schweizern) gegen den Widerstand der Minderheit (Juden) vorgeschlagen und durchgeführt.

3. Fazit

Die Schweiz wird oft als das Model eines multikulturellen Landes betrachtet. Ihre Verfassung garantiert seit 1874 die Kultus- und Gewissensfreiheit und die Gleichheit aller vor dem Gesetz. Der Fall des «Schächtverbots» zeigt aber, dass eine Mehrheit auch mit der demokratischen Methode der Volksabstimmung in der multikulturellen Gesellschaft Hegemonie ausüben kann.

Daraus lassen sich zwei Thesen ableiten. Erstens: «Religion» bleibt nach wie vor eines der stärksten Kriterien für Grenzziehungen innerhalb einer Gesellschaft. «Religion» wird dabei häufig mit «Kultur» gleichgesetzt oder ersetzt. Der Begriff der Kultur lässt sich dabei noch schwerer definieren als Religion und bildet somit ein sehr dehnbares Kriterium. Dies gilt auch in einer demokratischen Gesellschaft.

Zweitens: Grenzziehungen innerhalb einer Gesellschaft können sich durch Auseinandersetzungen, Debatten und Konflikte immer wieder verändern. Dabei hängt es immer von der politischen, wirtschaftlichen und gesellschaftlichen Konstellation ab, wie die Debatten verlaufen und wo am Ende die Grenzen gezogen werden.

Yoko Akiyama
akiyama@desk.c.u-tokyo.ac.jp

La « Nouvelle Hanse » de Björn Engholm a-t-elle vraiment ete un echec ?

Nicolas Escach
Centre interdisciplinaire d'études et de recherches sur l'Allemagne, École normale supérieure de Lyon

Les années 1980 et 1990 ont été des années d'intense maturation en matière de reconstruction d'une unité baltique tant par les chercheurs que par les politiques. Alors que de nombreuses villes des espaces riverains s'étaient associées dans le cadre de jumelages dès 1975 et que la « Convention d'Helsinki pour la protection de la mer Baltique » avait été signée dès 1974, Björn Engholm, président du *Land* Schleswig-Holstein, futur président du SPD et futur candidat au poste de chancelier lance l'idée à Kiel en 1988 d'une « Nouvelle Hanse », faisant ainsi référence à une période historique glorieuse au cours de laquelle les comptoirs de la Baltique avaient activement coopéré pour sécuriser les approvisionnements maritimes et lutter contre la piraterie. Un retour du mythe de la Hanse aurait, selon lui, après plusieurs années de division au sein de l'Europe, une visée mobilisatrice tant les mémoires hanséatiques pourraient constituer une part indispensable à l'accomplissement des projets européens. Les villes de la Baltique semblent donc avoir redécouvert, en partie grâce à lui, depuis une trentaine d'années, l'héritage matériel et immatériel de la Hanse du Moyen Âge, qu'elles ont tenté d'ériger en ressource afin de fonder des réseaux économiques, politiques, institutionnels. Ces réseaux de villes, au cœur d'une gouvernance européenne de plus en plus multiscalaire et multi-niveau, sont une manière de dépasser les frontières étatiques et les ferveurs nationalistes, constituant des espaces de coopération transnationaux fondés sur une prétendue identité hanséatique régionale.

Pourtant, malgré ces nombreux apports, le personnage et son projet ont été, depuis son retrait politique en 1994, fortement critiqués à tel point que Rainer Burchart et Werner Knobbe, deux journalistes allemands, ont choisi comme titre pour leur biographie de Björn Engholm, *Récit d'un espoir déçu*. Accusé de nationalisme et de réactivation d'idées nazies, lâché par son camp politique le Ministre-Président a dû répondre de son action politique. La « Nouvelle Hanse », critiquée par plusieurs gouvernements et intellectuels des espaces riverains de la Baltique a-t-elle rassemblée ou divisée la région dans son ensemble ? Au-delà du concept en lui-même, il semble que le parcours, les idées et les actions de Björn Engholm aient permis d'esquisser théoriquement l'émergence d'une région baltique qui s'est développée en pratique par la suite.

Eurostudia — Revue Transatlantique de Recherche sur l'Europe
Vol. 7, No.1-2 (2011), 73-86

Les définitions de la région et donc du processus de régionalisation peuvent varier[1] : nombre limité d'États liés par une relation géographique et par un degré d'interdépendance mutuelle pour le géopoliticien Joseph Nye, unité d'aspects géographiques, politiques, économiques ou culturels et/ou une identité régionale qui sont caractérisés par un certain degré d'homogénéité et/ou de fonctionnalité pour le professeur en sciences politiques de l'université de Iéna Helmut Hubel[2]. Les années 1980 voient en effet le retour du concept de région permis par la fin d'un monde bipolaire. Or ces régions sont indéniablement construites par les politiques. Joseph Nye affirmait que les régions sont « ce que les politiciens et le peuple veulent qu'elles soient »[3]. Marko Lehti, chercheur finlandais, va dans ce sens lorsqu'il définit la construction régionale comme un processus politique où images et truismes sont construits politiquement[4]. Iver B. Neumann, spécialiste des relations internationales et géopoliticien ayant travaillé à l'Institut des affaires internationales de Norvège, s'inscrit donc dans cette lignée : « Les qualités spécifiques individuelles comme des particularités culturelles, économiques, géographiques et ou des événements historiques sont choisis consciencieusement pour imaginer sur leur base une identité temporelle et spatiale autour de l'unité ou de la communauté »[5]. Les régions sont définies par des actes de langage politiques (*speech acts*) qui les font exister. Ce qui est présenté par les politiques comme pertinent culturellement est plus important que les similitudes culturelles elles-mêmes. On comprend alors mieux l'ouvrage de Karl Schröder qui parlait de « Spacing Story » dans *Im Raume, lesen wir die Zeit*.

En parlant de la Baltique comme d'une région unie culturellement, économiquement et politiquement, Björn Engholm a rendu possible l'existence de cette unité. L'école de Kiel qu'il a créée, à travers la *Denkfabrik*[6], véritable centre de planification stratégique de l'unification baltique, a rendu possible l'élaboration de pistes de réflexion qui ont mené plus tard à de réelles avancées dans le processus de régionalisation. Le rôle du Schleswig-Holstein et de Björn Engholm dans la construction d'une région baltique (*region-building*) est essentiel. Le *Land* fut qualifié régulièrement de « livreur d'idées » (*Ideenlieferant*). Parallèlement, Björn Engholm a offert une nouvelle définition de la région, plus vaste. Il existe plusieurs définitions de « l'espace baltique » ou de la région baltique : la mer Baltique elle-même, le bassin hydrographique de la Baltique et l'ensemble des espaces de ce bassin du golfe de Finlande jusqu'aux détroits Skagerak/Kattegatt, la région fonctionnelle formée par les

[1] Nathalie Blanc-Noël (dir.), *La Baltique. Une nouvelle région en Europe* (Paris : L'Harmattan, 2002).

[2] Helmut Hubel et Stefan Gänzle, *The Council of the Baltic Sea States (CBSS) as a Sub-Regional Organization for "soft security risk management" in the North-East of Europe*, Report to the Presidency of CBSS, 18 May 2001 (Iéna: Friedrich-Schiller-Universität, 2001).

[3] Joseph S. Nye Jr. (dir.), *International Regionalism Readings* (Boston: Little Brown, 1968).

[4] Hiski Haukkala (dir.), *Dynamic Aspects of the Northern Dimension* (Turku: Turku University Press, 1999).

[5] Iver-B. Neumann, « A Region-Building Approach to Northern Europe », *Review of International Studies* 20 (1991): 59.

[6] Littéralement: « la fabrique à pensées ».

échanges économiques et les investissements, la région humaine définie par les densités de population, la région institutionnelle définie par les projets INTERREG IV-B et l'approche macro-régionale et la région historique fondée à partir des routes des Varègues puis celle des *Hanseaten* et des comptoirs hanséatiques (pouvant aller jusqu'au Portugal). En réalité, la Baltique tout comme l'espace hanséatique sont des « espaces-valise » ou « espaces-nomade ». « L'espace-nomade ou espace-valise apparait donc comme un espace que l'on peut tirer à soi et que l'on peut déformer à sa guise car ce dernier n'a jamais été précisément délimité et ne pourra probablement pas l'être. L'espace est fantasmé, imaginé, recrée, recadré par les acteurs dans la perspective de leurs propres stratégies »[7]. La Baltique de Björn Engholm, comme toute région historique et culturelle, est à géométrie variable, sanguine et réticulaire, espace de la circulation et du flux. Elle pose autant de points d'interrogation qu'elle apporte de réponses toute faites. Ces éléments sont-ils suffisants pour réhabiliter l'œuvre de Björn Engholm ? La « Nouvelle Hanse » a-t-elle un avenir ?

1. La Nouvelle Hanse, un projet pour la mer Baltique ?

Björn Engholm : la vision d'un « Hanseat » social-démocrate

Björn Engholm adhère au parti social-démocrate d'Allemagne dès 1962. Il cumule ensuite sous cette étiquette des fonctions nationales (élu député du *Bundestag* en 1969, Secrétaire d'État parlementaire du Ministre fédéral de l'Éducation et des Sciences dès 1977, puis ministre dès 1981, Ministre de l'Agriculture en 1982, Président fédéral du SPD en 1991 puis candidat à la chancellerie) et régionales (élu Ministre-Président du Schleswig-Holstein de 1988 à 1993 après avoir été longtemps dans l'opposition).

Son intérêt pour la Baltique et les pays scandinaves est en adéquation avec une position traditionnelle des sociaux-démocrates allemands sur l'Europe et sur la politique étrangère allemande. Depuis la fin de la Seconde Guerre mondiale, il est vrai que l'Allemagne avait peu coopéré avec les pays baltiques. Les contacts les plus étroits avec les pays d'Europe du Nord s'étaient justement réduits à ceux tissés par Willy Brandt, de par son exil en Norvège et en Suède et de par ses origines nord-allemandes[8], alors que du côté nordique, les tendances à l'isolement de la Suède ou de la Finlande s'étaient multipliés. Or Willy Brandt est un objet de fascination pour Björn Engholm qui publie en 1992 un recueil de textes lui rendant hommage : « Sa patrie politique, la social-démocratie doit rester comme elle a toujours été : ouverte au monde, européenne, patriotique, réformatrice, de gauche et libre »[9]. Les discours de Björn Engholm sont véritablement pétris par des références sociales-démocrates. Il insiste sur la formule « l'Allemagne est notre patrie, l'Europe notre futur », cite Paul-

---

[7] Nicolas Escach, *Une nouvelle Hanse en Europe, Brême, Gdansk, Riga* (Berlin: Trafo Verlag, 2010), 175.

[8] Leena-Kaarina Williams, *Zur Konstruktion einer Region. Die Entstehung der Ostseekooperation zwischen 1988 und 1992* (Berlin: Berliner Wissenschafts-Verlag, 2007).

[9] Björn Engholm, *Dank an Willy Brandt* (Marburg: Schüren Verlag, 1992), 75.

Henri Spaak, Helmut Schmidt, Bruno Kreisky et défend un travail collégial où la concertation prime sur la hiérarchie verticale.

La deuxième raison qui a poussé Björn Engholm à s'intéresser aux pays scandinaves et à l'espace baltique est à trouver dans ses origines. Il loue chez Brandt « l'homme de Lübeck », expression qui sera reprise pour le qualifier. Rainer Burchart et Werner Knobbe n'hésitent pas à lui attribuer le titre d'*Hanseat*. Résolument nord-allemand, distant et distingué, humaniste, modeste à l'excès, fier des traditions hanséatiques et de l'architecture de la « Perle de la Baltique », l'homme évoque de manière récurrente sa patrie baltique. Il se définit lui-même comme un Nord-européen, aspirant au consensus, préférant la pratique à de longs discours, recherchant la justice et le juste milieu.

Le constat d'une Baltique en marginalisation, la peur d'une Europe à deux vitesses…

Björn Engholm mène dès son élection à la tête du *Land* du Schleswig-Holstein en 1988 d'intenses réflexions sur l'espace baltique. Il entrevoit le danger dans une future Europe réunifiée d'une accentuation du modèle centre/périphérie. Dans cette perspective, les centres seraient l'Isthme européen s'étalant de Londres à Milan, la *Sunbelt* européenne connectant Milan à Lyon et la région (éventuellement) « post-socialiste » associant Prague, Budapest, Dresde et Leipzig. Les régions du Nord, subissant la concurrence de celles du Sud de l'Europe, se trouveraient, dans ce schéma, marginalisées. Afin d'éviter une « périphérisation » des pays nordiques, il serait pour lui urgent d'établir une coopération étroite dans le but de rassembler le potentiel de la région : une forte productivité, une force d'innovation, un haut standard écologique, la concentration de 20% du commerce mondial et de 70 millions d'habitants. Cette étroite association des pays baltiques est d'autant plus essentielle qu'elle doit répondre à un certain nombre de défis futurs : rendre les états baltiques assez forts pour que les négociations futures d'entrée dans l'UE et pour que la formation d'un marché économique commun arrivent à leur terme, présenter les intérêts communs baltiques d'une seule voix, notamment auprès de l'UE, coordonner les liaisons et les flux de transports dans le Nord de l'Europe afin que la régionalisation passe par des mobilités accrues au sein des espaces riverains, proposer une impulsion économique en se basant sur la très forte culture entrepreneuriale du nord de l'Europe (visible notamment dans le grand nombre de PME qui sont autant de potentiels d'innovation), aider les petites et moyennes entreprises, encourager un développement écologique, mener une coopération culturelle intense afin que l'identité baltique trouve une assise populaire.

Parallèlement, l'Europe s'accorde sur les valeurs communes de démocratie, de liberté, de pluralisme, de justice indépendante, et sur la fin du parti unique, de la censure et de l'économie planifiée. Si les blocs de l'Ouest et de l'Est ne sont plus une forme d'organisation, de classement et de structuration, selon quels critères, à partir de quelles règles les rapports entre les États vont-ils s'organiser ? C'est ce vide qu'occupe l'idée d'une régionalisation baltique.

La coopération proposée par Björn Engholm pourrait s'appuyer sur une forme de caractère et d'habitudes communs des populations baltiques : « Ce qui nous relie, ce sont bien les mêmes standards sociaux, un tempérament et un caractère commun, des conditions de vie communes liées au paysage, aux températures, au climat, à l'influence maritime, aux formes de peuplement. Nous sommes calmes, absolument pas brutaux, souvent têtus mais dignes de confiance. Nous avons un sentiment aigu de la justice sociale »[10]. À côté de cette « nature nordique », les pays riverains partageraient aussi une histoire commune, l'histoire hanséatique, la mémoire de mille ans de coopération, mémoire au cœur de la pensée de Björn Engholm.

Le retour du concept de « Nouvelle Hanse »

La redécouverte de la Hanse en Europe débute le 31 Octobre 1978 lorsque la ville de Zwolle lance un appel à 57 villes hanséatiques dont Bergen et Londres. La ville précise dans son invitation que l'idée de Hanse est un élément important car elle rappelle l'époque d'une coopération économique qui allait au-delà des frontières nationales. Zwolle organise ainsi du 23 au 27 août 1980 les premières journées de la Hanse (*Hanstage*) que la presse évoque à l'image du *Westfälische Rundschau* et d'autres journaux qui titrent : « La Hanse vit à nouveau ». Ces rencontres marqueront la naissance du réseau de villes « Hanse des Temps Nouveaux ».

Dès le milieu des années 1980, certains élus du Schleswig-Holstein et politiques allemands promeuvent des collaborations économiques plus étroites entre le *Land* et les pays européens tels le Danemark et autres pays baltiques. C'est le cas d'Egon Bahr, originaire de l'Est, et du ministre du Schleswig-Holstein pour les affaires sociales, la santé et l'énergie, Günter Jansen. Egon Bahr milite dès les années 1970 pour des liens approfondis avec la Scandinavie et pour l'inclusion des pays de l'Est dans une « Hanse moderne ». A côté des intérêts économiques, cette initiative présente également un objectif de réconciliation et de pacification. Cependant, les soutiens politiques restent peu nombreux tout comme l'attention portée au concept[11].

Björn Engholm a une certaine vision de la Hanse. Pour lui, la Hanse représente une forme d'unité économique ancienne, une organisation flexible, sans date de création ni « contrat », qui a favorisé une forme de stabilité et de paix en Europe. La Ligue hanséatique serait synonyme de libertés intérieures, d'uniformisation des règles de commerce et du droit autour de la Baltique, de division internationale du travail et d'apparition d'un marché global d'échanges sans frontières ni barrières, qui aurait rapproché les hommes et les cultures. Sa vision de la Hanse n'est pas seulement spatiale mais reflète véritablement une « communauté de valeurs essentielles ». Le concept de « Nouvelle Hanse », utilisé à de multiples reprises au cours du XXe siècle, doit exprimer l'urgence d'une coopération et être directement mobilisateur : « La chance de coopérer est plus grande qu'auparavant, c'est la configuration la plus

---

[10] « Die Neue Hanse », *NordEuropaForum* 04 (1991): 10.

[11] Williams, *Zur Konstruktion einer Region.*

idéale depuis le début de la Guerre de Trente ans »[12]. Björn Engholm donne de la Hanse une définition spatiale large, l'étendant jusqu'à Londres à l'Ouest, jusqu'à Cologne au Sud, jusqu'à Novgorod à l'Est et jusqu'au *Norden* scandinave au Nord.

Le concept de « Nouvelle Hanse », tel qu'il l'utilise, établit une véritable vision de la coopération baltique qui s'inscrit dans les prémices d'une « Europe des régions ». Le fait que l'idée vienne du Ministre-Président d'un *Land* allemand n'est pas étranger à une conception de la coopération supranationale, décentralisée et réticulaire. La région baltique n'est plus conçue comme un espace divisé par des frontières étatiques mais comme une entité historique, géopolitique réticulaire définie par la métaphore de la Hanse. Elle devient dans l'esprit de ses créateurs un réseau non hiérarchisé et supranational. Björn Engholm est très attaché à cette absence de hiérarchie : « Il ne s'agit pas de rappeler la domination germanique en Baltique. Bien au contraire, nous voudrions que le concept de Hanse soit associé à l'idée d'une coopération décentralisée, supranationale et régionale. Dans la future Europe des régions, ce ne seront pas les État-nations mais les unités régionales indépendantes qui coopéreront ensemble »[13]. L'horizontal doit donc remplacer le vertical dans un ensemble qui s'oppose à une « société en pyramide ». Les acteurs non étatiques sont aussi présents que les acteurs étatiques.

De cette nouvelle vision de l'espace, découle une définition « postmoderne » de la région. Contrairement à la région moderne qui est territoriale, basée sur l'État, la région « postmoderne » est fondée sur le lien, les flux et le réseau. La question décisive de la région « postmoderne » est « être ou non relié ». L'État-nation aurait été une interprétation subjective et datée de la politique spatiale. Ces éléments fondent la différence entre l'ancien régionalisme (« Old Regionalism »), constitué d'organisations intergouvernementales, et de relations multilatérales et le nouveau régionalisme (« New Regionalism ») que les intellectuels de la *Denkfabrik* entendent bâtir se concentrant sur la mise en réseau des acteurs des pays riverains, la *soft security* et une consultation de la société civile. Björn Engholm promeut la gouvernance et non le gouvernement, le *bottom up* plutôt que le *top down*, le processus plutôt que la structure, l'ouverture et non la fermeture, la coopération plutôt que la coordination, la confiance plutôt que la responsabilité, la décentralisation plutôt que la concentration ; en somme un modèle « néo-médiéval » et non « néo-westphalien ».

2. La « Nouvelle Hanse », l'histoire d'un echec ?

L'échec de la « Nouvelle Hanse » coïncide avec la chute de l'homme

Dès 1992-1993, Björn Engholm connaît des difficultés personnelles et entre dans une période de grave crise politique qui aboutira à son départ de la vie politique en 1994. Cette crise est d'abord celle de la social-démocratie qui l'a porté ; or de cette

[12] Ibid., 9.
[13] Ibid., 10.

social-démocratie, il est une forme d'incarnation. Les arguments politiques s'appuyant sur la récession mondiale, sur la fin de la guerre froide, sur une nouvelle politique à l'Est et sur l'instauration de la démocratie sont dépassés. Candidat à la chancellerie, Björn Engholm ne propose pas un véritable programme et la politique européenne du SPD, fer de lance de la vision social-démocrate, ne s'est pas adaptée à la réalité du traité de Maastricht et des processus monétaires et économiques engagés. Il finit par démissionner de son poste de Ministre-Président le 13 mai 1993 suite à « l'affaire Barschel » qui parachève sa chute. Il doit en effet en 1993 reconnaître avoir menti devant une commission d'enquête du *Landtag* à propos de l'espionnage électoral dont il avait été victime de la part du Ministre-Président Uwe Barschel lors des élections de 1987. En 1994, il démissionne de son mandat parlementaire régional et se retire de la vie politique.

Une critique du concept de « Nouvelle Hanse » autour de la Baltique

Dès 1994, le concept de « Nouvelle Hanse » n'est plus autant utilisé par les élus même si l'idée d'une coopération dans la région demeure forte. En Scandinavie, côté danois et norvégien, la Hanse est surtout perçue comme une période de domination et de tutelle allemande à ne pas reproduire. La Hanse de Björn Engholm parait idéalisée. Plus qu'une période de paix et d'unification, elle semble avoir profondément divisée la région. Dès 1397, les royaumes de Suède, du Danemark et de Norvège signent « l'Union de Kalmar » pour lutter contre la suprématie de la Hanse en baltique. La Hanse a mené de nombreuses guerres en Baltique comme celle contre Waldemar IV, roi du Danemark, aboutissant à la paix de Stralsund. Uffe Ellemann-Jensen, ministre des affaires étrangères danois ne se prive pas de le rappeler en 1992 : « Nous avons, nous Danois, mené une guerre contre la Hanse. Il faut rappeler que la Hanse avait comme centre Lübeck, comme langue l'allemand, et que son influence s'étendait de Novgorod à Londres »[14].

L'idée de « Nouvelle Hanse » apparait donc ambiguë. Cette interprétation est renforcée par deux éléments : certains propos tenus par Björn Engholm lui-même et le passé historique du concept de « Nouvelle Hanse ». Lors d'un discours à Brême le 29 mai 1991, Björn Engholm a la maladresse de situer l'Allemagne au centre du processus baltique : « Je n'évoque pas une Europe faible avec en son centre une Allemagne devenue plus grande mais une Europe forte dans laquelle l'Allemagne devenue plus grande injecte toute sa force »[15]. Cette rhétorique nationaliste n'est pas sans rappeler un autre passé.

Depuis la chute de la Hanse historique à l'époque moderne, et particulièrement dès le XIXe siècle, le mythe hanséatique est réapparu à de nombreuses reprises souvent sous forme d'une manipulation politique ou idéologique. Il s'agissait alors

---

[14] Rainer Burchart et Werner Knobbe, *Björn Engholm: Die Geschichte einer gescheiterten Hoffnung* (Stuttgart: Deutsche Verlags-Anstalt, 1993), 209.

[15] Alfred Gertler, *Björn Engholm im Gespräch* (Berlin: Bouvier Verlag, 1991), 209.

d'évoquer une unité culturelle fictive au sein de la Baltique, alors même que les pays qui la composaient étaient de nature différente. Jusqu'à la Seconde Guerre mondiale, cette unité baltique a plutôt servi les intérêts germaniques. Alfred Rosenberg, futur « Ministre du Reich pour les territoires occupés de l'Est » vit dans la Hanse une manière de démontrer, nature à l'appui, la légitimité des Allemands à occuper la région. Hinrich Lohse, haut dignitaire nazi, membre de la Commission pour les territoires occupés à l'Est, déclara ainsi en 1942 : « Les fluctuations de l'histoire reviennent comme un reflet et témoignent toujours de la domination allemande (...) notre Baltique est redevenue une mer allemande »[16]. La Hanse vint en appui au concept hitlérien d'espace vital (*Lebensraum*) constituant une période de forte expansion allemande. L'entre-deux-guerres fut marqué, quant à lui, par les œuvres de l'historien Fritz Rörig. Celui-ci déclare en 1937 : « Ce qui était appelé "ville" dans la Baltique restait immature et la plupart du temps primitif. Lübeck était mature »[17]. Il évoqua l'unification de la Baltique sous les traits allemands : « Ce n'est qu'après 1250, c'est-à-dire après que les villes allemandes eurent été fondées, que l'on put parler de région baltique (*Ostseeraum*) dans le sens d'une unité économiquement pleinement organisée »[18]. Fritz Rörig rapprochait l'apparition d'une région baltique de l'unification sous domination germanique. Il parlait de l'Allemagne comme d'une « porteuse de culture » et compta comme « quantité négligeable » la contribution des régions du Nord et de l'Est de l'Europe.

Une coopération trop « économique » : une « éco-Hanse » ?

Une critique inattendue de la « Nouvelle Hanse » se cristallise également autour de la candidature verte aux élections régionales du Schleswig-Holstein de 1992. Pour eux, le concept de « Nouvelle Hanse » prenant comme ancrage symbolique une période de prospérité économique s'accompagne d'une vision de la croissance baltique anti-écologique : « Des slogans comme la "Nouvelle Hanse", la région baltique, la Mare Balticum sont souvent utilisés. Les gouvernements et acteurs privés de Kiel à Stockholm et de Copenhague à Riga voient la région baltique comme une région de croissance économique au sein de l'Europe. Il est extrêmement contestable que cette vision de la croissance soit capable de résoudre les problèmes écologiques de la région. Il y a des raisons de penser qu'une expansion de la croissance en Baltique entrainera des dommages environnementaux supplémentaires et une détresse sociale »[19]. Cette revendication des écologistes allemands a donné lieu à une conférence intitulée « Des observations vertes pour la région baltique » organisée à

[16] Thomas Hill, « Die Neue Hanse : Rückblick eines Historikers auf einen Mythos », in *Mare Balticum 1996* (Lübeck: Ostsee Academie, 1996), 20.

[17] Jörg Hackmann, « Not only Hansa. Images of History in the Baltic Sea Region », in *Mare Balticum 1996* (Lübeck: Ostsee Academie, 1996), 27.

[18] Fritz Rörig, « Hanse, Ostseeraum und Skandinavien », in *Völker und Meere, Aufsätze und Vorträge*, dir. Egmont Zechlin et al. (Leipzig: O. Harrassowitz, 1944), 141.

[19] Williams, *Zur Konstruktion einer Region*, 217.

Copenhague au moment même où un Conseil des États de la Baltique était créé, en 1992.

3. Rehabiliter la « Nouvelle Hanse », est-ce possible ?

La « Nouvelle Hanse » : le projet d'un Land

La « Nouvelle Hanse » a d'abord eu un effet concret à l'échelle locale. Grâce à Björn Engholm, le Schleswig-Holstein est le premier de deux *Länder* allemand à voir dans la région baltique une ressource possible. De 1988 à 1992, en développant le concept de « Nouvelle Hanse » à l'échelle subrégionale, il critique fortement la politique du gouvernement CDU qui l'avait précédé et qui s'était plutôt concentré sur les partenariats avec l'Asie autour des marchés *high-tech* et des nouvelles technologies (Chine, Corée, Japon, Indonésie). La proximité géographique des pays de la Baltique avec le *Land* est un argument essentiel pour une réorientation : « Les contacts avec les pays scandinaves sont en retard depuis plusieurs années. La Scandinavie est pour nous le partenaire le plus proche. Je n'ai rien contre les relations avec la Chine mais Copenhague se situe plus près de nous que Pékin, c'est pourquoi nous voulons faire le premier pas »[20]. De son côté, l'opposition CDU insiste sur le caractère rétrograde d'une référence quelconque à la Hanse, morte depuis l'époque de la découverte de l'Amérique. L'avenir du Schleswig-Holstein se situerait plutôt en Europe de l'Ouest ou dans les zones pacifiques ou est-asiatiques.

Björn Engholm a une ambition pour son *Land* : le voir un jour devenir une plaque tournante des échanges maritimes et terrestres en mer Baltique. Il cherche donc à replacer le Schleswig-Holstein au centre de la région. Dans un contexte de réunification, il compte parmi les plus pauvres *Länder* d'Allemagne et a intérêt à construire des intérêts en mer baltique indépendamment de Bonn ou Berlin[21]. La structure fédérale de l'Allemagne est alors un atout pour cette construction. Le concept de « Nouvelle Hanse » devient synonyme de coopération autour de la Baltique renforcée avec le Schleswig Holstein comme pays-pont entre les régions de la Baltique, et de l'Europe de l'Ouest et du Centre. L'objectif est notamment de créer un axe Allemagne du Nord / Baltique qui viendrait contrecarrer l'axe Nord-Sud, passant par Hambourg, lequel évite les *Länder* du Schleswig-Holstein et du Mecklembourg-Poméranie-Occidentale.

Dans cette volonté de transformer le *Land* en plaque tournante, rien n'est négligé. Le vocabulaire utilisé est sans appel : « porte », « espace de transit » (*Umschlagplatz*), « plaque tournante », « hub », « centre », « espace du *Norden* », « région de l'Europe des régions ». Ces métaphores traduisent le besoin d'un discours du centre voire de la centralisation et même du centralisme qui doivent faire oublier l'effective situation

---

[20] Ibid., 62.

[21] Reinhold Wulff et Manfred Kerner, « Die Neue Hanse, » *Arbeitspapiere des Instituts für Internationale Politik und Regionalstudien* 1 (Institut für Internationale Politik und Regionalstudien des Fachbereichs Politische Wissenschaft der Freien Universität Berlin, 1994).

de périphérie et de marginalisation que connait le *Land*. La géographie européenne est recomposée pour mettre en avant un atout de localisation du *Land* : il ne se situerait pas en marge mais au cœur du *Norden*, possédant des ouvertures vers la Scandinavie et pays de l'Est. Il pourrait être un guide montrant la voie de l'Est au Danemark, à la Norvège, à la Suède ou à la Finlande.

Björn Engholm : le moteur de l'insertion allemande en Baltique ?

L'Allemagne réunifiée s'est montrée hésitante dans ses relations extérieures avec la Baltique. Quatre raisons peuvent expliquer ce changement de position de l'Allemagne (par l'intermédiaire du ministère des affaires étrangères) dans la région baltique. Tout d'abord, l'Allemagne a longtemps refusé de prendre position dans la démarche entreprise par les États baltes afin d'intégrer l'OTAN et l'UE ainsi que sur le contentieux de Kaliningrad pour ménager ses relations avec la Russie. En réalité, la République fédérale a été dans un premier temps favorable à la reconnaissance de l'indépendance des États baltes et fut même parmi les premiers pays à la proclamer en 1991 par l'intermédiaire de Hans Dietrich Genscher, connu pour son engagement envers l'Est de l'Europe[22]. L'Allemagne, qualifiée alors d'avocat des Baltes (*Anwalt der Balten*) soutient la candidature des pays baltes dans la Conférence sur la sécurité et la coopération en Europe (CSCE), le Conseil européen, le Conseil de coopération de l'OTAN, le Conseil des États de la mer Baltique. Cependant, cet engagement décroît avec le départ de Hans Dietrich Genscher du ministère des affaires étrangères (1982-1992) et l'arrivée de Klaus Kinkel (1992-1998). Pour ménager la Russie, l'Allemagne soutient alors les candidatures de la Pologne, de la République Tchèque et de la Hongrie mais pas celle des Pays baltes. Une deuxième raison au retrait allemand est à trouver dans la perception allemande du partage des partenariats européens[23]. La République fédérale aurait reçu la responsabilité d'un parrainage des pays de l'Europe médiane et orientale comme la République tchèque ou la Hongrie alors que les relations avec les pays baltiques incomberaient aux pays nordiques (Norvège, Suède, Finlande) à travers les outils de coopération nordiques ou nordico-baltiques. Une troisième raison à cette indifférence est lisible dans la géographie de la Baltique elle-même. D'un côté, la Baltique est longtemps restée un marché étroit de seulement 50 à 60 millions d'habitants et d'un autre côté, l'Allemagne comme la Russie ou la Pologne ne possède qu'une petite partie de son territoire en Baltique (Hambourg, le Schleswig-Holstein et le Mecklembourg-Poméranie Occidentale ne représentent que 11% de la superficie allemande et moins de 8% des habitants) et est partagée entre mer Baltique et mer du Nord (où se situent la plupart des grands ports allemands). Enfin, un dernier handicap de l'espace baltique notamment depuis 2004 est que celui-

[22] Helge Dauchert, « Deutschlands Baltikumpolitik, zwischen europäischer Integration und Annäherung an Russland », *Nordeuropa Forum* 2/2008: 54-73.

[23] Nikolaus Werz, Jenny Bonin, Jeanette Edler, Ute Fabricius, Christoph Krüger et Heribert Saldik, « Kooperation im Ostseeraum, Eine Bestandsaufnahme der wissenschaftlichen und politischen Kooperation unter besonderer Berücksichtigung der neue Bundesländer », *Rostocker Informationen zu Politik und Verwaltung* 24 (2005).

ci recoupe peu ou prou l'espace européen. L'Allemagne a ainsi longtemps cru qu'il suffisait de s'investir dans les institutions européennes pour finalement s'investir dans la zone baltique elle-même. Même les rapports avec la Russie pourraient être réglés par la politique de voisinage de l'UE. Même lorsque les intérêts allemands en Baltique ont été reconnus, la politique menée dans la région n'a pas été visible : Gerhard Schröder a ainsi déclaré que la Baltique représentait une part aussi importante de la politique extérieure allemande que les USA et le Japon mais il était toujours question dans les médias du Japon et des USA et peu de la Baltique.

Ce relatif détachement envers la Baltique est spécifique à l'Allemagne si l'on compare l'ensemble des pays riverains et a longtemps mis les *Länder* du Nord de l'Allemagne en porte-à-faux par rapport à l'échelle fédérale comme le précise Nikolaus Werz : « Il existe une asymétrie dans l'intérêt porté par les pays riverains à l'espace baltique. L'Allemagne qui borde la Baltique grâce à seulement deux Bundesländer n'y voit pas un centre économique ce qui freine les efforts entrepris par le Mecklembourg-Poméranie-Occidentale, le Schleswig-Holstein et Hambourg pour porter leurs intérêts dans la région »[24]. Cette situation a d'autant plus gêné les *Länder* du Nord que l'Allemagne fédérale est en principe responsable juridiquement de la politique extérieure. Le paragraphe 3 de l'article 32 de la constitution allemande mentionne la possibilité pour les *Länder,* avec l'approbation du gouvernement fédéral et dans la mesure de leur compétence législative, de conclure des traités avec des États étrangers. Ce paragraphe de l'article 32 a donné lieu à une variété d'interprétations allant du parallélisme affirmé entre *Bund* et *Länder* à l'affirmation d'une suprématie absolue de l'échelle fédérale. L'accord de Lindau, conclu en 1957, précise ce point en prévoyant que lorsque la fédération conclut des traités qui, de l'avis des *Länder,* touchent à leurs compétences législatives exclusives, le consentement des *Länder* est nécessaire avant que le traité ne devienne obligatoire en droit international. La constitutionnalité de l'accord n'est cependant pas reconnue de manière unanime. A l'échelle européenne, les transformations de la loi fédérale en 1992 et notamment le texte de l'article 23 renforcent ce flou juridique.

Puisque la RFA fut longtemps absente des processus de régionalisation baltique, les *Länder* ont dû se substituer à l'échelon fédéral pour défendre leurs intérêts dans la région. Ils se sont un temps comportés comme des États à part entière. Le Schleswig-Holstein, premier des deux *Länder* à avoir entamé une politique offensive dirigée vers la Baltique, par l'intermédiaire de son Ministre-Président, Björn Engholm, a en effet souvent mené une politique étrangère indépendante[25]. Si l'idée d'un « Conseil des États de la mer Baltique » provient tout d'abord en 1990 de Mats Hellström, ministre suédois, auteur d'un « Plaidoyer pour un Conseil des États de la mer Baltique », celle-ci a été développée et exploitée en coopération avec Björn Engholm. En avril 1991, Björn Engholm, Werner Jann et Bernd Rohwer de la *Denkfabrik* se rencontrent à

---

[24] Ibid., 160.
[25] Williams, *Zur Konstruktion einer Region*, 57.

Kiel. Le Ministre-Président du Schleswig-Holstein accuse directement l'État fédéral : « Cela est, pour notre part, d'une importance toute particulière car à l'échelle nationale, il n'y a ni intérêt, ni compréhension pour l'urgence de la coopération régionale »[26]. Il enchaîne les déplacements officiels : à la Commission européenne pour rencontrer Jacques Delors ou à Moscou où il participe, en septembre 1991, avec Pierre Mauroy, Pertti Paasio et Alfonso Guerra, Mikhaïl Gorbatchev, Boris Eltsine et Eduard Schewardnadse, à la mise sur pied d'un Conseil qui réunirait le Schleswig-Holstein (et non le *Bund*), la Scandinavie, les Pays Baltes et la Russie. Björn Engholm se rend ensuite en Pologne afin de s'entretenir avec Lech Wałesa et son ministre des Affaires étrangères. Un voyage dans les Pays Baltes est cependant interdit par l'État fédéral qui rappelle au Ministre-Président qu'il ne peut pas inviter les chefs de gouvernements d'États nationaux à une conférence des présidents et chefs de gouvernements sans son accord préalable. Dérogeant à cette règle, Engholm envoie des invitations, avant que les Affaires étrangères ne finissent par se rallier à l'idée d'un sommet. De nombreux débats opposent alors le ministre Genscher et Engholm sur la place que pourraient occuper les *Länder* dans un Conseil d'États de la mer Baltique. Genscher propose que la délégation allemande à ce Conseil comporte un représentant des *Länder*. Le premier Conseil des États de la mer Baltique a finalement lieu les 5 et 6 Mars 1992 à Copenhague.

Grâce à l'action de Björn Engholm, de nombreuses institutions baltiques ont été mises en place notamment en collaboration avec d'autres gouvernements sociodémocrates comme celui d'Ingvar Carlsson en Suède, vice-ministre d'Etat de 1982 à 1991. L'*Ars Baltica,* réseau culturel autour de la Baltique est imaginé en juillet 1989. Cette plate-forme doit permettre de rapprocher les cultures baltiques : « Il s'agit d'un pas important afin de montrer et de faire prendre conscience de la similitude des formes artistiques et culturelles dans le passé, présent et futur. Les participants voient en *Ars Baltica* un renforcement culturel de l'espace baltique»[27]. En collaboration avec Pehr Gyllenhammar, le président du Land créé également en septembre 1990 le Club Nord Européen (*North European Club*) à Stockholm. L'objectif du NEC est de renforcer politiquement et économiquement l'unité baltique et le rapprochement entre l'Allemagne, les pays scandinaves, les pays de l'Est et les Pays Bas. Les trois grands thèmes de débats sont : les infrastructures de transport, la protection de l'environnement et les infrastructures sociales. Les membres du Club sont des chefs d'entreprises influents : Ulf Sundquist, directeur de la banque STS à Helsinki ou Harald Norvik, directeur de Statoil à Stavanger. À compter de mars 1989, apparaissent les *Forums du Schleswig-Holstein* qui permettent une réflexion et une rencontre entre de nombreux acteurs baltiques. Le premier forum sur le thème *Mare Balticum* attire des délégations de Pologne, des pays scandinaves et de RDA autour de Paulina Mürl (SPD). Björn Engholm a enfin largement contribué à la création en 1991 à Helsinki de la Conférence des parlementaires de la mer Baltique (BSPC) et, nous

[26] Ibid., 171.
[27] Ibid., 146.

l'avons vu, à celle du Conseil des États de la Baltique (Copenhague, 1992). Ce dernier reste un lieu privilégié d'échanges entre le Bund et les *Länder* sur la coopération baltique. Les *Länder* y sont représentés au sein de la délégation allemande par un *Land* différent chaque année (le Schleswig-Holstein, le Mecklembourg-Poméranie-Occidentale, ou Hambourg).

Une nouvelle vision de la coopération baltique

Grâce à Björn Engholm, la régionalisation baltique a avancé dans trois directions principales. Tout d'abord, celui-ci a théorisé, comme d'autres avant lui, une forme d'unité baltique. Il a mis en avant les similitudes des régions et pays riverains, après de longues années de division. Ensuite, il a offert la possibilité à des élus, chefs d'entreprise et artistes de se rencontrer à travers des plateformes accélérant la prise de contact ; or ces contacts serviront plus tard à élaborer de nouveaux projets. Enfin, par la métaphore de la Hanse, il a défini d'une nouvelle manière la région baltique. Celle-ci adopte des limites floues mais extensibles. Les réflexions autour de la création du Club Nord Européen posent la question de l'intégration potentielle des Pays-Bas. Björn Engholm l'affirme sans détour : « Nous ne devons pas oublier que les Pays-Bas ont avec nous une conscience régionale commune ou qu'ils l'auront par cette institution »[28]. Cette phrase montre bien que Björn Engholm a davantage cherché à élargir l'espace baltique par l'institution qu'à recouvrir une conscience commune préexistante par l'institutionnalisation. L'institution crée la région et non l'inverse. Le Conseil des états de la Baltique comprend quant à lui la Russie. Les réseaux hanséatiques se sont étendus au Moyen Âge de manière large en Belgique, Pays-Bas, Russie, Biélorussie, Angleterre. Björn Engholm ne fait pas de la Baltique une région figée : il a souvent l'habitude de la représenter sous le trait de cercles concentriques.

4. Conclusion

La coopération baltique avait pris son essor suite à la chute du rideau de fer mais connait une crise depuis quelques années. La critique du concept de « Nouvelle Hanse » permit aux nordiques de rappeler leurs spécificités. Ces ambitions furent très vite déçues notamment face à la formulation d'une stratégie intégrée pour la mer Baltique dès 2006 et cela bien que celle-ci travaille en collaboration avec la « dimension septentrionale ». Le gouvernement suédois a fait de cette stratégie macro-régionale baltique, qui exclut directement la Russie, une priorité pour sa présidence de l'Union Européenne en 2009 avant de s'y désintéresser. La Baltique reste donc une région sans centre et la relance apparait dès lors délicate.

Est-ce l'occasion, une nouvelle fois, de réveiller la métaphore hanséatique délaissée au milieu des années 1990 ? La vision de Björn Engholm, qui n'a pas vraiment pu lui survivre, a-t-elle une chance de revoir le jour ? La métaphore de la Hanse, récur-

[28] Ibid., 152.

rente dans l'esprit des penseurs baltiques, n'aurait-elle pas un rôle de relance dans des moments où la coopération s'épuise… La Hanse serait-elle la régulation presque biologique donnant l'impulsion à « des cycles d'unification baltique » ? Tout comme la construction européenne, la construction de l'unité baltique, plus politique que naturelle, davantage créée que remémorée, n'est pas une ligne continue mais s'avère cyclique, connaissant flux et reflux.

En se débarrassant du mot « Hanse » trop polémique, la coopération baltique doit être perçue davantage comme un ensemble de cercles (grappes des coopérations nordiques, baltiques, baltes, bilatérales, de Barents, européennes) se recoupant ou non que comme une région à proprement parler uniforme et bornée. Il faut rappeler la forme réticulaire des coopérations baltiques qui fait la force de la région. En dehors de l'Europe, la Baltique fonctionnelle intègre la Russie ou la Biélorussie. « L'unité d'une région baltique » est un concept trop simple. La Baltique mérite d'être pensée dans la complexité : elle offre l'occasion d'un emboitement des aires de coopérations se recoupant en graphes au gré des rayons convergents.

Nicolas Escach
nicoescach@hotmail.com

Helen Williams
Institute for German Studies, University of Birmingham

The past decade has been a period of upheaval for citizenship and naturalisation policy (CNP) in the UK and Germany, with elite discursive shifts reflecting accompanying evolutions in their respective national identities. Germany has gone from insisting that it was not a country of immigration in the 1990s to widespread recognition of its long-resident foreign population and the pressing need to increase integration. The UK, on the other hand, has shifted from elite discursive acceptance of immigration – even, at times, despite public opposition – to increasingly open hostility and continual changes to requirements for naturalisation.

This article examines the shift in perspectives on integration in the UK and Germany and the resulting implications for national identity. Throughout the changes in both countries, there is evidence of conscious construction and alteration of the national narrative that has led to a re-conceptualisation of the borders between "insiders" and "outsiders." The result has been greater inclusion in Germany and greater exclusion in the UK. This article, though drawn from theory-driven research, focuses on describing the changes to CNP in the UK and Germany over the past ten years, examining elite discursive shifts that indicate changing national identities in the face of long-term migration. It ultimately argues that, despite the popularity of convergence literature,[1] the empirical data supports a growing body of literature indicating continued divergence of British and German CNP.[2] This article briefly defines key terms used throughout before presenting the United Kingdom and Germany, respectively, as case studies before offering analysis and conclusions about the lack of apparent convergence.

---

[1] See Simon Bulmer, "Germany, Britain and the European Union: Convergence through Policy Transfer?," *German Politics* 16, 1 (2007); Simon Green, *Policy Convergence in the UK and Germany* (London: Routledge, 2007); Hans Marig and Andreas Wimmer, "Country-Specific or Convergent? A Typology of Immigrant Policies in Western Europe," *Journal of International Migration and Integration* 1, 2 (2000); Edward Turner and Simon Green, "Understanding Policy Convergence in Britain and Germany," *German Politics* 16, 1 (2007).

[2] Simon Green, "Divergent Traditions, Converging Responses: Immigration and Integration Policy in the UK and Germany," *German Politics* 16, 1 (2007); Edward C. Page, "Conclusions," *German Politics* 16, 1 (2007).

EUROSTUDIA — REVUE TRANSATLANTIQUE DE RECHERCHE SUR L'EUROPE
Vol. 7, No.1-2 (2011): 87-103

1. Key terms

The terms "citizenship" and "nationality" are frequently used interchangeably, though they are separate concepts. When used precisely, citizenship describes not just one's nationality but also the rights and duties accompanying the legal status.[3] In Germany, politicians consistently employ the term "nationality," but in the UK, usage is far more mixed, due in part to its complicated colonial history and the resulting six main forms of British nationality, including British citizenship.[4] One could argue that more recent discussions in both countries revolve more around citizenship than nationality, as recent legislation seeks to codify rights and obligations as well as possession of a passport. However, this article's use of the terms reflects the usage in the respective countries.

Discourse in this article is very broadly defined, encompassing the use of written and spoken language, including diction and repetition. Discursive shifts occur when there are changes to popular phrases; previously unacceptable ideas become mainstream; or the words used to frame a debate on contentious issues are modified, causing a change in the focus of the debate.

2. United Kingdom

After a long history of formally unrestrictive policies, recent UK immigration and nationality policies reveal a growing conservative trend, with restrictive changes made to nearly every criterion for naturalisation since 2000 in the UK.[5]

This research does not argue that restrictive discursive shifts have not happened before in the UK: They have occurred several times in post-war British immigration policy, most notably in the aftermath of Enoch Powell's infamous "Rivers of Blood" speech in 1968, which pushed Heath to a more conservative policy.[6] Such a shift in discourse is again evident in the period in question. After a few decades of carefully constructed scripts and elite shunning of anti-immigrant rhetoric, the discursive shifts between the 2002 and 2009 immigration bills indicate a growing number of mainstream politicians expressing worries about "thresholds," "limits," and lack of integration.

This section analyses the identity discourse evident in responses to external pressures, debates surrounding limits on immigration, the imposition of language requirements, and the Knowledge of Life in the UK Test. Each of these makes clear the shifting discursive scripts and ideas behind British CNP. A common trend is

---

[3] Kay Hailbronner, *Country Report: Germany*, April ed. (Florence: EUDO Citizenship Observatory, 2010), 1.

[4] For a history of British nationality legislation, see Randall Hansen, *Citizenship and Immigration in Post-War Britain: The Institutional Origins of a Multicultural Nation* (Oxford: Oxford University Press, 2000).

[5] See Table 1.

[6] Hansen, *Citizenship and Immigration*, 190.

identifiable throughout: the executive introduces a proposal for change; the proposal is rejected as contrary to British identity as a liberal country of immigration; the plan is dropped; the proposal is reintroduced some time later, passing with little comment.

External pressures

The governmental agenda shifted during this period in response to pressures on other policy areas and the electoral rewards of a restrictive stance. Discourse during debates in Parliament about the three nationality law bills between 2000 and 2010 indicates the influence of exogenous factors in causing a rapid, unplanned response to events external to CNP. Like many other policy areas during this time period, the most commonly cited exogenous factors were related to the effects of radical Islam. The terrorist attacks in the USA on 11 September 2001 directly occasioned the addition of clauses altering laws regarding deprivation of citizenship.[7] Even more clearly, the London bombings on 7 July 2005 led to the late introduction of clauses affecting the deprivation of citizenship to a bill that was intended to legislate immigration and asylum, not nationality.[8] However, both of these cases affected only policy on the deprivation of citizenship; acquisition remained largely untouched by these events.

The UK also faced race riots in 2001 that prompted a debate about integration, especially of non-white minorities. This resulted in a Home Office review and the publication its report on community cohesion.[9] David Blunkett became Home Secretary around the same time, entering with a pre-set legislative agenda,[10] and the recommendations from the report simply served to reinforce his proposals.

Discursive shifts

During the 2002 Nationality, Asylum and Immigration (NIA) Bill debates, limits on immigration were discussed, but permanent settlement were generally confined to Conservative politicians, such as Peter Lilley, who did not receive a great deal of sympathy for their views.[11] Several chastisements were given during the Immigration, Asylum and Nationality (IAN) Bill (2006) debates for behaviour politicising immigration during the 2005 General Election campaigns.[12] However, by the time of

---

[7] UK Parliament, *Parliamentary Debates (Hansard): House of Lords Official Report*, 5th Ser., vol. 637, cc. 12, 440-512, 524, 530-554, 565-576, 588-636, 661-678, 844, 689-714, 727-758, 773-814, 963-977, 999-1032, 1233-1243, 1257-1305, 1322-1388 (London: HMSO, 2002).

[8] UK Parliament, *Parliamentary Debates (Hansard): House of Commons Official Report on Standing Committee E*, 5th Ser., vol. SCE, cc. 001-316 (London: HMSO, 2005).

[9] Ted Cantle (ed.), *Community Cohesion: A Report of the Independent Review Team* (London: Home Office, 2001).

[10] Helen Williams, "Interview with Senior Home Office Official," Jan. 2010.

[11] UK Parliament, *Parliamentary Debates (Hansard): House of Commons Official Report*, 5th Ser., vol. 384, cc. 341-436 (London: HMSO, 2002), cc. 378-81.

[12] UK Parliament, *Parliamentary Debates (Hansard): House of Commons Official Report on Standing*

the Borders, Citizenship and Immigration (BCI) Bill (2009) debates, scripts had shifted. Although actors coupled demands for "limited immigration" with the catchphrase "firm but fair" throughout the decade,[13] the 2005-2006 and 2009 debates show increasing anti-immigration rhetoric.[14] Naturalisation was discussed in terms of immigration policy, with ministerial claims of "making migration work for Britain" closely intertwined with increasing the requirements for naturalisation.[15] There were fewer mentions of the positive contributions of migrants and more expectations placed on them. Lord West, the Labour minister in the House of Lords during the BCI Bill, encapsulates the argument:

> We want to encourage those with the right values to become citizens. With rights come responsibilities, and those responsibilities must first be demonstrated, ensuring that the benefits of British citizenship are earned. This is at the heart of the Government's firm-but-fair system.[16]

Nationality acquisition policy remains tied to a discourse of numbers, functioning more as an extension of immigration policy than a policy in its own right in the UK.[17] Because of its colonial history and its post-colonial involvement with the Commonwealth, the UK has never developed a free-standing citizenship policy. Arguments widely used in the 1960s about strains on resources, lack of space, and panic about numbers have resurfaced, with many of the statements following the general formula of, "I'm not a racist, but the UK simply cannot take on more people." It is increasingly acceptable to say, "The problem is simply one of numbers. There is clearly some limit."[18] The fact that the same arguments were put forth when the national population was around a third lower than today encourages scepticism.[19]

Committee E, cc. 30, 171, 297.

[13] UK Parliament, *Parliamentary Debates (Hansard): House of Commons Official Report*, c. 379; ibid., c. 885; UK Parliament, *Parliamentary Debates (Hansard): House of Lords Official Report*, c. 523; UK Parliament, *Parliamentary Debates (Hansard): House of Commons Official Report*, 5th Ser., vol. 496, cc. 177-257, 801 (London: HMSO, 2009), c. 255; UK Parliament, *Parliamentary Debates (Hansard): House of Commons Official Report on Public Bill Committee*, 5th Ser., vol. PBC Borders, Citizenship and Immigration Bill, cc. 001-256 (London: HMSO, 2009), c. 156.

[14] UK Parliament, *Parliamentary Debates (Hansard): House of Commons Official Report*, 5th Ser., vol. 436, cc. 188-275 (London: HMSO, 2005), c. 275; UK Parliament, *Parliamentary Debates (Hansard): House of Commons Official Report*, 5th Ser., vol. 493, cc.169-241 (London: HMSO, 2009), c. 190, 193, 207; UK Parliament, *Parliamentary Debates (Hansard): House of Lords Official Report*, 5th Ser., vol. 707, cc. 1128-1213, WA215-216 (London: HMSO, 2009), c. 1172.

[15] UK Parliament, *Parliamentary Debates (Hansard): House of Commons Official Report*, c. 174; UK Parliament, *Parliamentary Debates (Hansard): House of Lords Official Report*, c. 1130-1131.

[16] UK Parliament, *Parliamentary Debates (Hansard): House of Lords Official Report*, c. 1130.

[17] Ann Dummett, "United Kingdom," in *Acquisition and Loss of Nationality: Policies and Trends in 15 European States. Volume 2: Country Analyses*, ed. Rainer Bauböck et al. (Amsterdam: Amsterdam University Press, 2006).

[18] Peter Lilley, *UK Parliament, Parliamentary Debates (Hansard): House of Commons Official Report*, c. 378.

[19] Hansen, *Citizenship and Immigration*, 182-190, 210; Ipsos MORI, "Immigration Poll," (London: Ipsos MORI for *The Sun* newspaper, 2007).

With the uptake of citizenship averaging around 150,000 people a year in the years leading up to 2010,[20] the discourse of numbers reflects the delayed influence of policy outcomes, which policy-makers can no longer control. Around a quarter of naturalisations are consistently granted on the basis of marriage; a further quarter of acquisitions are the registrations of minor children on the basis of a parent's nationality. The other roughly fifty per cent of naturalisations are granted on the basis of residence, including both people given refugee status in the UK and highly skilled migrants.[21]

Naturalisations granted on the basis of marriage are difficult for a liberal democracy to regulate. Although the UK has tightened language and integration requirements for spouses, it cannot prevent British citizens from marrying non-Britons. This is a reflection of at least four conventions: everyone has the right to marry whom they choose and that the naturalisation of a foreign spouse is facilitated by marriage.[22] The recent disregard of international treaties in favour of domestic politics reveals the prioritisation of domestic political concerns over international commitments. The UK also has little power to restrict naturalisations and registrations of minors, and it has been forced to extend gender equality to registration, which had historically been restricted to the mother's nationality.[23]

A deeper look at trends in citizenship uptake based on residence reveals a roughly five-year delay between the sudden increase in asylum seekers in the UK around 2000 and recent applications for citizenship.[24]

The UK experienced a peak in asylum applicants in 2002, at which time the highest numbers of applicants and people granted refugee status were from Iraq, Zimbabwe, Somalia, and Afghanistan.[25] Five years later, these same people had fulfilled the residency requirements to apply for citizenship, which large numbers did, creating panic about the numbers of people acquiring citizenship, though the UK can reasonably expect these numbers to decrease in the coming years as a reflection of the decrease in refugees after 2002.

---

[20] Philip Danzelman, *British Citizenship Statistics: United Kingdom 2008* (Research, Development and Statistics Directorate: Home Office Statistical Bulletin, 2009), 1.

[21] Idem.

[22] Council of Europe, *European Convention on Nationality*, 1997; United Nations, *The Universal Declaration of Human Rights*, 1948; United Nations, *Convention on the Reduction of Statelessness*, 1961; United Nations, *International Covenant on Civil and Political Rights*, 1966.

[23] For an overview of changes prior to the decade here discussed, see Dummett, "United Kingdom," and Hansen, *Citizenship and Immigration*.

[24] See Figure 1.

[25] David Matz, Rachel Hill, and Tina Heath, "Asylum Statistics: United Kingdom 2000," *Home Office Statistical Bulletin* 17, 1 (2001): 23-24.

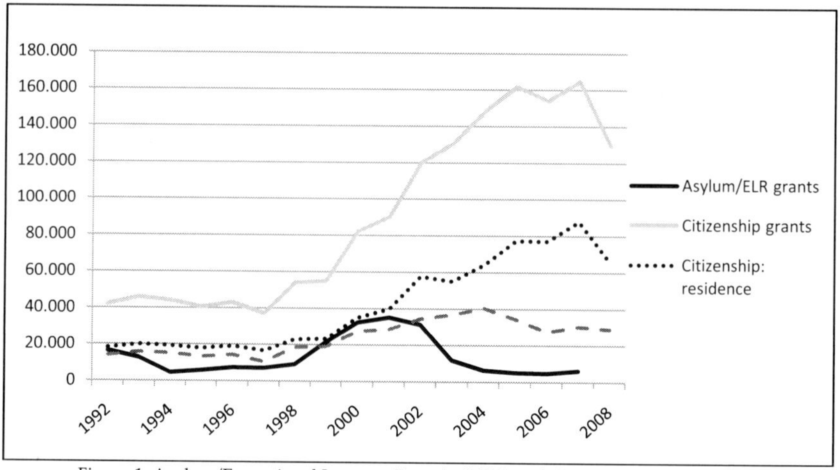

Figure 1. Asylum/Exceptional Leave to Remain (ELR) and Citizenship Grants, UK, 1992-2008.

Change in ideas

The use of minimum standards of language proficiency as a component of CNP exemplifies changes in ideas as well as behavioural scripts during the past decade. When the government introduced language requirements in the BNA (1981) for naturalisation applications on the basis of residency many organisations and parliamentarians expressed concerns about the potentially discriminatory nature of such a requirement. By 2002, however, the introduction of clauses requiring more formal proof of language ability led to expressions of support and assertions that the previous requirements had been too casual. The extension of these language requirements to spouses of British citizens received intense criticism from some parliamentarians and organisations, though. Some expressed fears that it would interfere with rights of family life; others felt that it would exclude spouses.

Parliamentary debates from the Nationality, Immigration and Asylum (NIA) Bill (2002) indicate conscious discursive construction by the parliamentarians and clearly defined discursive scripts from which few strayed. The direction of the discussions exhibits a lack of acceptance of greater restrictions on spouses, especially the introduction of a formal language requirement. Before 2002, the general assumption was that spouses of British citizens would naturally acquire language skills in the course of marriage, but the government cited evidence that linguistic integration was not as high as it had been assumed or hoped.[26] Even so, the introduction of a language requirement for spouses of British citizens proved very controversial. Several hours were spent discerning whether it was just or discriminatory to enforce such a requirement.

[26] UK Parliament, *Parliamentary Debates (Hansard): House of Lords Official Report*, 5th Ser., vol. 636, cc. 1087-1180 (London: HMSO, 2002), c. 1168.

Some of the legislators still expressed concern about having a language requirement for anyone: "It worries me deeply that there is a requirement to learn English;"[27] "I do not believe that we should impose conditions which are not at present imposed on the citizens of this country."[28] However, there was a general consensus that economic migrants should be required to prove their proficiency. Discourse surrounding spousal language requirements suggested that it was interfering with British citizens' right to chose a spouse: "I have to say that the suggestion from a Labour Member of Parliament [...] that prospective spouses coming to Britain for arranged marriages should be required to learn English was rightly criticised as being a case of the state dictating who was to marry whom."[29]

The new clause passed, however, and by 2009 the politicians no longer questioned the existence of such a requirement but were more concerned that the standard of proficiency was too low. In fact, some politicians congratulated themselves on the positive impact of having enforced the spousal language requirement because of preliminary results indicating that it decreased the social isolation of spouses from non-Western cultures. While those in support of language requirements claimed that they were justified for naturalisation applicants in 2002, the discursive shift by 2009 had led to requirements not only that immigrants must show language proficiency but to proposals to test visa applicants in their home countries before granting entry clearance, akin to the model used in the Netherlands. Such proposals did not draw as much outrage as ten years prior, even though they have the potential to detract significantly from family life and will affect women, the poor, and the least educated the most because of limited access to English courses in their home countries. The Conservative government formally announced the implementation of such requirements starting 29 November 2010.[30]

Integration/naturalisation tests

Around the period in question, the idea of naturalisation tests became fashionable in Western Europe. Though long used in the USA, Canada and Australia, the Netherlands was the only country in Europe to have a naturalisation/integration test in 2000. Since then, many countries have implemented them, including Denmark, Estonia, Germany, Latvia, Lithuania and the United Kingdom; and France and Belgium are contemplating following suit. This has led to a growing body of literature evaluating the liberal or restrictive nature of these tests.[31]

---

[27] Ibid., c. 445.

[28] Ibid., c. 451.

[29] Ibid., c. 1167.

[30] UK Border Agency, "New English Language Requirement for Partners" http://www.ukba.homeoffice.gov.uk/sitecontent/newsfragments/26-english-language-partners, accessed 10.09.2010.

[31] See Rainer Bauböck and Christian Joppke (eds.), "How Liberal Are Citizenship Tests?," EUDO Citizenship Observatory, *EUI Working Paper* RSCAS 2010/41; especially the contribution by Sergio

The Knowledge of Life in the UK Test was originally brought in as a naturalisation exam before being applied as a requirement for settlement status. Its introduction is a clear example of the technique mentioned above – introducing a change, receiving criticism, withdrawing it, and reintroducing the same change at a later date. As Table 1 shows, this test was not a requirement at the starting point in 2000. It was brought in after much heated debate in the 2002 Nationality, Immigration and Asylum Act. Major objections were made on the grounds of it being discriminatory against non-EU nationals.[32] The government convinced the parliamentarians that it was not discriminatory, however, on the grounds that the test was not required for visa applications but only for naturalisation, and EU nationals were subject to the same criteria as non-EU nationals in the naturalisation process.[33] Several of the objecting Members subsequently withdrew their objections on the grounds of these reassurances.

In 2006, the government changed the point of application of the Knowledge of Life in the UK Test,[34] making it compulsory for anyone applying for settlement in the UK.[35] Such a requirement was directly contrary to the assurances given during the 2002 debates that the test was not discriminatory against non-EU nationals, as EU nationals do not need to apply for settlement status in the UK because of their right to live in any EU member state. The UK government continued with this tactic in 2009, presenting the possibility of using the Knowledge of Life in the UK Test as a hurdle for settlement and a second exam focused on civics and history for applicants for naturalisation.[36] This was justified on the grounds that the Knowledge of Life Test examines applicants on topics that are important to settlement, while a civics exam would make sure that applicants understood the political system and how to exercise the rights of citizenship, such as voting, to which applicants had not previously had access.

Summary

This brief overview indicates the breadth and depth of changes in nationality acquisition and the connected discursive shifts in the UK between 2000 and 2010. The process of change in the UK is particularly interesting because it follows a clear pattern of testing an idea, withdrawing it after a negative reaction, then subsequently re-introducing the idea successfully when the initial aversion has worn off. This

---

Carrera and Elspeth Guild, "Are Integration Tests Liberal? The "Universalistic Liberal Democratic Principles" as Illiberal Exceptionalism," 29-34.

[32] UK Parliament, *Parliamentary Debates (Hansard): House of Commons Official Report*, 5th Ser., vol. 388, cc. 440-554 (London: HMSO, 2002).

[33] UK Parliament, *Parliamentary Debates (Hansard): House of Commons Official Report on Select Committee E*, 5th Ser., vol. SCE cc. 001-064 (London: HMSO, 2002), c. 020.

[34] UK Parliament, "Immigration, Asylum and Nationality Act," (2006). http://www.opsi.gov.uk/acts/acts2006/pdf/ukpga_20060013_en.pdf (accessed 10 Aug. 2009).

[35] See Table 1.

[36] UK Border Agency, "Earning the Right to Stay: A New Points Test for Citizenship," (2009), 6.

method becomes apparent through an overview of government publications, documentation of public and parliamentary response, and parliamentary debates.

The discursive shift between 2000 and 2010 indicates movement towards a more restrictive position. Despite expressions of concern from a wide array of immigrants' rights associations, the UK government lengthened the residence requirement for labour migrants and those on the protected route, for whom the path to citizenship could now take eight years from the time of acquisition of a qualifying residence status.[37] This drew harsh criticism especially from the UN High Commissioner for Refugees, whose office has long demanded that the path to citizenship for recognised refugees should take no more than five years.[38] The domestic political rewards for a restrictive citizenship policy have clearly outweighed the international punishment for behaviour in violation of treaties of which the UK is a signatory.

3. Germany

Germany, on the other hand, has moved from a very restrictive citizenship regime for much of the twentieth century to a more liberal regime that attempts to fulfil treaty obligations and to further integration. After decades of naturalisation being the exception rather than the rule, even for second- and third-generation immigrants, Germany now officially encourages naturalisation, and policies are intended to increase integration and naturalisation rates. Although some of the German policy changes have been similar to the UK, others now make Germany more liberal than the UK.[39] It is Germany's discourse, however, that presents the strongest evidence of the liberalising shift. From widespread statements that Germany was *not* a country of immigration in 2000 to open acceptance that it *is* a country of immigration in 2010, this reflects a broader discursive shift. Politicians are now punished for politicising integration, and there is a broad consensus in favour of easing naturalisation.

Even in the first years after the landmark changes to the Staatsangehörigkeitsgesetz (StAG) came into effect on 1 January 2000, both academic and public discourse continued to focus on the xenophobic, ethno-cultural German identity. Yet the past decade shows evidence of discursive, legislative and administrative shifts that commentators ten years ago largely dismissed as impossible. This section examines the historical influences on German discourse and policy, the politicisation of immigration, the roles of public opinion and the media, and finally the shift towards positive public discussion of integration and greater "constitutional patriotism" replacing the ethno-cultural model.

---

[37] See Table 1.

[38] UNHCR, *Borders, Citizenship and Immigration Bill: Parliamentary Briefing, House of Commons Second Reading* (London: United Nations, 2009), 2.

[39] See Table 1.

Discursive scripts

Discursive scripts play a very important role in the construction of the perceived reality in Germany. Shifts in scripts have accompanied the change in national understanding of what it means to be German in the slow transformation from an inherited characteristic to a community that rallies around a common constitution and set of accepted societal values. The path of the Immigration Act from 2001 to 2004 and the Integration Summits of the Merkel chancellorship provide excellent examples of changing scripts. The rate of changing norms was different on the left than the right, and each merits its own discussion.

SPD discursive scripts showed the greatest period of change before the introduction of the Immigration Act in 2001, but the debates between 2001 and 2004 show evidence of the solidification of the new scripts. In 1998, Minister of the Interior Otto Schily famously said, "The capacity for immigration in Germany has been exceeded,"[40] a quote that CDU/CSU politicians cited during the 2002 debates.[41] However, in 2002, he was much more careful about his phrasing: "The limitation of immigration, taking into account the capacity for absorption and the willingness of the Federal Republic of Germany, must be the goal of this law."[42] With this he implied that the threshold had not been exceeded but simply that the absorptive capacity needed to be recalled. At the same time, he clearly stated that immigration must continue, citing the report of the Müller Commission: "Managed migration of skilled workers is, therefore, very much in the interest of our national economy and thus of the entire country."[43]

The years between 2000 and 2005 were an important transitional period in elite discourse because it was during this time that most of the politicians agreed to stop consciously politicising immigration-related policies in recognition of the great damage inflicted for minor electoral gains. Before this tacit – and sometime explicit – agreement, several politicians expressed frustration at the acceptance of the need for a coherent Immigration Act and comprehensive action on integration measures when speaking privately accompanied by outright rejection and insistence on an irreconcilable gulf between the parties when speaking publicly about the policy options.[44]

---

[40] "Die Grenze der Belastbarkeit Deutschlands durch Zuwanderung ist überschritten," in "Der Rechtsextremismus ist die größte Gefahr, " *Der Tagesspiegel*, 15.11.1998, 4.

[41] Deutscher Bundestag, "Deutscher Bundestag: Stenographischer Bericht," *Verhandlungen des Deutschen Bundestages* BT Drs. 14/222, 1 Mar (2002): c. 22031.

[42] "Die Begrenzung der Zuwanderung unter Berücksichtigung der Aufnahmefähigkeit und der Bereitschaft der Bundesrepublik Deutschland muss das Ziel des Gesetzes sein." Otto Schily, ibid., c. 22045.

[43] "Eine gesteuerte Zuwanderung qualifizierter Fachkräfte liegt daher durchaus im Interesse unserer Volkswirtschaft und damit des gesamten Landes," ibid.

[44] Kay Hailbronner disagrees that pleas for non-politicisation pay anything more than rhetorical lip-service (Hailbronner, *Country Report: Germany*, 26).

Sigmar Gabriel named this a "*Vieraugengesellschaft*,"[45] underscoring the discrepancies between scripts employed for public consumption and the content of discussions behind closed doors.[46]

Although scripts were changing, the 2001-2002 parliamentary speeches are filled with speeches by CDU/CSU politicians decrying Germany's status as a country of immigration and rejecting multiculturalism of any definition. In this context, the perceived meaning of integration varied widely, from visions of full assimilation to the harmonious parallel existence of multiple cultures. Christian Union members generally agreed that Germany was *not* a country of immigration.

However, Chancellor Merkel laid out a new agenda for integration when the CDU/CSU returned to power in 2005, signalling a change and ushering in a series of integration summits with representatives from a wide variety of NGOs, immigrant groups and practitioners. Her leadership seemed to indicate a deviation from the traditional Christian Democratic understanding of integration. However, with the stark drop in popularity of the black-yellow coalition following the September 2009 elections and the euro crisis as well as the public discussion ignited by the publication of controversial Federal Bank chairman Thilo Sarazzin's book in summer 2010, the Christian Union appeared poised for a shift to the right. Some argue this is exactly what happened when Angela Merkel announced on 16 Oct 2010 that "multiculturalism has absolutely failed."[47] In itself, this statement seems to constitute a return to the Christian Union Parties' adherence to German culture as a leading culture and rejection of multiculturalism as the model for integration. However, it could also be interpreted as a response to the intra-party rebellion, which has shown more politicians criticising the centrist shift under Merkel, blaming the party for leaving the right wing open by abandoning its conservative core.[48] After a summer focused on party unity, Merkel's statement could simply be an excellent example of Gabriel's disjuncture between scripts created for public – or party – consumption and those behind closed doors during policy negotiations. What the situation certainly indicates is that this discursive script is still under negotiation.

Change in ideas

Changes in ideas certainly play a role in the institutional change of CNP in Germany. In interviews, multiple parliamentarians mentioned the Netherlands as a country to whom Germany looked for ideas to promote integration.[49] The FDP in particular considered the Dutch model at the beginning of the 2000s as "very appeal-

[45] Lit., a "four-eyed society," the closest English idiomatic equivalent is "behind closed doors."

[46] Deutscher Bundesrat, "Bundesrat: Stenographischer Bericht," *Verhandlungen des Deutschen Bundesrates* BR Drs. 14/774, (2002): c. 143.

[47] "Integration: Merkel erklärt Multikulti für gescheitert," *Spiegel Online*, 16.10.2010.

[48] Daniela Vates, "Weniger Konservatismus wagen," *Berliner Zeitung*, 13.01.2010.

[49] Helen Williams, "Interview with Dr. Max Stadler, FDP," 23 Apr. 2009; Helen Williams, "Interview with Stephan Mayer," 7 May 2009.

ing, but Germany wasn't ready."[50] However, Dutch policies afterwards took a more restrictive direction, and "in the end, Germany chose its own path."[51]

Even the long-held idea that naturalisation should be the end-point of the integration process is beginning to break down. "While the ruling Social Democratic Party in 1999 considered the acquisition of German nationality to be an essential instrument in achieving integration, the opposition Christian Democratic Parties (CDU/CSU) argued that naturalisation should complete the process of integration rather than pave the way towards it."[52]

Integration/naturalisation tests

Germany's integration test was announced with the EU Directives Implementation Act[53] and implemented on 5 August 2008 to allow time for the test's development.[54] Its form exemplifies the mixed character of integration tests. On the one hand, the creation of a federally designed exam finally standardised the naturalisation process, which had previously been different in each state, leading to vastly different naturalisation rates and requirements. On the other hand, there are always arguments that such exams raise the bar for naturalisation. However, Germany's use of integration tests appears not to act as an instrument of exclusion, as initial figures indicate a ninety-nine per cent pass rate,[55] far higher than the UK's seventy-one per cent pass rate for its Life in the UK Test.[56] Whether these changes are liberal or restrictive, the exchange of new ideas about integration and naturalisation tests has certainly resulted in the institutional change of CNP in both Germany and the UK.

National identity

Although discussions in Germany have revolved around citizenship as the end-point of integration – a reward for taking on German values – German identity discourse has shifted substantially in the past ten years. After successful right-wing campaigns against foreigners in the 1990s, parties who have subsequently strayed from the newly established discursive scripts have been punished rather than rewarded by voters.[57] From Brubaker's famous prophecy that Germany's policy process was too path dependent to be able to institute an *ius soli* (birthright) system

---

[50] Williams, "Interview with Dr. Max Stadler, FDP."

[51] Williams, "Interview with Stephan Mayer."

[52] Hailbronner, *Country Report: Germany*, 19.

[53] Bundesgesetzblatt, "EU-Richtlinienumsetzungsgesetz," *BGBl I*, 28.08.2007.

[54] Bundesgesetzblatt, "Verordnung zu Einbürgerungstest und Einbürgerungskurs (Einbürgerungstestverordnung)," *BGBl I*, 05.08.2008.

[55] Christoph Wöhrle, "Deutschland: Einbürgerungstest wird fast immer bestanden," *Migration und Bevölkerung* 1 (2009).

[56] Helena Wray, "United Kingdom: 29.1 Percent of Migrants Taking the Citizenship Test Fail," EUDO Citizenship Observatory, accessed 01.09.2010, http://eudo-citizenship.eu/citizenship-news/314-uk-291-percent-of-migrants-taking-the-citizenship-test-fail-.

[57] Karl-Heinz Meier-Braun, *Deutschland, Einwanderungsland* (Frankfurt am Main: Suhrkamp, 2002), 102.

of citizenship[58] to a system more liberal than France and widely accepted by the German public,[59] discourse surrounding national identity is strongly indicative of dramatic change.

Changes in ideas about the German national identity have resulted directly in changes to CNP. Once an institution that focused on descent as the main criterion for nationality – for the many reasons discussed above – the growth of Germany's non-German population and status as a *de facto* country of immigration forced a national debate about identity. Two competing conceptions have emerged: the more conservative view that one can only hold loyalties to one country, a model that rejects multiple nationality; and a "republican" or "constitutional patriotic" concept, which rallies around compliance with the rule of law and respect for the principles of the Basic Law.[60] The widespread, continuing debates about terms like "integration" and *Leitkultur* show that a new discursive equilibrium has not yet been reached.[61]

The changing national identity is reflected most starkly by the dividing line of the Nationality Act (1999). Hailbronner writes,

> Since 1 January 2000, naturalisation and acquisition of German nationality is considered as being in the public interest of Germany rather than as an unavoidable fact. This change in nationality law also reflects a substantial change in the perception of migration. The original assumption that the migrant workers recruited in the early 1970s would return eventually to their home countries has been abandoned.[62]

Changes in discourse about whether Germany is, in fact, a country of migration have accompanied this. The ethnocentric discursive script began to break down in the 1990s, with the early 2000s acting as a transition period during which acceptance of Germany's status as a country of immigration was still limited. By the time Angela Merkel came into office in 2005, however, the debate was largely settled, and even the CDU and much of the CSU openly admitted that Germany *is* a country of immigration.[63] As chancellor, Merkel made a national discussion of integration a priority, inviting many different migrant interest groups, including the major Turkish societies, to a series of Integration Summits, where a National Integration Plan was created. Although the summits have been subject to criticism for producing little in the way of concrete changes, they still mark a turning point in German CNP. As Reimman points out, "[…] the very idea behind the events was revolutionary. It was

---

[58] Rogers Brubaker, *Citizenship and Nationhood in France and Germany* (Cambridge, MA: Harvard University Press, 1992), 185.

[59] Dietrich Thränhardt, "Include or Exclude: Discourses on Immigration in Germany," *Journal of International Migration and Integration* 3, 3-4 (2002): 359.

[60] Hailbronner, *Country Report: Germany*, 25-26.

[61] Ibid., 26.

[62] Ibid., 17.

[63] Karl Forster, "Heiner Geißler im Gespräch: "Man muss vor Menschen keine Angst haben"," *Süddeutsche Zeitung*, 11.12.2004; Anna Reimann, "Vor dem Gipfel: Integratives Kuscheln," *Spiegel Online*, 12.07.2006.

the first time that the federal government officially sat down with migrants and Muslims."[64]

Integration starts at home

By 2005, 18.9 per cent of the population in Germany had an immigrant background, rising to close to 40 per cent in Germany's large cities.[65] Amongst those under the age of 15, the proportion was 30 per cent and almost 45 per cent of those in large cities.[66] Such statistics have become common knowledge in much of Germany and, rather than fuelling arguments that the country was too full, they have begun to support arguments that a greater effort must be made by the Germans to facilitate integration.

The new catchphrase in Germany has become "integration starts at home,"[67] emphasising the importance of the local community.[68] This reflects the growing consensus that federal legislation can only set the framework for integration, while the local institutions must take charge of the actuality of policy administration.[69] Federal Chancellor Angela Merkel has recognised the need for greater dialogue about integration, convening a series of integration summits to which practitioners, immigrants, and various interest groups were invited to discuss the state of integration and how to improve it. Although these summits have drawn criticism and have suffered from the decisions of key groups to boycott them, they still symbolise a shift towards greater form of inclusion and consultation, a radical step in German policy. Following the federal example, local authorities have sought the opinions and suggestions of immigrants and minorities more in the policy-making process.[70] People of migrant origin are spoken of now as "policy partners," reflective of a paradigmatic change at both the local and national levels.[71] Some cities have begun openly recruiting people with migration origin for public service jobs.[72]

---

[64] Anna Reimann, "Integrationspolitik: Die Entdeckung der Einwanderer,"*Spiegel Online*, 30.12.2009.

[65] Statistisches Bundesamt Deutschland, *Mikrozensus 2005* (Wiesbaden: Bundesregierung Deutschland, 2006).

[66] "7. Bericht der Beauftragten der Bundesregierung für Migration, Flüchtlinge und Integration über die Lage der Ausländerinnen und Ausländer in Deutschland" (Berlin: Die Beauftragte der Bundesregierung für Migration, Flüchtlinge und Integration, 2007).

[67] "Integration findet vor Ort statt."

[68] Bundesregierung Deutschland, *Nationaler Integrationsplan: Neue Wege - Neue Chancen*, July 2007 (Berlin: Presse- und Informationsamt der Bundesregierung, 2007).

[69] Hartmut Häußermann and Andreas Kapphan, "Integrationspolitik der Städte - Ein Paradigmenwechsel," in *Migrationsreport 2008*, ed. Michael Bommes and Marianne Krüger-Potratz (Frankfurt: Campus Verlag, 2008), 15-16.

[70] Lena Wundenberg, "Bilanz der bisherigen Integrationsgipfel: Ernüchterung, wenn es ins Detail geht," *Tagesschau*, 06 Nov. 2008.

[71] Häußermann and Kapphan, "Integrationspolitik der Städte," 23.

[72] Ibid., 25."

Summary

Germany has learned in recent decades that citizenship policy, while not a routine issue like the annual budget, cannot be ignored because countries must address the situation of the millions of foreigners living within their borders, as it has become clear that they are not temporary migrants looking to leave soon. As a consequence, it has realised the necessity of higher levels of naturalisation.[73] Higher levels of naturalisation cannot be realised simply through legal and administrative changes, however: uptake of German citizenship continued at levels seen as disappointing after an initial surge in response to the 1999 changes. Uptake must be encouraged through greater public acceptance, higher incentives for naturalisation, and a discursive shift from an ethno-cultural national identity to a more civic identity.

Both "foreigners" and Germans seem to have a tacit understanding that the acquisition of German citizenship is not simply a membership to the state and all its civic responsibilities but also indicative of a cultural understanding.[74] This cultural membership seems to be a form of expression of loyalty to the German state, a central theme in many of the policy discourses in the 1990s in Germany.[75] German integration efforts have focused increasingly on linguistic unity whilst moving away from ethnic identity. With this has also come a growing emphasis on constitutional patriotism similar to the American model: creating a national identity through loyalty to the political institutions and democratic ideals rather than through a common ethnic history. Where integration in Germany previously meant something closer to assimilation, requiring the immigrant to lose any previous identity and become virtually undistinguishable from ethnic Germans, discourse in Germany has sought to re-define this term. The National Integration Plan proposes that "Integration means integration into the social, economic, intellectual, cultural and legal fabric of the host country without giving up one's own cultural identity."[76] For the first time, there is widespread discussion of reciprocal adaptation in place of an expectation that immigrants must make all of the changes.[77]

4. Conclusions

The British and German cases show several common responses and the impact of popular ideas during the past decade: both are renegotiating their national identities; both have instituted integration/naturalisation tests and citizenship ceremonies; and both have formalised language requirements. However, these seemingly similar changes do not indicate a convergence of policy trajectories. The methods of policy

---

[73] Simon Green, *The Politics of Exclusion: Institutions and Immigration Policy in Contemporary Germany* (Manchester: Manchester University Press, 2004), 142.

[74] Brubaker, *Citizenship and Nationhood in France and Germany*, 178.

[75] Green, *The Politics of Exclusion*, 104.

[76] Bundesregierung Deutschland, 127.

[77] Ibid.; Häußermann and Kapphan, "Integrationspolitik der Städte," 18.

implementation and the intentions of the changes have led to divergent outputs and outcomes. While German rhetoric has grown more inclusive, British has grown more exclusive. The initial statistics for the German naturalisation exam indicate a 99 per cent pass rate, while the Knowledge of Life in the UK test pass rate is less than 75 per cent, with results varying widely between different ethnicities. Immigrants are required to pay for citizenship ceremonies in the UK, and acquiring British nationality is nearly four times more expensive than German nationality, acting as an effective deterrent to many. The length of time required to acquire nationality is now nearly identical.

Despite the similar current requirements in the two countries, the evidence does not seem to point towards convergence; rather, a comparison indicates that perhaps Germany and the UK have crossed paths on trajectories headed in opposite directions, a finding contrary to convergence studies in many other policy areas. However, this supports the conclusions of several policy experts in a special issue on policy convergence in the UK and Germany.[78] Though there is evidence of policy sharing with regards to popular ideas like naturalisation ceremonies and swearing of oaths according to a more American or Dutch model, in terms of requirements likely to affect the ability of the foreigners to naturalise, Germany is in many ways now more liberal than the UK, which has tightened the criteria for naturalisation to such an extent that it is only more liberal than Germany in its widespread acceptance of multiple nationality. Yet the UK retains its reputation for liberal policy in much of the national discourse, while Germany continues with its post-war pattern of self-criticism.

While Britain seems to be reviving the sentiments of the 1960s, indicating a discursive shift towards exclusion and greater assimilation rather than reciprocal integration, Germany seems to be shaking off its ethno-cultural model and building a linguistic and constitutional patriotism. Germany has now largely dropped slogans like "the boat is full," while British discourse increasingly cites overburdening of the infrastructure and welfare system. Anti-immigrant discourse is becoming more acceptable in the UK at all levels, with restrictive immigration policies featuring in the campaign manifestos of the major political parties and in parliamentary debates without backlash and even with reward, while attempts to politicise immigration and integration in Germany have increasingly resulted in punishment of the responsible actors. For the time being, it appears that British identity discourse will continue to accept certain levels of anti-immigrant speech, and policies will continue in a restrictive direction; on the other hand, German discourse appears to be growing more liberal and more stable, and the country appears to be establishing a new discursive norm that is more inclusive and exhibits more elements of reciprocal integration.

Helen Williams
mrshelenmwilliams@gmail.com

[78] *German Politics* 16, 1 (2007).

Table 1. Comparative table of naturalisation requirements, 2000-2010.

	UK				Germany		
Criterion	**2000**	**2002**	**2006**	**2009**	**2000**	**2005**	**2007**
Good character	Yes	Yes	Yes	Yes	Fines up to 180 days wages, prison sentences up to 6 months	Fines up to 180 days wages, prison sentences up to 6 months	**Fines up to 90 days wages, prison sentences up to 3 months**
Language	Casual, none for spouses	**Yes, including spouses**	Yes	Yes	Yes/No†	Yes/No†	**Yes, CEFR B1**
Citizenship oath/pledge	Oath	**New oath and pledge**	Oath and pledge	Oath and pledge	No	No	**Yes**
Citizenship ceremony	No	***Yes***	Yes	Yes	No	No	***Yes***
Integration /naturalisation test	No	**Yes**	**Yes, for settlement**	**Yes, possible second test**	No	**Yes, law and society test**	**Yes, plus naturalisation test**
Cost	Approx. £150	Approx. £150	**Approx. £575**	**Approx. £800**	500DM (adult) /100DM (child) /reductions possible	€255 (adult)/€51 (child)/ reductions possible	€255 (adult)/€51 (child)/ reductions possible
Length of residence	3 yrs (spouses), 5 yrs (residence)	3 yrs (spouses), 5 yrs (residence)	3 yrs (spouses), 5 yrs (residence)	**3-5 yrs (spouses), 6-8 yrs (residence)**	*8 years*	*8 years/7 years**	*8 Years/7 years*/6 years***
Absences from country	Avg. 90 days/yr, 90 days in final year	Avg. 90 days/yr, 90 days in final year	Avg. 90 days/yr, 90 days in final year	**Absolute 90 days/yr**	Up to 6 months	Up to 6 months	Up to 6 months
Activity (UK)/ Optionsmodell (DE)	No	No	No	**Yes**	**Yes**	Yes	Yes

Restrictive changes indicated in bold. *Liberal changes indicated in italics.*

* Upon successful completion of integration course. ** In cases of "extraordinary integration," especially linguistic.

† Proof of sufficient German knowledge required for naturalisation by right (*Anspruch*) but not for naturalisation by discretion (*Ermessen*).

SOZIALE MARKTWIRTSCHAFT, MODELL DEUTSCHLAND UND POLDERMODELL

Wirtschaftspolitische Leitbilder als Merkmale nationaler Identität und Europäisierung

Hanco Jürgens
Duitsland Instituut Amsterdam, Universiteit van Amsterdam

Seit der Kreditkrise bewegen sich die Debatten über die Zukunft der niederländischen und deutschen „sozialen Marktwirtschaft" in eine neue Richtung. Nicht nur haben die politischen Parteien alte ideologische Stellungnahmen aufgemöbelt, auch der Blickwinkel der Debatten hat sich verschoben. Die Idee, dass der alte, hinfällige Rheinländische Patient krank sei und nur durch Liberalisierung, Privatisierung, Deregulierung und Steuerreform wieder gesunden könne, hat die politischen Debatten lange dominiert. Seit den achtziger Jahren, vor allem aber nach dem Fall der Mauer, war das angelsächsische Modell des Kapitalismus ein Vorbild für die niederländische und die deutsche Wirtschaft. Ironischerweise wehte die Bankenkrise aus den Vereinigten Staaten herüber und damit ist die transatlantische Orientierung abhanden gekommen. Alte Orientierungen, seien es die soziale Marktwirtschaft, das Modell Deutschland, das Poldermodell, angelsächsischer oder Rheinischer Kapitalismus, werden jetzt neu formuliert. Da das Schreckgespenst des grenzenlosen Turbokapitalismus mit der Kreditkrise ein Gesicht erhalten hat und die Politik vor großen Herausforderungen steht, ist zu erwarten, dass es zu einer Re-Ideologisierung kommen wird, zu einem neuen Links-Rechts-Schema, das auch die europäische Union nicht unberührt lassen kann.

Die Kreditkrise war aber nicht nur eine wirtschaftliche, sondern auch eine wirtschaftswissenschaftliche Krise: Es hat kaum Experten gegeben, die diese rasche Entwicklung vorausgesagt haben.[1] Politiker sind mehr als gefordert, nicht nur weil stets sofortige Lösungen geboten waren und sind, sondern auch, weil ständig neue Probleme auftauchen. Es stellen sich Fragen nach einer Neuorientierung, vielleicht sogar einer neuen Ideologie, zumindest aber nach einem von der Politik angeregten Wertewandel im Wirtschaftsleben. Die Antworten auf diese Fragen müssen sich noch herauskristallisieren.

1. WECHSELBEZIEHUNGEN

Die Kreditkrise könnte sich als Rettung der Europäischen Union erweisen. Bei den Bürgern Europas, nicht zuletzt den niederländischen, hat in den neunziger

[1] Siehe auch: Alexander Nützenadel, „Economic Knowledge, Experts and the German Public Sphere in Postwar Germany," *Forschungsberichte aus dem Duitsland Instituut Amsterdam, Universiteit van Amsterdam* 5 (2009): 62-73. Für das Korrekturlesen sei Angelika Wendland ganz herzlich gedankt.

EUROSTUDIA — REVUE TRANSATLANTIQUE DE RECHERCHE SUR L'EUROPE
Vol. 7, No.1-2 (2011): 105-117

Jahren die Idee Fuß gefasst, dass Europäisierung mit Privatisierung und Deregulierung gleichzusetzen sei. Weil die Europäische Union die Sozialpolitik überwiegend den Mitgliedstaaten überlassen hat, wird die EU tatsächlich als ein neoliberales Projekt betrachtet. Globalisierung, Privatisierung und Europäisierung gelten als Bedrohungen der erworbenen sozialwirtschaftlichen Rechte. Die zahlreicher werdenden Kritiker des Neoliberalismus wurden auf diese Weise einfach auch Kritiker der Vertiefung und Erweiterung der EU: In Deutschland die Wählerschaft der Linken, in den Niederlanden die der SP.

Nach dem negativen Ausgang des französischen und des niederländischen Referendums über den europäischen Verfassungsvertrag im Jahr 2005 engagierten sich die Politiker in Europa weit weniger für mehr Konvergenz in der EU. Das Zustandekommen und die Ratifizierung des Lissabonner Vertrags wurde überwiegend als eine technisch-bürokratische Angelegenheit aufgefasst, ohne dass die europäische Öffentlichkeit genau wusste, was mit dem Vertrag tatsächlich ratifiziert worden ist.

Seit der Kreditkrise aber ist Europa wieder ins Zentrum der politischen Debatte gerückt. Die Bürger realisieren mehr denn je, dass die Sozialpolitik der Mitgliedstaaten ohne die EU kaum noch umzusetzen ist. Gerade Letzteres kann für das schwächere Engagement für die „Idee Europa" große Folgen haben.

Die Kreditkrise hat nicht nur neue Ansichten zu den Gegenwartsproblemen generiert, sondern auch neue Perspektiven auf die Zeitgeschichte aufgezeigt.[2] Nicht die Glaubwürdigkeit, sondern die Deutungshoheit der wirtschaftspolitischen Leitbilder, wie soziale Marktwirtschaft und Poldermodell, ist gewachsen. Besonders nach dem Fall der Mauer fungierten sie als Muster und Modelle für Politiker mit ihrer eigenen Agenda. Dabei wurde die niederländische und deutsche Sozialpolitik mehrfach als Identitätsfrage politisiert. Obwohl ein gesunder Sozialstaat oft als eine nationale Angelegenheit dargestellt wird, gibt es weitreichende transnationale Querverbindungen. Diese finden sich beispielsweise in den Niederlanden mit der Einführung des Kurzarbeitergeldes 2009 nach deutschem Beispiel und in Deutschland mit der Rettung der Commerzbank 2008, zwei Monate, nachdem der niederländische Staat den Allfinanzkonzern ING auf ähnliche Weise gerettet hatte.

Dieser Beitrag konzentriert sich auf die transnationalen Wechselbeziehungen, die zwischen Experten, Politikern und Öffentlichkeit bestehen, darauf, wie sich die niederländische und die deutsche Sozialpolitik zur nationalen und europäischen Identitätsbildung verhält und welche Momente der transnationalen Adaption es gab. Wichtig ist ebenfalls die Rolle, die Sozialwirtschaftler und ihre Modelle in der niederländischen und deutschen Gesellschaft dabei gespielt haben. Wie haben die Politiker die unterschiedlichen sozialwirtschaftlichen Modelle instrumentalisiert?

---

[2] Anselm Doering-Manteuffel und Lutz Raphael, *Nach dem Boom, Perspektiven auf die Zeitgeschichte seit 1970* (Göttingen: Vandenhoeck & Ruprecht, 2008).

Und auf welche Weise haben die Modelle die Identität der Niederländer und Deutschen geprägt? Anders gefragt: Was ist ihre bindende Kraft gewesen?

Es gab bereits zahlreiche Überlegungen zur Frage der Industrialisierung und Urbanisierung, zur politischen Machtverteilung oder zur institutionellen Pfadabhängigkeit und zum Wandel.[3] Die normative Orientierungskraft und Wirkungsgeschichte von Begriffen wie soziale Marktwirtschaft, Modell Deutschland, Poldermodell und Rheinischer Kapitalismus dagegen sind bisher kaum Forschungsgegenstand gewesen. Der vorliegende Beitrag betont die komplexen Wechselwirkungen zwischen den Personen, die sich politische Begriffe aneignen, um Politik zu machen, die Institutionen, die das Rahmenwerk der Sozialpolitik bilden, und die Ideen, die durch Leit- oder Gegenbilder gestaltet werden.

Die politische Aktualität könnte Politiker zwingen, sich neue Begriffe anzueignen oder alte neu anzuwenden. So hat Angela Merkel 2003 die Initiative Neue Soziale Marktwirtschaft mit großer Überzeugung aufgegriffen und sich von der alten distanziert. Seit der Kreditkrise erkennt sie dem Erbe Erhards einen anderen Stellenwert zu und instrumentalisiert die ordoliberale Idee vom Staat als Hüter der Märkte auch im europäischen Raum. Der ehemalige Parteichef der niederländischen Sozialdemokraten Wouter Bos hat sich im Januar 2009 in einem ideologisch geprägten Vortrag vom dritten Weg, dem Weg der „Neuen Mitte," distanziert, dessen Exponent er einst selbst war. Als Alternative schlug er einen „breiten Wohlstandsbegriff" vor.[4] Diese Begriffe dienen als Leitbilder in der Politik.

Es zeigt sich, dass Politikwissenschaftler und Politikhistoriker in ihren Analysen der Zeitgeschichte Ideen, Ideale und Utopien oft zu wenig ernst genommen haben. Kein Politiker kann – wie es beispielsweise der niederländische Ministerpräsident Wim Kok versuchte – die ideologischen Federn einfach abschütteln.[5] Die Relevanz der Ideen bleibt bestehen und es gibt weder nur pragmatische *managerial politics* noch nur Symbolpolitik.

Zugegeben, die sozialwirtschaftlichen Leitbilder tragen beides in sich. Sie sind pragmatisch und verwaltungstechnisch geprägt, weil sie als Modelle funktionieren und weil ihre Darstellung eine wirtschaftswissenschaftliche Praxis ist. Verknüpft ist mit ihnen aber auch ein besonderer Symbolwert, da Begriffen wie Modell Deutschland oder Poldermodell tatsächlich eine eigene Deutungshoheit zukommt. Nicht zu unterschätzen ist, dass dieser Symbolwert sowohl normativ als auch zukunftsweisend ist und dass die Modelle als Metaphern ideologisch geprägt sind.

---

[3] Günther Schulz, „Der Wohlfahrtstaat und institutionelle Kontinuitäten," *Vierteljahresschrift für Sozial- und Wirtschaftsgeschichte* 4 (2006): 481.

[4] Wouter Bos, „De derde weg voorbij," J.M. den Uyl-lezing, 25 January 2010, eingesehen am 9. Dezember 2010, http://nu.pvda.nl/binaries/content/assets/documenten/De+Derde+Weg+Voorbij.pdf

[5] Wim Kok, *We laten niemand los* (Amsterdam: Stichting Dr J.M. den Uyl-lezing, 1995).

2. Grenze und Grenzüberschreitungen

Dieser Beitrag betrachtet Deutschland und die Niederlande als einen offenen Gesamtraum, ohne dabei die Unterschiede, insbesondere was die Größe und die Verwaltungsstrukturen beider Länder betrifft, aus den Augen zu verlieren.[6] Die Unterschiede in den sozialstaatlichen Systemen sind wichtig, weil die Systeme selbst Ausgangspunkt für Reformen sind und oftmals auch die Grenzen der Reformen aufzeigen und erklären können. Die Niederlande sind keine föderale Republik, sondern ein dezentralisierter Einheitsstaat. Das Bruttoinlandsprodukt der Niederlande ist vergleichbar mit dem BIP des größten deutschen Bundeslandes. Auf der IMF-Liste der Länder nach dem Bruttoinlandsprodukt standen die Niederlande 2008 auf dem sechzehnten Platz. Nordrhein-Westfalen würde umgerechnet den siebzehnten Platz einnehmen. Weitreichende Unterschiede in beiden Staaten zeigen sich dagegen in den Sektoren Landwirtschaft, Industrie und Dienstleistung, obwohl man die Unterschiede auch wieder nicht überbewerten sollte. In modernen Industriestaaten macht der Dienstleistungssektor 70% bis 80% des Bruttoinlandsprodukts aus, in Deutschland 69%; in den Niederlanden 79%. Die Gewerkschaften in Deutschland sind aufgrund der starken Industrie besser organisiert und anders vernetzt: In den Niederlanden kennt man keine Arbeitermitbestimmung im Vorstand der Unternehmen; in Deutschland dagegen fehlt ein zentrales Beratungsgremium von Arbeitnehmern, Arbeitgebern und der Regierung wie der niederländische soziale Wirtschaftsrat, der SER. Nicht zuletzt hat man in den Niederlanden nicht die Kosten der Wiedervereinigung tragen müssen. Die Folgen des Mauerfalls aber sind auch in den Niederlanden spürbar als Folge der neuen geografischen bzw. geopolitischen Lage des Landes innerhalb der europäischen Union und der fortschreitenden Europäisierung.

Zwei Gesichtspunkte der transnationalen Querverbindungen sind wichtig. Es gibt erstens mancherlei Modernisierungsprozesse, die in beiden Ländern gleichzeitig stattgefunden haben: der Aufbau des Sozialstaates in den fünfziger Jahren und die Krise des Sozialstaates in den achtziger und neunziger Jahren, aber auch technische Revolutionen wie beispielsweise die vom Transistor über die Bildröhre zum Computer. Weiterhin zeigte sich in beiden Ländern eine kritische Herausforderung des Fortschrittsoptimismus in den sechziger und siebziger Jahren, eine konservative Wende in den Achtzigern und eine Krise der Volksparteien nach dem Ende des Kalten Krieges. Gerade im Bereich der individuellen Lebensstile, der Mode, Emanzipation, Schulbildung, Freizeitbeschäftigung usw. sind die Unterschiede zwischen den Ländern verwischt. Viele Entwicklungen in der Mentalitäts-, Sozial-, Wirtschafts- und Politikgeschichte kennen keine staatlichen Grenzen mehr.

---

[6] Die Unterschiede werden thematisiert in: G.M.M. Gelauff und C. den Broeder, *Governance of stakeholder relationships, The German and Dutch experience* (Den Haag: CPB Netherlands Bureau for Economic Policy Analysis, 1996) und in: H.A.M. Klemann und C.W.A.M. van Paridon, *In voor en tegenspoed… Verleden, heden en toekomst van de Nederlands-Duitse economische betrekkingen* (Den Haag: Stichting Maatschappij en Onderneming, 2008).

In Bezug auf die Geschichte der Sozialstaaten sind die Wechselwirkungen nicht nur in der Gleichzeitigkeit der Entwicklungen zu suchen, sondern zweitens auch in den grenzüberschreitenden Orientierungen übernationaler *best practices*. Nach dem Wiederaufbau hat es immer eine Art Systemkonkurrenz gegeben, nicht nur zwischen Ost und West, sondern auch unter den kapitalistischen Staaten. Die nationalen Behörden verglichen in zunehmendem Maße den wirtschaftlichen Fortschritt und die Sozialpolitik der EU-Länder miteinander. So war in den Siebzigern die deutsche Wirtschaft ein Vorbild für die Niederlande, später war die Orientierung genau umgekehrt.[7]

Wenn man die Debatten über die wirtschaftspolitischen Leitbilder analysiert, wird aber schnell deutlich, wie wenig ausgereift diese Debatten sind. Ein Beispiel: *The Economist* veröffentlichte 2009 einen Artikel über die Erfolge des französischen Modells.[8] Die französische Wirtschaft hat unter der Kreditkrise relativ gesehen weit weniger gelitten als beispielsweise Großbritannien. Ein wichtiger Grund liegt darin, dass die französischen Banken traditionell ihre Wertpapiere defensiv angelegt und sich deswegen viel weniger an den amerikanischen *subprime* Hypotheken übernommen haben. Was kürzlich noch als ein Zeichen der Schwäche gesehen wurde, die defensive Strategie, wird in diesem Artikel genau umgekehrt als ein Zeichen der Stärke betont. Im Frühjahr 2010 befand sich der Rheinische Kapitalismus in der Defensive. Angela Merkel wurde von Frankreich und den Vereinigten Staaten wegen ihrer Sparpolitik kritisiert. Im Sommer 2010 dagegen zeigte sich die Schwungkraft der deutschen Industrie. In der Öffentlichkeit verblasste die Kritik: Die deutsche soziale Marktwirtschaft hat sich – vielleicht nur zeitweilig – als vielversprechendes Modell erwiesen. Über das französische Modell wurde kaum mehr geschrieben.

Neben der Flüchtigkeit der Analyseergebnisse zeigt sich ein zweiter Nachteil in der Debatte über die wirtschaftspolitischen Leitbilder als Modelle für die Gesellschaft: Ausgangspunkt sind nicht die offenen und sich schnell ändernden Wirtschaftssysteme, sondern eher die statischen Körper und geschlossenen Räume der Nationalstaaten, die den offenen Wirtschaften Unrecht tun.[9] Durch Globalisierung nähern sich die nationalen Varianten einander an. Es ist die Frage, ob man die amerikanische Gesundheitsreform Obamas als eine Rheinische Wende kennzeichnen kann. Laut dem ehemaligen niederländischen Ministerpräsidenten Jan Peter Balkenende haben Obama und er sehr wohl über das niederländische Gesundheitswesen gesprochen. Balkenende präsentierte dies als ein Beispiel des

---

[7] W.A.F. Camphuis, *Tussen analyse en Opportuniteit, de SER als adviseur voor de loon- en prijspolitiek* (Nijmegen: Aksant, 2009) und Maarten van Bottenburg, *„Aan den Arbeid!" In de wandelgangen van de Stichting van de Arbeid 1995-1995* (Amsterdam: Bert Bakker, 1995), 163.

[8] „The French Model: Vive la différence! The French way of doing things looks pretty good — at least in these troubled economic times," *The Economist*, 7 May 2009.

[9] Dazu: Jelle Visser und Anton Hemerijck, *Ein holländisches Wunder? Reform des Sozialstaates und Beschäftigungswachstum in den Niederlanden* (Frankfurt/Main: Campus, 1998).

Lernens voneinander.[10] Bereits kurz nach diesem Treffen aber sprach Obama aus innenpolitischen Gründen von „a uniquely American way of providing care. So I'm not in favor of a Canadian system. I'm not in favor of a British system. I'm not in favor of a French system. That's not what Max is working on."[11] Obama meinte, dass es zerstörerisch wäre, wenn das amerikanische System nicht zum Ausgangspunkt genommen würde. Gesundheitsreformen sind immer ein gutes Beispiel für transnationale Geschichte, weil sie sowohl von nationalen Organisationsstrukturen, als auch von transnationalen Modernisierungsprozessen und *best practices* geprägt sind.

3. Das Umsetzen der Ausgangspositionen

Die Ausgangsposition nach dem Zweiten Weltkrieg und die darauffolgende Wiederaufbauphase haben das Verhältnis zwischen Wirtschaft und Staat in den Niederlanden und Deutschland geprägt.[12] Die Vorstellungen vom Aufbau des Sozialstaates nach 1945 und die Rolle der Experten als Ansprechpartner für die Politik dienen bis heute als Muster für Politiker, Wirtschaftler und Experten. In der Forschung über Erinnerungskulturen ist die sozialwirtschaftliche Pfadabhängigkeit bisher allerdings kaum beachtet worden. Interessanterweise waren die Ausgangspositionen in beiden Ländern unterschiedlich. In Deutschland plädierten die Vertreter der Freiburger Schule wie Walter Eucken für eine ordoliberale Politik. Dabei sollte sich der Staat weniger auf die Steuerung der Wirtschaftsprozesse konzentrieren, sondern vielmehr als Hüter der Wirtschaft agieren und auf die Gestaltung der Wirtschaftsordnung achten. Vollständiger Wettbewerb ist nach Eucken nur möglich, wenn der Staat durch einen entsprechenden Rechtsrahmen die Spielregeln vorgibt und die Wirtschaftsordnung wahrt.

Die Ideen der Freiburger Schule wurden als eine Antwort auf den Dirigismus der Nationalsozialisten gesehen, auf die Machtkonzentration und die Kartellbildung in den Jahren 1933-1945. Die Politik bemühte sich intensiv um die Aufteilung der großen Industriekonzerne wie Krupp und die I.G. Farben in kleinere Unternehmen und förderte eine aktive Mittelstandspolitik. Außerdem wurde 1951 die Mitbestimmung der Arbeitnehmer im Vorstand der Kohle- und Stahlindustrie (Montanindustrie) gesetzlich festgelegt.

---

[10] „Remarks by president Obama and Prime Minister Balkenende of the Netherlands after meeting, the White House," *Office of the Press Secretary*, eingesehen am 9. Dezember 2010, http://www.whitehouse.gov/the-press-office/remarks-president-obama-and-prime-minister-balkenende-netherlands-after-meeting.

[11] Barack Obama, „President Obama Holds Town Hall in Belgrade, Montana, Transcript," *Washington Post*, August 14, 2009.

[12] Für Deutschland siehe Werner Abelshauser, *Deutsche Wirtschaftsgeschichte seit 1945* (München: C.H. Beck, 2005); für die Niederlande siehe Herman de Liagre Böhl, „Consensus en polarisatie. Spanningen in de verzorgingsstaat, 1945-1990," in *Land van kleine gebaren. Een politieke geschiedenis van Nederland 1780-1990*, hg. Remieg Aerts, Herman de Liagre Böhl, Piet de Rooy und Henk te Velde (Nijmegen: SUN, 1999), 265-314.

Der Ordoliberalismus der Freiburger Schule richtete sich auf den Rahmen der Gesellschaft, auf qualitative Probleme und weniger auf Fragen der Quantität. Quantitative Wirtschaft und Prognosen betrachtete sie als Instrumente sozialistischer Planung. Auch Adenauer war wenig von der Wirtschaftsmathematik angetan, ganz einfach, weil er Professoren als Politikberatern misstraute. Erst nach dem Ende seiner Kanzlerschaft 1963 wurde der Sachverständigenrat zur Begutachtung der gesamtwirtschaftlichen Entwicklung gegründet. Obwohl diesem Rat – bekannt als die Fünf Weisen – oftmals eine nahezu päpstliche Autorität zugeschrieben wurde,[13] so ist doch die statistische Politik- und Unternehmensberatung in Deutschland im Gegensatz zu den Niederlanden wesentlich vielschichtiger und verteilt sich auf eine Vielzahl mehr oder weniger großer Institute.

Im Gegensatz zu Deutschland wurde in den Niederlanden bereits in den Nachkriegsjahren versucht, eine Planungspolitik durchzuführen. Das Zentrale Planungsbüro unter Leitung des späteren Nobelpreisträgers Jan Tinbergen wurde 1945 gegründet. Schon 1947 wurde das Gesetz zur Vorbereitung und Feststellung eines zentralen wirtschaftlichen Plans angenommen. Obwohl die niederländische Wirtschaft damit noch keine Planwirtschaft war, ist damit die Rolle der Experten gleich nach dem Krieg in den Niederlanden und Deutschland sehr unterschiedlich gewesen. Während die deutschen Wirtschaftswissenschaftler einen Ordnungsrahmen als Modell schafften, bauten die niederländischen Wirtschaftsmathematiker ihre quantitativen mathematischen Modelle und beeinflussten damit auch die Wirtschaftssprache der Politik.[14] Auf Dauer führte die Verwissenschaftlichung der politischen Agenda zu einer Entideologisierung und Objektivierung der Wirtschaftspolitik. Selbstverständlich war das nicht nur ein niederländisches Phänomen, doch wurde die Entpolitisierung in den Niederlanden verstärkt durch eine typisch niederländische Form der konzertierten Aktion, durch die sogenannte *overlegeconomie*. Das ist ein kontinuierlicher Abstimmungsprozess zwischen Arbeitnehmern und Arbeitgebern, die sich 1945 in der ‚Stiftung der Arbeit' zusammenschlossen und sich seit 1950 im sozialwirtschaftlichen Rat (SER) treffen. Dieser setzt sich aus Vertretern des Staates, der Arbeitgeber und Arbeitnehmer zusammen.

4. Erfolgsgeschichten?

Obgleich der Nachhall der Leitbilder soziale Marktwirtschaft, Modell Deutschland oder Poldermodell noch immer groß ist, stellt sich die berechtigte Frage, inwieweit die Ideen hinter den Leitbildern tatsächlich realisiert worden sind. In der deutschen Historiographie wird die Kontinuität des bismarckschen Sozialstaats

[13] Siehe auch Nützenadel, „Economic Knowledge, Experts and the German Public Sphere."

[14] Gerard Alberts und Jaren van Berekening, *Toepassingsgerichte initiatieven in de Nederlandse wiskundebeoefening 1945-1960* (Amsterdam: Amsterdam University Press, 1998); Frans van Lunteren, Bert Theunissen und Rienk Vermeij (Hg.), *De opmars van de deskundigen, Souffleurs van de samenleving* (Amsterdam: Amsterdam University Press, 2002).

betont.[15] Die Kontinuitätsthese wird durch die Tatsache bekräftigt, dass der Begriff „soziale Marktwirtschaft" zum ersten Mal 1946 in dem Buch *Wirtschaftslenkung und Marktwirtschaft* des Nationalökonomen und früheren überzeugten NSDAP Mitglieds Alfred Müller-Amrack benutzt wurde. Schon 1947 bekannten sich die CDU und CSU zu diesem Konzept, das als gutes Marketinginstrument des neuen Kapitalismus, unbelastet von alten ideologischen Konnotationen, galt.[16] Trotz anfänglich politisch-ideologischer Deutungshoheit der ordoliberalen Variante des Kapitalismus hat sich die deutsche Wirtschaft schnell der Wirtschaft ihrer westeuropäischen Nachbarn angepasst. Es gibt drei Gründe, weshalb der Ordoliberalismus nicht standhielt. Erstens ließ sich das Modell aus verschiedenen Gründen in der Praxis nicht aufrechterhalten, zweitens gab es letztendlich auch in der Bundesrepublik Deutschland eine Planungseuphorie, und nicht zuletzt war die Westbindung vor allem auch im wirtschaftlichen Sinne erfolgreich. Das größte Problem des Ordoliberalismus in der Praxis war die klare Trennung zwischen Markt und Staat. Der Staat selbst war und blieb ein wichtiger Spieler auf dem Markt: 1960 hatte er 40% der Montanindustrie in den Händen, 62% der Elektrizitätswerke und auch 62% des Bankensektors.[17] Durch die Verflechtung des Bankensektors mit dem Wirtschaftsleben hat die Trennung niemals wirklich funktioniert. Zudem zeigte der schnelle Aufbau des Sozialstaats, wie utopisch die Ideale der Ordoliberalen waren.

Angeregt durch den wissenschaftlichen Austausch mit den amerikanischen Universitäten, entstand auch in der Bundesrepublik eine neue Richtung der mathematischen Wirtschaftswissenschaft, die Ökonometrie.[18] Die Planungseuphorie fand ihre Bestätigung mit der Gründung des Sachverständigenrates 1963 und dem Planungsgesetz 1967. Sowohl die Westbindung als auch die Systemkonkurrenz mit dem Osten beflügelten die neue quantitative Wirtschaftswissenschaft. Gerade durch die europäische Integration musste sich die deutsche Politik mit der französischen *planification économique* auseinandersetzen, da de Gaulle diesen französischen Stil als Vorbild für die europäische Wirtschaftsgemeinschaft sah. Die Systemkonkurrenz mit der DDR war ebenfalls von beträchtlichem Einfluss: Die Bundesrepublik wollte unbedingt das bessere und stärkere Deutschland sein und bleiben.

---

[15] Sandrine Kott, „Der Sozialstaat," in *Deutsche Erinnerungsorte II*, hg. Etienne François und Hagen Schultze (München: Beck, 2001), 485-501; und Werner Abelshauser, *Deutsche Wirtschaftsgeschichte*, 28-44.

[16] Mark Spoerer, „Wohlstand für alle? Soziale Marktwirtschaft," in *Modell Deutschland, Erfolgsgeschichte oder Illusion?*, hg. Thomas Hertfelder und Andreas Rödder (Göttingen: Vandenhoeck & Ruprecht, 2007), 32.

[17] Herman van der Wee, *Prosperity and Upheaval, The World Economy 1945-1980* (Harmondsworth: Penguin Books, 1986), 307.

[18] Hier folge ich Alexander Nützenadel, *Stunde der Ökonomen, Wissenschaft, Politik und Expertenkultur in der Bundesrepublik 1949-1974* (Göttingen: Vandenhoeck & Ruprecht, 2005); als Beispiel für die neue Modellierung der westdeutschen Wirtschaft siehe: Gerhard Gehrig, *Ein makroökonomisches Modell für die Bundesrepublik Deutschland* (Berlin: Duncker & Humblot, 1963).

Abgesehen von dem so erfolgreichen Wirtschaftswunder hatte das ordoliberale Projekt Erhards ideologisch gesehen wenig Erfolg. Sogar so wenig, dass die Bundesrepublik in späteren Analysen des Wohlfahrtskapitalismus, wie in jene von Gøsta Esping-Andersen und Michel Albert, als eine eher konservative Variante des Kapitalismus, wenn nicht gar als Gegenpol zum Neoliberalismus, gesehen wurde.[19]

Die Erklärung dafür liegt teilweise in der Erfolgsgeschichte der westdeutschen Wirtschaft, die seit 1966 mehr und mehr von sozialdemokratischer Politik gekennzeichnet war. Der weit verzweigte Sozialstaat und das Mitbestimmungsgesetz für Arbeitnehmer im Vorstand von Kapitalgesellschaften wurden 1976 als neue Erfolgsgeschichte präsentiert und im Wahlkampf von der SPD als „Modell Deutschland" propagiert. Gleichzeitig aber wurde es zu einem negativem Modell in Bezug auf den Sicherheitsstaat, die Berufsverbote und die „eigentümliche Verquickung von ‚Wohlfahrtsstaat' und dem technisch perfektionierten "Überwachungsstaat"."[20] Später wurde der Begriff auch als Argument in der Krisenrhetorik verwendet. Die politische Instrumentalisierung des Begriffs ist vergleichbar mit dem des niederländischen Poldermodells, das 1997 plötzlich als Modewort in der niederländischen Öffentlichkeit auftauchte. Beide Begriffe sind mit eine Erfolgsgeschichte assoziiert, beide wurden aber ebenso als Illusion abgewertet und mit Worten wie „Reformstau" und *stroperigheid* (Zähflüssigkeit) verknüpft.

Obwohl die beiden letzten Begriffe nicht ganz zufällig mit der sozialdemokratischen Politik assoziiert wurden, haben sie genauso viel mit der Christdemokratie zu tun. Beiden Begriffen haftet eine nationale Prägung an: Sie wurden in einer Periode der Zeitgeschichte verwendet, als die Frage der nationalen Identität in der Öffentlichkeit noch nicht so stark diskutiert wurde. Weil Nationalstolz und Chauvinismus noch tabu waren, suchte man Bestätigung in anderen Qualitäten wie dem Fußballspiel, dem Sozialstaat oder der Zivilmacht. In den Niederlanden führte der Begriff Poldermodell sogar zu einer neuen Geschichtsschreibung. Das Abkommen von Wassenaar, die 1982 geschlossene Vereinbarung zwischen Arbeitnehmern und Arbeitgebern, auf Lohnerhöhungen zu verzichten, wurde als Anfangspunkt des Poldermodells betont. Es wurde als eine neue Erfolgsgeschichte der niederländischen Wirtschaft wahrgenommen.[21]

Der Literaturwissenschaftler Herman Pleij zog sogar eine direkte Verbindung zwischen der mittelalterlichen Kultur des Verhandelns und dem heutigen Poldermodell. Im ewigen und existentiellen Kampf gegen das Meer und für den Bau und Unterhalt der Deiche und Polder gab es in den Niederlanden keinen Raum für

---

[19] Gøsta Esping-Andersen, *The Three Worlds of Welfare Capitalism* (Cambridge: Polity Press, 1990) und Michel Albert, *Capitalisme contre Capitalisme* (Paris: Éditions du Seuil, 1991).

[20] Joachim Hirsch, *Der Sicherheitsstaat, Das „Modell Deutschland," seine Krise und die neuen sozialen Bewegungen* (Frankfurt am Main: Europäische Verlagsanstalt, 1980), 8; K. Farin und H.J. Zwingman (Hg.), *Modell Deutschland? Berufsverbote* (Karlsruhe: DOKU-Verlag, 1978).

[21] Für eine kritische Ausarbeitung siehe: Dennis Bos, Maurits Ebben und Henk te Velde (Hg.), *Harmonie in Holland, Het poldermodel van 1500 tot nu* (Amsterdam: Bert Bakker, 2007).

die üblichen Hierarchien; die Bewohner waren gezwungen, auf gleicher Ebene zusammenzuarbeiten. Nach Pleij hat bereits der Philosoph Erasmus das wissenschaftliche und spirituelle Fundament zu diesem Kommunikationsmodell gelegt, weil er die Gewissensfreiheit, die Kritik und die Anerkennung Andersdenkender berücksichtigte. In einem Interview bestätigte Pleij die Deutungshoheit und politische Prägung seiner Interpretation: „Wer gegen das Poldermodell ist, ist gegen die Niederlande.“[22]

So wurde das Poldermodell am Ende des zwanzigsten Jahrhunderts eine neue *Invention of Tradition*. Beflügelt von der Bewunderung im Ausland realisierte die niederländische Öffentlichkeit nicht, dass selbst die sozialwirtschaftlichen Verhältnisse der fünfziger Jahre, auf die sich das Modell so vielfältig bezog, ganz andere waren als die in den achtziger und neunziger Jahren. Damals diktierte der Staat den sozialen Partnern die Tarifpolitik, *geleide loonpolitiek* genannt. Von einer fast „herrschaftsfreien Kommunikation“ zwischen Arbeitnehmern, Arbeitgebern und Staat konnte keinesfalls die Rede sein. Und gerade die freiwillige Zusammenarbeit der sozialen Partner war in den Neunzigern so gepriesen worden.

5. Europäisierung

Ein wichtiger Unterschied zwischen den Begriffen Modell Deutschland und Poldermodell liegt in ihrer Entstehungsgeschichte. Während die deutsche Variante ein Slogan der SPD war, hat der Begriff Poldermodell die Niederländer mehr oder weniger überfallen, nachdem Ministerpräsident Wim Kok 1997 beim G-8 Gipfel neben Bill Clinton saß und die Erfolgsgeschichte des niederländischen dritten Weges erläutern konnte. Im gleichen Jahr zeichnete die Bertelsmann Stiftung die niederländische Stiftung der Arbeit mit dem Prestigepreis aus. Die deutschen Gastgeber waren überrascht, als sie bemerkten, dass der Arbeitgebervorsitzende Hans Blankert und der Arbeitnehmervorsitzende Lodewijk de Waal zusammen in einem Auto zur Preisverleihung gefahren waren – für deutsche Verhältnisse undenkbar.[23]

Niederländische Sozialdemokraten wie Thijs Wöltgens und Ad Melkert hatten den Begriff Poldermodell zuvor noch nicht benutzt, da sie sich eher mit dem Begriff Rheinischer Kapitalismus identifiziert hatten. Wöltgens schrieb 1996 in einem Aufsehen erregenden Artikel zur Lage der niederländischen Sozialdemokratie, dass seine Partei die europäische Identität vorantreiben und stärken müsse. Der niederländischen Öffentlichkeit sollte deutlich gemacht werden, dass die Niederlande wirtschaftlich gesehen bereits einem Bundesland der Bundesrepublik

---

[22] Herman Pleij, *Erasmus en het poldermodel – essay* (Amsterdam: Bakker, 2005); siehe auch: Wilma Kieskamp, „Herman Pleij: Wie tegen het poldermodel is, is tegen Nederland,“ *Trouw* 15 (1995).

[23] Henk te Velde, *Van regentenmentaliteit tot populisme, Politieke tradities in Nederland* (Amsterdam: Bert Bakker, 2010), 210; siehe auch: Maarten van Rossem, *Het poldermodel in internationale context* (Utrecht: Universiteit Utrecht, 1998).

ähnelten, vergleichbar mit Nordrhein-Westfalen: „Man könnte sogar über die Frage diskutieren, ob die Niederlande als ein Bundesland der Bundesrepublik gemeinsam mit Nordrhein-Westfalen nicht mehr Einfluss auf Europa ausüben könnten, als ihnen das zur Zeit als einem von vielen Mitgliedstaaten der Europäischen Union möglich ist. In jedem Fall müsste die Berliner Regierung den Forderungen eines solchen Westverbunds verstärkt entsprechen."[24] Obwohl es Wöltgens um einen westlich orientierten, sozialwirtschaftlichen und vor allem ideologischen Schwerpunkt in Europa ging, wurde sein Artikel in den Medien kurzerhand als seltsamer Vorschlag zu einem niederländischen „Anschluss" gewertet.

Nach der internationalen Anerkennung des Poldermodells schwenkten sowohl Wöltgens als auch Melkert um: Wöltgens erklärte nun das Poldermodell zum nationalen Erbe und sah die Sozialdemokratie als dessen Hüter. Und als Sozialminister wollte Melkert, Journalisten zufolge, das Poldermodell an Europa weitergeben. Als dann 2003 dem ehemaligen Ministerpräsidenten Wim Kok von der Universität Münster die Ehrendoktorwürde verliehen wurde, standen die Vorträge im Zeichen von Pragmatismus, Brückenbauen und handelten von der europäischen Herausforderung sozialer und wirtschaftlicher Reformen.[25]

Das niederländische „Beschäftigungswunder," so genannt von der Bertelsmann Stiftung, wurde in Deutschland vom Wirtschaftswissenschaftler bis hin zum Politiker gepriesen.[26] Es war tatsächlich ein Vorbild für das 1996 gegründete Bündnis für Arbeit und die späteren Hartz-IV-Reformen. Konzepte aus europäischen Nachbarländern lassen sich jedoch nicht einfach übernehmen. Das Scheitern des Bündnisses und die krisenhafte Lage der SPD nach der Einführung der Hartz-IV-Reformen zeigen das deutlich. Die SPD konnte die wichtigsten Reformen des deutschen Sozialstaats seit Jahrzehnten politisch nicht nutzen.

Die Modelle sind weniger als Beschreibungsmuster der gesellschaftlichen Verhältnisse interessant, man sollte sie vor allem als politisches Instrument analysieren. Für kurze Zeit wollte Gerhard Schröder Tony Blairs „Dritten Weg" umsetzen. Er war aber sowohl aus innen- wie auch aus außenpolitischen Gründen nicht in der Lage, die deutsch-englische Freundschaft ideologisch zu stärken.[27] Die niederländischen Sozialdemokraten unter Wouter Bos orientierten sich vor allem an der englischen und amerikanischen Politik, kaum an der deutschen.[28] Obwohl die Krise der Sozialdemokratie in den Nachbarländern ganz ähnliche Züge trägt, sind

---

[24] Thijs Wöltgens, „Beginselen in een nieuwe context," *Socialisme & Democratie* 7/8 (1996): 375.

[25] Friso Wielenga und Loek Geeraerdts (Hg.), *Wim Kok: Soziale und wirtschaftliche Reformen, Eine europäische Herausforderung. Festrede* (Münster: Waxmann, 2003).

[26] Bodo Hombach, *Aufbruch. Die Politik der neuen Mitte* (München: Econ, 1998); Anke Hassel, „Soziale Pakte in Europa," *Gewerkschaftliche Monatshefte* 10 (1998): 629-638; Werner Eichhorst, „Bündnis für Arbeit, Chancen vergeben?," *Sozialer Fortschritt* 51 (2002): 274-281.

[27] Siehe auch: Franz Walter, *Vorwärts oder abwärts? Zur Transformation der Sozialdemokratie* (Berlin: Suhrkamp, 2010).

[28] Illustrativ dazu ist Wouter Bos' J.M. den Uyllezing, siehe Fußnote 4.

die sozialdemokratischen Parteien SPD und PvdA so sehr mit ihren eigenen Problemen beschäftigt, dass sie diese Ähnlichkeiten kaum berücksichtigen.

Die Frage ist interessant, inwieweit die europäische Integration zu dieser Krise beigetragen hat. Die Begriffe Modell Deutschland und Poldermodell dienten nicht nur als Leitbild für die sozialwirtschaftliche Gesellschaftsordnung, sondern auch als bindende Kraft. In links-liberalen Kreisen wurde es seit dem Zweiten Weltkrieg als problematisch empfunden, stolz auf den eigenen Staat zu sein. Die Leitbilder aber lieferten Gründe, wenigstens stolz auf die staatlichen Institutionen und Regelungen zu sein. Vor allem in den Niederlanden zeigte sich ein umgekehrter Nationalismus: Man war stolz darauf, nicht nationalistisch zu sein. Als am Anfang dieses Jahrhunderts das Poldermodell vehement kritisiert wurde und mit der Einführung des Euros die Europäische Union nicht mehr aus der niederländischen Wirtschaft wegzudenken war, herrschte unter progressiven Intellektuellen ein Gefühl von Orientierungslosigkeit, ein Bedürfnis nach unbestrittener Führung anstelle des aus ihrer Sicht ewig abwägenden und zögerlichen Ministerpräsidenten Balkenende. Nicht zuletzt zeigte sich ein wachsendes Klagen über die Begleiterscheinungen der multikulturellen Gesellschaft.

Außerdem wurden andere sozialwirtschaftliche Leitbilder in der niederländischen Öffentlichkeit aktuell: Der Gegensatz zwischen dem Rheinischen Kapitalismus und dem neoamerikanischen Modell, auf Niederländisch *Rijnlands* und *Angelsaksisch model*, erhielt einen großen politischen Stellenwert – nicht als Beschreibung der realen wirtschaftlichen Systeme, sondern als Richtungsanzeiger für entweder soziale oder (neo)liberale Politik.[29] Dies ist vergleichbar mit den im 21. Jahrhundert vehement diskutierten Varianten der sozialen Marktwirtschaft in Deutschland, sei es die kranke, die neoliberale oder die soziale Marktwirtschaft.[30]

Das europäische Projekt wurde in der Öffentlichkeit zu Unrecht mit dem Neoliberalismus gleichgesetzt. Zum einen, weil die Europäische Union von Anfang an auch sozialen Interessen gedient hat. Ein interessantes Beispiel dafür ist die Gleichberechtigung von Frauen auf dem Arbeitsmarkt, auch in Bezug auf ihre Rentenansprüche.[31] Zum zweiten, weil die für die EU so wichtige Agrarpolitik kaum mit der freien Marktideologie zu verknüpfen ist. Da die Agrar-, Fischerei- und

---

[29] Zum Beispiel: L. Bovenberg und C.N. Teulings, „Rhineland exit?," *CPB Discussion Paper* (Den Haag: Tinbergen Institute, 2008); W.S.P. Fortuyn (Hg.), *Voor en tegen de Markt* (Zwolle: Kluwer, 1986) und Werner Abelshauser, *Kulturkampf. Der deutsche Weg in die neue Wirtschaft und die amerikanische Herausforderung* (Berlin: Kulturverlag Kadmos, 2003).

[30] Zum Beispiel: R. Schettkat und J. Langkau (Hg.), *Aufschwung für Deutschland. Plädoyer international renommierter Ökonomen für eine bessere Wirtschaftspolitik* (Bonn: Dietz, 2007); Hans-Werner Sinn, *Can Germany be saved? The Malaise of the World's First Welfare State* (Cambridge Mass: MIT Press, 2007); siehe auch: Michael S. Aßlander und Peter Ulrich (Hg.), *60 Jahre Soziale Marktwirtschaft, Illusionen und Reinterpretationen einer ordnungspolitischen Integrationsformel* (Bern: Haupt, 2009).

[31] Anna van der Vleuten, *The Price of Gender Equality. Member States and Governance in the European Union* (Aldershot: Ashgate, 2007).

Umweltpolitik noch immer 42% des EU-Haushalts ausmachen, ist es sehr verwunderlich, warum diese nicht konsequenter diskutiert werden. Das wichtigste Argument aber, warum die EU nicht nur als ein neoliberales Projekt gesehen werden sollte, liegt darin, dass die EU die Sozialpolitik den Mitgliedstaaten überlässt. Und damit müssen die verschiedenen sozialwirtschaftlichen Modelle, sei es das Rheinische, Polder-, Pariser oder Englische Modell, eher als Varianten der europäischen sozialwirtschaftlichen Ordnung gesehen werden.

Dieses Argument wird durch eine neue Entwicklung im Europäisierungsprozess verstärkt. Zahlreiche europäische Agenturen, die der Verwaltung der Mitgliedstaaten auf dem Fuße folgen, sammeln und vergleichen Daten. Auch durch diesen Datenvergleich wachsen die Wirtschaften der Mitgliedstaaten zusammen. Es hängt von der Perspektive ab, wie groß die europäischen Unterschiede tatsächlich noch sind. Der englische Historiker Tony Judt betont in seinem Buch *Postwar* eine europäische soziale Solidarität gegenüber einem amerikanischen Stil wirtschaftlicher Flexibilität.[32] Seit Obamas Gesundheitsreform nähern sich auch diese beiden Wirtschaftsstile – soziale Solidarität und wirtschaftliche Flexibilität – einander an.

Gerade weil die sozialwirtschaftlichen Leitbilder politisch leicht instrumentalisiert werden können, ist es wichtig, die Sprache der Politik, die unterschiedlichen Wirtschaftssysteme und die transnationalen Querverbindungen untereinander kritisch zu hinterfragen. Deutschland als Modell konnte erst innerhalb der Strukturen der Europäischen Union wirklich erfolgreich werden: Die Europäische Zentralbank wurde nach dem Vorbild der Deutschen Bundesbank aufgebaut.

Die vehementen Debatten über die soziale Marktwirtschaft, das Modell Deutschland und das Poldermodell als Leitbilder der nationalen Wirtschaftspolitik können so gesehen nur noch als Rückzugsgefechte gegen Globalisierung und Europäisierung gekennzeichnet werden. Obwohl die nationalen Ökonomien gerade durch Globalisierung und Europäisierung mehr und mehr miteinander verflochten sind, bietet die nationale Volkswirtschaft Halt und Identität. Nach der Kreditkrise aber wird die Zusammenarbeit und Kohärenz in der EU verstärkt und der europäische Steuerungsmechanismus der Wirtschaft innerhalb der EU weiterentwickelt. Durch die Orientierung auf gegenseitige *best practices* werden die Unterschiede weiter verblassen. Es gibt keinen Weg zurück.

Hanco Jürgens
h.j.jurgens@uva.nl

[32] Tony Judt, *Postwar, A History of Europe since 1945* (London: Pimlico, 2005), 793-795.

John Leslie
Victoria University of Wellington

Anne L. Clunan
Naval Postgraduate School, Monterey, CA

This paper seeks to draw attention to a neglected but essential element of institutions: their boundaries.[1] Boundaries permit actors to organize the world around them into categories and groups and to establish arenas of authority or jurisdiction. Scholars too often assume that boundaries between groups are firm and clear, and assume that these distinctions form the basis for social hierarchies and divisions of labor.[2] However, the *nature* of boundaries is no less important to institutional operation and social organization than is the fact of their existence. As the first step in a larger research program, we set out to elaborate here not only the importance that the *existence* of boundaries has in creating and regulating social organization, but also the political significance that the *varying nature* of boundaries has. We draw on our own work from very different sub-disciplines of political science to highlight what boundaries do and how they vary, as well as to raise a set of theoretical questions to guide further investigation.

Our interest in institutional boundaries arose from puzzles arising out of our research. One of us has focused on political parties, and found that despite similar structural conditions, actors responded by creating very different boundaries between political parties and labor unions. The other one of us focuses on international institutional change, and realized that IR theorists' ability to understand and explain such change largely centers on how they conceptualize the boundaries of key institutions, in particular those of the sovereign state. What we present here is our first effort at laying out the rationale for an investigation of institutional boundaries. We view this paper as the initial step in developing a research program that examines how and why boundaries matter as well as how they arise and change. We

[1] The views expressed in this document are those of the authors and do not represent the official position of the Department of Defense or the U.S. government.
[2] Explanations of nationalism such as those of Karl W. Deutsch, *Nationalism and Social Communication*, 2nd ed. (Cambridge, MA: MIT Press, 1966); Ernst Gellner, *Nations and Nationalism* (Ithaca, NY: Cornell University Press, 1983); Ernst Haas, *Nationalism, Liberalism and Progress* (Ithaca, NY: Cornell University Press, 1997); Benedict Anderson, *Imagined Communities* (London: Verso, 1983) are obvious exceptions to this.

EUROSTUDIA — REVUE TRANSATLANTIQUE DE RECHERCHE SUR L'EUROPE
Vol. 7, No.1-2 (2011): 119-131

conclude by asking whether the nature of boundaries substantially affects the mechanisms of institutional change that are likely to operate.

We believe that a study of boundaries can aid institutional analysis in a number of ways. First, institutional analyses have emphasized how institutions create relations of authority; we hope to demonstrate that the *bounds* of authority, or jurisdiction, are as important to understanding political outcomes. Second, like relations of authority, boundaries or jurisdictions reflect the circumstances in which they are created. As a consequence, boundaries will vary in politically significant ways. We believe that a critical dimension on which boundaries vary is in their permeability. Finally, we propose as subject for further research that this variance is most likely related to particular types of institutional change.

We proceed first to discuss how the literature on institutions has neglected the question of boundaries. We suggest that this neglect has shaped current institutionalist accounts of institutional reproduction and change, institutional stability or durability, as well as institutional capacity to shape actors' behavior. We develop in greater depth how our proposed attention to boundaries can yield a better understanding of institutional reproduction and institutional capacity, as well as institutional change.

1. The New Institutionalisms and Institutional Borders

The new institutionalisms have focused on the authority relations that institutions create rather than their boundaries. Consider, for example, two well-known definitions of institutions from international relations and comparative political economy. Stephen Krasner defines institutions, or—more accurately—"international regimes," as "sets of implicit or explicit principles, norms, rules, and decision-making procedures around which actors' expectations converge in a given area of international relations."[3] Peter Hall refers to them as "the formal rules, compliance procedures, and standard operating practices that structure the relationship between individuals in various units of the polity and economy."[4] Both authors emphasize the authoritative and hierarchical aspects of institutions rather than the limits of institutions' authority, or jurisdiction. For Krasner, regimes are bounded by a group of actors' expectations and an issue area. Hall leaves institutional boundaries even less well-defined, as "various units." This neglect of the limits that boundaries place on the authority relations inside institutions represents a significant gap in these literatures and in our understanding of institutions. Institutions are embedded in "societies"[5] with other institutions and, because actors navigate not only within

---

[3] Steven Krasner, "Structural Causes and Regime Consequences: Regimes as Intervening Variable," in *International Regimes*, ed. Stephen Krasner (Ithaca, NY: Cornell University Press, 1983), 2.

[4] Peter Hall, *Governing the Economy* (New York and Oxford: Oxford University Press, 1986), 19.

[5] Note that "society" and "social" refer to particular groupings of actors. "Society" can refer to the community of individuals bounded by a state or it can refer to the anarchical "society" of nation

institutions but also between them, it is important to understand not only how the "rules of the game" work, but also how far they extend.[6] By recognizing that institutions create not only authority relations but also "jurisdictions" we can increase our understanding of how institutions come into being, how they reproduce themselves, and how they shape the behavior of actors.

2. Institution Boundaries and Institutional Origins

The recognition that institutions not only create authority relations but also bound those relations entails the recognition that institutions are a product of forces in tension. Institutions are simultaneously the product of cooperation and conflict, an outcome that traditional perspectives do not permit. Traditional approaches to group formation have tended to emphasize the role of either cooperation or conflict, but not their union. For example, pluralists and rationalists of various bents observe that individuals form groups and institutions to pursue common interests.[7] From this perspective, cooperation is limited only by the bounds of rationality and the boundaries of groups and institutions can expand, potentially, without limit. Traditional structuralists, on the other hand, argue that structure limits cooperation and that conflict is central to institutional construction. They argue that real cleavages divide societies and create boundaries across which cooperation and voluntary institutions do not extend. For Marxists, boundaries that parallel class divisions are real, while those that separate organizations on either side of a social divide are transitory.[8] Structural realists in international relations recognize the explanatory power of states and the borders between them, but not of institutions that cross state boundaries or exist wholly within them.[9] These two perspectives view social organization differently, one as the reflection of interest and the other as the reflection of power. There is either harmony or conflict but little room for strategic interaction in organizing societies.

The new institutionalisms arose to explain cooperation in circumstances where there is strategic interaction, but cooperation is problematic.[10] Even while they recognize the complexities imposed by strategic interaction, however, new institutionalists neglect boundaries, causing them to limit their understanding of the forms of

states. Hedley Bull, *The Anarchical Society* (New York: Columbia University Press, 1977).

[6] Mark Granovetter, "Economic Action and Social Structure: The Problem of Embeddedness," *American Journal of Sociology* 91 (1985): 481-510.

[7] David B. Truman, *The Governmental Process* (New York: Alfred A. Knopf, 1963); Robert Keohane, *After Hegemony* (Princeton, NJ: Princeton University Press, 1984).

[8] Ira Katznelson, "Working-Class Formation: Constructing Cases and Comparisons," in *Working-Class Formation,* eds. Ira Katznelson and Aristide Zolberg (Princeton, NJ: Princeton University Press, 1986), 3-41.

[9] Kenneth Waltz, *Theory of International Politics* (Reading, MA: Addison-Wesley Publishing Company, 1979).

[10] Douglass North, *Institutions, Institutional Change, and Economic Performance* (Cambridge, UK: Cambridge University Press, 1990), 16.

cooperation. The central problem for the new institutionalisms was how to explain cooperation among actors with common interests but different preferences. For rational choice institutionalists, conflict is a dysfunctional consequence of information asymmetries, transaction costs, and coordination problems that institutions permit actors to overcome. It is assumed that a universal definition of rationality or utility bridges these conflicts, potentially extending boundaries of institutions out infinitely. Clever institutional designers, it is implied, can always find the common ground and manage conflicts.

Historical institutionalists bring structure and conflict back into the spotlight in institutional construction, but they offer a truncated set of options for the institutional management of conflict. They recognize that institutional construction is embedded in social structures that generate ideas and interests as well as constraints on resources and power. However, they confine the influence of structure and conflict to the construction of an institution's authority relations. Structure, conflict, and power ultimately determine whose preferences are favored by authoritative rules, but they ignore the possibility that actors may decide to limit institutional jurisdiction, leaving some actors or actions beyond the reach of its authority relations. They may create parallel sets of authoritative rules and then seek to regulate their interactions. This is not quite cooperation, nor is it conflict, but rather an "agreement to disagree" or "peaceful coexistence."[11] The institutional nature of such arrangements becomes apparent, however, only when one focuses on boundaries.

Recognition that institutional construction is socially embedded points to the dual role that boundaries play "inside" and "outside" institutions and the "critical" nature of the junctures in which they are often created. They designate who may, or must, conform to rules defining authority "within" an institution. But they also demarcate the extent of those rules and how one institution, and its members, interact with other institutions. Defining such relations is critical not only to the institution's own survival but also to the survival of other institutions and, perhaps, the survival of society.[12] This interdependence points to the fact that the boundaries of important institutions are likely to crystallize at the same time and as part of a larger process. Actors reach "settlements" that create full-fledged cooperation in some institutions even as they embed conflicting values in other institutions that exist parallel to one another. In establishing one area of authority and jurisdiction

[11] Günther Roth, *The Social Democrats in Imperial Germany* (New York: Arno Press, 1979) describes the "negative integration" of Social Democrats in Wilhelmine Germany. This issue is also central to literature on "consociationalism." See for example Arend Lijphart, *Democracy in Plural Societies* (New Haven and London: Yale University Press, 1977) and Kurt Richard Luther, "A Framework for the Comparative Analysis of Political Parties and Party Systems in Consociational Democracy," in *Party Elites in Divided Societies*, eds. Kurt Richard Luther and Kris Deschouwer (London: Routledge, 1999).

[12] This has been the focus of the population ecology school in organizational theory. See Michael T. Hannan and John Freeman, "The Ecology of Organizational Founding: American Labor Unions, 1836-1985," *The American Journal of Sociology* 92 (1987): 910-943.

where certain actors have specified powers and roles, boundaries also create the negative of the institution in establishing realms where such authority, jurisdiction, powers and roles do not apply.[13] Subsequently, institutional boundaries regulate the limits of institutional authority and the conduct of institutional interactions.

3. BOUNDARIES, SOCIAL ORDER, AND INSTITUTIONAL SURVIVAL

The dual role of boundaries points to a source of legitimacy and support for institutions that institutionalists have neglected. For rational choice and historical institutionalists, institutions thrive when they reproduce and extend the interests they were constructed to promote directly.[14] From this perspective, it is the interests of actors organized within the institution or the interests of groups or other institutions that deal directly with it that support its survival. For economic institutionalists, actors will seek to design institutional boundaries so as to economize on transactions costs. They do not investigate how the social environment or "background conditions" form and implicate the drawing of boundaries.[15] Historical institutionalists tell us how the institutions come into being and how their boundaries may differ, but tell us little about how these boundaries reinforce or undermine the existing social order. Institutions contribute to the reproduction of societal values and social stability generally. Because they transmit values from the level of society to the level of individual actors, institutions are important to the reproduction of the values around which societies are organized. But the embeddedness of institutions in a society and the dual role of their boundaries point to a far broader base of support.

Institutional boundaries do a number of things: they protect the institution; they provide institutional continuity; they define who belongs to the institution; they establish rights of institutions, placing them in particular positions *vis-à-vis* each other within a society; and they constrain actors' behavior across and within institutions. As such, it is the boundaries of institutions that make social order possible.[16] Boundaries are established to shield institutions from external pressures and influences as much as to create internal authority relations. They help ensure institutional survival because they provide a measure of security and a legal basis on which to challenge incursions and violations.[17] Sovereignty functions in this manner at the international level, helping to ensure the survival of weak states.[18] In the United States, the boundaries of non-profit status allow 501(c)(3) organizations to guard

---

[13] One might think of the "pillar" structure of the European Union from the Maastricht Treaty to the Lisbon Treaty as a particularly transparent example.

[14] Paul Pierson, "Increasing Returns, Path Dependence, and the Study of Politics," *American Political Science Review* 94 (2000): 251-268.

[15] W. Richard Scott, *Institutions and Organizations*, 2nd edn. (Thousand Oaks, CA: Sage, 2001), 103.

[16] K. J. Holsti, *Taming the Sovereigns: Institutional Change in International Politics* (Cambridge: Cambridge University Press, 2004), 116-118.

[17] Holsti, *Taming the Sovereigns*, 116-117.

[18] Robert H. Jackson, *Quasi-States: Sovereignty, International Relations and the Third World* (Cambridge: Cambridge University Press, 1990); and Holsti, *Taming the Sovereigns*.

against their take-over by potentially more powerful political interests, serving thereby to enable institutional survival as well as broader social goals of public interest. Boundaries also help to guarantee institutional continuity, by designating the institution rather than actors within it as the carriers of autonomy. Political parties continue to exist despite changes in leadership and states survive when governments change or are not recognized.[19]

Institutional boundaries encourage social order by determining whether and how institutions "fit" into the "societies" of which they are part. In short, boundaries define how settlements regulating conflicts and cooperation *within* an institution conform to broader patterns of conflict and cooperation that define "societies."[20] They organize the myriad institutions within a social space. They place an institution and its rules in superordinate, subordinate, and competitive relationships with other institutions and groups and they transmit these relations to the level of individuals. In doing so, they establish particular roles and rights both within, and between, institutions and societies.[21] For example, a basic institution of international society is diplomatic immunity, which designates the person, property, residence and embassy of a foreign ambassador as falling not within the jurisdiction of the host country, but rather the home country. To belong to international society, sovereigns must accept that within their territory there are bounded areas and actors outside of their authority and control. The boundaries of this institution are clearly specified and are designed to preserve the overarching institution of sovereign equality.[22] When such institutional boundaries are violated, as when the revolutionary Iranian government held US and Canadian diplomats hostage in the 1979-1980 hostage crisis, the violator is viewed as not belonging to international society and is often punished.

Rules defining boundaries bring individuals in line with the decision-making mechanisms that make collective action possible within the institution.[23] At the same

---

[19] Holsti, *Taming the Sovereigns*, 117.

[20] March and Olsen distinguish between two different logics at work in much of international relations theorizing, a logic of consequences and a logic of appropriateness. Most structuralists and pluralists and rationalists adhere to the logic of consequences – that the ends produced explain the means pursued, or in our case, the boundaries built. However, we argue that boundaries are defined not only according to the consequences, but they also reflect and create logics of appropriateness. James G. March and Johan P. Olsen, "The Institutional Dynamics of International Political Orders," *International Organization* 52 (1998): 943-69.

[21] March and Olsen, "Institutional Dynamics."

[22] The institutions of diplomacy were spelled out in the Vienna Convention on Diplomatic Relations, which entered into force in 1964, but which codified five centuries of practice. The International Court of Justice ruled in 1980 that the Iranian government had violated not only a contract in the form of the Vienna Convention, but also the broader obligations of a state in international society. See Ian Brownlie, *Principles of International Law* 6th ed. (Oxford: Oxford University Press, 2003), 342. On diplomacy as one of the fundamental institutions giving rise to an international *society* of states, see Hedley Bull, *The Anarchical Society*, ch. 3.

[23] Ira Katznelson, "Periodization and Preferences: Reflections on Purposive Action in Comparative Historical Social Science," in *Comparative Historical Analysis in the Social Sciences*, eds. James Mahoney

time, they force individual behavior to conform to rules governing relationships between one institution and others. They provide authoritative rules about behavior that tell individuals how to navigate complex social environments where groups and institutions pursue different preferences.[24] The government of Iran was cast out by international society for failing to prevent and then approving the actions of militant students, not government officials, which were contrary to international society's values of maintaining inter-state interaction and the inviolability of sovereigns. Iran was punished for not forcing its individual citizens to conform to the rules governing relations among states within international society. While Iran continues to pursue values at odds with many other states, it no longer pursues behaviors that directly challenge the core values of an international society of sovereign states.[25]

Boundaries in the German Union Federation's (DGB) have evolved to place similar constraints on the behavior of German unionists. Article 8 of the DGB's postwar statute mandated "neutrality," obligating the federation and its unions to operate independently of the influence from government, parties, religious communities, public administrations and employers, although the exact meaning of union "independence"—initially—remained ambiguous.[26] In the first years of the Federal Republic the conservative government of Chancellor Konrad Adenauer resisted successfully DGB attempts to influence directly government policy. Social Democratic unionists responded by purging the DGB leadership and mobilizing the union movement to support the Social Democratic Party (SPD) in the 1953 federal elections.[27] In turn, Catholic and Christian unionists threatened to desert the DGB and found a rival Christian federation. Unwilling to reactivate the ideological schisms of Weimar era unions, Social Democratic unionists backed down and the DGB placed clear boundaries on the use of union resources for political campaigns and the partisan activities of peak-level DGB and union officials.[28] DGB and union members pursue interests opposed to other social groups, but they do so within boundaries.

---

and Dietrich Rueschemeyer (Cambridge University Press, 2002) 295; Charles Taylor, "Modernity and Identity," in *Schools of Thought*, eds. Joan W. Scott and Debra Keates (Princeton, NJ: Princeton University Press, 2001), 139-53.

[24] Frederik Barth, "Introduction," in *Ethnic Groups and Boundaries*, ed. Frederik Barth (Oslo: Universitaetsforlaget, 1969), 15-17; Katznelson, "Periodization and Preferences," 295.

[25] Brownlie, *Principles of International Law*, 342.

[26] Theo Pirker, *Die blinde Macht: Die Gewerkschaftsbewegung in Westdeutschland* (Munich: Mercator Verlag, 1960) vol.2, 77.

[27] Pirker, *Die blinde Macht*, v.2, 23ff; Kurt Klotzbach, *Der Weg zur Staatspartei* (Berlin and Bonn: J.H.W. Dietz Nachfolger GmbH, 1982), 250-251.

[28] A partisan *Proporz* ("proportionality") distributes positions in the DGB executive among Social Democrats and Christian unionists. Lower level DGB and union officials hold Bundestag mandates for various parties, but strong norms prevent members of the DGB Executive and union presidents from representing parties in parliament or government. Both SPD- and CDU/CSU-led governments consult union leaders in selecting individuals for cabinet positions, especially the Minster for Labor and Social Policy, but unionists relinquish union functions while holding such portfolios. See Anton Pelinka, *Gewerkschaften im Parteienstaat* (Berlin: Duncker & Humblot, 1980), 95-6, 99, 109-10, 114.

Institutional boundaries in domestic and international political arenas force individual behavior to conform to higher-level values embedded in social structure. The boundaries of institutions, therefore, reflect conflicts and compromises not only between the members of an institution, but also between the protagonists of different values in society.

Institutions win legitimacy and broader support by reinforcing social values.[29] By organizing social space and transmitting the hierarchy of societal values through to the level of individuals, institutional boundaries act as a critical part of the "settlements" that prevent societies from disintegrating. This means those interested in supporting and enforcing the boundaries of a particular institution extends beyond actors who participate in or interact with it directly to a broader set of societal actors. To the extent that an institution contributes to the reproduction of social values, the maintenance and enforcement of its rules, particularly its boundaries, become a matter of social stability. They matter not only to members of the institution and those who interact with it directly, but also to society more generally.[30] This represents the growth of "legitimacy" and may be the result of different processes.[31] Rationalists stress that institutions perform functions that make them indispensable to the reproduction of values that keep society together.[32] Sociological perspectives argue that some institutions have symbolic or cognitive value that makes their survival essential to the legitimacy and survival of other institutions in society.[33] Regardless of its source, this legitimacy provides a reason for even those actors who are not directly affected by its actions to enforce its rules.

A contemporary example arises from the sometimes furious debate over the separation between church and state in the United States. This boundary is often cast as a foundational value of U.S. society, preventing both the establishment of a hierarchy of religions or ideologies within the United States and the state-sanctioned subordination of minority religious views to majority ones. Churches and religions as institutions are deeply socially embedded in this particular fashion in the United States and their limited boundaries are understood within a broader frame of ordering and preserving fundamental societal values.

Similarly, the evolution of DGB "neutrality," described above, is intimately linked to the unionists' desire to support parliamentary democracy in the fledgling

---

[29] Mary Douglas, *How Institutions Think* (Syracuse: Syracuse University Press, 1986).

[30] Wolfgang Streeck and Kathleen Thelen, "Introduction: Institutional Change in Advanced Political Economies," in *Beyond Continuity*, eds. Wolfgang Streeck and Kathleen Thelen (Oxford and New York: Oxford University Press, 2005).

[31] Arthur Stinchcombe, *Constructing Social Theories* (Chicago: University of Chicago Press, 1968), 163.

[32] See for example, James Fearon and David Laitin, "Explaining Interethnic Cooperation," *American Political Science Review* 90 (1996): 715-735.

[33] Paul DiMaggio and Walter Powell, "Introduction," in *The New Institutionalism in Organizational Analysis*, eds. Paul DiMaggio and Walter Powell (Chicago and London: University of Chicago Press, 1991); and W. Richard Scott, *Institutions and Organizations*, 77.

Federal Republic. Contrary to many unionist hopes, the Adenauer government asserted a doctrine of "parliamentary sovereignty," delegitimizing extra-parliamentary pressure (e.g. strikes) for political ends and limiting the ability of unionists to influence policy.[34] Unionists accepted "parliamentary sovereignty"—and a consequent division of labor that left parties as the representatives of employees' interests in policy arenas and unions as the employees' representatives in labor markets—as the price of stabilizing institutions of West German democracy against subversion. German unions became a "pillar" (*Ordnungsfaktor*) of the democratic order rather than a "principled opposition" (*Gegenmacht*), supporting, and supported by, other groups carrying democracy in West German society.[35] Thus, the examples of separation of church and state in the US and the acceptance of "parliamentary sovereignty" in the FRG demonstrate how institutions acquire legitimacy and broad support in the societies of which they are part because boundaries project "settlements" about societal values over individuals' behavior.

4. Institutional boundaries, variance, and behavior

The new institutionalisms' neglect of boundaries also blinds them to important effects of institutions on actor behavior. A central focus of historical institutionalists, in particular, has been explaining how actors construct similar institutions—unions, for example—differently in different places.[36] Likewise, constructivists have sought to explain how variations on the institution of the nation-state affect the nature of inter-state interaction.[37] Differing institutional structures then become an explanation for variance in actor behavior. The historical institutionalist and constructivist argument about the origins of behavioral variance can be applied to institutional boundaries. Doing so provides insights into behaviors that an exclusive focus on authority relations within institutions might overlook.

These explanations of institutional variance neatly extend to institutional boundaries. Although all institutional boundaries organize social settlements over individual behavior, similar institutions can have different rules that govern their boundaries. Institutions that exist in the same society as well as those that perform

---

[34] This use of the term "parliamentary sovereignty" should not be confused with the use of the term in the context of British politics where it indicates that parliament acts without formal constraint by a written constitution or the acts of previous parliaments.

[35] Eberhard Schmidt, *Ordnungsfaktor oder Gegenmacht: Die politische Rolle der Gewerkschaften* (Frankfurt a.M.: Suhrkamp, 1971).

[36] Kathleen Thelen and Sven Steinmo, "Historical Institutionalism in Comparative Politics," in *Structuring Politics*, eds. Sven Steinmo, Kathleen Thelen and Frank Longstreth (Cambridge U.K. and New York: Cambridge University Press, 1992), 1-32.

[37] John Gerard Ruggie, "Territoriality and Beyond: Problematizing Modernity in International Relations," *International Organization* 47 (1993); Thomas Risse-Kappen, *Cooperation Among Democracies* (Princeton: Princeton University Press, 1995); Peter J. Katzenstein (ed.), *The Culture of National Security: Norms and Identity in World Politics*, 1st ed. (New York: Columbia University Press, 1996); Alexander Wendt, *Social Theory of International Politics* (Cambridge: Cambridge University Press, 1999).

similar roles in different societies may have different boundaries. For example, the Austrian Trade Union Federation's (ÖGB) statute contains a neutrality clause almost identical to the DGB's, but institutional boundaries permitted complete interpenetration of party and union organizations and direct integration of unions into policy making.[38] Such diversity is the consequence of the different value preferences that distinguish social "settlements" across societies and "path dependence."[39] Path dependent arguments suggest that events in one time influence future events. Social structure and the distribution of power vary across time and place, pushing individual societies toward particular conflicts, and resolutions of them, and different institutional structures. For example, different distributions of power among social groups might lead to the creation of governance institutions based on representative democracy in one place or authoritarianism in another. Or, to extend the comparison above, differences in the Allied administration of Austrian and German occupation, permitted unions in the former—but not the latter—to exploit their strength in the immediate postwar era to institutionalize their influence in economic policy making. Once in place, however, institutions tend to reinforce certain interests and outcomes, cementing the relationships that led to their structure in the first instance. Thus, institutions project the impact of particular conflicts, distributions of power, and social choices across time. This same process produces variance in institutional boundaries. Because they come into being under different circumstances, the boundaries of institutions look very different from one another.

Existing analyses provide an explanation for *why* institutional boundaries vary, but—so far—they have not examined *how* they vary. We suggest that, most simply, boundaries vary in their permeability, whether they permit outside actors to exercise influence within an institution and whether they permit actors within the institution to wield influence in other arenas. Does society condone, through particular boundary regulations, the influence of some actors or institutions on the decision making of other institutions or not? How are the authority relations inside the institution related to the hierarchies that govern other institutions and society itself? Do boundary regulations create privileged channels of influence for some types of actors or do they seek to limit them, forcing contests to influence institutional decision making into more transparent or competitive arenas? As a concrete example, one might consider the different means of integrating markets across national boundaries: managed trade, harmonization and mutual recognition.[40] These questions are not new, but the concerns of an "old" institutionalism of Montesquieu and Madison. This "old" institutionalism recognized explicitly that institutional boundaries are mechan-

---

[38] Pelinka, *Gewerkschaften im Parteienstaat*, 104; Fritz Klenner, *Das Unbehagen in der Demokratie* (Vienna: Verlag der Wiener Volksbuchhandlung, 1956), 54ff.

[39] Paul Pierson, "Increasing Returns;" James Mahoney, "Path Dependence in Historical Sociology," *Theory and Society* 29 (2000): 526-7.

[40] Miles Kahler, "Trade and Domestic Differences," in *National Diversity and Global Capitalism*, ed. S. Berger and R. Dore (Ithaca, NY: Cornell University Press, 1996), 300.

isms that enforce societies' preferences over individual behavior, elevating some values while subordinating others. While the "old" institutionalism focused on the boundaries of formal governmental institutions, however, we see the problem of boundaries extending wherever there are institutions. Classically, four mechanisms have permitted actors to influence decision making across institutional boundaries: 1) formal rules that specify such influence (often backed up by state power); 2) control over resources critical to an institution; 3) the personal union of decision-making roles in different institutions; and 4) ideological affinity. Boundaries that proscribe such mechanisms are relatively impermeable, such as anti-trust laws that prohibit collusion among firms. Those that condone them are more permeable, such as the overlapping jurisdictions in federal systems.

The relative permeability of institutional boundaries touches on many types of behavioral outcomes. Boundary regulations have perhaps their greatest impact on the coordination of decision making between institutions and organizations. Between functionally differentiated institutions, permeable boundaries may permit coordination as between the "pillarized" institutions of plural societies. Impermeable or solid boundaries between interest groups and parties, on the other hand, may enforce a division of representational labor between them, such as between parties and unions in postwar West Germany. Between undifferentiated organizations, permeable boundaries may invite collusion while solid boundaries enforce competition. In the structural realist conception of states as unitary actors, bounded by sovereignty, these actors are functionally the same as their core purpose is vying for survival in an anarchic system.[41] Boundary regulations may also shape flows of information. The price mechanism of the mythical, perfectly competitive market relies on borders between firms that guarantee all equal access to information. Conversely, the success of collusion often depends on the maintenance of opacity around decision making. These are areas of behavior shaped as much by the limitations placed on authoritative rules as by the rules themselves.

We have focused on the stabilizing and reproductive elements of institutional boundaries here, though we recognize that variance in institutional boundaries also facilitates institutional change and can undermine stability. Permeability in particular opens the possibility for boundary shifts that may significantly alter the institution itself and its internal relations, but also its relations with external institutions.[42] These boundary changes in turn can trigger societal change. Attention to how a boundary gets drawn or the nature and outcome of boundary disputes will bring more attention to how such changes can feed back into society to alter fundamental institutions and values as well as the overall organization of society. Small changes in institution-

---

[41] Waltz, *Theory of International Politics*, ch. 4.

[42] For an empirical example of permeability in the boundary of sovereignty leading to broader institutional change, see Anne L. Clunan, "Redefining Sovereignty: Humanitarianism's Challenge to Sovereign Immunity," in *Negotiating Sovereignty and Human Rights: Actors and Issues in Contemporary Human Rights Politics*, ed. Noha Shawki and Michaelene Cox (Farnham, UK: Ashgate, 2009), 7-26.

al boundaries can ultimately have large societal effects, as small changes in the drawing of jurisdictions can have reverberations for overall societal order. This is an issue we raise here primarily with an eye to further research, as our main focus has been on how boundaries matter and how they vary.

5. Conclusion

We have sought to highlight how the nature of, and change in, the boundaries of discrete institutions has important consequences for broader social organization and order. Institutional boundaries deserve attention because they are what structure – in very different ways – the amount and ease of access between institutional domains. In defining that access, they can serve to reproduce or alter institutions.

The nature of boundaries determines whether, and which, actors are able, or unable, to operate legitimately within, and across, institutional jurisdictions. Boundaries transmit social and institutional rules internally, as in the interactions between unions and political parties and between sovereign governments and their citizens, but they also transmit social rules between institutions, as in the preservation of sovereign immunity.[43] In these ways, boundaries can protect institutions and contribute to institutional survival and continuity. They also organize and stabilize social orders, fostering collective action in some realms and regulating conflict in others.

We have also suggested that the creation of boundaries, or their change, can reverberate throughout other institutions in society, shaping their relations and the overall degree of institutionalization of the values on which a society is founded. Boundaries transmit social values and roles to institutional and societal actors and individuals. For these reasons, we think that more attention needs to be paid to the boundaries of institutions. Without understanding how these borders come into being and what the consequences of their creation and alteration are, we are likely to miss how the nature of a boundary or its change can ripple through society, potentially producing major institutional as well as societal change.

An important focus of future research is the way in which boundaries can vary and the consequences of that variance. We suggest that the variance in the permeability of boundaries is particularly worthy of further research for three reasons. First, the permeability of an institution's boundaries is likely to have significant impact not only on relations within, and between, institutions, but also on the overall pattern of power and authority within society. This is because permeability determines which actors have power and influence within, and across, institutions. Second, the permeability of boundaries determines the likelihood of political struggles over those boundaries and therefore the likelihood of institutional change. Third, as a consequence, permeable boundaries are more likely to be associated with fundamental transformation of the values underpinning society. We suggest that the tools of

---

[43] Clunan, "Redefining Sovereignty."

historical institutional and constructivist analysis are particularly appropriate for understanding when, and how, boundaries come into being, how they facilitate collective action among like, and unlike, actors; and, more broadly, for understanding the relationship between institutional and social change.

John Leslie
john.leslie@vuw.ac.nz

Anne L. Clunan
alclunan@nps.edu

Zur Rekonfiguration politischer Herrschaft

Jens Wissel
Institut für Sozialforschung, Frankfurt am Main

Zwar gibt es in der Europaforschung eine große Anzahl von Untersuchungen zu den unterschiedlichen Aspekten des weitverzweigten Systems der EU, eine staatstheoretische Einordung der Prozesse fällt aber noch schwer.[1] Diese Schwierigkeiten drücken sich auch in der Suche nach adäquaten Begriffen aus. Es wird von einer „europäischen Staatlichkeit"[2] gesprochen, von einem „post modern state,"[3] einem „quasi state,"[4] oder einem „international state,"[5] um nur einige Versuche zu nennen. „Der Nachteil vieler dieser Charakterisierungen liegt in der Statik einer Momentaufnahme; sie ermöglicht nicht, die Evolution der EU in einer dynamischen Perspektive über die Zeit zu erfassen."[6] Bezüglich des Nationalstaates wird von einem „Zerfaserungs-" und „Anlagerungsprozess" neuer Institutionen und Akteure an den Staat ausgegangen[7] oder umgekehrt von einer Einbindung dieses Staates in transnationale „Politikregime."[8] Um der Gefahr zu entgehen, die Perspektive auf die neue Konstellation mit alten Begriffen zu verstellen, wird die EU aufgrund ihrer „multi-level governance"-Struktur auch als Organisation „sui generis"[9] zu fassen versucht. Der multi-level governance-Ansatz hat zweifellos das

[1] Die staatstheoretischen Prämissen dieses Artikels gehen auf ein gemeinsam mit Sonja Buckel und John Kannankulam konzipiertes und von der DFG gefördertes Forschungsprojekt zurück („Die Transnationalisierung des Staates im Prozess der Entstehung einer gemeinsamen europäischen Migrationskontrollpolitik").

[2] Hans-Jürgen Bieling, „Transnationale Vergesellschaftung und die "neue Sozialdemokratie"," in *Ein neuer Kapitalismus?*, hg. Mario Candeias und Frank Deppe (Hamburg: VSA, 2010); Elmar Altvater, *Konkurrenz für das Empire. Die Zukunft der Europäischen Union in der globalisierten Welt* (Münster: Westfählisches Dampfboot, 2007); siehe auch Sonja Puntscher-Riekmann (Hg.), *The State of Europe. Transformation of Statehood from a European Perspective* (Frankfurt am Main: Campus, 2004).

[3] James Caporaso, "The European Union and Forms of the State: Westphalian, Regulatory or Post-Modern?," *Journal of Common Market Studies* 34, 1 (1996).

[4] William Wallace, „Government without Statehood," in *Policy-Making in the European Union*, hg. Helen Wallace and William Wallace, 4. Auflage (Oxford: University Press, 1996).

[5] Alexander Wendt, „Der Internationalstaat: Identität und Strukturwandel in der internationalen Politik," in *Perspektiven der Weltgesellschaft*, hg. Ulrich Beck (Frankfurt am Main: Suhrkamp, 1998).

[6] Wolfgang Wessels, „Theoretischer Pluralismus und Integrationsdynamik: Herausforderung für den "acquis academique"," in *Theorien der europäischen Integration*, hg. Hans-Jürgen Bieling und Marika Lerch (Wiesbaden: VS-Verlag, 2005).

[7] Stephan Leibfried und Michael Zürn, „Von der nationalen zur post-nationalen Konstellation," in *Transformation des Staates?* (Frankfurt am Main: Suhrkamp, 2006), 41-42.

[8] Ulrich Beck und Edgar Grande, *Das kosmopolitische Europa: Gesellschaft und Politik in der Zweiten Moderne* (Frankfurt am Main: Suhrkamp, 2004), 56.

[9] Markus Jachtenfuchs, „Die Europäische Union – ein Gebilde sui generis?," in *Projekt Europa im*

EUROSTUDIA — REVUE TRANSATLANTIQUE DE RECHERCHE SUR L'EUROPE
Vol. 7, No.1-2 (2011): 133-151

Verdienst, die neue räumliche Ausdifferenzierung politischer Prozesse in Europa erkannt und beschrieben zu haben. Problematisch ist allerdings der „Problemlösungsbias“[10] und die hieraus folgende Ausblendung politischer Herrschaft.[11] In der Beschreibung einer neuen Form der Steuerung, in der die Akteure in einem „nicht-hierarchischen Verhältnis“ zueinander stehen,[12] wird übersehen, dass die Rekonfiguration der alten Hierarchien keineswegs heißt, dass Hierarchien verschwinden. Ich gehe davon aus, dass ein Rückgriff auf die Debatten um die „Internationalisierung des Staates,“[13] dazu beitragen kann, die Rekonfiguration Europas als ein neues Staatsprojekt zu begreifen, in dessen Rahmen sich neue Hierarchien zwischen den unterschiedlichen Staatsapparaten und Institutionen auf europäischer und nationaler Ebene in einer neuen skalaren Struktur herausbilden. Eine solche Perspektive ermöglicht es, sowohl die Dynamik des Integrationsprozesses, als auch die Veränderung von politischer Herrschaft in den Blick zu nehmen. Bei der Entfaltung werde ich mich zentral auf die Arbeiten von Nicos Poulantzas beziehen.

In einem ersten Schritt wird sein Ansatz kurz dargestellt, um dann zu der Frage zu kommen, inwiefern seine theoretischen Grundlegungen bei der Analyse der aktuellen Prozesse in der EU weiterführen können. Meine These ist, dass sich innerhalb der EU ein Ensemble aus nationalen Staatsapparaten, europäischen quasi-Staatsapparaten und internationalen Organisationen herausgebildet hat, dessen organisatorische Kohärenz und Anordnung weniger durch seine – selbst noch umkämpfte – formale Struktur sichergestellt werden kann, als vielmehr das Ergebnis eines hegemonialen Projektes ist. Um der These eines entstehenden europäischen Staatsapparateensembles nachzugehen, werde ich die Europäisierung von Migrationskontrollpolitiken im Rahmen der EU analysieren, weil die Kontrolle von

Übergang?, hg. Klaus Dieter Wolf (Baden-Baden: Nomos, 1997), 15-35.

[10] Renate Mayntz, „Zur Selektivität der steuerungstheoretischen Perspektive,“ in *MPIfG Working Paper* 01/2 (Köln: Max-Planck-Institut für Gesellschaftsforschung, 2001).

[11] Vgl. Christoph Görg, „Multi-Level Environmental Governance. Transformation von Staatlichkeit – Transformation der Naturverhältnisse,“ in *Multi-Level-Governance*, hg. Achim Brunnengräber und Heike Walk (Baden-Baden: Nomos, 2007); Markus Wissen, „Internationalisierung, Naturverhältnisse und Politics of Scale. Zu den räumlichen Dimensionen der Transformation des Staates,“ in *Staatstheorie vor neuen Herausforderungen. Analyse und Kritik*, hg. Jens Wissel und Stefanie Wöhl (Münster: Westfälisches Dampfboot, 2008).

[12] Markus Jachtenfuchs, „Regieren jenseits der Staatlichkeit,“ in *Die neuen Internationalen Beziehungen. Forschungsstand und Perspektiven in Deutschland*, hg. Gunther Hellmann, Klaus Dieter Wolf und Michael Zürn (Baden-Baden: Nomos, 2003).

[13] Vgl. Robert W. Cox, *Production, Power and World Order. Social Forces in the Making of History* (New York: Columbia University Press, 1987); Nicos Poulantzas, „Die Internationalisierung der kapitalistischen Verhältnisse und der Nationalstaat,“ in *Die Zukunft des Staates*, hg. Joachim Hirsch, Bob Jessop und Nicos Poulantzas (Hamburg: VSA, 2001); Joachim Hirsch, *Der nationale Wettbewerbsstaat* (Berlin und Amsterdam: ID-Verlag, 1995); Bob Jessop, *State Power. A Strategic-Relational Approach* (Cambridge: Polity Press, 2008).

Bevölkerung und Territorium bisher zu den Kernbereichen nationaler Staatlichkeit gehörte.

Der Rückgriff auf Poulantzas' Staatstheorie zur theoretischen Einordnung der veränderten Konstellation bietet sich aus verschiedenen Gründen an. Zum einen verstand es Poulantzas in seiner Staatstheorie die Vermittlung von gesellschaftlichen Auseinandersetzungen und staatlichen Veränderungen in den Blick zu nehmen. Begreift man den Staat als „materielle Verdichtung eines gesellschaftlichen Kräfteverhältnisses,"[14] vermeidet man den heute weitverbreiteten Funktionalismus, beziehungsweise Ökonomismus, der die politischen Prozesse in Europa als „spill over"[15] des gemeinsamen europäischen Marktes versteht. Gleichzeitig verfällt man nicht in eine politizistische Erkärung, in der gesellschaftliche Prozesse weitgehend ausgeblendet bleiben.[16] Zum anderen hat Poulantzas schon früh ein Konzept zur Analyse von Internationalisierungsprozessen entwickelt und es verstanden, dieses mit seinem Begriff der „inneren Bourgeoisie" staatstheoretisch zu fundieren.

1. Eine neue Form der US-Hegemonie in Europa

Im Unterschied zu vorhergehenden Phasen des Kapitalismus analysierte Poulantzas in den 1970er Jahren das Verhältnis zwischen den Staaten des kapitalistischen Zentrums nicht als ein äußerliches. Die Hegemonie der USA war demnach keine, die Europa von außen aufgezwungen wurde oder die aus einem bestimmten Interessenskalkül von „den Europäern" akzeptiert wurde, vielmehr zeichnete sich die neue Situation dadurch aus, dass das US-amerikanische Kapital Europa durchdrang und die unterschiedlichen nationalen Machtböcke von innen heraus veränderte.[17]

Die europäischen Metropolen blieben dabei selbst Zentren der Kapitalakkumulation mit einer eigenen Peripherie und standen weiterhin in einem Konkurrenzverhältnis zu den USA. Möglich wurde diese Durchdringung durch eine neue Form der internationalen Arbeitsteilung, in der immer mehr amerikanische Direktinvestitionen nach Europa flossen. Der entscheidende Schritt, um die interiorisierte amerikanische Hegemonie in Europa zu begreifen, lag in einem neuen

---

[14] Nicos Poulantzas, *Staatstheorie. Politischer Überbau, Ideologien, Autoritärer Etatismus* (Hamburg: VSA 2002).

[15] Vgl. Leon N. Lindberg, *The Political Dynamics of European Economic Integration* (Stanford, CA: Stanford University, Press 1963).

[16] Die Folgen einer politizistischen Theorie zeigten sich deutlich in der integrationstheoretischen Ratlosigkeit nach dem Scheitern der Referenden zum Verfassungsvertrag. Jürgen Neyer kritisiert in diesem Zusammenhang, dass der Begriff der Gesellschaft in der „Integrationstheorie noch immer ein Fremdwort ist:" Jürgen Neyer, „Die Krise der EU und die Stärke einer deliberativen Integrationstheorie," *Zeitschrift für Internationale Beziehungen* 2, 12 (2005): 380; siehe auch Anne Faber und Wolfgang Wessels, „Die Verfassungskrise der EU als Krise der Integrationstheorie," *Zeitschrift für Internationale Beziehungen*, 2 (2005): 358.

[17] Poulantzas, *Die Internationalisierung*, 28.

Verständnis der Transformation der nationalen Machtblöcke. Bisher standen zur Analyse von Herrschafts- und Abhängigkeitsverhältnissen im internationalen Zusammenhang zwei Begriffe zur Verfügung. Bei einer relativ eigenzentrierten Entwicklung[18] ging man von einer starken nationalen Bourgeoisie mit eigenständiger Reproduktionsbasis aus, während zur Analyse von Abhängigkeitsverhältnissen schon früh der Begriff der Kompradorenbourgeoisie geprägt wurde. Insbesondere in der Dependenztheorie[19] wurden mit diesen beiden Begriffen Zentrum-Peripherieverhältnisse analysiert. Die Kompradorenbourgeoisie verfügte über keinerlei eigene Reproduktionsbasis und galt als Träger ausländischer Kapitalinteressen. Beide Begriffe sind, so Poulantzas, nicht geeignet, die veränderte Konstellation zu fassen, weil in Europa eine Bourgeoise entstanden ist, die weder als eine rein nationale noch als eine völlig abhängige Statthalter-Bourgeoisie zu charakterisieren ist.

Um diese Entwicklung begreifen zu können, kreierte Poulantzas den Begriff der „inneren Bourgeoisie." Die innere Bourgeoisie ist eine Bourgeoisie, die zwar innerlich durch die Einlagerung „ausländischen" Kapitals internationalisiert ist, gleichzeitig aber nach wie vor eine eigene Reproduktionsbasis besitzt und wesentlich auf den Nationalstaat bezogen bleibt. Die Widersprüche, die sich aus Herrschaft und Abhängigkeit ergeben, sind gewissermaßen in der inneren Bourgeoisie eingelagert. In diesem Sinne handelt es sich bei ihr nicht mehr um eine autozentrierte Bourgeoisie, vielmehr verlaufen die Beziehungen untereinander „über den Umweg des in ihnen eingelagerten amerikanischen Kapitals."[20] Der US-amerikanische Kapitalexport hat also die Machtverhältnisse in den jeweiligen Ländern verändert, weil das amerikanische Kapital Teil der gesellschaftlichen Kräfteverhältnisse in den europäischen Nationalstaaten wurde. Die Position der inneren Bourgeoisie ist demnach wesentlich ambivalenter als die der nationalen Bourgeoisien, und ihre Stellung in den gesellschaftlichen Machtverhältnissen ist konjunkturabhängiger. Wechselnde Bündnisse mit den Resten der nationalen Bourgeoisie oder Teilen der Kompradorenbourgeoisie sind keineswegs ausgeschlossen oder unwahrscheinlich. „Das erklärt eine ganze Reihe von Verwerfungen auf der Ebene der Hegemonie in diesen Blöcken an der Macht."[21] Die europäischen Machtblöcke sind nicht mehr auf der nationalen Ebene zu erfassen, die „Staaten nehmen nicht nur die Interessen ihrer inneren Bourgeoisien wahr, sondern gleichfalls die Interessen des herrschenden

---

[18] Darunter versteht man eine Situation, in der sich aufgrund einer relativ eigenständigen nationalen Bourgeoisie und einem entsprechenden politischen Projekt in einem Nationalstaat ein eigener Entwicklungsweg herausbildet.

[19] U.a. Samir Amin, *Die ungleiche Entwicklung* (Hamburg: Hoffmann und Campe, 1975); Fernando H. Cardoso und Enzo Faletto, *Abhängigkeit und Entwicklung in Lateinamerika* (Frankfurt: Suhrkamp, 1976).

[20] Poulantzas, *Die Internationalisierung*, 58; zum Begriff der inneren Bourgeoisie siehe auch John Kannankulam und Jens Wissel, „Stichwort innere Bourgeoisie," in *Historisch-Kritisches Wörterbuch des Marxismus* (Hamburg: Das Argument, 2004).

[21] Poulantzas, *Die Internationalisierung*, 56.

imperialistischen Kapitals und die anderer imperialistischer Kapitale, wie sie innerhalb des Internationalisierungsprozesses verbunden sind."[22]

Die veränderte internationale Arbeitsteilung, der Kapitalexport und die Veränderung der Eigentumsverhältnisse in Europa, die, so Poulantzas, die Machtbefugnisse des amerikanischen Kapitals in Europa ausweiteten,[23] betrafen „jedoch nicht nur die Produktionsverhältnisse." Sie veränderten die europäischen Gesellschaftsformationen grundsätzlich.[24] Diese Entwicklung führte zu dem, was heute gemeinhin als Amerikanisierung beschrieben wird und in der Regulationstheorie als Verallgemeinerung des Fordismus charakterisiert wurde.[25]

Für Poulantzas hat sich der Nationalstaat in diesen Prozessen wesentlich verändert. Er bleibt aber insofern Nationalstaat, als die innere Struktur der einzelnen Staatsapparate, das Verhältnis und die Hierarchie der Staatsapparate zueinander sowie das Rechtssystem um ihn zentriert sind. Zwar werde die „juristische Begriffssetzung der nationalen Souveränität" durch diese Entwicklungen in Frage gestellt,[26] Poulantzas beharrt jedoch darauf, dass kein Staat über den bereits existierenden Nationalstaaten entstehe. Auch den Institutionen und Apparaten, die im europäischen Kontext entstanden sind, gesteht Poulantzas keine Eigenständigkeit zu. „Man kann die verschiedenen Interventionen und ihre Aspekte nicht vom Staat trennen, indem man die Möglichkeit der *wirklichen Übertragung* der "ökonomischen Funktionen" auf die supranationalen oder überstaatlichen Apparate ins Auge fasst, wobei der Nationalstaat nur eine repressive und ideologische Rolle innehielte. Es handelt sich zuweilen höchstens um ein *Delegieren* dieser Funktionen."[27]

Die Internationalisierung und die Durchdringung der europäischen Gesellschaften führt für Poulantzas weniger zu einer Supra-Nationalisierung des Staates, als zu einer inneren Fragmentierung und der Tendenz „zur inneren Auflösung der europäischen Gesellschaftsformationen und ihrer Ökonomien."[28]

2. Die Entwicklung der europäischen Integration

Poulantzas' Analyse stammt aus den 1970er Jahren, insofern kann nicht unvermittelt an sie angeschlossen werden. Die heutige Situation stellt sich in vielerlei Hinsicht anders dar.

Die von Poulantzas beschriebenen Durchdringungsprozesse betreffen nicht mehr nur Europa, sondern seit den 1980er Jahren ebenso die USA. Auch in den USA ist eine innere Bourgeoisie entstanden. In der Folge lassen sich die inneren Bourgeoisien

---

[22] Ebenda.
[23] Ebenda, 48.
[24] Ebenda, 49.
[25] Vgl. Alain Lipietz, *Mirages and Miracles. The Crisis of Global Fordism* (London: Verso, 1987), 69-71.
[26] Vgl. Poulantzas, *Die Internationalisierung*, 61.
[27] Ebenda, 62-63; Hervorhebung im Original.
[28] Ebenda, 61-62.

nicht mehr ausgehend von einer expandierenden nationalen Bourgeoisie analysieren. Die inneren Bourgeoisien haben sich transnationalisiert, das heißt, es ist ein neues Innen-Außen-Verhältnis entstanden, in dem die Bindungen der inneren Bourgeoisien an spezifische Nationalstaaten schwächer werden.[29] Zudem hat sich die globale Arbeitsteilung verändert. In den 1990er Jahren hat ein neuer Internationalisierungsschub eingesetzt. Dabei haben sich die Internationalisierungsprozesse nicht nur beschleunigt, vielmehr sind in diesem Prozess „dauerhafte und dichte sozialräumliche Verflechtungszusammenhänge" entstanden, „die über mehrere nationalstaatliche Räume beziehungsweise Territorien hinweg aufgespannt sind."[30] Dies betrifft sowohl ökonomische als auch politische und kulturelle Prozesse.[31] Mit anderen Worten: Poulantzas beschrieb eine historische Phase, die mit dem Begriff der Internationalisierung noch adäquat gefasst werden konnte. Heute befinden wir uns in einer Phase, in der Prozesse an Bedeutung gewonnen haben, die über eine einfache Internationalisierung hinausgehen, weil sie nicht mehr ohne Weiteres auf die involvierten Nationalstaaten zu reduzieren sind. Dies äußert sich auch in der Organisierung eines europäischen Blocks an der Macht, für den europäische und transnationale Institutionen und Organisationen zunehmend an Bedeutung gewinnen. Dazu zählt mittlerweile eine weitverzweigte Institutionalisierung auf europäischer (EuGH, Europäische Kommission, unzählige europäische Agenturen etc.) und auf globaler Ebene (WTO, IWF, UNO, NATO etc.), aber auch ein dichtes Netz zur transnationalen Interessenorganisation in Form von Think Tanks, Verlagen, Instituten etc.[32]

---

[29] Ausführlich Jens Wissel, *Die Transnationalisierung von Herrschaftsverhältnissen* (Baden Baden: Nomos, 2007), 102-108. Das heißt keineswegs, die transnationalisierten inneren Bourgeoisien seien jetzt die einzig relevanten Kräfte in den Machtblöcken, aber nationale und Kompradorenbourgeoisien haben an Bedeutung verloren. Vgl. Gregory Albo, „The Old and New Economics of Imperialism," in *Socialist Register 2004. The New Imperial Challenge*, ed. Leo Panitch and Colin Leys (London: Merlin Press, 2003).

[30] Ludger Pries, *Die Transnationalisierung der sozialen Welt* (Frankfurt: Suhrkamp, 2008), 45.

[31] Siehe hierzu auch Holm-Detlev Köhler, „Lokale Vernetzung in der globalen Produktion am Beispiel der Automobilkonzerne," in *Der Global Player und das Territorium*, hg. Ulrich Mückenberger und Markus Menzl (Opladen: Leske und Budrich Verlag, 2002), 126-129; Boy Lüthje, Wilhelm Schumm und Martina Sproll, *Contract Manufacturing. Transnationale Produktion und Industriearbeit in der IT-Branche* (Frankfurt am Main und New York: Campus, 2002), 69-70; Mario Candeias, *Neoliberalismus, Hochtechnologie, Hegemonie. Grundrisse einer transnationalen kapitalistischen Produktions- und Lebensweise. Eine Kritik* (Hamburg: Argument, 2004); William I. Robinson, *A Theory of Global Capitalism. Production, Class, and State in a Transnational World* (Baltimore and London: John Hopkins University Press, 2004), 33-37.

[32] Vgl. Bastiaan van Apeldoorn, „Transnationale Klassen und europäisches Regieren: Der European Round Table of Industrialists," in *Die Konfiguration Europas*, hg. Hans-Jürgen Bieling und Jochen Steinhilber (Münster: Westfälisches Dampfboot, 2000); Hans-Jürgen Bieling, „Die neue europäische Ökonomie: Transnationale Machtstrukturen und Regulationsformen," in *Eurokapitalismus und globale politische Ökonomie*, hg. Martin Beckmann, Hans-Jürgen Bieling und Frank Deppe (Hamburg: VSA, 2003), 48-50; Bernhard Walpen, *Die offenen Feinde und ihre Gesellschaft* (Hamburg: VSA, 2004); Andreas Nölke, Henk Overbeek and Bastiaan van Apeldoorn, „Marketization, Transantionalisation, Commodification and the Shift in Corporate Governance Regulation," in *The Transnational Politics of*

Das heißt keineswegs, dass heute eine einheitliche europäische oder gar globale Klasse entstanden ist. Vielmehr unterscheiden sich die inneren Bourgeoisien aufgrund ihrer verschiedenen regionalen Schwerpunktsetzungen zum Teil erheblich voneinander. Zwar sind tatsächlich globale Produktionsnetzwerke entstanden, gleichzeitig aber haben sich viele transnationale Konzerne – bezüglich der Produktion wie auch des Marktes – auf eine bestimmte Region konzentriert. Die inneren Bourgeoisien behalten zudem privilegierte Beziehungen zu einzelnen Nationalstaaten und stehen – wie jede Bourgeoisie – in einem inneren Konkurrenzverhältnis zueinander. Diese nationalen und regionalen Fragmentierungen in den Inter- und Transnationalisierungsprozessen haben auch dazu beigetragen, dass keine europäische (nationale) Bourgeoisie entstanden ist.

Auch die Europäische Union unterscheidet sich wesentlich von der EWG (Europäische Wirtschaftsgemeinschaft), über die Poulantzas schrieb. Selbst in der Krisen- und Stagnationsphase zwischen 1973 und 1985 wurden wichtige Schritte zu einer tiefer gehenden Integration unternommen. Erstmals wurde die EG (Europäische Gemeinschaft, bis 1993 EWG) mit einem eigenen Haushalt ausgestattet. Um die innereuropäische Solidarität zur gemeinschaftlichen Absicherung der Wechselkurse sicherzustellen, wurde 1979 das Europäische Währungssystem (EWS) geschaffen. Im gleichen Jahr wurde das Europäische Parlament zum ersten Mal direkt gewählt, und der Europäische Rat wurde als regelmäßiges Treffen der Staats- und Regierungschefs eingerichtet.[33] In derselben Zeit begann sich der Charakter der europäischen Integration zu wandeln. Durch die Inter- und Transnationalisierungsprozesse verschoben sich die Kräfteverhältnisse in den meisten Nationalstaaten zuungunsten der Subalternen. Nachdem die veränderte globale Konstellation nach dem Ende des Bretton-Woods-Systems die verschiedenen nationalen Krisenbewältigungsstrategien, insbesondere nationale Konjunkturprogramme, zunehmend ins Leere laufen ließ, setzte sich in Europa schrittweise eine neoliberale Integrationsweise durch, die geprägt war durch „die Absage an alle eurokeynsianischen Strategien und eine monetaristische Neuausrichtung der Wirtschaftspolitik."[34] Diese Veränderungen liefen parallel zu einer Interiorisierung von internationalen und europäischen Kräfteverhältnissen in den jeweiligen nationalen Gesellschaftsformationen.

1985 bekam der Integrationsprozess hierdurch einen erneuten Schub. Die Einheitliche Europäische Akte (EEA) war das erste Ergebnis dieser Entwicklung, in der der „europäischen Ebene von Staatlichkeit" eine erhebliche Aufwertung zuteil

---

Corporate Governance Regulation, ed. Andreas Nölke, Henk Overbeek and Bastiaan van Apeldoorn (London und New York: Routledge, Chapman & Hall, 2007), 216; Jessop, *State Power*, 216-217.

[33] Stephan Heidbrink, „Geschichtlicher Abriss der europäischen Integration," in *Welt-Macht Europa. Auf dem Weg in weltweite Kriege*, hg. Tobias Pflügler und Jürgen Wagner (Hamburg: VSA 2006), 52.

[34] Patrick Ziltener, *Strukturwandel der europäischen Integration* (Münster: Westfälisches Dampfboot, 1999), 195.

wurde.[35] Schon früher hatten europäische Konzerne damit begonnen, ihre Interessen in Bezug auf Europa zu organisieren. „1984 erstellte Wisse Dekker vom Philips-Konzern ein Thesenpapier („Europe 1990"), das dann durch den *European Round Table of Industrials* gebilligt wurde. Seine Vorschläge zielten auf den Abbau aller tarifären und nicht-tarifären Handelshindernisse in Westeuropa, also die Bildung eines einheitlichen Marktes für Güter, Dienstleistungen, Kapital und Arbeitskräfte sowie die Öffnung des öffentlichen Beschaffungswesens und die Harmonisierung der indirekten Steuern. Sie bildeten das Herzstück des Weißbuches, das 1985 von der Kommission dem Rat vorgelegt wurde."[36]

Das Binnenmarktprojekt, das so von den europäischen transnationalen Konzernen entwickelt wurde, stand, so Ziltener, im Zusammenhang mit einem zunehmenden „Außendruck" durch die US-amerikanische und japanische Konkurrenz.[37]

Mit dem Vertrag von Maastricht, der am 10. Dezember 1992 von den Staats- und Regierungschefs beschlossen wurde, gelang abermals eine Vertiefung der Europäischen Integration. Zentrales Element des Vertrages war der Einstieg in die Wirtschafts- und Währungsunion.[38]

Nachdem 1997 in Amsterdam noch keine Einigung über die zukünftige institutionelle Beschaffenheit der erweiterten EU erzielt werden konnte, wurden vier Jahre später mit dem Vertrag von Nizza die entsprechenden institutionellen Reformen zur Aufnahmefähigkeit der EU vorgenommen. Im Mittelpunkt standen dabei die Abstimmungsmodalitäten des Ministerrats und die Zusammensetzung und Ernennung der Kommission.[39]

Ende Februar 2002 wurde ein Konvent zur Zukunft der Union zwecks Erarbeitung eines Verfassungsentwurfs ins Leben gerufen. Die Tatsche, dass ein Entwurf vorgelegt wurde, war angesichts diverser ungelöster Probleme ein spektakulärer Erfolg. Die wesentlichen Neuerungen bestanden in einer Reduktion der Kommissionsmitglieder. Ihr Präsident sollte in Zukunft auf Vorschlag des Rats vom Parlament gewählt werden. Die Ratspräsidentschaft sollte nicht mehr halbjährlich rotieren, sondern mit einer Amtszeit von zweieinhalb Jahren ausgestattet werden. Es sollte das Amt eines Außenministers geschaffen und die Rolle des Parlaments aufgewertet werden. Die wichtigste Änderung bestand aber in der Veränderung des Abstimmungsmodus.[40]

---

[35] Ebenda, 138.

[36] Ziltener, *Strukturwandel*, 136

[37] Ebenda.

[38] Vgl. Ingeborg Tömmel, *Das politische System der EU* (München und Wien: Oldenbourg Verlag, 2008), 31-33.

[39] Ausführlich Tömmel, *Das politische System*, 43.

[40] Vgl. Ingeborg Tömmel, „Eine Verfassung für die EU. Institutionelle Anpassung oder Systemreform?," in *Integration* 27, 3 (2004): 202-210.

Nachdem der Verfassungsvertrag in den Niederlanden und Frankreich in Referenden scheiterte, wurde aus dem Verfassungsvertrag ein Reformvertrag, und alle Begriffe und Symboliken, die auf einen europäischen Staat hindeuten könnten, wurden gestrichen. Die Veränderungen waren im Wesentlichen kosmetischer Natur.[41]

Der Vertrag wurde trotz anfänglicher Schwierigkeiten in allen Mitgliedsstaaten ratifiziert und trat am 1. Dezember 2009 in Kraft. Damit wurde die EU zu einer Rechtspersönlichkeit und hat auch rechtlich den Status eines supranationalen Gebildes.[42]

All diese Veränderungen haben zu tiefgreifenden Verschiebungen in der politischen Konstellation Europas geführt. Nicht nur die Rahmenbedingungen für nationalstaatliche Politik und die institutionelle Zusammensetzung im europäischen Rahmen haben sich verändert, vielmehr haben sich die nationalen Staatsapparate selbst im Integrationsprozess transformiert.

Der europäische Integrationsprozess veränderte die nationalen Staatsapparate, sodass diese immer stärker von der „Implementierung europäischer Vorgaben und der Anpassung nationalen Rechts an europäisches" in Beschlag genommen wurden. Die nationalen Bürokratien werden segmentiert durch die Herausbildung einer „Verwaltungselite der Europaexperten." Schon durch die supranationalen Hoheitsfunktionen und transnationalen Vernetzungen durchbricht diese neue Verwaltungselite „die herkömmlichen nationalen Bürokratiestrukturen."[43]

3. Materialistische Staatstheorie und europäische Integration

In den Debatten um den europäischen Integrationsprozess spielt materialistische Staatstheorie seit Ende der 1970er Jahre kaum noch eine Rolle. Dies liegt zum einen an einer allgemeinen Marginalisierung politik-ökonomischer Ansätze, aber auch daran, dass in den Debatten innerhalb der materialistischen Staatstheorie der Integrationsprozess lange Zeit unterschätzt wurde. In den letzten Jahren hat sich mit dem neogramscianischen Ansatz der Internationalen Politischen Ökonomie allerdings ein kritischer Ansatz in die Diskussionen um den Integrationprozess eingemischt.[44]

---

[41] Vgl. Steve Peers, „Statewatch Analysis. EU Reform Treaty: Analysis 1: Version 3," *JHA Provisions*, 22. October 2007; Tömmel, *Das politische System*, 51.

[42] Vgl. Tömmel, *Das politische System*, 51.

[43] Maurizio Bach, „Eine leise Revolution durch Verwaltungsverfahren. Bürokratische Integrationsprozesse in der Europäischen Gemeinschaft," *Zeitschrift für Soziologie* 21 (1992): 26; vgl. Ziltener, *Strukturwandel*, 204.

[44] Zum Verhältnis von Neogramscianismus und an Poulantzas orientierten Arbeiten siehe auch Ulrich Brand, „Globalisierung als Krise des Fordismus und ihrer Überwindung. Poulantzas' Überlegungen zur Internationalisierung von Politik und Ökonomie," in *Das Staatsverständnis von Nicos Poulantzas. Der Staat als gesellschaftliches Verhältnis*, hg. Alex Demirovic, Stefan Adolphs, und Serhat Karakayali

Es ist kein Zufall, dass es an Gramsci orientierte AutorInnen waren, die sich frühzeitig mit der Transnationalisierung gesellschaftlicher Verhältnisse und mit dem europäischen Integrationsprozess auseinandersetzten.[45] Gramsci legt den Schwerpunkt seiner theoretischen Arbeiten auf die Bedeutung gesellschaftlicher Kräfteverhältnisse.[46] So konnten frühzeitig Veränderungen in den Kräfteverhältnissen und vor allem die Orientierung maßgeblicher Akteure auf europäische und transnationale Zusammenhänge registriert werden. Zwar markiert Gramscis Arbeit einen entscheidenden Wendepunkt in den von der Marxschen Theorie inspirierten Debatten über den bürgerlichen Staat, indem er mit dem Begriff des erweiterten Staates, der die zivilgesellschaftlichen Auseinandersetzungen einbezieht, den Fokus auf die Formveränderung bürgerlicher Macht richtete;[47] eine ausgearbeitete Staatstheorie hat er gleichwohl nicht hinterlassen. Auch in den neogramscianischen Arbeiten wurde keine systematische Staatstheorie entwickelt. Dies hat auch dazu geführt, dass viele Analysen voluntaristisch erscheinen. Zumindest blieb das Verhältnis von Struktur und Handlung meist ungeklärt. Poulantzas' Vermittlung von gesellschaftlichen Kräfteverhältnissen und strukturellen Verfestigungen sowie institutionellen Verselbständigungen blieb in diesem Zusammenhang weitgehend unberücksichtigt. Erst Arbeiten, die wieder stärker auf staatstheoretische Erkenntnisse zurückgriffen, haben diese Situation verändert.[48]

Betrachtet man den Integrationsprozess als eine Rekonfiguration von nationalen Staatsapparaten, europäischen Institutionen und Organisationen, in dem neue europäisierte Staatsapparate (Europäische Zentralbank), oder quasi-Staatsapparate (europäische Agenturen, beispielsweise FRONTEX) entstehen, dann liegt die Aktualität von Poulantzas' Staatstheorie auf der Hand. Poulantzas begriff den Staat nie als einen einheitlichen Block oder als Subjekt. Veränderungen in den

(Baden-Baden: Nomos, 2010).

[45] Vgl. Cox, *Production*; Stephen Gill, „The Emerging World Order and European Change. The Political Economy of European Union," in *New World Order? Socialist Register 1992*, ed. Ralph Miliband and Leo Panitch (London: Merlin Press, 1992), 157-196; Hans-Jürgen Bieling und Frank Deppe „Gramscianismus in der internationalen politischen Ökonomie," *Das Argument* 217 (1996); einen Überblick bietet Dorothee Bohle, „Neogramscianismus," in *Theorien der europäischen Integration*, hg. Hans-Jürgen Bieling und Marika Lerch (Wiesbaden: VS Verlag, 2005).

[46] Zum Begriff der Kräfteverhältnisse siehe Jens Wissel, „Stichwort Kräfteverhältnisse," in *Historisch-Kritisches Wörterbuch des Marxismus*, hg. W.F. Haug, Band 6 II (Hamburg: Das Argument, 2010).

[47] Joachim Hirsch, John Kannankulam und Jens Wissel, „Die Staatstheorie des westlichen Marxismus. Gramsci, Althusser, Poulantzas und die sogenannte Staatsableitung," in *Der Staat der Bürgerlichen Gesellschaft* (Baden-Baden: Nomos, 2008).

[48] Siehe Ulrich Brand, *Globalisierung als Krise*; Bob Jessop, „Die Zukunft des Nationalstaates – Erosion oder Reorganisation? Grundsätzliche Überlegungen zu Westeuropa," in *Jenseits der Nationalökonomie? Weltwirtschaft und Nationalstaat zwischen Globalisierung und Regionalisierung*, hg. Steffen Becker und Thomas Sablowski (Hamburg: Das Argument, 1997); Bernd Röttger, *Neoliberale Globalisierung und eurokapitalistische Regulation* (Münster: Westfälisches Dampfboot, 1997); Ziltener, *Strukturwandel*; Bieling, *Die neue europäische Ökonomie*; Leo Panitch and Sam Gindin „American Imperialism and Eurocapitalism: The making of neoliberal globalisation," in *Studies in Political Economy* 71/72 (2003).

gesellschaftlichen Kräfteverhältnissen übertragen sich niemals eins zu eins auf den Staat, weil dieser über eine relative Autonomie verfügt. Gleichzeitig können solche Veränderungen den Staat und seine Apparate jedoch nicht unberührt lassen. Die Kräfteverhältnisse passen „sich der Materialität der verschiedenen Apparate an," das heißt, sie kristallisieren „sich im Staat nur in gebrochener und differenzierter, den Apparaten entsprechender Form."[49] Weder die einzelnen Staatsapparate noch der Staat als Ganzes lässt sich als hierarchisch strukturiertes einheitliches Machtdispositiv begreifen, vielmehr handelt es sich um ein komplexes Ensemble aus konkurrierenden Knoten, Macht- und Entscheidungszentren innerhalb von staatlichen Apparaten und zwischen diesen, bestehend aus einer „Vielzahl zerstreuter Mikropraktiken."[50] Die Einheit des Staates ist nicht durch ein institutionelles Korsett festgeschrieben, sondern gründet sich auf ein Staatsprojekt.[51] Auch wenn ein solches meist von einem hegemonialen Projekt dominiert wird, schreiben sich eine Vielzahl von politischen Projekten, die im Machtblock um Führung ringen, in das Staatsprojekt ein. Bei den gesellschaftlichen und apparativen Auseinandersetzungen wird bestimmt, wie die einzelnen Apparate oder Abteilungen in diesen angeordnet sind, welche Position sie in der Hierarchie der Apparate einnehmen und auf welchem Terrain Auseinandersetzungen ausgetragen werden.

Die EU ist also als neues Staatsprojekt zu betrachten, in dessen Rahmen sich neue Hierarchien zwischen den unterschiedlichen Staatsapparaten und Institutionen auf europäischer Ebene und auf den nationalen Ebenen herausbilden. Das europäische Staatsprojekt, das sich im Rahmen der „Internationalisierung des Staates" herausbildete, konkurriert dabei mit den unterschiedlichen nationalen Staatsprojekten. Die Positionen und die Verhältnisse der einzelnen europäischen und nationalen Apparate zueinander sind relativ flexibel und das Ergebnis eines permanenten Aushandlungsprozesses, weil es noch keinen hegemonialen Konsens über die Hierarchie der räumlichen Bezugsebenen gibt. So sind die Europäische Union und die jeweiligen nationalen und europäischen Apparate nicht nur von den gesellschaftlichen Widersprüchen durchzogen, sondern in stärkerem Maße auch von den Konkurrenzen der verschiedenen räumlichen Bezugsebenen untereinander.[52] Die unterschiedlichen *scales* stehen nicht in einem äußerlichen Verhältnis zueinander, sondern sind aufgrund der gegenseitigen Durchdringung ineinander verschränkt. Das europäische Staatsapparateensemble hat dabei noch keineswegs eine ähnlich

---

[49] Nicos Poulantzas, *Staatstheorie*, 162.

[50] Ebenda, 167.

[51] Bob Jessop, *State Theory. Putting Capitalist State in its Place* (Cambridge: Polity, 1990), 315-316; siehe auch Sonja Puntscher-Riekmann (ed.), *The State of Europe*.

[52] Der Europäische Ministerrat, der für das intergouvernementale Element der EU steht, wacht beispielsweise darüber, dass die Kommission als supranationales Element nicht zu mächtig wird. Ein Ergebnis dieser Konstellation sind die europäischen Agenturen, die formal nicht klar in die institutionelle Struktur der EU eingeordnet sind, weil der Rat nicht will, dass mit der Kommission eine Superbehörde entsteht. Effekt ist, dass die Agenturen keine formal übergeordnete Institution haben, die sie kontrollieren könnte vgl. Tömmel, *Das politische System*, 159.

gefestigte Struktur wie ein funktionierender Staat. Zwar kommt es in Staaten immer zu Auseinandersetzungen, in deren Rahmen sich die Hierarchien der einzelnen Staatsapparate zueinander verändern können, aber zumindest die zentralen Terrains und Abläufe der Auseinandersetzung unterliegen einer stärkeren Reglementierung und Tradierung. Die Kohärenz und Einheit des neuen Ensembles ist dagegen noch keineswegs gegeben.

4. Das europäische Staatsapparateensemble

Die Frage, ob aus Europa ein supranationaler Staat wird, lässt sich theoretisch nicht beantworten. Festzustellen ist aber, dass im europäischen Kontext ein Ensemble aus nationalen und europäischen (Staats-)Apparaten und einer europäisierten rechtlichen Struktur entstanden ist. Dabei haben sich nicht nur eine Reihe von Vernetzungen zwischen Staatsapparaten verschiedener Nationalstaaten herausgebildet, vielmehr haben sich die nationalen Staatsapparate selbst in unterschiedlicher Intensität „innerlich" europäisiert. Die nationalen Gewaltmonopole wurden in diesem Prozess zu einem Teil der europäisierten Konstellation. Mit anderen Worten: Es gibt kein europäisches Gewaltmonopol, aber die nationalen Gewaltmonopole ordnen sich dem neuen Projekt unter.

In jüngster Zeit ist eine Entwicklung zu beobachten, in der es zu einer Vergemeinschaftung von Kernbereichen nationaler Staatlichkeit kommt. Gingen viele Autoren bisher davon aus, dass der Vergemeinschaftungsprozess auf die *low politics*-Bereiche (Wirtschafts-, Währungs- und Kulturpolitik) beschränkt bliebe, so muss heute konstatiert werden, dass auch in den zentralen Bereichen staatlicher Herrschaft qualitative Veränderungen eingesetzt haben.

Mit dem Vertrag von Amsterdam vom 2. Oktober 1997 wurden auch Mechanismen vergemeinschaftet, die Territorialität, das heißt Ein- und Ausschlussverhältnisse, organisieren. Unter dem neuen Titel IV („Raum der Freiheit, der Sicherheit und des Rechts") wurden Migration und Asyl in die erste, das heißt vergemeinschaftete, Säule[53] der EU überführt sowie der Schengen-Besitzstand, der bist dahin nur ein völkerrechtlicher Vertrag zwischen einigen Mitgliedsstaaten war, in den Rahmen des Gemeinschaftsrechts integriert. Die Bedeutung dieses Vorgangs ist nicht zu unterschätzen,[54] denn die „Gemeinschaft verfügt nunmehr über alle erforderlichen Rechtsgrundlagen und Instrumente, um eine moderne Migrationspolitik führen und umsetzen zu können."[55] Durch die, an die

[53] Die Europäische Union besteht aus drei Säulen. Die erste vergemeinschaftete Säule besteht aus den Europäischen Gemeinschaften (Europäische Gemeinschaft und Europäische Atomgemeinschaft). Die zweite Säule der gemeinsamen Sicherheits- und Außenpolitik und die dritte Säule der polizeilichen und justiziellen Zusammenarbeit sind intergouvernemental organisiert.

[54] Jürgen Bast, „Transnationale Verwaltung des europäischen Migrationsraums," in *Der Staat* 46 (2007): 1.

[55] Röben, „Art. 61 et seq." EG. in *Das Recht der Europäischen Union. Kommentar*, hg. Eberhard Grabitz und Meinhard Hilf (München: C. H. Beck, 2005), Art. 63, Rdnr. 45.

Unionsbürgerschaft anknüpfenden Freizügigkeitsregelungen für Staatsangehörige aus Mitgliedsstaaten unterliegt schon jetzt der Aufenthalt der Hälfte der ausländischen Wohnbevölkerung unmittelbar dem EU-Recht.[56]

Neue staatsapparative Gebilde sind in allen Politikbereichen innerhalb der EU entstanden. Ein markantes Beispiel hierfür sind die vielen Agenturen,[57] die in der EU gegründet wurden. Seit den 1990er Jahren besitzen die Agenturen hoheitliche Entscheidungsbefugnisse. „Insgesamt führt die Ausgründung von Agenturen mithin zu einer Verselbständigung administrativer Apparate und bedeutet in der Konsequenz eine zunehmende Unabhängigkeit der Agenturen vom politischen Einfluss von Rat und Kommission – und parlamentarischer Mitwirkung [...]. Die neueren Agenturen sind, zumindest soweit dies die Agenturen der inneren Sicherheit einschließlich des Grenzschutzes betrifft, ihrem rein technisch-regulativen Gewand entwachsen."[58]

Diese Agenturen sind in den europäischen Gründungsverträgen nicht vorgesehen, sondern lediglich sekundärrechtlich geschaffene, auf mehr als vagen Rechtsgrundlagen basierende, selbständige Verwaltungseinrichtungen.[59] Wie weit sich die Agenturen von ihren ursprünglichen Unterstützungsaufgaben entfernt haben, zeigt die europäische Grenzschutzagentur FRONTEX, mit der versucht wird, die Kontrolle der europäischen Grenzen unter die organisatorische Hoheit der EU zu bringen. Ihre Zuständigkeit erstreckt sich auf die EU-Mitgliedsstaaten, die Schweiz und die im Schengener Abkommen assoziierten Länder. Sie wurde auf der Grundlage der VO (EG) 2007/2004 gegründet. Ihre Aufgaben liegen unter anderem im Bereich des Schutzes der Außengrenzen, der Unterstützung der Mitgliedsstaaten bei der Ausbildung von Grenzbeamten sowie der Risikoanalyse. Die Agentur nahm am 3. Oktober 2005 den operativen Betrieb auf. FRONTEX soll nicht nur explizit mit Europol, auf dessen Daten sie Zugriff hat, sowie mit Drittstaaten und Geheimdiensten zusammenarbeiten (Art. 13, 14 VO) und umfangreiche Durchführbarkeitsstudien „effektiveren Grenzschutzes" in Auftrag geben, sondern

---

[56] Günter Renner, *Ausländerrecht. Kommentar*, 8. neuberarb. und erweiterte Aufl. (München: C. H. Beck, 2005), Vorbem. Rdnr. 5; siehe auch Sonja Buckel, John Kannankulam und Jens Wissel, „Die Transnationalisierung des Staates im Prozess der Entstehung einer gemeinsamen europäischen Migrationskontrollpolitik. Projektantrag bei der Deutschen Forschungsgemeinschaft" (2007). Das schließt nicht aus, dass auch die juridische Struktur nach wie vor umkämpft ist, wie das Beispiel der – gegen Europäisches Recht verstoßenden – italienischen und französischen Sonderverfügungen gegen rumänische Staatsbürger zeigt.

[57] Die über Agenturen organisierte mittelbare Gemeinschaftsverwaltung befindet sich in permanentem Wachstum. In der Europäischen Union gibt es eine große Anzahl von Gemeinschaftsagenturen und Exekutivagenturen, die der ersten Säule zugeordnet sind. Hinzu kommen Agenturen im Rahmen der zweiten Säule in der gemeinsamen Außen- und Sicherheitspolitik sowie der dritten Säule der polizeilichen und justiziellen Zusammenarbeit in Strafsachen. Andreas Fischer-Lescano und Timo Tohidipur „Europäisches Grenzkontrollregime. Rechtsrahmen der europäischen Grenzschutzagentur FRONTEX," *Zeitschrift für ausländisches öffentliches Recht und Völkerrecht* 67 (2007): 1219-1276.

[58] Fischer-Lescano und Tohidipur, *Europäisches Grenzkontrollregime*, 1234.

[59] Ebenda, 1231.

auch selbst operative Einsätze durchführen. Seit 2006 gab es verschiedene Grenzschutzaktionen (*Joint Operation*/JO) vor der afrikanischen Küste im Mittelmeer: JO HERA (315 Tage 2008) vor Spanien, JO Nautilus (332 Tage 2008) um Italien und Malta, und JO Poseidon (217 Tage 2008) in der Ägäis – und viele andere an Land auf den Flughäfen.[60] Inzwischen sieht eine Änderungsverordnung von 2007[61] die Bildung von sogenannten „schnellen Eingreifteams (RABIT)" vor. Darin sollen Grenzschutzbeamte aus EU-Mitgliedsstaaten für gemeinsame grenzpolizeiliche Einsätze auf Anforderung eines Staates bereitstehen. Während die bisherigen Einsätze unter Art. 8 der VO bloße „Unterstützungseinsätze" darstellten, bei denen die FRONTEX-Beamten und die durch FRONTEX koordinierten nationalen Unterstützungsteams keine eigenen exekutiven Kompetenzen innehatten, sollen den „schnellen Eingreifteams" in Zukunft exekutive Befugnisse im jeweiligen Mitgliedsstaat übertragen werden.[62] Bisher wurden diese Interventionsteams nur bei Übungen eingesetzt. Im Oktober 2010 hat Griechenland FRONTEX um Unterstützung bei der Überwachung der türkisch-griechischen Grenze gebeten und den Einsatz von RABITs angefragt. Kurz darauf startete der erste RABIT-Einsatz.[63]

Die fragwürdige Rechtsgrundlage für diese sich verselbständigende Grenzpolizeieinheit, eine kaum durchschaubare Zuständigkeits- und Statusstruktur der agierenden Beamten an den Außengrenzen, intransparente und beschränkte Rechtsschutzmöglichkeiten sowie die Tendenz, die Kontrollmaßnahmen zu exterritorialisieren, um sich darüber von Menschenrechtsbindungen zu entpflichten, führen zu „strukturellen rechtsstaatlichen und demokratischen Defiziten."[64]

Während Binnenmarkt und Währungsunion im Wesentlichen von mächtigen ökonomischen Interessen angetrieben wurden, stellt sich bezüglich des Ausbaus des europäischen Grenzregimes die Situation anders dar. Es ist davon auszugehen, dass über die grundsätzliche Notwendigkeit der Regulation von Migration, trotz aller Differenzen, ein gesellschaftlicher Konsens in der Europäischen Union existiert.

---

[60] FRONTEX, „General Report 2008, Warsaw" (2009) http//www.frontex.europa.eu/annual_report, 35; Bernd Kasparek und Fabian Wagner, „Technology of Bordering. The European Union's Border Agency FRONTEX and the European Migration Management Project," Contribution to the International Workshop Disciplining Global Movement Migration Management and its Discontents, Institute for Migration Research and Intercultural Studies, 13. November 2010.

[61] VO EG 863/2007, ABl. EU Nr. L 199/30 vom 11. Juli 2007.

[62] Andreas Fischer-Lescano, Tillman Löhr und Timo Tohidipur, „Border Controls at Sea: Requirements under International Human Rights and Refugee Law," *International Journal of Refugee Law* 21, 2 (2009): 258.

[63] Siehe Europäische Kommission, „Press Releases RAPID: Statement by Cecilia Malmström, European Commissioner in Charge of Home Affairs on the Request of the Greek Government to get Assistance via Rapid Border Intervention Teams at the Land Border between Greece and Turkey," MEMO/10/516, 24. 10. 2010; FRONTEX, „News Release. Frontex to Deploy 175 Specialist Border Personnel to Greece," 29. 10. 2010.

[64] Fischer-Lescano und Tohidipur, *Europäisches Grenzkontrollregime*, 1273; siehe auch Sonja Buckel und Jens Wissel, „State Project Europe: The Transformation of the European Border Regime and the Production of Bare Life," in *International Political Sociology* 4, 1 (2010).

Dieser wird allenfalls von einer relativ kleinen Gruppe von *No Border*-AktivistInnen grundsätzlich in Frage gestellt. Die konkrete Gestalt des Grenzregimes, das Verhältnis von nationalen und europäischen Kompetenzen und seine Selektivität sind aber höchst umstritten. Während sich Großbritannien, Irland und Dänemark aus grundsätzlichen Erwägungen nicht beteiligen, drängen insbesondere Staaten wie Belgien, die Bundesrepublik Deutschland und Österreich, die keine EU-Außengrenze haben, auf den Ausbau der europäischen Grenzkontrollen. Hinzu kam Frankreich, das den Vorschlag einer europäischen Grenzschutzbehörde unterstützte. Aber auch Spanien und Italien, die eine lange europäische Außengrenze haben und von verschiedenen Migrationsrouten gekreuzt werden, setzten sich für stärkere Abwehrmaßnahmen ein.[65] Auch die Frage, in welchem Verhältnis nationale Territorien und das europäische Territorium stehen, bleibt umkämpft. Viele Mitgliedstaaten waren zwar der Auffassung, dass die EU-Außengrenzen besser geschützt werden sollten, bevorzugten hierfür aber bilaterale Regelungen. Das Europäische Parlament versuchte, in den entsprechenden Auseinandersetzungen die Rolle als demokratisch legitimierte Instanz einzunehmen. Widerstände gegen eine Europäisierung zeigten sich auch hier, letztlich sprach es sich aber für einen „stärkeren gemeinschaftlichen Charakter" der Grenzschutzagentur aus und forderte eine vollständige Einbeziehung von Kommission und Parlament.[66] Der Versuch hierdurch eine Rechenschaftspflicht und Kontrolle der Agentur sicherzustellen misslang allerdings.[67] Mit FRONTEX und den RABITs beginnt sich eine europäische Grenzschutzpolizei, die noch 2003 am Widerstand der Mitgliedstaaten scheiterte, durch die Hintertür zu formieren.[68] Die Auseinandersetzungen um das entstehende Grenzregime machen auch deutlich, dass die Vergemeinschaftung der Migrationskontrollpolitiken nicht als „spill over" des Binnenmarktes oder des Schengener Abkommens, sondern als Ergebnis gesellschaftlicher Strategien und apparativer Praktiken zu verstehen ist.

Zwei Entwicklungen sind in den staatstheoretisch zentralen Bereichen der Migrationskontrolle und des Grenzschutzes zu beobachten: Erstens entstehen in diesen Bereichen genuin europäische Strukturen, und zweitens ist eine Multiplizierung von staatlichen Kontrollapparaten und eine Restrukturierung des

---

[65] Siehe W. Andrew Neal, "Securitization and Risk at the EU Border: The Origins of FRONTEX," *JCMS Journal of Common Marked Studies* 47, 2 (2009): 340.

[66] Europäisches Parlament, „Bericht über den Vorschlag für eine Verordnung des Rates zur Errichtung einer Europäischen Agentur für die operative Zusammenarbeit an den Außengrenzen" (Endgültig A5-0093/2004), 33.

[67] Siehe Sergio Carrera, "The EU Border Management Strategy. Frontex and the Challenges of Irregular Immigration in the Canary Islands," in *CEPS Working Document* No. 261/March (2007), 14; auch Johannes Pollak und Peter Slominski, "Experimentalist but not Accountable Governance? The Role of Frontex in Managing the EU`s External Borders," *West European Politics* 32, 5 (2009).

[68] Vgl. Sabine Hess und Vassilis Tsianos, "Europeanizing Transnationalism! Provincializing Europe! – Konturen eines neuen Grenzregimes," in *Turbulente Ränder*, hg. Transit Migration Forschungsgruppe (Bielefeld: Transcript, 2007), 35.

Verhältnisses von Wissen und Macht im europäischen Maßstab zu beobachten. Die europaweite Vernetzung vormals nationaler Kontrollapparate sowie die Bildung neuer Apparate dienen nicht nur der erweiterten Überwachung der Außengrenzen. Vielmehr wird durch den Ausbau des interbehördlichen Informationsaustauschs sowie der Einrichtung neuer Informationsbeschaffungsprogramme beziehungsweise Agenturen (SIS, SIS II, SIRENE, VIS, EURODAC, ARGO) auch das Wissen über große Teile der Bevölkerung innerhalb der Union kontinuierlich erweitert. Diese Form der Informationsbeschaffung war seit dem 18. Jahrhundert (in Form von demografischen und statistischen Erhebungen) ein wesentliches Kennzeichen der sich entwickelnden Nationalstaaten.[69]

Ein Ergebnis dieser europaweiten Rekonfigurierung von nationalen Staatsapparaten und europäischen staatsapparativen Gebilden äußert sich in spezifischen Machttechnologien, die zu einer Erweiterung informeller Politikformen und damit zur Distanzierung der Bevölkerung von den Entscheidungszentren führen.[70] Dabei ist eine permanente Verschiebung von Machtrelationen und Kompetenzen im europäisch erweiterten Staatsapparateensemble zu registrieren. Entscheidungsprozesse werden wesentlich unübersichtlicher als im relativ klar aufgebauten Nationalstaat des Fordismus. Sogenanntes *forum-shifting* und *scale-jumping* lässt Initiativen zur Beteiligung an politischen Entscheidungen immer wieder ins Leere laufen.[71] Ein Beispiel hierfür stellt der Versuch dar, exterritoriale Lager an den Rändern der EU zu errichten. „Obwohl dieser Vorschlag exterritorialer Lager von Kommission und Parlament abgelehnt wurde, wird er von den EU-Innenministern kontinuierlich umgesetzt. Bei ihrem Treffen im Oktober 2004 wurde der Aufbau von fünf "Aufnahmezentren für Migranten" in Algerien, Libyen, Mauretanien, Marokko und Tunesien beschlossen. Im November 2004 bereiste eine Delegation aus Mitarbeitern der Innenministerien und Beamten der EU-Grenzpolizeien in Begleitung von Interpol im Auftrag der EU-Kommission als technische Mission Libyen."[72]

Parallel hierzu verändert sich das Verhältnis von Staatsapparaten und privaten Organisationen sowie Institutionen. Mittlerweile werden viele Aufgaben im Rahmen des entstandenen europäischen Grenzregimes, die vormals staatlich organisiert wurden, von internationalen Organisationen wie etwa der IOM (International Organisation for Migration) oder dem UNHCR (United Nations High Commissioner

---

[69] Buckel, Kannankulam und Wissel, „Die Transnationalisierung des Staates."

[70] Poulantzas, *Staatstheorie*, 87; für Europa siehe Helen Schwenken, *Rechtlos, aber nicht ohne Stimme* (Bielefeld: Transcript, 2006), 137; Birgit Sauer, „Vom Nationalstaat zum europäischen Reich? Staat und Geschlecht in der Europäischen Union," in *Feministische Studien* 1 (2001); Jürgen Neyer, „Die Krise der EU und die Stärke einer deliberativen Integrationstheorie," *Zeitschrift für Internationale Beziehungen* 2, 12, (2005): 381.

[71] Vgl. Wissel, *Transnationalisierung*, 161-181; siehe auch Adrienne Héritier, *Policy-Making and Diversity in Europe: Escaping Deadlock* (Cambridge: Cambridge University Press, 1999).

[72] Christoph Marischka, „Militarisierte Bevölkerungspolitik – zum Umgang der EU mit Flüchtlingen," in *Welt-Macht EUropa* (Hamburg: VSA, 2006), 305.

for Refugees) durchgeführt. Sabine Hess und Serhat Karakayali sehen in diesem Zusammenhang eine „NGOisierung" der Politik, „zum einen im Sinne des Outsourcing und Subcontracting ehemals staatlicher Aufgaben an nichtstaatliche Akteure, aber auch im Sinne eines Formwandels der klassischen politischen Akteure und ihrer Praxen selbst."[73] In diesem Prozess zieht sich der Staat nicht zurück, vielmehr dehnt er sich immer weiter aus.[74]

Ein europäischer Staat ist gleichwohl nicht entstanden. Insofern spricht tatsächlich vieles dafür, die Europäische Union als Organisation *sui generis*[75] zu beschreiben, in der sich die Nationalstaaten nicht aufgelöst haben, gleichwohl aber von einem europäischen Territorium sowie europäischen politischen Arenen und Apparaten und einer europäischen juridischen Struktur mit dem Europäischen Gerichtshof im Zentrum überlagert werden.[76] Durch diese Entwicklung wird die EU zu einer neuen Ebene räumlicher Fragmentierung im kapitalistischen Weltsystem. Gleichzeitig findet innerhalb der EU ein Prozess des *rescaling of state* statt,[77] indem lokale und regionale Zusammenhänge gegenüber den Nationalstaaten aufgewertet werden. Poulantzas interpretierte diese Entwicklung als Tendenz zur inneren Fragmentierung der europäischen Nationalstaaten. Das ist zwar nicht falsch, übersieht aber, dass im europäischen Kontext eine neue Struktur entsteht.

Der neue EU-Vertrag, der am 1. Dezember 2009 in Kraft trat, führt zu einem weiteren qualitativen Sprung. Der Vertrag besteht zu 96% aus dem Text der in Frankreich und den Niederlanden durch Volksentscheide abgelehnten EU-Verfassung. Die wenigen Änderungen sind nicht wesentlich.[78] Mit der Grundrechtscharta und der Tatsache, dass der Europäische Gerichtshof nicht nur von der letzten nationalen Gerichtsinstanz angerufen werden könnte, wird die europäische Juridifizierung eine noch größere Dynamik annehmen.

---

[73] Sabine Hess, und Serhat Karakayali, „New Governance oder die imperiale Kunst des Regierens. Asyldiskurs und Menschenrechtsdispositiv im neuen EU-Migrationsmanagement," in *Turbulente Ränder*, hg. Transit Migration Forschungsgruppe (Bielefeld: Transcript, 2007), 53.

[74] Ebenda.

[75] Jachtenfuchs, *Die Europäische Union*.

[76] Siehe Jessop, *State Power*, 217-222; Ingeborg Tömmel, „Governance und Policy-Making im Mehrebenensystem der EU," in Die Europäische Union. Governance und Policy-Making, *PVS Sonderheft* 40 (2007): 29-32.

[77] Eric A. Swyngedouw, „Neither Global nor Local: Globalization and the Politics of Scale," in *Spaces of Globalization. Reasserting the Power of the Local*, hg. Kevin R. Cox (New York: Guilford Pubn, 1997), 155; Neil Brenner, *New State Spaces* (Oxford und New York: Oxford University Press, 2004); Markus Wissen, "Internationalisierung, Naturverhältnisse und Politics of Scale. Zu den räumlichen Dimensionen der Transformation des Staates," in *Staatstheorie vor neuen Herausforderungen. Analyse und Kritik*, hg. Jens Wissel und Stefanie Wöhl (Münster: Westfälisches Dampfboot, 2008); zu Europa siehe Chris Rumford, „Rethinking European Spaces: Territory, Borders, Governance," in *Comparative European Politics* 4 (2006).

[78] Vgl. Steve Peers, „Statewatch Analysis."

5. Schluss

Poulantzas hatte recht, als er insistierte, dass sich die Nationalstaaten im Prozess der Internationalisierung nicht auflösen. Dennoch hat sich die Situation seit Poulantzas' Analyse grundlegend gewandelt. Es ist sehr wohl eine Struktur oberhalb der europäschen Nationalstaaten entstanden. Dadurch verändert sich die Position des Nationalstaates in Europa. Die Nationalstaaten werden Teil eines sehr viel weiter gefassten Ensembles von Apparaten und verlieren so tendenziell ihre privilegierte Stellung in der Regulation gesellschaftlicher Verhältnisse. Bei der Organisierung von Legitimation sowie der Identitätsstiftung in sich gespaltener Gesellschaften bleiben die Nationalstaaten zentral, auch wenn die angedeutete Fragmentierung nationaler Räume dies erschwert. Zwar sind Institutionen wie die Unionsbürgerschaft und der mit ihr im Zusammenhang stehende Ausbau von sozialen Rechten identitätsbildend, und auch das neue europäische Grenzregime konstruiert über die Herstellung eines gemeinsamen Außen eine europäische Identität. Hinzu kommen mittlerweile eine Reihe weiterer Entwicklungen – von der gemeinsamen Währung, Europafahnen auf den Autokennzeichen bis zu europäischen Studienaustausch- und Forschungsprogrammen etc. – womit sich die Herausbildung einer europäischen Identität andeutet.[79] Auch die Debatten um die europäische Verfassung oder um einen möglichen EU-Beitritt der Türkei lassen sich als Versuche deuten, eine europäische Identität zu konstruieren. Im Vergleich zu den nationalen Identitäten in Europa ist diese aber noch relativ schwach ausgeprägt.

Die Internationalisierungsprozesse, von denen Poulantzas spricht, haben in den 1990er Jahren eine neue Qualität angenommen, die in einem komplexen Wechselverhältnis zu den Nationalstaaten und der Europäischen Union sowie den transnationalen Netzwerken und Machtverdichtungen steht. Versteht man diese Prozesse als gleichermaßen politisch wie ökonomisch, so kann die Europäische Union als eine regionale Antwort auf die Globalisierung von ökonomischen und politischen Verhältnissen betrachtet werden. Dabei setzt sich in der neoliberalen Integrationsweise eine neue „Form der Artikulation von Politik und Ökonomie [durch], die sich dadurch auszeichnet, dass sich die Vermittlung zwischen dem Politischen und dem Ökonomischen zunehmend in der restringierten Begriffswelt der Ökonomie vollzieht."[80]

Die Entstehung einer europäischen Staatlichkeit hat dazu geführt, dass die Europäische Union mehr ist als ein Vertrag zwischen Nationalstaaten. Gleichzeitig sprechen die mehrere räumliche Bezugsebenen einschließende flexible skalare Struktur und die Konkurrenz der unterschiedlichen Ebenen nach wie vor dagegen, die Europäische Union als Staat zu begreifen. Dies würde tatsächlich auch der

---

[79] Vgl. Alex Demirovic, „Erweiterter Staat und europäische Integration," in *Die Konfiguration Europas*, hg. Hans-Jürgen Bieling und Jochen Steinhilber (Münster: Westfälisches Dampfboot, 2000), 68.

[80] Michael Felder, *Die Transformation von Staatlichkeit. Europäisierung und Bürokratisierung in der Organisationsgesellschaft* (Wiesbaden: Westdeutscher Verlag, 2001), 137.

Dynamik der beschriebenen Prozesse nicht gerecht. In welche Richtung sich das Staatsprojekt Europa bewegen wird, entscheidet sich in den gesellschaftlichen und apparativen Auseinandersetzungen. Die Möglichkeit des Scheiterns ist hier immer mit eingeschlossen.

Die beschriebene Konstellation hat das Terrain der Auseinandersetzung in Europa grundlegend verändert. Gesellschaftliche Kämpfe um demokratische Partizipation können sich nicht mehr auf die Nationalstaaten konzentrieren (sofern das jemals sinnvoll war), vielmehr müssen die Auseinandersetzungen in ihrer transnationalen Dimension gesehen werden. Gerade an der EU kann die Multidimensionalität und Diversifizierung von Herrschaft gezeigt werden. Partizipation, die auf den Nationalstaat beschränkt bleibt, droht nicht nur ihr emanzipatorisches Potenzial zu verlieren, weil die neoliberale Globalisierung die „vormals zum Teil progressiven Elemente des national-sozialen Staates ausgehöhlt hat,“[81] vielmehr lassen sich national organisierte Kompromisse in der beschriebenen Struktur leicht aushebeln.

Jens Wissel
J.Wissel@soz.uni-frankfurt.de

[81] Stephan Adolphs und Serhat Karakayali, „Die Aktivierung der Subalternen – Gegenhegemonie und passive Revolution,“ in *Hegemonie gepanzert mit Zwang*, hg. Sonja Buckel und Andreas Fischer-Lescano (Baden-Baden: Nomos, 2007), 137.

STADT – FLUSS – GRENZE
Geteilte Städte an der deutsch-polnischen Grenze

Elżbieta Opiłowska
Willy Brandt-Zentrum für Deutschland- und Europastudien der Universität Breslau

"[...] Östlich davon der blutende Grenzfluss
die Oder – Völker trennend.
In der Mitte die scharf bewachte
Trennlinie.
Dichter, polnische, deutsche,
zogen am Fluss entlang,
davon träumend, Fährmann zu sein –
Lange Zeit ein vergeblicher Traum.

Ich wurde Fährmann,
übertrug kostbare Fracht –
polnische Dichtung –
ins Deutsche,
in die Buchstabenwelt.

Sperrig blieb für die Menschen
der Fluss lange Zeit.
Lange neidete ich Vögeln und Fischen
das lockere Hin und Her.
Nun aber fahre ich selber
locker hinüber, herüber –
Fährmann grenzenlos."

Henryk Bereska, *Auf dem Poetdampfer zwischen Frankfurt und Eisenhüttenstadt, September 1996*

Mit diesen Worten beschreibt Henryk Bereska – Dichter und Übersetzer polnischer Literatur in Deutschland – den Fluss, der lange Zeit für Menschen gesperrt war und den nur Vögel und Fische überqueren durften. Ursprünglich gab es nur eine Stadt am Fluss, der als Transportweg den Handel und die Entwicklung begünstigte. Im Jahre 1945 wurde der Fluss, der bis dahin zwei Stadtufer miteinander verband, zur hermetischen Grenze zwischen zwei Staaten. Die Stadt am Fluss wurde geteilt; der eine Teil setzte die Geschichte fort, in dem anderen fing 1945 eine neue Geschichtstradition an, ohne sich auf die gemeinsame Vergangenheit zu beziehen. Die Stadt als Raum musste neu definiert werden, man versuchte neue Identifikationsmuster zu schaffen. Ein polnischer Journalist der parteilichen Tageszeitung *Trybuna Ludu* schrieb 1947: „Zwei Jahre nach dem Ende des Krieges fuhr ich auf einem Schiff von Wrocław nach Szczecin über die

EUROSTUDIA — REVUE TRANSATLANTIQUE DE RECHERCHE SUR L'EUROPE
Vol. 7, No.1-2 (2011): 153-166

Oder. Ich erinnere mich nicht an die ausgestorbenen Städte auf beiden Seiten des Flusses, nicht an wilde Felder, die das Gras überwuchs. [...] Im Gedächtnis sind Massen von Menschen an beiden Ufern haften geblieben, die auf ein paar geschmückte Boote schauten. [...] Es waren schweigende Massen, Menschen auf beiden Flussufern, die einander in Stille, ungläubig und misstrauisch ansahen. Das war ein Fluss, der teilte und nicht verband."[1]

An den europäischen Grenzen gibt es mehr als 60 solcher Doppelstädte, die unmittelbar benachbart sind und zwei verschiedenen Staaten angehören. Infolge der Grenzziehung an Oder und Neiße wurden ca. 50 Dorfgemeinden und sieben Städte geteilt, wovon drei als Doppelstädte fungieren; sie wurden Doppelstädte wider Willen. Geteilte Städte sind „Wunden der Geschichte, die großen Schmerzen im Bewusstsein der Welt."[2]

Deutschland : Einwohner	**Polen : Einwohner**	**Formen der Zusammenarbeit**
Bad Muskau : 3.937	Łęknica : 2.686	Partnerschaftsabkommen seit 1995
Forst : 20.596	Zasieki : 300	Partnerschaft mit Gemeinde Brody seit 2000-2002 Eröffnung der deutsch-polnischen Grenzbrücke Forst-Zasieki
Frankfurt (Oder) : ca. 60.000	Słubice : 16.800	Städtepartnerschaft seit 1975
Görlitz : ca. 56.000	Zgorzelec: ca. 32.000	Europa-Stadt seit 1998
Guben : 20.000	Gubin : 17.000	Europa Stadt seit 1998
Gemeinde Küstriner Vorland : 2.873 Festungsstadt Küstrin : ca. 870	Kostrzyn : 17.674	
Zittau : 28.906	Porajów : 1.500	Grenzübergang 1993

Abb. 1: Geteilte Städte an der Oder/Neiße-Grenze

Die Doppelstädte sind zumeist mittelgroß und liegen an der Peripherie des Landes, weit vom wirtschaftlichen und politischen Zentrum entfernt. Die Zusammenarbeit beider Stadthälften ergibt sich demnach aus dem Bedürfnis, dem Charakter der Randlage zu entgehen. Das Grenzüberschreitende, das Binationale charakterisiert sie und hierdurch versuchen sie, sich von den anderen durchschnittlichen, „national homogenen" Mittelstädten zu unterscheiden und Aufmerksamkeit auf sich zu lenken, wie z. B. Görlitz und Zgorzelec, als sie sich gemeinsam um den Titel der Europäischen Kulturhauptstadt bewarben.

[1] Zit. n. Cezary Trosiak, „Proces formowania się pogranicza polsko-niemieckiego w latach 1945-1993," [Der Prozess der Entstehung des deutsch-polnischen Grenzlandes in den Jahren 1945-1993] *Przegląd Zachodni* 3 (1993): 81-103.

[2] Vgl. Dagmara Jajeśniak-Quast und Katarzyna Stokłosa, *Geteilte Städte an Oder und Neiße. Frankfurt (Oder) – Słubice, Guben – Gubin und Görlitz – Zgorzelec 1945-1995* (Berlin: Spitz, 2000), 9.

Die Osterweiterung der Europäischen Union am 1. Mai 2004 war die Stunde der Doppelstädte, schreibt Helga Schultz. Von Frankfurt/Słubice an der Oder und Görlitz/Zgorzelec an der Neiße bis Gorizia/Nova Gorica am italienisch-slowenischen Isonzo eilten hochrangige Politiker in die krisengeschüttelten Grenzstädte, um die Rhetorik der überwundenen Grenzen zu pflegen. Dieses politische Ereignis war begleitet von Volksfesten, die für „eine hochgestimmte Nacht die Völkerverbrüderung probten."[3] Bevor Brücken die beiden Flussufer miteinander verbanden, hatte der Fluss jedoch lange Zeit eine unüberwindbare Grenze gebildet.

Im Folgenden möchte ich mich auf die drei größten geteilten Städte an der deutsch-polnischen Grenze konzentrieren – Frankfurt (Oder)/Słubice, Guben/Gubin und Görlitz/Zgorzelec – und versuchen, verschiedene Entwicklungsstadien der deutsch-polnischen Grenzregionen und der Wahrnehmung ihrer Bewohnerschaft zu skizzieren.

Wenn man der Typologie der Interaktionsmodelle für Grenzregionen nach Martinez[4] folgt, die unten dargestellt ist, dann scheinen die deutsch-polnischen Grenzregionen die ersten zwei Etappen hinter sich gebracht zu haben und momentan zunehmend dem Muster der „kooperierenden Grenzregionen" entgegenzustreben (siehe S. 166).

1. Gesprengte Brücken, geteilte Städte, der Fluss als Grenze

Die Symbolik der gesprengten Brücken des Jahres 1945 ist für alle drei Grenzstädte typisch. In Frankfurt (Oder), Guben und Görlitz wurden die Brücken kurz vor der Kapitulation Deutschlands vernichtet. Frankfurt (Oder) und Guben wurden im Krieg völlig zerstört. Am 26. Januar 1945 wurde Frankfurt (Oder) zur Festung erklärt und die Bevölkerung evakuiert. General Theodor Busse und Stadtkommandant Oberst Biehler ließen am 19. April die Oderbrücke in die Luft sprengen. Anschließend bombardierte die Rote Armee die Festung. Es kam zu Plünderungen und Brandschatzungen, was dazu führte, dass 65 Prozent der Stadtgebäude einschließlich der historischen Altstadt zerstört wurden.[5] Eine Frankfurterin erinnert sich: „Es hätte niemand sagen dürfen, dass die Polen und die Russen die Stadt zerstört haben. Denn soviel wir jetzt wissen, ist es ja doch so gewesen, dass die Stadt zur Festung erklärt worden ist, also völlig leer gezogen war. [...] Es hat auch auf jeden Fall Plünderungen gegeben. Aber wir wissen auch, dass die Leute, die etwas eher

---

[3] Vgl. Helga Schultz, „Doppelstädte als Laboratorien der Integration," in *Stadt – Grenze – Fluss. Europäische Doppelstädte*, hg. Helga Schultz (Berlin: Spitz, 2005), 13-26.

[4] Oscar J. Martinez, "The Dynamics of Border Interaction," in *Global Boundaries. World Boundaries*, ed. Clive H. Schofield, Vol. 1 (New York: Routledge, 1994), 2-4.

[5] Wolfgang Stribrny und Fritz Zöpke, *Frankfurt (Oder). Porträt einer Brückenstadt* (Berlin/Bonn: Westkreuzverlag, 1991), 90-93.

hier gewesen sind, in die Wohnungen ihrer Nachbarn eindrangen und dort klauten. [...] Und da sind die Russen gekommen. Da waren auch Polen."[6]

Infolge der Bombardements stand Guben im Februar 1945 in Flammen. Die Altstadt östlich der Neiße war zu 88% zerstört. Im westlichen Teil betrugen die Zerstörungen etwa 21%.[7] Zu den Kriegszerstörungen kamen noch Plünderungen hinzu, was sich im Gedächtnis der Einwohner stark einprägte: „Die Plünderer in dieser Stadt nahmen, was und wann sie nur konnten. [...] Gubin war zerstört, ja, aber das alles konnte man wiederaufbauen. Man nahm es faktisch auseinander und fuhr das Material weg. [...] Aber die erste Phase war so, dass man nicht wusste, ob das alles polnisch bleibt. Deswegen musste man es zerlegen und wegtransportieren. Als man schon wusste, dass es polnisch bleibt, da gab es dann kein Geld."[8]

Im Unterschied zu Frankfurt (Oder) und Guben blieb Görlitz samt historischer Altstadt wie eine Insel unzerstört. Nur die Neißebrücken und Eisenbahnbrücken wurden vernichtet. Es sind 37 Häuser mit Totalschäden verzeichnet, die 1945 zerstört wurden.[9]

Franz Scholz, der als Pfarrer in den Jahren 1940-1946 im Ostteil der Stadt eingesetzt war, schrieb am 25. Mai 1945 in sein Tagebuch: „Die ersten von Osten ankommenden Polen berichten uns, dass Görlitz die erste nicht vom Krieg zerstörte Stadt sei; weiter östlich läge fast alles in Trümmern, jedenfalls Brieg, Breslau, Liegnitz, Bunzlau, Lauban."[10]

In allen drei Städten wurden sowjetische Stadtkommandanturen eingerichtet und provisorische Brücken über die Flüsse gebaut. Von allen Seiten strömten Flüchtlinge herbei, die in der Hoffnung, in die Heimat zurückkehren zu können, an der Grenze blieben. Ein Interviewpartner aus Guben erinnert sich an Folgendes: „Und es waren ja viele, die hier in Guben bleiben wollten, dann auf der Westseite, weil sie ja gar nicht glaubten, dass sie nicht mehr zurückkönnen. Sie haben ja wochen- und monatelang die Hoffnung noch gehabt, na ja die Polen haben uns vielleicht rausgeschmissen, nur um drüben zu plündern, und dann lassen sie uns wieder rein in unsere Häuser, und es war sehr viel zerstört, aber es war ja nicht so. Die Grenze war dann endgültig, nicht."[11]

---

[6] Interview mit Frau Albeshausen, Frankfurt (Oder), 9.1.1997, zit n. Jajeśniak-Quast und Stokłosa, *Geteilte Städte*, 20.

[7] Jajeśniak-Quast und Stokłosa, *Geteilte Städte*, 22.

[8] Interview mit Herrn Pantkowski, Gubin 19.3.1997, zit. n. ebenda, 24.

[9] Vgl. Peter Wenzel, „Kriegsschäden 1945 in Görlitz," in *Denkmalpflege in Görlitz. Eine Schriftenreihe,* hg. Stadtverwaltung Görlitz, Bd. 11 (Görlitz – Zittau: Oettel, 2002), 31-37.

[10] Franz Scholz, *Görlitzer Tagebuch. Chronik einer Vertreibung 1945/1946* (Frankfurt am Main, Berlin: Ullstein, 1993), 46.

[11] Zit. n. Dariusz Galasiński und Ulrike H. Meinhof, „Looking across the river. German-Polish border communities and the construction of the Other," *Journal of Language and Politics* 1, 1 (2002): 23-58.

Es herrschte Chaos, Hunger und Überfüllung. Krankheiten verbreiteten sich schnell, weil es nicht genug Ärzte und Medikamente gab. Die Selbstmordrate war überdurchschnittlich hoch.

Noch bevor die Friedenskonferenz in Potsdam begann, versuchten die kommunistischen Machthaber in den Nord- und Westgebieten, die offiziell „wiedergewonnene Gebiete" genannt wurden, die Politik der „vollendeten Tatsachen" umzusetzen. Anfang Mai kamen im östlichen Teil aller drei Städte Vertreter der polnischen Administration zusammen, um diese Stadthälften von der sowjetischen Kommandantur zu übernehmen und jeweils eine polnische Stadt einzurichten. Nun wurde die angekündigte Teilung der Städte an Oder und Neiße Realität. In Frankfurt (Oder) und Görlitz lag die historische Altstadt auf der westlichen Seite des Ufers, während der östliche Teil nur eine Vorstadt bildete. Umgekehrt in Guben – die Altstadt war im Osten, aber alle infrastrukturellen Einrichtungen, Fabriken, Betriebe und der Bahnhof befanden sich westlich der Neiße. So sollten sich die Städte östlich des Flusses zu einem selbständigen Stadtorganismus entwickeln, während sie von ihrer wirtschaftlichen Basis abgeschnitten wurden.

Mit der Errichtung der polnischen Administration bekamen die östlichen Städte ihre Namen – Słubice, Gubin und Zgorzelice (dann in Zgorzelec umbenannt). Im Juni 1945 wurden die deutschen Bewohner hinter den Fluss ausgesiedelt. Frankfurt (Oder) zählte 1939 fast 84.000 Einwohner, davon wohnten 15.600 im östlichen Teil der Stadt.[12] Etwa 13.500 Gubener und 7.500 Görlitzer mussten den östlichen Stadtteil verlassen.[13] Theodor Treu, ein Görlitzer, notierte in seinem Tagebuch: „Immer häufiger verbreitete sich auch das Gerücht, dass die ganze Oststadt geräumt werden müsste – ich konnte und wollte es nicht glauben – und schließlich am 21. Juni 1945 an einem Donnerstag – wurde es zur furchtbaren Wirklichkeit: Um 6.30 Uhr früh kam der Befehl, (v. Haus zu Haus) durch die "deutsche Polizei," zur Räumung der Oststadt: Es war eigentlich eine Plünderungsaktion der Polen! Vergeblich versuchte ich bei der polnischen Kommandantur ein Erlaubnisschein zum Bleiben zu bekommen. Ich ging im Talar hinüber! Alles war erfolglos!"[14]

Man könnte sicher meinen, dass es die deutschen Aussiedler in den Grenzstädten leichter hatten als andere, weil sie den Wohnsitz nur innerhalb ein und derselben Stadt wechseln mussten. Andererseits war ihre Situation umso schwieriger, weil sie jahrelang voll Nostalgie über die Flüsse auf ihre verlorene Heimat blicken mussten.

---

[12] Vgl. Wolfgang Bauwert, „Festung Frankfurt (Oder). Eine Stadt am Kriegsende," in *Brandenburg im Jahre 1945. Studien,* hg. Werner Stang und Kurt Arlt (Potsdam: Brandenburgische Landeszentrale für Politische Bildung, 1995), 68.

[13] Vgl. Jajeśniak-Quast und Stokłosa, *Geteilte Städte*; vgl. auch Elżbieta Opiłowska, *Kontinuitäten und Brüche deutsch-polnischer Erinnerungskulturen. Görlitz/Zgorzelec 1945-2006* (Dresden: Neisse Verlag, 2009).

[14] Theodor Treu, *Auszug aus dem Tagebuch meines Vaters Theodor Treu Pfarrer an der Peterskirche zu Görlitz 1945*, hg. Toni Treu (Görlitz: Selbstverlag, 1993), 15.

Die Grenze wurde abgeriegelt, die Stadthälften isoliert: „Die Bewohner des östlichen Guben begaben sich oft auf die Westseite [...] Doch dann kam der 13. Juni 1945! Wieder wollten einige - auch ich gehörte zu ihnen – die Neiße in Richtung Ostteil passieren. [...] Doch nun stand da ein polnischer Wachposten und der ließ uns nicht passieren [...] Es gab hierzu eine Bekanntmachung, die wir nicht kannten. Diese hatte folgenden Wortlaut: Der Kommandant der Stadt Guben gibt bekannt, dass durch die Grenzfestlegung ab 13. Juni 1945 das Passieren der Neiße verboten ist!"[15]

Die Städte auf beiden Uferseiten gehörten zu einer etwa 30 Kilometer breiten Grenzzone. Dieses Gebiet wurde von Grenzschutzsoldaten besetzt, was die Bewegungsfreiheit und die Ansiedlung der Bürger beeinträchtigte. Hinzu kam die Unsicherheit der Westgrenze. Für die Einreise in die Grenzzone brauchte man spezielle Genehmigungen. Eine Frankfurterin hat folgendes Bild in Erinnerung: „Aus meiner Kindheit habe ich die Situation in Frankfurt und an der polnischen Grenze so in Erinnerung, dass sie eine ausgesprochen streng abgeschottete Grenze war. Wenn man z. B. Wanderungen, Schulausflüge oder private Spaziergänge in Richtung Lebus machte, musste man immer gegenwärtig sein, dass Grenzkontrollen waren, also man musste den Ausweis vorzeigen. Man konnte dann natürlich, wenn man einen Ausweis eingesteckt hatte und wenn man nicht besonders auffällig war, ganz ruhig weiter wandern, aber die Landschaft jenseits der Oder war für uns natürlich ganz weit weg."[16]

Eine Interviewpartnerin aus Zgorzelec erzählte von Schwierigkeiten bei Familienbesuchen: „Man musste Einlassscheine haben, es gab Grenzkontrollen und das war nicht angenehm. Wenn man ausreiste, musste man von den Grenzschutzsoldaten kontrolliert werden. Es gab schlechte Verbindungen. Meine Familie aus Warschau und Kielce besuchte uns oft. Meine 70-jährige Tante vergaß einmal irgendwelches Papier und sie wurde unter Begleitung der Grenzschutzsoldaten durch die ganze Stadt zum Arrest geführt, weil sie verdächtig war."[17]

Während die westlichen Teile von Flüchtlingen und Aussiedlern überfüllt waren, wurde im jeweiligen Ostteil erst eine Ansiedlungsaktion organisiert. Zu den ersten Bewohnern der Nord- und Westgebiete Polens gehörten die rückkehrenden Zwangsarbeiter, die Insassen der befreiten Konzentrationslager sowie Remigranten aus Westeuropa und die Militärsiedler. Dann folgten Umsiedler aus den an die Sowjetunion gefallenen Ostgebieten und Zugezogene aus Zentralpolen sowie den südlichen Woiwodschaften. Ein Gubiner betonte im Gespräch die Unsicherheit der neuen Ansiedler: „Diese Straße Piastowska, die entlang der Neiße nach oben bis WOP (Grenzschutzsoldaten) führt, sie war für die Zivilisten geschlossen. Das war hier der Eiserne Vorhang, so nannten wir sie, dort lag sie, nicht wahr [...] auf jeden

---

[15] Gubener Heimatbrief 1 (1995): 12-13.

[16] Interview mit Frau Alsbeshausen, Frankfurt (Oder), 9.1.1997, zit. n. Jajesniak-Quast und Stokłosa, *Geteilte Städte*, 68.

[17] Interview mit Frau M.G. aus Zgorzelec, 16.12.2003, Privatarchiv der Autorin.

Fall blühte das Leben wie nötig. Dort [in Guben] konnte man gleich nach dem Krieg den Wiederaufbau beobachten, das, weil sie sich dort als Besitzer fühlten und wir hier wie auf einer Bombe gesessen haben. In jedem Moment konnten wir erwarten, dass wir diese Gebiete werden verlassen müssen."[18]

An der Grenze trafen sich Sieger und Verlierer, schreibt Anna Wolff-Powęska, Pioniere des Aufbaus, die auf diesem Terrain ein neues Leben anfingen, sowie Grundeigentümer, die Haus und Hof hatten verlassen müssen. Plünderer (*szabrownicy*) auf der Suche nach leichter Beute mischten sich mit denen, die im Kriege alles verloren hatten. Ehrgeizige Zukunftsplaner fanden sich in Gesellschaft leichtlebiger Abenteurer, die im „wilden Westen" überleben wollten, wo Rechtlosigkeit, Korruption und das Faustrecht über die weitere Entwicklung der Region entschieden. Alle diese Menschen wurden mit unterschiedlichen Ideologien, Traditionen und Plänen für die Verwendung dieser Gebiete konfrontiert.[19]

Nach dem Krieg versuchten die kommunistischen Machthaber, die Erinnerungskulturen auf beiden Seiten des Flusses zu bestimmen und zu monopolisieren. In deutschen Stadtteilen war die neue Geschichtspolitik mit dem Mythos vom Antifaschismus verbunden. Die Abgrenzung vom Nationalsozialismus bildete die Grundlage für die politische Machtbildung in der SBZ/DDR. Dabei wies der Antifaschismus zwei Komponenten auf: eine historische, die auf Aussagen zur Geschichte der kommunistischen Opposition gegen das NS-Regime beruhte (Geschichtskonstruktion), und eine legitimatorische, die die Staatsgründung der DDR mit der ersten Komponente rechtfertigte. Widerstand und Opfertod erhielten also ihren Sinn nicht nur aus dem historischen Kontext des Nationalsozialismus, sondern aus der gesellschaftlichen Ordnung der DDR.[20] Somit bildete die schnelle Entnazifizierung die Priorität der neuen Macht.

In den östlichen Städten war die Polonisierung des übernommenen Landes, offiziell „Repolonisierung" genannt, die wichtigste Aufgabe. Dabei spielte die piastische Staatenkonzeption, die zu einem Mythos[21] heranwuchs, eine wichtige Rolle bei der Begründung der Angliederung der deutschen Gebiete an den Westen Polens. Es wurden die Lebendigkeit und Dauerhaftigkeit der piastischen Traditionen in den neuen Nord- und Westgebieten betont. Man sprach von der „Rückkehr der

---

[18] Interview Nr. 24, zit. n. Julita Makaro, *Gubin – miasto graniczne* [Guben – eine Grenzstadt] (Wrocław: Wydawnictwo Uniwersytetu Wrocławskiego, 2007), 179.

[19] Anna Wolff-Powęska, „Die doppelte Identität in den Nord- und Westgebieten Polens," in *Deutschlands Osten – Polens Westen,* hg. Matthias Weber (Frankfurt/Main: Peter Lang, 2001), 17-29.

[20] Vgl. Jürgen Danyel, „Die Opfer- und Verfolgtenperspektive als Gründungskonsens? Zum Umgang mit der Widerstandstradition und der Schuldfrage in der DDR," in *Die geteilte Vergangenheit. Zum Umgang mit Nationalsozialismus und Widerstand in beiden deutschen Staaten,* hg. Jürgen Danyel (Berlin: Akad.-Verlag, 1995), 31-46.

[21] Zur Entstehungsgeschichte des Piasten-Mythos vgl. Jerzy Strzelczyk, „Die Piasten – Tradition und Mythos in Polen," in *Mythen in Geschichte und Geschichtsschreibung aus polnischer und deutscher Sicht,* hg. Adelheid von Saldern (Münster: Lit, 1996), 113-131.

Piasten-Länder," die nur von den Deutschen „okkupiert" gewesen waren. Die „wiedergewonnenen Gebiete" wurden von der kommunistischen Macht als einer von wenigen Faktoren betrachtet, die die Gesellschaft an die neue Macht binden sollten.[22] Bereits im Jahre 1944 rief man im Manifest des Polnischen Komitees für Nationale Befreiung (PKWN) vom 22. Juli alle Polen zum Kampf um die Rückkehr der vormals polnischen Gebiete wie Pommern, Oppelner Schlesien, Ostpreußen auf, um einen breiten Zugang zum Meer zu bekommen und polnische Grenzsäulen an der Oder zu errichten.[23]

Um das Ziel der Polonisierung zu erreichen, versuchte man alle Spuren des Deutschtums aus der Öffentlichkeit und auch aus dem Privatleben zu entfernen. Es handelte sich hier um Kulturgüter wie Denkmäler, Bücher, Andachtstafeln etc.,[24] aber auch um deutsche Inschriften auf Geschirr, Kleidern, Aschenbechern und anderen Gegenständen des täglichen Bedarfs. Die „Repolonisierungsaktion" sollte auch Kirchen, Kapellen, Friedhöfe und Straßenkreuze umfassen. In Vergnügungslokalen war das Singen oder Abspielen von deutschen Liedern streng verboten.[25] Doch die ersten Aktionen beruhten meistens auf wilden Zerstörungen, die oft aus Rachegefühlen hervorgingen. So wurden auch Grabsteine auf den Friedhöfen und sogar Gebetsbücher zerstört.

Auch deutsch klingende Vor- und Nachnamen sollten geändert werden. Die Änderung der Vornamen betraf meistens Kinder, deren Eltern Angst vor Diskriminierung hatten. Eine Frau erzählt folgende Episode: „Heute war ich mit meiner Mutter in einem Amt, es hieß – Starostei. Man sagte, dass mein Vorname Hildegard deutsch ist und dass ich ihn in einen polnischen Vornamen ändern muss. Die Geschwister haben bestimmt schon polnische Vornamen, da nur ich hingegangen bin. Sie heißen: Aniela, Wanda, Hubert, Bernard. Ein Mann von dem Amt fragte, ob mir Halina gefällt und ob ich so heißen möchte. Ich sagte ja. Und so bin ich ab heute Halina. Vielleicht ist es besser so? Wenn ich gut Polnisch spreche,

---

[22] Vgl. Krystyna Kersten, *Narodziny systemu władzy. Polska 1943-1949* [Die Geburt des Machtsystems. Polen 1943-1949] (Poznań: SAWW, 1990), 147.

[23] Vgl. Ryszard Sudziński, „Taktyka i propaganda władz komunistycznych w stosunku do ziem odzyskanych w latach 1944-1949," [Strategie und Propaganda der kommunistischen Macht in Bezug auf die wiedergewonnenen Gebiete in den Jahren 1944-1949] in *Władze komunistyczne wobec ziem odzyskanych po II wojnie światowej. Materiały z konferencji* [Das Verhältnis der kommunistischen Machthaber zu den Wiedergewonnenen Gebieten nach dem Zweiten Weltkrieg. Konferenzmaterialien], hg. Stanisław Łach (Słupsk: Wydawnictwo WSP, 1997), 8.

[24] Vgl. Zbigniew Mazur, „Die Einleitung," in *Wokół niemieckiego dziedzictwa kulturowego na Ziemiach Zachodnich i Północnych* [Vom deutschen Kulturerbe in den West- und Nordgebieten], hg. Zbigniew Mazur (Poznań: Instytut Zachodni, 1997), I-XXVI.

[25] Staatsarchiv Wrocław: Urząd Wojewódzki Wrocławski, Wydział Społeczno-Polityczny, Sprawy repolonizacji, interwencja 1949, Sign. VI/750: *Rundschreiben Nr. 18 des Ministeriums für Wiedergewonnene Gebiete betr. Verstärkung der Repolonisierungsaktion in den Wiedergewonnenen Gebieten*, 26.4.1948.

werden alle denken, dass ich eine echte Polin bin. Nun aber wenn ich weiterhin Hildegard heiße, dann weiß jeder, dass es ein deutscher Vorname ist."[26]

Neben einer starken Propaganda auf Grundlage der „Piasten-Legende" wurde ein negatives Bild von Deutschland, den Deutschen und der Gefahr des Revisionismus verbreitet, was als Integrationsfaktor für die polnische Gesellschaft dienen sollte.[27]

Da die polnischen und deutschen Kommunisten im sowjetischen Block mit der Entstehung der DDR auf den Aufbau von nachbarschaftlichen Beziehungen angewiesen waren, wurde dieses negative Bild nur auf Westdeutschland bezogen. Die Grenzregionen und insbesondere Grenzstädte wie Frankfurt (Oder)/Słubice, Guben/Gubin und Görlitz/Zgorzelec bildeten Sonderfälle, denn sie konnten nach Kriegsende ohne eine gewisse Zusammenarbeit nicht funktionieren. Nachdem der frühere Stadtorganismus geteilt wurde, blieben z. B. die Gasanlage in Zgorzelec, das Elektrizitätswerk und Wasserwerk aber in Görlitz.[28]

Die verlorene Heimat wurde auf beiden Seiten tabuisiert. Weder deutsche Flüchtlinge und Vertriebene, noch polnische Umsiedler aus „Kresy" durften von ihrem Schicksal sprechen.

2. Der Fluss als Grenze der Freundschaft und des Friedens

Die große Anzahl an Flüchtlingen und Vertriebenen in der SBZ/DDR beeinflusste auch die Einstellung der KPD/SED in der Frage der Grenze zu Polen. In den ersten Nachkriegsjahren ging die Führungsspitze der SED von der Vorläufigkeit der Gebietszuweisungen nach der Potsdamer Konferenz aus.[29] Doch unter dem Druck Moskaus musste die DDR die Grenze an Oder und Lausitzer Neiße akzeptieren. Am 6. Juli 1950 wurde in Zgorzelec der Grenzvertrag unterschrieben. Beide Seiten stellten in Artikel 1 fest: „...dass die festgelegte und bestehende Grenze, [...] die Staatsgrenze zwischen Deutschland und Polen bildet."[30]

---

[26] *Erinnerungen der Siedler*, in Archiv des Westinstituts Posen, Sign. P 577, 12.

[27] *Deutschland – von Polen gesehen. Zu den deutsch-polnischen Beziehungen 1945-1990*, hg. der Polnischen Stiftung für Internationale Angelegenheiten/Mieczysław Tomala (Marburg: Schüren Verlag, 2000), 25.

[28] Vg. Archiwum Ministerstwa Spraw Zagranicznych [Archiv des Ministeriums für Außenbeziehungen], z. 3, w. 1, t. 1: Bericht des Mitglieds der Kommission für Grenzstudien bei dem Komitee für Auslandsangelegenheiten der Wiedergewonnenen Gebiete, aus den Erkundungen in der Grenzzone Gubin – Zittau für den Zeitraum vom 31. 01. bis 5.02.1947, zit. n. *Polska wobec Radzieckiej Strefy Okupacyjnej maj 1945 – październik 1949* [Polen gegenüber der Sowjetischen Militäradministration Mai 1945 – Juli 1949], hg. Jerzy Kochanowski und Klaus Ziemer Klaus (Warszawa: Neriton, 2006), 206-212.

[29] Vgl. Andreas Malycha, „Die SED und die Oder-Neiße-Grenze bis zum Görlitzer Vertrag 1950," in *Grenzen im Ostblock und ihre Überwindung*, hg. Helga Schultz (Berlin: Spitz, 2001), 81-111.

[30] Staatsarchiv Wrocław, Filiale in Lauban, Miejska Rada Narodowa i Zarząd Miejski w Zgorzelcu, Sign. 37/6: *Chronik der Stadt Zgorzelice*.

Die Unterzeichnung des Vertrages wurde von einer starken Propaganda über Freundschaft und Frieden begleitet, die sich symbolisch auch in den Straßennamen der Städte widerspiegelte: In Guben wurde die Alte Poststraße in Cyrankiewicz-Straße umbenannt, in Gubin erhielt eine Straße den Namen Ulica Wilhelma Piecka.[31] In Frankfurt (Oder) wurden der Posener Ring in Cyrankiewicz-Platz, der Bromberger-Ring in Bierut-Ring[32] umbenannt. Die Promenaden und Brückenstraße in Görlitz hießen nun Bolesław-Bierut-Straße, der Otto-Müller-Park wurde in Park des Friedens umbenannt.

Doch die Vertriebenen taten sich schwer mit der Anerkennung der deutsch-polnischen Grenze im Görlitzer Vertrag. So war im Jahre 1953 während des Aufstands vom 17. Juni in Görlitz der Ruf nach einer Revision der Oder-Neiße-Grenze zu hören. Dieselbe Forderung kam von der intellektuellen Opposition im Jahre 1956: Wolfgang Harich sprach sich in seinem Memorandum zur weltgeschichtlichen Situation für die Rückkehr der größeren Teile Pommerns, der östlichen Mark Brandenburg, Schlesiens und Ostpreußens in das Gebiet der DDR aus.[33]

Für manche polnischen Bewohner der Grenzstädte brachte der Vertrag eine gewisse Sicherheit, doch die Mehrheit lebte bis in die 1970er Jahre hinein in Angst vor der Rückkehr der Deutschen. Ein Gubiner erzählt: „Am schlimmsten für diese Stadt war, dass jeder mehr oder weniger auf gepackten Koffern saß. [...] Die Mehrheit der Einwohner fühlte sich unsicher. Der morgige Tag war ungewiss. Es war unklar, wie die Politik sein wird, ob die Grenze hier verlaufen wird, oder ob Gubin deutsch wird, weil sich die Grenzen ändern."[34]

Anfang der 1950er Jahre begann man, Brücken und Eisenbahnviadukte aufzubauen und die Stadtverwaltungen knüpften für die gemeinsame Nutzung von Wasser- und Gaswerken die notwendigsten Kontakte. Mit dem „Tauwetter" nach 1956 kam eine gesteuerte Liberalisierung der Grenze.[35] Es wurden vor allem offizielle Treffen von Parteisekretären, Delegationen von Arbeitern und Jugendlichen abgehalten. Mit Einladungsschreiben durfte man nun die Grenze überschreiten. Auch wurden Kultur- und Sportveranstaltungen organisiert. Für die propagierte Freundschaft zwischen der DDR und der VR Polen bildete sich in folgenden Jahren

---

[31] Vgl. Jajeśniak-Quast und Stokłosa, *Geteilte Städte*, 66.

[32] Stadtarchiv Frankfurt (Oder), „Stadtverordnetenversammlung und Rat der Stadt Frankfurt (Oder)," zit. n. ebd.

[33] Vgl. Werner Mittenzwei, *Die Intellektuellen. Literatur und Politik in Ostdeutschland von 1945 bis 2000* (Leipzig: Faber & Faber, 2001), 141.

[34] Zit. n. Katarzyna Stokłosa, *Grenzstädte in Ostmitteleuropa. Guben und Gubin 1945 bis 1995* (Berlin: Spitz, 2003), 135.

[35] Vgl. Hieronim Szczegóła, „Polsko-niemiecka współpraca przygraniczna w latach 1945-1990," [Die deutsch-polnische grenzüberschreitende Zusammenarbeit in den Jahren 1945-1990] *Rocznik Lubuski* 17 (1992): 185.

der Begriff „zwangsverordnete Freundschaft"[36] heraus: „Es gab eine Zeit, als auf der Brücke Gras wuchs. Aber weil sie die Brücke der Freundschaft genannt wurde, trafen sich von Zeit zu Zeit, während für uns unverständlicher Festtage [...], auf ihrer Mitte beide Nationen. [...] Für uns waren das Begegnungen der Dritten Art. Wir wunderten uns, dass ein typischer Deutscher keinen Helm oder keine Handgranaten trägt und sich ruhig verhält."[37]

Im Jahre 1967 wurde ein Abkommen unterzeichnet, wonach polnische Bürger, insbesondere Frauen, in den Grenzregionen der DDR beschäftigt werden konnten. Aufgrund dieses Abkommens wurden viele polnische Frauen im Feinoptischen Werk sowie im Kondensatorenwerk in Görlitz, im Chemiefaserkombinat in Guben und im Halbleiterwerk in Frankfurt (Oder) beschäftigt.

Dennoch bedeutete erst die nächste Etappe in der Geschichte der Grenze, also die Jahre 1972-1980, einen Durchbruch in den Beziehungen zwischen den Nachbarn an der Grenze. Die Öffnung der deutsch-polnischen Grenze am 1. Januar 1972 für den pass- und visafreien Verkehr wird oft als „Wunder an der Oder" bezeichnet. Das Abkommen zwischen den neuen Machthabern Edward Gierek und Erich Honecker hatte vor allem einen politischen Charakter. Nach Aussage von Gierek sollte die Öffnung der Grenze auch einen weiteren Schritt in der deutsch-polnischen Versöhnung nach dem Muster Bundesrepublik – Frankreich darstellen.[38]

Diese Periode brachte für die Grenzgebiete eine neue Realität. Die Einwohner der geteilten Stadt durften erstmals lernen, was Nachbarschaft bedeutet. Und das Interesse daran war groß: In den Jahren 1972-1979 passierten polnische und deutsche Bürger die deutsch-polnische Grenze über 100 Millionen Mal.[39] Die deutschen Grenzraumbewohner begaben sich auf „Heimwehreisen," um ihre alten Häuser und Höfe, Schulen und Kirchen anzuschauen. Diese Besucher lösten bei manchen Polen Angst aus, wurden von anderen jedoch herzlich empfangen. Es wurden viele Bekanntschaften und Freundschaften begründet. So wurden in den Jahren 1972-1974 40 Ehen zwischen Bürgern aus Słubice und Frankfurt (Oder) geschlossen,[40] für

[36] Vgl. Ludwig Mehlhorn, „Zwangsverordnete Freundschaft? Zur Entwicklung der Beziehungen zwischen der DDR und Polen," in *Zwangsverordnete Freundschaft? Die Beziehungen zwischen der DDR und Polen 1949-1990*, hg. Basil Kerski, Andrzej Kotula und Kazimierz Wóycicki (Osnabrück: Fibre, 2003), 35- 40.

[37] Stanisław Lisiecki, „Słubice jako miasto pogranicza," [Słubice als Grenzstadt] in *Słubice 1945-1995*, hg. Maria Rutowska (Poznań: Urząd Miejski, 1996).

[38] Vgl. Jerzy Kochanowski, „Socjologiczny zwiad po otwarciu granic PRL-NRD," [Das soziologische Interview nach der Öffnung der Grenze zwischen der VR Polen und der DDR] *Polski Przegląd Dyplomatyczny* 2 (2001): 229-255.

[39] Vgl. Hieronim Szczegóła, „Polsko-niemiecka współpraca przygraniczna w latach 1945-1990," [Die polnisch-deutsche grenzüberschreitende Zusammenarbeit in den Jahren 1945-1990] *Rocznik Lubuski* 17 (1992): 190.

[40] Maria Rutowska, „Die regionale Zusammenarbeit in den deutsch-polnischen Grenzregionen in den Jahren 1945-1990," in *Grenze der Hoffnung. Geschichte und Perspektiven der Grenzregion an der Oder*, hg. Helga Schultz und Alan Nothnagle (Potsdam: Verlag für Berlin-Brandenburg, 1996), 46.

Görlitz und Zgorzelec waren es 1963-1979 85 Ehen[41] und für Guben und Gubin 1972-1979 64 Ehen.[42]

Doch was diese Zeit prägte, waren nicht die Heimatreisen und die deutsch-polnischen Eheschließungen. In das Gedächtnis der beiden Gesellschaften gingen vielmehr die massiven Einkäufe deutscher Produkte durch polnische Touristen ein, bedingt durch die schlechte Versorgung in polnischen Geschäften. Dies wurde oft mit Schwarzhandel in Verbindung gebracht und rief unter der deutschen Bevölkerung großen Unmut hervor. In der DDR kursierte folgender Polenwitz: „Um 12 Uhr wird nun in den Kaufhäusern die polnische Nationalhymne gespielt, die Masse der Polen steht dann stramm, und wir können unsere Einkäufe erledigen."

Adam Krzemiński, Publizist der Wochenzeitschrift *Polityka*, beurteilt in seinem Artikel „Der Oder-Neiße-Komplex" die Kontakte zwischen den Bürgern der DDR und der VR-Polen sehr kritisch. Seiner Meinung nach behielten die Deutschen nur Scharen von Polen in Erinnerung, die die DDR-Geschäfte leer kaufen wollten, und die Polen Schikanen von Grenzbeamten, deren Uniformen – besonders ältere Menschen – an die Wehrmacht erinnerten. Weder im deutschen noch im polnischen Bewusstsein seien Spuren von Versuchen zu finden, literarische Brücken über die Oder und Neiße zu bauen, obwohl es in der DDR-Literatur eine Periode gab, in der man sich vom „polnischen Anderssein" durchaus faszinieren ließ. Für die Polen wohnten die „echten Deutschen" westlich der Elbe. Die offene Grenze habe gezeigt, wie es den beiden Gesellschaften an einer gemeinsamen Sprache fehlte. Nach der Schließung der Grenze 1980 versuchte die DDR-Propaganda, das eigene Volk zu überzeugen, dass die Polen, die noch kurz zuvor als Freunde bezeichnet und der ewigen und lebendigen Freundschaft versichert worden waren, Friedensstörer seien. Und wenn wir noch ergänzen, dass Honecker mit seinen Panzern gerne über die Oder und Neiße nach Osten marschiert wäre – was die Polen sicher gespürt haben – wundert es nicht, dass das Bild der DDR in den Augen der Polen negative Züge bekam.[43]

Soziologische Forschungen dieser Zeit zeigen sowohl positive, als auch negative Folgen der Grenzöffnung. Das Image der Grenzregion ist in dieser Zeit besser geworden. Viele verordnete Dienstkontakte entwickelten sich zu Privatkontakten. Jedoch entstanden auch neue Stereotype über das Einkaufsverhalten von Polen in deutschen Geschäften.[44]

---

[41] „Zusammenarbeit zwischen den Städten Zgorzelec und Görlitz, 5.7.1979," Ratsarchiv Görlitz, Beziehungen zu Novy Jicin (CSSR), Zgorzelec (VR-Polen) u. SUL Garnison Lodenau, Görlitzer Schulen (1976-89), Sign. 1086.

[42] Vgl. Makaro, *Guben*, 105.

[43] Adam Krzemiński, „Kompleks Odry i Nysy," [Der Oder-Neiße-Komplex] *Polityka*, 3 September 1994, 12-13.

[44] Andrzej Kwilecki, „Socjologiczne aspekty otwarcia granicy między Polska a NRD (raport z badań)," [Soziologische Aspekte der Öffnung der Grenze zwischen Polen und der DDR. Ein Forschungsbericht]

Die wachsende Bedeutung der Solidarność-Bewegung in Polen führte dazu, dass am 20. Oktober 1980 die Grenze geschlossen wurde.

3. Die Grenze überwinden – die Zusammenarbeit im Rahmen der Euroregionen

Die politische Transformation in Polen und Deutschland eröffnete neue Chancen für die Grenzstädte. Anfang der 1990er Jahre wurden schnell Partnerschaftsabkommen unterzeichnet. Vorgesehen war die Zusammenarbeit in den Bereichen Schulwesen und Gesundheitswesen, zwischen Feuerwehren, ebenso eine gemeinsame Kommunalwirtschaft in der Wasser- und Energieversorgung sowie die Kooperation in der Umwelt- und Stadtplanung.[45] Wenig später kam es zur Gründung von Euroregionen: Am 21.12.1991 entstand die Euroregion Neiße, der Zgorzelec und Görlitz angehören; am 21.09.1993 die Euroregion Spree-Neiße-Bober, der die Städte Guben und Gubin angehören, und am 21.12.1993 die Euroregion Pro Europa Viadrina, zu der Słubice und Frankfurt (Oder) gehören. Im Bildungswesen schritt die Zusammenarbeit zügig voran: Im Jahre 1994 entstanden in Frankfurt (Oder) ein deutsch-polnischer Kindergarten, die Europa-Universität Viadrina und das Collegium Polonicum. In Guben wurde eine Europa-Gesamtschule eingerichtet. Heutzutage lernen in Sachsen ca. 1700 Schüler Polnisch als Fremdsprache und Görlitz ist die einzige Stadt in Deutschland, wo Schüler Polnisch von der ersten Klasse bis zum Abitur lernen können. Auch in Sachsen wurden im Jahr 2008 ergänzende Unterrichtsmaterialien für das Fach Geschichte „Geschichte verstehen – Zukunft gestalten" gemeinsam von polnischen und deutschen Historikern herausgegeben, die vor allem in den Schulen in Sachsen und Niederschlesien genutzt werden.[46]

Durch die europäische Integration und Förderprogramme für Grenzregionen, wie z. B. INTERREG, durch die Maastricht-Verträge und das Schengen-Abkommen wurden viele Grenzbarrieren abgebaut. Allerdings wurden die Barrieren nach Osten verlegt. Die Einführung der Visumspflicht und insbesondere der hohe Preis für ein Visum, wie es Anna Tomaszewska in ihrem Beitrag in diesem Heft darstellt, erschweren jetzt die Grenzüberschreitung zwischen Polen und der Ukraine.

Die Doppelstädte versuchten, in der europäischen Identität einen Ausweg aus nationalen Antagonismen zu finden. Während der Europawoche vom 2. bis 9. Mai 1998 wurde am 5. Mai in einer gemeinsamen Stadtratssitzung die Europastadt

---

in Archiwum Akt Nowych, Urząd Rady Ministrów (Archiv der Neuen Akte, Ministerrat), Sign. 2.7/6, k. 30-55; hier nach Kochanowski, *Socjologiczny zwiad,* 240-255.

[45] Vgl. Czesław Osękowski und Hieronim Szczegóła, *Pogranicze polsko-niemieckie w okresie transformacji 1989-1997* [Das deutsch-polnische Grenzgebiet in der Transformationszeit 1989-1997] (Zielona Góra: Wydawnictwo WSP, 1999), 211.

[46] Vgl. Katrin Schröder, „Język polski na pograniczu. Portret saksońskiej inicjatywy edukacyjnej," *Dialog* 94 (2010-2011): 95-97.

Görlitz/Zgorzelec proklamiert, deren Ziel „eine Stadt – zwei Völker" sein sollte. Im selben Jahr entstand die Eurostadt Guben-Gubin.

In den Doppelstädten an der deutsch-polnischen Grenze sprechen Lokalpolitiker immer häufiger von der Überwindung der Grenze und von grenzüberschreitender Kooperation. Eine europäische Identität wird als neues Identifikationsmuster für die Stadtbewohner beiderseits des Flusses angeboten. Doch ohne eine Auseinandersetzung mit den tabuisierten Problemen wird das europäische Image der Grenzstädte lediglich als neue Floskel der Politiker empfunden.

Grenzüberschreitende Zusammenarbeit entwickelt sich nicht automatisch. Gute Voraussetzungen dafür bilden eine gemeinsame Geschichte, Bilingualität, gemeinsame Interessen und letztendlich die gemeinsame Identifikation mit der Doppelstadt und die gemeinsame Identität der Bewohner dieser Stadt. Für die Doppelstädte an der deutsch-polnischen Grenze sind dies noch Aufgaben der Zukunft.

Elżbieta Opiłowska
opilowska@wbz.uni.wroc.pl

*****

a) *Isolierte Grenzregionen* – Regionen, die praktisch ohne Verbindungen zwischen den beiden Seiten der Grenze existieren. Die Regionen können sich im Kriegszustand befinden und sich politisch und ideologisch stark voneinander unterscheiden. Die Grenze wird streng kontrolliert, es gibt keine Zusammenarbeit; die ganze Grenzzone ist schwach besiedelt und bewirtschaftet.

b) *Koexistierende Grenzregionen* – es existieren Starke emotionale Barrieren zwischen den beiden Grenzgesellschaften, die aus den Erfahrungen des Krieges oder ungelösten Grenzproblemen resultieren.

c) *Kooperierende Grenzregionen* – bilden eine Symbiose der Grenzregionen; Einwohner und Wirtschaftssubjekte entwickeln eine enge grenzüberschreitende Zusammenarbeit, Einwohnermigration und freier Warenverkehr sind typisch. Eine gute Voraussetzung für die Herausbildung einer kooperierenden Grenzregion ist ein vergleichbares wirtschaftlich-gesellschaftliches Niveau, denn schwächere Regionen werden immer benachteiligt.

d) *Integrierte Grenzregionen* – Grenzregionen dieser Art entstehen, wenn zwischen den Nachbarstaaten die Barrieren im Handel und in gesellschaftlichen Beziehungen verschwinden, wenn es keine großen politischen Unterschiede gibt und freier Verkehr von Arbeitskräften, Waren, Dienstleistungen und Kapital herrscht. Die Idee eines gemeinsamen Zusammenlebens ersetzt nationale Ideen. Die Regionen verzichten zugunsten gemeinsamer Ziele freiwillig auf einen Teil ihrer Souveränität. Dieser Typ der Grenzregion ist heutzutage in Lothringen an der deutsch-französischen Grenze zu finden.

Quelle: Oscar J. Martinez, „The Dynamics of Border Interaction," in *Global Boundaries. World Boundaries*, hg. Clive H. Schofield, Vol. 1 (New York: Routledge, 1994), 3.

DIE POLNISCHE OSTGRENZE ALS NEUE EU-AUßENGRENZE

Paradigmenwechsel zwischen der EU und der Ukraine

Anna Tomaszewska
Willy Brandt-Zentrum für Deutschland- und Europastudien der Universität Breslau

Die Erweiterung der Europäischen Union ist nicht nur für die Mitgliedsstaaten eine Herausforderung, sie schafft auch eine neue Situation für die Nachbarn der EU: Neue Mitgliedsstaaten, die den *acquis communitaire* übernehmen, verschärfen ihre Grenzregime.

Seit dem EU-Beitritt hat der polnische Grenzschutz die Aufgabe übernommen, die Außengrenze der EU zu schützen. Das war für die EU eine große Veränderung – die neuen Mitgliedsstaaten sollten von jetzt an für die Sicherheit der ganzen Gemeinschaft sorgen. Für Polen war der Schritt noch wichtiger, weil er auch bedeutete, dass die Kontakte zu den wichtigsten Nachbarn im Osten neu bestimmt werden mussten. Mit dem EU-Beitritt im Jahr 2004 hat sich Polen verpflichtet, auch dem Schengen-Raum beizutreten und alle notwendigen Veränderungen durchzuführen. Dabei war es unter anderem notwendig, die Struktur des Grenzschutzes anzupassen und seine Aufgaben neu zu definieren (jeweils unterschiedlich an der Westgrenze zu Deutschland und an der Ostgrenze). Mit der Unterstützung der EU-Mitgliedsstaaten, insbesondere Deutschlands, konnte der Grenzschutz auch die technische Ausstattung auf den neuen Stand bringen. Bis jetzt hat sich der polnische Grenzschutz bei der Erfüllung seiner Aufgaben einen guten Ruf erworben. Der Schengen-Beitritt war für Polen eindeutig positiv; es gab aber auch einige Probleme, die die östlichen Nachbarn betrafen, insbesondere die Ukraine. So musste die Visumspflicht für die Ukraine 2003 wieder eingeführt werden, wobei die Visa entgeltlich vergeben werden sollten. Gleichzeitig einigte man sich auf ein Abkommen über Erleichterungen bei Visa-Erteilung. Was die ukrainische Seite heute als problematisch meldet, sind die Wartezeiten für die Visa-Erteilung, die steigende Zahl von Absagen und die niedrige Zahl von Mehrfachvisa für längere Zeiträume. All das beeinträchtigt das Bild der EU in der Ukraine und hinterlässt den Eindruck unfairer Behandlung.

In meinem Text möchte ich genauer nachprüfen, ob die Schengen-Erweiterung eine Auswirkung auf den Grenzverkehr hatte, und wenn ja, welche. Ich werde die Frage der Visumspflicht in den Kontext der Nachbarschaftspolitik stellen und zu zeigen versuchen, wie sich die Veränderungen auf bilaterale Beziehungen zwischen Mitglieds- und Nichtmitgliedsstaaten bzw. auf die Beziehungen der EU zu Drittstaaten auswirken.

EUROSTUDIA — REVUE TRANSATLANTIQUE DE RECHERCHE SUR L'EUROPE
Vol. 7, No.1-2 (2011): 167-174

Dieser Text und der Text von Elżbieta Opiłowska, der auch in diesem Heft zu finden ist, ergänzen sich thematisch. Sie stellt die westliche Grenze vor, mit den Problemen der Teilung, mein Text beschreibt, wie sich die Situation im Osten entwickelt. Die gegenseitigen Kontakte an der polnischen Westgrenze waren jahrelang durch Misstrauen und Kontrolle geprägt, bevor die Grenze geöffnet wurde. Die Ostgrenze schließt sich immer mehr. Hoffentlich wird sich an ihr die Geschichte der Teilung nicht wiederholen und die Grenze zu einem Faktor werden, der die Zusammenarbeit zwischen Polen und der Ukraine fördert.

1. Die Ostverschiebung der EU-Außengrenze und die Konsequenzen

Das Verlegen der Außengrenze der EU war ein langer, mehrere Jahre andauernder Prozess. Dabei war der 21. Dezember 2007, an dem die Grenzkontrollen durch Kompensationsmaßnahmen ersetzt wurden, nur ein symbolischer Moment. Am 15. August 2001 verabschiedete das polnische Komitee für Europäische Integration einen Schengen-Aktionsplan. Dieses Dokument beinhaltete einen detaillierten Plan, der die schrittweise Übernahme des Schengen-Regimes vorsah. Ab dem Jahr 2000 gab es auch eine Strategie für eine integrierte Grenzverwaltung,[1] die bestimmte, welche Aufgaben Polen vor dem Schengen-Beitritt erfüllen musste und wie die Aufgabenverteilung nach dem Beitritt verlaufen sollte.[2] Dieses Dokument zeigt auch, dass die Aufgaben für Polen politisch nicht leicht durchzuführen waren: „Die wichtigste Annahme war, dass Polen einen angemessenen Schutz der EU-Länder vor unerwünschten Personen und Gütern gewährleistet und gleichzeitig gute Kontakte zu den Nicht-EU-Ländern pflegt."[3]

Einerseits sollte Polen also die Grenze so undurchlässig wie möglich halten, andererseits sollten sich die Kontakte zu den Nachbarn nicht verschlechtern. Wie sollte das möglich sein? Polen war verpflichtet, die Visumspflicht für die Ukrainer einzuführen, was am 1. Oktober 2003 geschah. Dabei bemühte sich die polnische Seite, dies so liberal wie möglich zu tun: Die Visa waren kostenlos. Leider wurden jedoch die Wartezeiten zu einem echten Problem. Direkt nach der Einführung der Visumspflicht standen bis zu 2.000 Personen in der Warteschlange vor dem polnischen Konsulat in Lemberg, was 14 Tage Wartezeit bedeutete. Nach sechs Monaten (März 2004) gingen die Schlangen auf 100-200 Personen am Tag zurück.[4]

In der polnischen Öffentlichkeit war die Wiedereinführung der Visumspflicht für Ukrainer sehr umstritten: Einerseits gab es und gibt es immer noch Stimmen, die sagen, Polen solle die Ukraine unterstützen und leiste mit der Visumspflicht das Gegenteil von Unterstützung. Polen vergesse seine Wurzeln, lasse seine Verbündeten

---

[1] Auf Polnisch: *Strategia Zintegrowanego Zarządzania Granicą*.

[2] Adam Dudzic, *Polska w strefie Schengen* (Warszawa: Urząd Komitetu Integracji Europejskiej, 2009).

[3] Ebenda, 32.

[4] Karolina Stawicka und Aleksandra Zieleniec (Hg.) *Monitoring polskiej polityki wizowej- raport* (Warszawa: Fundacja im. Stefana Batorego, 2004), 64.

im Stich. Andererseits ist in der Presse nachzulesen, dass der EU-Beitritt Polen modernisiere und nur ein wirtschaftlich und politisch starkes Polen seine Nachbarn unterstützen könne. Kaum jemand ging darauf ein, dass Polen eigentlich keine Wahl hatte – die Visumspflicht für die Ukrainer war ein Teil des *acquis communitaire.*

In Polen und in der Ukraine wurde befürchtet, dass die Einführung der Visumspflicht einen erheblichen Einfluss auf den Grenzverkehr haben würde, denn die Visa-Prozeduren waren lang und bürokratisch. Doch wie die Statistik zeigt, waren die Befürchtungen unbegründet.

Im Jahr 2003 ist im Vergleich zu 2002 ein leichter Rückgang der Grenzübertritte zu beobachten (- 4,6%). Hier besteht aber nur ein geringer Zusammenhang mit der Visumspflicht, denn diese wurde erst im letzten Quartal eingeführt. Im Jahr 2004 ist eine leichte Steigerung zu erkennen; trotz Anfangsschwierigkeiten (Schlangen und lange Wartezeiten in polnischen Konsulaten) nahm der Verkehr wieder zu. Im Jahr 2005 kann man schon von einem Boom an der polnisch-ukrainischen Grenze sprechen, denn die Zahlen steigen fast um die Hälfte. Es gibt in diesem Jahr jedoch keine Visa-Erleichterungen, die eine solche Entwicklung des Grenzverkehrs erklären könnten.

Die ukrainische Regierung hat sich ihrerseits dafür entschieden, den visafreien Reiseverkehr für polnische Bürger beizubehalten. Die EU-Erweiterung hat also in dieser Hinsicht keine negativen Auswirkungen für Polen gehabt.

Der rasante Anstieg der Zahl der Grenzübertritte im Jahr 2005 ist schwer zu erklären. Auch die ökonomischen Werte machen das nicht leichter. Die Kursentwicklung, gemessen in Kaufkraftparität (engl. *Purchasing Power Parity*), war in beiden Ländern sehr unterschiedlich, stieg aber hier wie dort an. Erst im Jahr 2009 war wegen der Weltfinanzkrise in der Ukraine ein Rückgang und in Polen eine Abbremsung zu beobachten. 2005 ist weder in Polen noch in der Ukraine in der Wirtschaft etwas geschehen, was diese plötzliche Veränderung im Reiseverkehr erklären könnte.

Polen als ein sich schnell entwickelndes Land ist für die Ukraine das erste Ziel für Arbeitsmigration. Laut offiziellen Angaben werden jedes Jahr bis zu 3.000 Arbeitserlaubnisse für Ukrainer erteilt. Gleichzeitig übersteigt die Zahl der Visa, die polnische Konsulate in der Ukraine ausstellen, jährlich 500.000 (2004 waren es 589.000)[5]. Experten schätzen die Zahl der Schwarzarbeiter auf 50.000 bis 300.000. Man könnte das zunehmende Interesse an Grenzüberschreitung damit erklären, dass die Suche nach Arbeit die Menschen zu dieser Mobilität bewegt. Wenn man sich aber die Arbeitslosenstatistiken genauer anschaut und die Situation in beiden Ländern vergleicht, wird diese Erklärung entkräftet.

---

[5] Justyna Frelak, „Praca Ukraińców w Polsce," *Analizy i Opinie* 38 (Warszawa: Instytut Spraw Publicznych, 2005), 6.

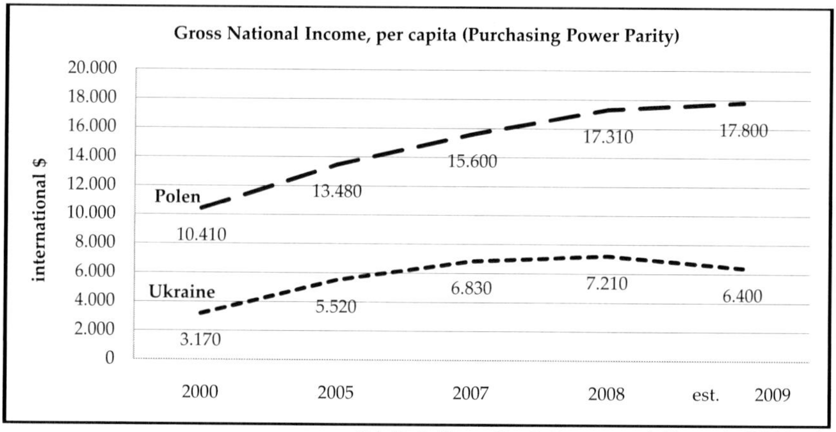

Tabelle 1: Eigene Bearbeitungen nach Daten der Weltbank.

Für Polen ist in den Jahren 2001-2004 eine hohe Arbeitslosenquote charakteristisch. Ab 2005 verbessert sich die Situation ein wenig, die Zahl der Arbeitslosen ist aber immer noch erheblich. Gleichzeitig sinkt ab 2000 in der Ukraine der Prozentsatz der Personen ohne Beschäftigung und liegt die ganze Zeit viel niedriger als in Polen. Trotzdem kann Polen für viele Ukrainer als Arbeitsmarkt attraktiv sein, weil das Lohnniveau dort entsprechend höher ist. Dennoch ist es unwahrscheinlich, dass gerade im Jahr 2005, als Polen selbst mit einer Arbeitslosigkeit von mehr als 18% zu kämpfen hat, das Land gleichzeitig bei den Nachbarn als Anziehungspunkt für Saisonarbeiter betrachtet wird. Diese Art der Beschäftigung dürfte eher für die Bewohner der Grenzregionen interessant sein.

Am 21. Dezember 2007 trat das Schengen-Regime offiziell in Kraft. Ab 2008 ist das auch in den Statistiken zu bemerken: Fast um 16% ist der Grenzverkehr zurückgegangen, was relativ beachtlich ist, weil in dieser Zahl sowohl die Ukrainer, als auch die Polen enthalten sind, die weiterhin einen visumsfreien Grenzverkehr genießen können. Das Jahr 2009 brachte einen weiteren Rückgang um 28%.

Die polnische Visapolitik war seit 2003 ziemlich liberal. Das Visum war entgeltlich zu haben; es gab zwar lange Wartezeiten, aber das Risiko, kein Visum zu bekommen, war sehr gering. Nur 1,7% aller eingereichten vollständigen Anträge wurden abgelehnt.[6] Ein Gespräch mit dem Konsul war eher die Ausnahme, die Prozedur beschränkte sich auf das Notwendigste. Der Schengen-Beitritt brachte nun auch eine gemeinsame Visapolitik mit sich. Die sog. Schengen-Prozedur ist viel komplizierter und erlaubt es kaum, das Visum noch am Tag der Antragstellung zu

[6] Stawicka und Zieleniec, *Monitoring polskiej polityki*, 116.

erteilen. 2005 schafften es die polnischen Konsulate, fast 70% alle Anträge direkt zu bearbeiten.[7]

ARBEITSLOSIGKEIT IN %		
	Polen	**Ukraine**
2000	14	12,4
2001	16,2	11,7
2002	19,7	10,3
2003	19,9	9,7
2004	19,5	9,2
2005	18,2	7,8
2006	16,2	7,4
2007	12,7	6,9
2008	9,8	6,9
2009	11	9,6

Quelle: Eigene Bearbeitungen nach Daten des polnischen „Central Statistical Office" und ukrainischen „State Statistics Committee."

Das neue Verfahren wurde vom Rat der EU festgelegt und ist als Gemeinsame Konsularische Instruktion[8] in Kraft getreten. Außer einer längeren Prozedur wurden auch relativ hohe Gebühren eingeführt. Ein Visum kostet jetzt 35 Euro,[9] was für einen durchschnittlichen Ukrainer ein Vermögen darstellt. Im Januar 2008 waren das 260 *Hrywnja* (UAH), im Juli 2009 schon 372 UAH, weil die Wirtschaftskrise die Ukraine besonders stark getroffen hat. Gleichzeitig war der Mindestlohn im Juli 2009 auf 630 UAH festgelegt, das Existenzminimum beträgt 669 UAH. Das Durchschnittseinkommen liegt im Jahr 2009 bei 1.906 UAH. Ein Schengen-Visum ist damit zum Luxusgut geworden.

Die oben gezeigten Statistiken erlauben die Schlussfolgerung, dass nicht die Einführung des Visums selbst und alle damit verbundenen Schwierigkeiten den polnisch-ukrainischen Grenzverkehr reiseunfreundlich machen und den gegenseitigen Kontakten schaden. Erst der Preis des Visums, zusammen mit der langen, komplizierten Prozedur, hat den Grenzverkehr auf den niedrigsten Stand seit 2003 gedrückt. Ein System wird nicht dadurch repressiver, dass es neue administrative Barrieren schafft. Das Zusammenspiel von Bürokratie und entgeltlichen Visa aber macht die Ostgrenze der EU für viele ihrer Nachbarn unzugänglich.

2. Erleichterungen im Rahmen von Schengen: Systeme, die es ermöglichen, die Grenze zwischen der Ukraine und Polen durchlässiger zu gestalten

Am 18. Dezember 2007 trat das Abkommen zwischen der Europäischen Gemeinschaft und der Ukraine über Erleichterungen bei der Erteilung von Visa[10] in Kraft. Dieses ermöglicht es den Ukrainern, ein Visum für 35 Euro anstatt von 60 Euro

---

[7] Joanna Liczner (Hg.), *Zmiany w polityce wizowej państw UE. Raport z monitoringu* (Warszawa: Fundacja im. Stefana Batorego, 2009), 56.

[8] „Gemeinsame Konsularische Instruktion an die Diplomatischen Missionen und die Konsularischen Vertretungen," *Amtsblatt der Europäischen Gemeinschaften*, 16.12.2002, C 313/1.

[9] 35 EUR stellen bereits eine Ermäßigung der Visumsgebühr dar, die sich vor dem Visumserleichterungsabkommen zwischen der Ukraine und der EU auf 60 EUR belief.

[10] „Abkommen zwischen der Europäischen Gemeinschaft und der Ukraine über Erleichterungen bei der Erteilung von Visa," *Amtsblatt der Europäischen Union*, 18.12.2007, L 332/68.

zu bekommen. Das bedeutet zwar eine Ermäßigung, ändert aber nichts an der Tatsache, dass das Visum nach wie vor teuer ist. Für manche Personengruppen sind die Visa immer noch unentgeltlich, dazu gehören Schüler, Studenten, Rentner oder Pensionäre sowie Teilnehmer an offiziellen Austauschprogrammen von Partnerstädten.

Ein Visum-Verfahren kann bis zu 10 Kalendertage dauern.[11] Einerseits schafft eine feste Frist Transparenz im Verfahren, anderseits bedeutet sie im Vergleich zu den polnischen Prozeduren aus dem Jahr 2003 eine beträchtliche Verlängerung.

Art. 5 des Abkommens enthält eine Liste von Personen, die ein Mehrfachvisum beantragen können, darunter Journalisten, Lkw- und Busfahrer, Geschäftsleute. Obwohl diese Möglichkeit vorgesehen ist, wird sie selten genutzt. Das gleiche Problem betrifft Langzeitvisa: Visa mit einer Gültigkeit über 3 Jahren werden kaum erteilt.[12]

Das Abkommen sieht als langfristiges Ziel für Staatsangehörige der Ukraine die Befreiung von der Visumspflicht vor. Es gibt aber derzeit keine Verhandlungen, die dieses Ziel näher bringen könnten.

Als eine Art von Erleichterung gilt ein Vertrag über den kleinen Grenzverkehr zwischen Polen und der Ukraine: Seit dem 1. Juli 2009 dürfen Ukrainer und Polen, die in einer 30 km-Zone leben, beim Grenzverkehr anstelle eines Passes eine andere Art von Dokument, eine sog. „Erlaubnis," benutzen.

Zweck des kleinen Grenzverkehrs ist es vor allem, das Leben der Einwohner auf beiden Seiten der Grenze leichter zu gestalten. Sie dürfen die Grenze beliebig oft überschreiten, z. B. aus kulturellen, sozialen oder familiären Gründen, nicht aber mit dem Ziel, einer bezahlten Arbeit nachzugehen. Eine Erlaubnis wird erteilt, wenn der Antragsteller einen gültigen Reisepass hat, seit mehr als 3 Jahren in der Grenzzone lebt, wenn er nachweisen kann, warum er die Grenze häufig überschreitet, wenn er nicht im SIS (*Schengen Information System*) registriert ist und nicht als Bedrohung für die Sicherheit, die Ordnung und die öffentliche Gesundheit in der Ukraine, in Polen oder in anderen Ländern der EU angesehen wird.

---

[11] Art. 7 in Ebenda, L 332/72.

[12] Sehe Wiaczesław Wojnarowski, „Schengen dla Ukrainy – spojrzenie z drugiej strony granicy. Przystąpienie Polski do strefy Schengen i jego konsekwencje dla Ukrainy," in *Polska w strefie Schengen. Refleksje po pierwszym roku członkostwa,* hg. Barbara Radzikowska-Kryśczak und Anna Sadownik (Warszawa: MSWiA, 2008), 121; und Jakub Boratyński, Grzegorz Gromadzki, Oleksandr Sushko und Anita Szymborska, *Questionable Achievement: EC- Ukraine Visa Facilitation Agreement* (Warsaw-Kyiw: Stefan Batory Foundation, 2006), 5.

3. Sollten Nachbarschaftspolitik und Visa-Politik anders als bisher miteinander verzahnt werden?

Die Nachbarschaftspolitik der EU gegenüber der Ukraine basiert auf der Vereinbarung über Partnerschaft und Zusammenarbeit (PCA) aus dem Jahre 1998. Seit 2008 verhandelt die EU mit der Ukraine über ein Dokument, das die PCA ersetzen soll. Es handelt sich dabei um ein Assoziationsabkommen. Um die Verhandlungen zu strukturieren, gibt es eine Assoziationsagenda 2010, die den früheren Aktionsplan abgelöst hat und das Inkrafttreten des Assoziationsabkommens vorbereiten soll. Im Bereich der Justiz und des Inneren gilt seit 2001 ein Aktionsplan, der die strategischen Ziele und Herausforderungen in diesem Bereich konkretisiert.

Die erste Hürde ist, dass die Nachbarschaftspolitik der Generaldirektion Außenbeziehungen (RELEX) unterliegt, wohingegen die Visapolitik der Generaldirektion Justiz, Freiheit und Sicherheit (JLS) zugeordnet ist. Das heißt nicht, dass diese zwei Themen nicht koordiniert sind, bedeutet aber, dass sie unterschiedlichen Zuständigkeiten unterliegen. Alle Dokumente der EU, die sich mit der Nachbarschaftspolitik beschäftigen, erwähnen die Frage der Visa, ohne sich jedoch näher damit zu befassen.[13] Nachbarschaftspolitik und JLS haben auch unterschiedliche Ziele: Während es bei der Nachbarschaftspolitik um mehr Zusammenarbeit mit den Nachbarländern geht, um ein Modell der lockeren Kooperation, konzentriert sich JLS auf Sicherheitsfragen und macht die Ostgrenze durch die Schengen-Maßnahmen immer undurchlässiger. Das erschwert die Entwicklung der Beziehungen zwischen der EU und der Ukraine sowie zwischen Polen und der Ukraine. Insbesondere das Bild einer kohärenten EU-Politik wird durch solche Unterschiede beschädigt.

4. Zusammenfassung

Entgegen landläufiger Ansichten hat die Einführung der Visumspflicht nicht zu einem Rückgang des Reiseverkehrs zwischen Polen und der Ukraine geführt. Für den Rückgang war vielmehr die Erhöhung der Kosten für das Visum verantwortlich. Dies zeigt, dass administrative Hürden allein nicht als Bremse für bilaterale Kontakte verantwortlich gemacht werden können. Es zeigt aber auch, dass die Ziele und Methoden des Schengen-*acquis* durchaus mit einer Verbesserung der bilateralen Zusammenarbeit zwischen dem EU- und Schengen-Mitglied Polen und dem Drittstaat Ukraine vereinbar wären. Damit ist auch die in Polen und der Ukraine häufig geäußerte Ansicht widerlegt, dass die Ausweitung des Schengen-Raumes auf Polen auf Kosten der bilateralen Kontakte gehen müsse. Die Migrationskontrolle und die Einhaltung der Schengen-Kriterien im Reiseverkehr mit Drittländern würden

[13] „Aktionsplan für den Bereich Justiz und Inneres in der Ukraine," *Amtsblatt der Europäischen Union*, 29.03.2003, C 77/1.

diese Kontakte nicht beeinträchtigen, wenn die Kosten für ein Visum angemessen niedrig lägen.

Demgegenüber stellt die unzureichende Verzahnung von Innen- und Außenpolitik der EU eher ein Image- und Koordinationsproblem dar. Probleme der grenzüberschreitenden Mobilität sind bei den Verhandlungen über eine PCA-Nachfolgelösung kaum ein Thema, obwohl sie für das polnisch-ukrainische Verhältnis, über das vor allem in den beiderseitigen Grenzgebieten entschieden wird, außerordentlich wichtig sind. Dies kann sowohl in Polen, als auch in der Ukraine den Eindruck erwecken, dass die EU eine vieldeutige und widersprüchliche Politik verfolgt: eine, die im Rahmen einer PCA-Nachfolgelösung Kontakte mit der Ukraine stimuliert und fördert, und eine andere, in deren Rahmen sie grenzüberschreitende Mobilität durch hohe administrative und finanzielle Hürden einschränkt.

Anna Tomaszewska
a.tomaszewska@feps.pl

David Simo
Université de Yaoundé 1

Die Literatur stellt eine Institution dar, in der Grenzen, Grenzziehung, aber auch Grenzüberschreitungen sowohl thematisch, als auch konzeptionell und diskursiv eine wichtige Rolle spielen. Gerade in Europa pendelt ihr Selbstverständnis zwischen Universalismus und Partikularismus, Nationalisierungstendenzen und Transnationalisierungsperspektive.

1. LITERATUR UND NATION ODER VERORTUNGSTENDENZEN DER LITERATUR

Kafka meinte zwischen der Literatur einer großen und der einer kleinen Nation unterscheiden zu können.[1] Als kleine Nation bezeichnete er eine religiöse oder ethnische Gemeinschaft, die unter einer repressiven Herrschaft lebt. Hier konstituiert sich das kollektive Gedächtnis als eine Widerstandsstrategie und als Mittel der Befreiung. Das Bewusstsein, eine Gruppe zu sein, ist alles andere als selbstverständlich. Das Bewusstsein, eine Gemeinschaft zu bilden, setzt eine diskursive Praxis voraus. Nur dadurch, dass man davon spricht, dass man eine Gemeinschaft bildet und sich entsprechend verhält, nimmt man sich als Gemeinschaft wahr. Die Wirklichkeit der Gemeinschaft muss erst sprachlich konstruiert werden, um eine Wirklichkeit an und für sich zu werden. Und die Literatur spielt dabei eine entscheidende Rolle, so zum Beispiel bei den historischen Fällen, die Kafka behandelt, nämlich dem Fall der tschechischen Minderheit in Prag und der jüdischen Minderheit in Warschau. Hier bildet die Literatur ein gemeinsames Gedächtnis sowie einen gemeinsamen geistigen Raum.

Aber nicht nur kleine und bedrohte Nationen rekurrieren auf die Literatur als Ort der Vergewisserung und Konsolidierung des Nationalbewusstseins. Die Geschichte zeigt, wie sehr auch starke Nationen die Literatur als Mittel der Darstellung und als Nachweis ihrer Größe verwenden.

Die indische Literaturwissenschaftlerin Viswanathan hat hierzu eine höchst interessante Studie durchgeführt.[2] Darin untersucht sie, wie die Engländer das Studium der englischen Literatur in Indien im 19. Jahrhundert als Herrschaftsmittel einführten, und zwar nicht nur, weil diese ethische Gedanken enthielt, die den kolonisierten einheimischen Völkern moralische Werte und Respekt gegenüber den

[1] Franz Kafka, *Tagebücher 1910-1923* (Frankfurt/M: Fischer Taschenbuch, 1973).
[2] Gauri Viswanathan, „The Beginning of English Literary Study in British India," in *The Post-colonial Studies Reader*, hg. Bill Ashcroft, Gareth Griffith, Helen Tiffin (London und New York: Routledge, 1995).

Gesetzen beibringen sollten, sondern auch, um der geistigen Größe und Überlegenheit Englands Ausdruck zu verleihen. Sie sollte den Einheimischen Respekt und Bewunderung einflößen und sie veranlassen, die Herrschaft Englands als natürlich und notwendig anzuerkennen.

Während die Literatur eines Landes im Ausland als Herrschaftsmittel verwendet wird, wird sie im Land selber zu einem Objekt, um das herum Kohäsion und Homogenität hergestellt wird. Für die Nachbarländer wird sie zum Ort der Sichtbarkeit der Alterität der Nationalidentität.

Der Literaturbetrieb, vor allem die Literaturkritik, die Literaturgeschichtsschreibung und der Literaturunterricht, partizipieren an der Tradierung des Nationalgeistes. Die Literaturgeschichte zeichnet den Weg nach, den die Gründungsväter der nationalen Literatur gewiesen haben, und zeigt, wie die nachfolgenden Generationen diesen Weg fortzusetzen haben. Im 19. Jahrhundert hatte für Gervinus die Literaturgeschichte, und zwar mehr noch als die Politikgeschichte, die Aufgabe, das sich konstituierende Nationalbewusstsein herauszuarbeiten und daraus die Verpflichtung der Zeitgenossen auf den Prozess der historischen Verwirklichung der Nation abzuleiten.[3]

Die Literatur insistiert aber auch gern, vor allem seit der literarischen Moderne, auf ihrer Autonomie. Die Eigenart des Ästhetischen wird gerade in seiner Alterität zu kulturellen Werten und somit zur Nation gesehen.

2. Die Moderne, die Entwurzelungserfahrung und Versuche der Entnationalisierung der Literatur

Kafka war einer der Protagonisten der literarischen Moderne. Deshalb reihte sich seine eigene literarische Produktion weder in die große noch in die kleine Literatur ein. Er schrieb nicht im Sinne der jüdischen Literatur, wie sie in Warschau funktionierte und die er als kleine Literatur charakterisierte. Er schrieb auch nicht nach der Tradition Goethes. Der Status des Fremden und Marginalisierten, den er als Jude hatte, und seine gleichzeitige Zugehörigkeit zur deutschen Kultur, die er genau kannte, verliehen ihm eine Freiheit und eine Fähigkeit zur Distanz und zur Verfremdung, die nicht alle hatten. Er konnte umso selbstverständlicher Positionen einnehmen, die andere, nicht-jüdische deutsche Schriftsteller nur mit großer Anstrengung erreichen konnten, weil sie für sie Bruch und Ablehnung der durch ihre Sozialisation verinnerlichten Werte und Denkmuster darstellten.

Das Bewusstsein einer existenziellen Entfremdung, der Entwurzelung, der Unmöglichkeit, an einer geteilten Wirklichkeit teilzuhaben, das Gefühl der Enge, all das drückten die avantgardistischen Schriftsteller aus. Für die Juden war dies erlebter Alltag. Kafkas Status als Jude brachte ihn dazu, eine Haltung zu entwickeln,

[3] Georg Gottfried Gervinus, *Geschichte der poetischen National-Literatur der Deutschen*, 5 Bde., 1835-1842 (Leipzig: Engelmann, 1846).

die nicht mehr eine rein jüdische Haltung darstellt, sondern dem Gefühl einer ganzen Generation von Deutschen entspricht, die – aus denselben Gründen wie die Juden oder aus anderen Gründen – dasselbe Unbehagen erleben wie sie. Aus dieser Haltung hat sich eine neue Vorstellung von Kunst herauskristallisiert, die jedem Versuch, sie zu vereinnahmen, Widerstand leistet. Gerade gegenüber der Nation als Anrufungsinstanz zeigt sich diese Kunstvorstellung kritisch. Die Behauptung der Autonomie der Kunst stellt einen Versuch dar, ihre Indienstnahme durch andere Felder, vor allem durch die Politik, zu verweigern.

Der Eintritt einer politisch, sozial und kulturell marginalisierten Gruppe in das literarische Feld hat also entscheidend dazu beigetragen, dieses Feld grundlegend zu verändern, neu zu strukturieren und ein Gegenmodell zu traditionellen Werten und zu Legitimationsinstanzen zu erarbeiten.[4]

Diese ästhetische Revolution erlebten nationalistische Kreise in Deutschland als einen Angriff auf heilige Werte, die sie verehrten, und zwar auf die Nation, die bestehende soziale und politische Ordnung sowie auf die Tradition. Die Revolution in der Schreibart, die Dekonstruktion der Kunst als Institution, die Einführung des Grotesken, des Hässlichen, des Abnormalen, des Irrationalen, des Unbewussten, des Maßlosen als ästhetische Kategorien durch Bewegungen wie den Naturalismus, den Futurismus, den Dadaismus, den Surrealismus und den Expressionismus wurden als antinationale, pazifistische, weltbürgerliche und kosmopolitische Bestrebungen bekämpft. Die literarische und künstlerische Moderne wurde also von konservativen Kräften als jüdische Bewegung betrachtet. Und für sie bedeutete dies, dass diese Bewegung antieuropäisch und antideutsch war.[5]

Dies hat Konsequenzen für die Literaturwissenschaftspraxis in Deutschland, aber auch in ganz Europa gehabt. Der durch die Moderne eingeschlagene Weg der Entortung der Literatur wurde nie konsequent verfolgt. Auch wenn das Prinzip der Autonomie immer wieder proklamiert wird, bleibt die Literaturwissenschaft weitgehend nationalphilologisch orientiert. Einige Ansätze aber versuchen, diese Tendenz zu überwinden. Hier soll nun auf einige dieser Ansätze eingegangen werden.

3. Interkulturelle Literaturwissenschaft

Der Begriff interkulturelle Literaturwissenschaft hat sich inzwischen als Grundlage der Profilierung einer neuen Disziplin oder einer neuen wissenschaftlichen Praxis auch in Deutschland durchgesetzt, nachdem die interkulturelle Literaturwissenschaft vor allem in den USA entwickelt worden war. Dabei stützen sich die Wissenschaftler auf sehr unterschiedliche historische, fachliche

[4] Vgl. Konrad Kwiet, Gunther E. Grimm, Hans Peter Bayerdörfer, „Einleitung," in *Im Zeichen Hiobs. Jüdische Schriftsteller und deutsche Literatur im 20. Jahrhundert*, ed. Gunther E. Grimm, Hans Peter Bayerdörfer (Königstein/Ts: Verlag Athenäum, 1985).

[5] Vgl., ibid.

und theoretische Traditionen und Erfahrungen und erarbeiten literaturhistorische und Textanalysemodelle, die stark divergierende Akzente setzen.

Mit der Interkulturalität als Kategorie der Literaturwissenschaft wird aber die traditionelle nationalphilologisch orientierte Literaturwissenschaft allgemein infrage gestellt. Literarische Texte werden nicht mehr als Ausdruck einer als homogen gedachten nationalen Kultur gelesen. Rekonstruiert werden nicht Kontinuität und Einheitlichkeit, Reinheit und Identität, Telos und Ethos, Wahrhaftigkeit und Genialität, Repräsentativität und Affirmation, Stimmigkeit und Totalität etc. Vielmehr werden alle diese Kategorien als Instrumentarien einer exegetischen Praxis betrachtet und behandelt, die sich selbst als kulturelle Gedächtnisarbeit in den Dienst einer wie auch immer verstandenen Perpetuierung oder gar Erneuerung der Nationalkultur stellt. Sie werden also als Symptome eines nationalistischen Bewusstseins historisiert und dekonstruiert. Die Grenzen einer traditionell nationalphilologischen Behandlung der Kultur hat der belgische Literaturwissenschaftler Marc Quaghebeur gerade an ihrer Unfähigkeit, die belgische Literatur und Kultur anders als in negativen Begriffen zu erfassen, demonstriert. An französischen Ansätzen analysiert er die Aporien gewohnter Kategorien und postuliert die Notwendigkeit, aber auch die Schwierigkeit, diesen kategorialen Rahmen zu überwinden und eine neue Sprache zu erfinden, die eine polyphone, polyglotte Literatur und Kultur wie die belgische, aber auch die schweizerische, zu erfassen vermag.

> La première question que pose la „culture belge" – et les cultures de Belgique –, c'est précisément cette question du droit à une autre histoire et donc, à un autre type d'identité. Ce qu'elle pose en outre comme question, c'est celle de savoir comment la dire, comment la dire en Europe aujourd'hui, et qui plus est, comment la dire en français. Il s'agit en effet de savoir […] comment écrire cela en français moderne, c'est-à-dire dans la langue dont le destin historique s'est identifié (et dont la vertu intrinsèque découle de) la construction de l'État-nation le plus centralisé du monde.[6]

> (Die erste Frage, die die „belgische Kultur" - und die Kulturen von Belgien - aufwirft, betrifft eben das Recht auf eine andere Geschichte und somit auf einen anderen Typus von Identität. Eine Frage, die sie außerdem stellt, betrifft die Art und Weise, wie man diese ausdrücken kann und zwar heute in Europa und, was noch komplizierter ist, in der französischen Sprache. Es geht in der Tat darum zu wissen, […] wie man dies in der modernen französischen Sprache schreiben kann, das heißt in der Sprache, deren historisches Schicksal darin bestanden hat (und deren intrinsische Tugend sich daraus ableitet), die zentralisierteste Staatsnation der Welt zu bilden.) [Übersetzung des Autors]

Die interkulturelle Literaturwissenschaft versucht, solche Aporien zu überwinden.

[6] Marc Quaghebeur, „Culture(s) belge(s), identité(s) et société," in *Cahiers francophones d'Europe centre-orientale* 5-6 (1995): 175.

Mit der Interkulturalität als Kategorie der Literaturwissenschaft wird nicht nur Distanz, sondern auch Nähe hergestellt. Und zwar die Nähe zum poststrukturalistischen Gestus der Überwindung westlicher metaphysisch-humanistischer Entwürfe, Nähe zur Diskursanalyse und ihrer Aufdeckung von Machtdispositiven, Machtverhältnissen und Strategien, zur postmodernen Geographie und ihrer Auffassung von Raum, zum symbolischen Interaktionismus, zur postkolonialen Theorie und Kritik etc. Aus diesen Ansätzen übernimmt die interkulturelle Literaturwissenschaft Kategorien und Denkmuster, mit denen Literaturgeschichte neu geschrieben werden kann, mit denen klassische und neuere Texte nach ihrem Verhältnis zu transnationalen und transkulturellen historischen Wirklichkeiten, Herausforderungen und Bestrebungen, zu interkulturellen Spannungen, Konflikten und Rivalitäten befragt werden. Befragt werden sie auch nach den Mitteln, mit denen sie in solchen Spannungskontexten alte Kulturmuster festzuschreiben versuchen oder neue kulturelle Paradigmen aushandeln.

Gerade in Bezug auf Literaturgeschichte hat sich die nationalphilologische Perspektive in der Literaturwissenschaft durchgesetzt. Die Literaturgeschichte ist weitgehend die Geschichte der Literatur von Nationen und zielt darauf ab, die Literatur als Ort der Manifestation eines nationalen Geistes zu erfassen, der sich zielstrebig durch eine interne Gesetzmäßigkeit zu immer höheren Leistungen entwickelt oder auch Höhepunkte und Tiefschläge erlebt. Die Entwicklung wird in jedem Fall auf interne soziale, wirtschaftliche und geistige Triebkräfte zurückgeführt. Eine solche Literaturgeschichte gründet auf einer Auffassung von Nation als primordiale Kulturgemeinschaft, die Denk-, Gefühls- und Erfahrungshorizonte festlegt und somit Verhaltensmuster aller Mitglieder vereinheitlicht und festschreibt.

Auch traditionelle komparatistische Ansätze betonen zwar das Moment des Kontakts und des Austausches, bleiben aber weitgehend diesem national-kulturellen Modell verpflichtet. Diesbezüglich schreibt Michael Böhler:

> Vorherrschend in der Theorie der transkulturellen Beziehungen und Phänomene war bis vor Kurzem eine am nationalstaatlichen Paradigma des 19. Jahrhunderts und der Idee einer Nationalkultur bzw. Nationalliteratur orientierte Vorstellung. Kulturelle Beziehungen und Austauschprozesse finden hier zwischen den Nationen oder zwischen Individuen qua nationale Repräsentationsfiguren statt. Nationale Kulturen werden dabei als in sich geschlossene, einheitliche Ensembles symbolhafter Handlungen und Riten, von Texten und Diskursen, Gegenständen und Begriffen verstanden, womit sich eine Gemeinschaft über sich selbst und andere verständigt. Dem Einheits- und Geschlossenheitsdenken dieses nationalen und Kulturbegriffs entsprechend stehen in einem solchen Modell kulturelle und literarische Austauschprozesse in einem Zusammenhang mit nationalen Identitätskonstrukten und werden vor allem unter dem Aspekt des Eigenen und Fremden bzw. der aneignenden Eingrenzung oder Ausgrenzung und der assimilierenden Homogenisierung konzeptualisiert.[7]

---

[7] Michael Böhler, „National-Literatur will jetzt nicht viel sagen, die Epoche der Weltliteratur ist an der Zeit, und jeder muss jetzt dazu wirken, diese Epoche zu beschleunigen," Überlegungen zu den

4. EUROPA IN BEWEGUNG

Der Postdamer Romanist Ottmar Ette hat kürzlich versucht, eine Theorie der europäischen Literatur jenseits gewohnter Territorialisierungen zu entwerfen. Ganz konsequent versucht er die vorherrschende Tradition, die den Werken einen bestimmten Wohnsitz zuschreibt und daher die europäische Literatur nur als additive Strukturen denken kann, zu überwinden. Er schlägt eine transversale Sichtweise der Literatur Europas vor, die deutlich machen soll, dass diese aus Werken besteht, die zwischen Innerhalb- und Außerhalbbefindlichkeit oszillieren. „Gerade die Literaturen ohne festen Wohnsitz, [...] verdeutlichen, in welchem Maße bei der Frage nach der europäischen Literatur eine Beschränkung auf die nationale oder die europäische Ebene obsolet geworden ist."[8] Ette muss jedoch feststellen, dass seine Idee, Europa in Bewegung und Europa als Bewegung zu denken, vorerst nur eine prospektive, zukunftsgerichtete Vision bleiben wird, zumal die europäische Literarturwissenschaft weiterhin mit Kategorien aus dem 19. Jahrhundert arbeitet. Es mehren sich aber Versuche, die europäische Literatur im Kontext der Globalisierung als eine Weltliteratur zu denken, die den Prozess der Globalisierung widerspiegelt und neue Räume produziert, die nicht national und nicht einmal kontinental gedacht werden können. So schreibt der spanische Autor Juan Goytisolo in der Besprechung von Emine Sevgi Özdamars Werk „Das Leben ist eine Karawanserei, hat zwei Türen, aus einer kam ich rein, aus der anderen ging ich raus:"

> Quite a long time ago, at a meeting of the French Institute in Madrid, I surprised the audience by coming out with the idea, that the future of French literature lay with writers from the Maghreb and Caribbean, English Literature with Pakistani and Hindu writers and German literature with Turks. My boutade was greeted with laughter [...] Now the joke is for real.[9]

Damit wären wir wieder bei der Situation angelangt, die zur Entstehung der Moderne und zum Versuch der Entnationalisierung der Literatur Ende des 19. Jahrhunderts führte. Wenn Nationen immer mehr Probleme mit der Inbesitznahme der Literatur haben, weil sich diese ihren gewohnten Kategorien entziehen, wenn Autoren aufgrund ihrer Biographie nicht mehr automatisch einer Volksgemeinschaft zugerechnet werden können, werden Kritiker und Wissenschaftler notwendigerweise neue Kategorien erfinden müssen, mit denen die Literatur geortet, geordnet und erfasst werden kann. Gerade solche Kategorien schlägt Ottmar Ette vor.

David Simo
dsimo@uycdc.uninet.cm

---

kulturtopographischen Raumstrukturen in der Gegenwartsliteratur. http://www.Goethezeitportal.de

[8] Ottmar Ette, „Europäische Literatur(en) im globalen Kontext. Literaturen für Europa," in *Wider den Kulturzwang. Migration, Kulturalisierung und Weltliteratur*, hg. Özkan Ezli, Dorothee Kimmich und Annette Werberger (Bielefeld: transcript, 2009), 292.

[9] Juan Goytisolo, Rezension: *Life is a Caravansaray* von Emine Sevgi Özdamar, *Times Literary Supplement*, 2. Dezember 1994, 12.

„GRENZT HIER EIN WORT AN MICH, SO LAẞ ICH'S GRENZEN."
Das Überschreiten der Grenze zum ersehnten Ideal in den späteren Gedichten Ingeborg Bachmanns

Ma Jian
Zentrum für Deutschlandstudien, Peking-Universität

Wir aber wollen über Grenzen sprechen,
und gehn auch Grenzen noch durch jedes Wort:
wir werden sie vor Heimweh überschreiten
und dann im Einklang stehn mit jedem Ort.[1]

So lautet die letzte Strophe des fünften Gedichts aus dem Gedichtzyklus Ingeborg Bachmanns „Von einem Land, einem Fluss und den Seen," den ihr 1956 veröffentlichter zweiter Gedichtband *Anrufung des Großen Bären* enthält. Es handelt sich bei diesem Gedichtzyklus um eine Landschaftsbeschreibung, nämlich um die Beschreibung ihrer eigenen Heimat Kärnten, und gerade diese Strophe ist für ein Verständnis der Dichterin von besonderer Bedeutung, denn zwei Einsichten von ihr sind hier wahrzunehmen: Zum einen stellen „Grenzen" zwar anscheinend einen geografischen und physischen Begriff dar, doch die ersten beiden Verse, insbesondere der zweite, zeigen, dass zwischen „Grenzen" und „Wort," nämlich sprachlichen Ausdrucksmitteln, eine enge Verknüpfung besteht, und somit misst ihnen diese Verbindung zwischen zwei im Wesentlichen voneinander unabhängigen Dingen einen außergewöhnlichen Sinn bei; zum anderen stehen „Grenzen," was die zweite Hälfte der Strophe expliziert, im Mittelpunkt zwischen der beschädigten Heimat der Gegenwart und einem ersehnten Ort, zu dem man bloß dadurch gelangt, dass man die Grenzen überschreitet. Eben in diesem Zusammenhang wohnt ihnen eine spezifische Bedeutung inne. Der zweimalige Gebrauch von „jede" – „jedes Wort" und „jedem Ort" – verdeutlicht darüber hinaus keine Willkür, sondern vielmehr Zuversicht und Bestimmtheit.

Aufschluss über die Frage nach dem Mittel, mit dem diese Grenzen überschritten werden können, gibt Bachmann in der letzten Strophe des achten Gedichts:

Wo ist Gesetz, wo Ordnung? Wo erscheinen
uns ganz begreiflich Blatt und Baum und Stein?
Zugegen sind sie in der schönen Sprache,
im reinen Sein ...[2]

---

[1] Ingeborg Bachmann, *Werke. Erster Band: Gedichte, Hörspiele, Libretti, Übersetzungen*, hg. Christine Koschel, Inge von Weidenbaum und Clemens Münster (München: R. Piper & Co., 1993), 89. Im Folgenden zitiert als *Werke I*.

EUROSTUDIA — REVUE TRANSATLANTIQUE DE RECHERCHE SUR L'EUROPE
Vol. 7, No.1-2 (2011): 181-190

Während „Sprache“ sich offenbar auf das „Wort“ in den oben zitierten ersten zwei Versen bezieht, vertieft „Sein,“ dieser philosophisch so stark geprägte Terminus, den implizierten Sinn der anderen zwei Verse. Indem sie das reine Sein „der schönen Sprache“ gleichsetzt, deutet Bachmann auf eine weitere Denkdimension hin – ihr durch intensive Beschäftigung mit der Philosophie geprägtes Verständnis von Sein und Sprache.

Bekanntlich hat Ingeborg Bachmann von 1945 bis 1950 an verschiedenen Universitäten wie Innsbruck, Graz und Wien Philosophie studiert und promovierte mit der Dissertation „Die kritische Aufnahme der Existenzialphilosophie Martin Heideggers.“ Danach befasste sie sich mit zunehmendem Interesse mit dem philosophischen Denken des österreichischen Philosophen Ludwig Wittgenstein. Dies dokumentieren ihre (Radio)-Essays „Ludwig Wittgenstein – Zu einem Kapitel der jüngsten Philosophiegeschichte“ (1953) und „Sagbares und Unsagbares – Die Philosophie Ludwig Wittgensteins“ (1954). Beide geben deutlich zu erkennen, wie tiefgreifend Bachmann von den philosophischen Gedanken Wittgensteins berührt und geprägt war, und in diesem Kontext lassen sich ihre Fragen nach den Grenzen der Sprache schlüssig klären.

Mit Wittgenstein ist Ingeborg Bachmann der festen Überzeugung, dass die Sprache des Menschen, das Denken total widerspiegelt, wie Wittgenstein feststellt: „Die Sprache selbst ist das Vehikel des Denkens,“[3] die Welt einerseits nur darzustellen und abzubilden vermag, andererseits aber gerade bei dieser Darstellung und Abbildung der Welt ihre Beschränktheit erfährt, wobei „Grenzen“ im Zentrum stehen. Dies zeigen zwei Zitate aus den beiden Essays: Das erste stammt aus „Ludwig Wittgenstein – Zu einem Kapitel der jüngsten Philosophiegeschichte:“

> Hier erfährt die Logik ihre Grenze, und da sie die Welt erfüllt, da die Welt in die Struktur der logischen Form eintritt, ist ihre Grenze die Grenze unserer Welt. So verstehen wir den Satz: "Die Grenzen meiner Sprache bedeuten die Grenzen meiner Welt."
>
> Diesseits der „Grenzen“ stehen wir, denken wir, sprechen wir. Das Gefühl der Welt als begrenztes Ganzes entsteht, weil wir selbst, als metaphysisches Subjekt, nicht mehr Teil der Welt, sondern „Grenze“ sind.[4]

Das zweite Zitat stammt aus dem Essay „Sagbares und Unsagbares – Die Philosophie Ludwig Wittgensteins:“

---

[2] Ebenda, 92.

[3] Ingeborg Bachmann, „Sagbares und Unsagbares – Die Philosophie Ludwig Wittgensteins,“ in *Werke. Vierter Band. Essays, Reden, vermischte Schriften*, hg. Christine Koschel, Inge von Weidenbaum und Clemens Münster (München: R. Piper & Co., 1993), 123. Im Folgenden zitiert als „Sagbares und Unsagbares.“

[4] Ingeborg Bachmann, „Ludwig Wittgenstein – Zu einem Kapitel der jüngsten Philosophiegeschichte,“ in *Werke. Vierter Band. Essays, Reden, vermischte Schriften*, hg. Christine Koschel, Inge von Weidenbaum und Clemens Münster (München: R. Piper & Co., 1993), 20f. Im Folgenden zitiert als „Ludwig Wittgenstein.“

> Und die logische Form ist die „Grenze," [...] denn sie ermöglicht zwar die Darstellung, kann aber selbst nicht mehr dargestellt werden. In ihr tritt etwas in Erscheinung, das über die Wirklichkeit hinausweist. Es weist insofern über die Wirklichkeit hinaus, als sich in der logischen Form etwas zeigt, das für uns undenkbar ist, und weil es undenkbar ist, läßt sich nicht darüber sprechen.[5]

Erkennbar sind die dreifachen Verhältnisse, auf die die eingangs zitierten Strophen anspielen: Erstens kommt aufgrund der mehrfachen Definitionen von „Grenze," sei es im Sinne von „wir" als metaphysisches Subjekt, sei es als „die logische Form," zum Ausdruck, dass sowohl das Subjekt, als auch das Denken und die Sprache ihre eigene Beschränktheit innehaben, während sich diese Beschränktheit, die „Grenze," eben durch sie herstellen lässt. Und gerade die mit solcher „Grenze" dargestellte Welt ist als „Ganzes" anzunehmen, was aber bei Ingeborg Bachmann große Unruhe stiftet, weil sie die Ansicht Wittgensteins teilt, dass diese Welt nur die Welt des Subjekts oder die Welt der subjektiven Wirklichkeit ist. Deswegen gilt: "Die Grenzen meiner Sprache bedeuten die Grenzen meiner Welt." Die Abhängigkeit der Grenzen von der Sprache liegt nahe.

Zweitens: Eben von diesem Standpunkt ausgehend, dass sich das Denken und die Sprache bei der Darstellung der Welt gleichzeitig ihre eigenen Grenzen ziehen, vertritt Bachmann mit Wittgenstein die Auffassung, dass alles, was man innerhalb der Grenzen denkt und sagt, einfach das Denkbare und das Sagbare ist und dass die Sprache selbst „nicht zu den Sachverhalten der Welt gehört, dass mit ihrer Hilfe etwas zwar sinnvoll gesagt werden kann, sie aber die Grenze des Sagbaren ist."[6] So zitiert Bachmann angesichts der Grenzsituation der Sprache mit Bewunderung in dem betreffenden Essay die zwei Leitsätze aus Wittgensteins *Tractacus logico-philosophicus*: "Was wir nicht denken können, das können wir nicht denken; wir können also auch nicht sagen, was wir nicht denken können."[7] Und noch direkter: "Wovon man nicht sprechen kann, darüber muß man schweigen."[8] Diese anscheinend keineswegs zu bezweifelnde These löst bei Bachmann starke Resonanz aus, weil sie nicht bloß auf die Beschränktheit des Denkens und der Sprache hinweist, sondern auch darauf hindeutet, wie man beim Erkennen einer solchen Grenzsituation verfährt. Ingeborg Bachmann hat wirklich „geschwiegen:" Nach der Veröffentlichung von *Anrufung des Großen Bären* im Jahr 1956 bis hin zu ihrem Lebensende im Jahr 1973, genauer gesagt, bis zu ihrer letzten Gedichtveröffentlichung 1968, verfasste sie weniger als 20 Gedichte, und in den letzten zehn Jahren ihres Lebens sind nicht mehr als sechs neue Gedichte entstanden. Darüber hinaus sagte sie 1971 in einem Fernseh-Interview in Rom: "Ich werde nie mehr Gedichte schreiben!" Dieses Schweigen ist wohl unter anderem ihrer „Grenzen"-Überlegung zuzuschreiben.

---

[5] „Sagbares und Unsagbares," 109.

[6] Ebenda. 109f.

[7] Ebenda. 109.

[8] „Ludwig Wittgenstein," 12.

Drittens ist offensichtlich Ingeborg Bachmann, die „in der schönen Sprache" das reine Sein ersehnt und wünscht, dennoch keineswegs mit der Grenzsituation zufrieden, denn auch angesichts der Grenze glaubt sie, dass etwas außerhalb der Grenzen vorhanden ist, was aber undenkbar und unsagbar ist. Auffällig ist hier ihre Formulierung „sich zeigen" in dem oben zitierten Abschnitt aus „Sagbares und Unsagbares – Die Philosophie Ludwig Wittgensteins." Auch diese übernimmt sie von Wittgenstein: „Es gibt allerdings Unaussprechliches. Dies zeigt sich, es ist das Mystische."[9] Unter dem „Mystischen" versteht sie eine unaussprechliche Erfahrung:

> Die Sprache kann nur über Tatsachen sprechen und bietet die Grenze unserer – meiner und deiner – Welt. Die Entgrenzung der Welt geschieht, wo die Sprache nicht hinreicht und daher auch das Denken nicht hinreicht. Sie geschieht, wo sich etwas „zeigt," und was sich zeigt, ist das Mystische, die unaussprechliche Erfahrung.[10]

Denkbar und undenkbar, sagbar und unsagbar, diese Begriffe vervollständigen sich gegenseitig. Mit einem Paradox, einer Problematik sieht sich Ingeborg Bachmann dabei konfrontiert: Eben dieses undenkbare „Mystische," das sich eigentlich nicht in der Sprache zeigen könnte, haftet immer noch an der Sprache, und zwar an der schönen Sprache, wo das Unaussprechliche sich dennoch ausspricht und die Grenze überschritten wird. Die späteren Gedichte Bachmanns, egal, aus welchen Anlässen verfasst, lassen sich daher wohl als ihr Versuch, sogar Unterfangen in dieser Hinsicht ansehen, die Grenzsituation der Sprache zu beschreiben und ihr Nachdenken darüber zum Ausdruck zu bringen, wobei, den erläuterten dreifachen Verhältnissen entsprechend, die Grenze und die damit zusammenhängenden Stichwörter wie Wort, Schweigen und Grenzenüberschreiten im Zentrum stehen. Vier Beispiele sind im Folgenden anzuführen: Während es sich in „Ihr Worte" um die Beschreibung der Grenzen von Worten, in „Keine Delikatessen" und „Wahrlich" um die Auseinandersetzung mit dieser schwierigen Situation und das poetische Selbstverständnis Bachmanns handelt, lässt sich ein vermeintlicher Ausweg aus dem Dilemma eventuell in „Böhmen liegt am Meer" wahrnehmen.

In dem Gedicht „Ihr Worte," das Bachmann 1961 der Dichterin und Freundin Nelly Sachs widmet und in dem sie das „Wort" so direkt aufgreift, als ob sie ein Zwiegespräch mit ihm führte, drückt sie durch eine Häufung von Imperativen ihre Reaktion auf die Grenzsituation der Worte aus:

> Ihr Worte, auf, mir nach!,
> und sind wir auch schon weiter,
> zu weit gegangen, geht's noch einmal
> weiter, zu keinem Ende geht's.
>
> Es hellt nicht auf.

[9] „Sagbares und Unsagbares," 118.
[10] Ebenda.

Das Wort
wird doch nur
andre Worte nach sich ziehn,
Satz den Satz,
So möchte Welt,
endgültig,
sich aufdrängen,
schon gesagt sein.
Sagt sie nicht.

Worte, mir nach,
daß nicht endgültig wird
– nicht diese Wortbegier
und Spruch auf Widerspruch!

Laßt eine Weile jetzt
keins der Gefühle sprechen,
den Muskel Herz
sich anders üben.

Laßt, sag ich, laßt.

Ins höchste Ohr nicht,
nichts, sag ich, geflüstert,
zum Tod fall dir nichts ein,
laß und mir nach, nicht mild
noch bitterlich,
nicht trostreich,
ohne Trost
bezeichnend nicht,
so auch nicht zeichenlos –

Und nur nicht dies: das Bild
Im Staubgespinst, leeres Geroll
von Silben, Sterbenswörter.

Kein Sterbenswort,
Ihr Worte![11]

Durch dreimal „mir nach" wird das Gedicht in drei Teile gegliedert, die die Phasen des literarischen Schaffens schildern und eng mit der Frage der Grenze zusammenhängen. Am Anfang hegt man den Wunsch – das ist ja vielleicht der Wunsch aller Dichter –, die Welt mit Worten als „endgültig," d. h. eine allerletzte Welt darzustellen, doch im Laufe des Schreibens erkennt man die Beschränktheit, die Grenze der Sprache, denn es geht „zu keinem Ende." Die mit den Worten dargestellte Welt kann also sowieso nicht die endgültige Welt sein, sondern setzt sich eben durch die sprachliche Fixierung ihre Grenze. Das entspricht eben dem, was die oben zitierte These Wittgensteins besagt – „Die Grenzen meiner Sprache bedeuten

---

[11] *Werke I*, 162f.

die Grenzen meiner Welt." Was bleibt zu tun? Das Schreiben aufgeben oder fortsetzen? Bachmann entscheidet sich festen Willens für das erstere und „befiehlt" den Worten, abzuwarten, bis ein neues Gefühl über die unendgültige Wortbegier hervortritt. Die Wiederholung von „laßt" betont die Gewalt des Wunsches und klingt wie ein Flehen, doch aufgehoben wird eigentlich die unerschöpfliche poetische Kraft, die dazu führt, dass große Ansprüche an die Sprache gestellt werden. Die auffällige Häufung der Negationen von entgegengesetzten Ausdrücken in der nächsten Strophe macht gerade die Schwierigkeiten deutlich, die entstehen, wenn man solchen Ansprüchen gerecht werden will, um die Grenze der Sprache zu überschreiten. Der Schlussvers „Kein Sterbenswort, / Ihr Worte!" deutet unverkennbar noch auf die feste Haltung Ingeborg Bachmanns gegenüber der Grenze hin, dass man eher schweigt und verstummt als ein „Bild im Staubgespinst" zu entwerfen.

Verwandelt wird das Zwiegespräch zwischen „ich" und „Worte" in einen Monolog von „ich" in dem wahrscheinlich 1963 entstandenen „Keine Delikatessen," wobei der ermüdenden und schmerzhaften Schöpfungstätigkeit zum Trotz die kompromisslose Haltung der Dichterin gegenüber den Grenzen und sogar gegenüber sich selbst radikal akzentuiert wird:

> Keine Delikatessen
>
> Nichts mehr gefällt mir.
>
> Soll ich
> eine Metapher ausstaffieren
> mit einer Mandelblüte?
> die Syntax kreuzigen
> auf einen Lichteffekt?
> Wer wird sich den Schädel zerbrechen
> über so überflüssige Dinge –
>
> Ich habe ein Einsehn gelernt
> mit den Worten,
> die da sind
> (für die unterste Klasse)
>
> Hunger
>   Schande
>   Tränen
> und
>   Finsternis.
>
> Mit dem ungereinigten Schluchzen,
> mit der Verzweiflung
> (und ich verzweifle noch vor Verzweiflung)
> über das viele Elend,
> den Krankenstand, die Lebenskosten,
> werde ich auskommen.

Ich vernachlässige nicht die Schrift,
sondern mich.
Die andern wissen sich
weißgott
mit den Worten zu helfen.
Ich bin nicht mein Assistent.

Soll ich
einen Gedanken gefangennehmen,
abführen in eine erleuchtete Satzzelle?
Aug und Ohr verköstigen
mit Worthappen erster Güte?
erforschen die Libido eines Vokals,
ermitteln die Liebhaberwerte unserer Konsonanten?

Muß ich
mit dem verhagelten Kopf,
mit dem Schreibkrampf in dieser Hand,
unter dreihundertnächtigem Druck
einreißen das Papier,
wegfegen die angezettelten Wortopern,
vernichtend so: ich du und er sie es

wir ihr?

(Soll doch. Sollen die andern.)

Mein Teil, es soll verloren gehen.[12]

Im Vergleich zu „Ihr Worte" wird hier der Vorgang des literarischen Schaffens – oder noch konkreter: das Abfassen eines Gedichts – viel eingehender dargestellt. Sowohl Metapher, Syntax, Vokal und Konsonant, Begriffe, die sich um die sprachlichen Ausdrucksmittel drehen und somit auf die Grenze der Sprache hinweisen, als auch Formulierungen wie „den Schädel zerbrechen," „Aug und Ohr verköstigen," „Libido erforschen" und „mit dem verhagelten Kopf," die auf Körperreaktionen und Sinneswahrnehmungen verweisen, das alles veranschaulicht die recht beschwerlichen und strapazierenden Arbeiten der Dichterin. Doch trotzdem: „Nichts mehr gefällt mir," denn je mehr Kraft die schöpferische Arbeit kostet, desto stärker fühlt man sich enttäuscht über die Unfähigkeit sowie Unmöglichkeit der Grenzüberschreitung. Dieser depressive Gemütszustand wird durch die dreierlei Gegenfragen an „mich" besonders deutlich.

Im Gegensatz zu der stark emotionsgeladen geäußerten Enttäuschung präsentiert das lyrische Ich aber noch durch einen Vergleich mit Anderen eine Art Resignation. Ähnliche Formulierungen wie in der sechsten Strophe finden sich in dem vermutlich im Jahr 1964 verfassten Gedicht „Wahrlich," das Bachmann der russischen Dichterin Anna Achmatova widmet:

---

[12] *Werke I*, 172f.

Wem es ein Wort nie verschlagen hat,
und ich sage es euch,
wer bloß sich zu helfen weiß
und mit den Worten –

dem ist nicht zu helfen.
Über den kurzen Weg nicht
und nicht über den langen.

Einen einzigen Satz haltbar zu machen,
auszuhalten in dem Bimbam von Worten.

Es schreibt diesen Satz keiner,
der nicht unterschreibt.[13]

Vor dem Hintergrund der Grenze ist klar: Denjenigen, die sich mit den Worten zu helfen wissen, ist deshalb nicht zu helfen, weil sie sich nur innerhalb der Grenze bewegen. Und sogar dieses Sich-zu-helfen-wissen stellt Bachmann mit der Formulierung mit „weißgott" im vorigen Gedicht sowie „Bimbam von Worten" in Frage. Es ist deswegen für sie nicht beneidenswert. Vielmehr leidet sie unter der Verzweiflung „vor Verzweiflung" – statt über das Elend im realen Leben zu verzweifeln, setzt sie sich unermüdlich für die „verzweifelte Bemühung um das Unaussprechliche"[14] ein, wie sie es auch an Wittgensteins Leistung schätzt. Fragwürdig ist nur, wie ein solcher einziger Satz aussieht, den man haltbar macht und mit dem man somit die Verzweiflung möglicherweise überwindet.

Eine Folge der Bemühung um das Unaussprechliche lässt sich am Gedicht „Böhmen liegt am Meer" ablesen, das im selben Jahr wie „Wahrlich" geschrieben wurde und ihre letzte Gedicht-Veröffentlichung war. Schon der Titel spielt auf Shakespeares Irrtum in „The Winter's Tale" an, in dem es in der dritten Szene des dritten Aufzugs heißt: „Böhmen, eine wilde Gegend am Meer." Eben diese der Wirklichkeit widersprechende Aussage kommt Ingeborg Bachmann hinsichtlich der Grenz-Überlegung zu Hilfe:

Sind hierorts Häuser grün, tret ich noch in ein Haus.
Sind hier die Brücken heil, geh ich auf gutem Grund.
Ist Liebesmüh in alle Zeit verloren, verlier ich sie hier gern.

Bin ich's nicht, ist es einer, der so gut wie ich.

Grenzt hier ein Wort an mich, so laß ich's grenzen.

Liegt Böhmen noch am Meer, glaub ich den Meeren wieder.
Und glaub ich noch ans Meer, so hoffe ich auf Land.

Bin ich's, so ist's ein jeder, der ist soviel wie ich.

---

[13] *Werke I*, 166.

[14] „Ludwig Wittgenstein," 13.

Ich will nichts mehr für mich. Ich will zugrunde gehn.

Zugrund – das heißt zum Meer, dort find ich Böhmen wieder.
Zugrund gerichtet, wach ich ruhig auf.
Von Grund auf weiß ich jetzt, und ich bin unverloren.

Kommt her, ihr Böhmen alle, Seefahrer, Hafenhuren und Schiffe
unverankert. Wollt ihr nicht böhmisch sein, Illyrer, Veroneser,
und Venezianer alle. Spielt die Komödien, die lachen machen

Und die zum Weinen sind. Und irrt euch hundertmal,
wie ich mich irrte und Proben nie bestand,
doch hab ich sie bestanden, ein um das andere Mal.

Wie Böhmen sie bestand und eines schönen Tags
ans Meer begnadigt wurde und jetzt am Wasser liegt.

Ich grenz noch an ein Wort und an ein andres Land,
ich grenz, wie wenig auch, an alles immer mehr,

ein Böhme, ein Vagant, der nichts hat, den nichts hält,
begabt nur noch, vom Meer, das strittig ist, Land meiner Wahl zu sehen.[15]

Im Zusammenhang mit den oben zitierten Gedichten kann das Gedicht als ein Selbstbekenntnis der Dichterin betrachtet werden, welches alle oben diskutierten Aspekte einbezieht: Unverändert bleiben zuerst die Grenze und das Wort, so dass sich das lyrische Ich immer noch mit der Grenze konfrontiert fühlt. Aber „Grenzt hier ein Wort an mich, so laß ich's grenzen." beschreibt zwar, dass das Ich die Beschränktheit der Sprache immer noch nicht abwirft, doch in dieser Resignation ist etwas positiv Freudiges versteckt; unverändert bleibt dann der Vergleich zwischen „Ich" und anderen, jedoch stellt die Steigerung von „einer" zu „ein jeder" ebenfalls eine Wandlung des Subjekts dar, dass nämlich das Ich sich selbst nicht mehr so prätentiös ansieht und somit glaubt, sich selbst zu helfen zu wissen. Unverändert bleibt immer noch der Wunsch, „im Einklang" „mit jedem Ort" zu stehen, doch statt des ungewollten Verlorengehens meines Teils will das Ich jetzt „zugrunde gehen." Das alles ist bloß darauf zurückzuführen, ans Meer zu glauben, an dem Böhmen liegt, und auf Land zu hoffen. Sowohl das Meer als auch das Land sind Sinnbilder für etwas, was über die Wirklichkeit hinausweist. So bedeutet das Zugrundegehen eine Rettung, so besteht das Ich „ein und das andre Mal" die Proben, die es „nie bestand," wenn auch voller Enttäuschung und Verzweiflung, so steht das An-Ein-Wort-Grenzen für das Grenzen „an ein andres Land" mit dem Namen „Böhmen," den utopischen Ort, zu dem man nur durch Grenzüberschreiten zu gelangen vermag. So glaubt Ingeborg Bachmann, dass das Ich das Mystische erlebt, die unaussprechliche Erfahrung, das reine Sein.

---

[15] *Werke I*, 167f.

In diesem Sinne ist es nicht mehr wichtig, ob das Ich die Grenze wirklich überschreitet oder nicht; wichtig ist vielmehr, dass Bachmann durch ihre Grenz-Überlegung, natürlich angeregt durch Ludwig Wittgenstein, sowie durch ihre schöpferische Praxis ein Ideal für sich und für andere entwirft, dessen Wesen und Sinn sie am 17. März 1959 bei der Verleihung des Hörspielpreises der Kriegsblinden in ihrer Rede mit dem Titel „Die Wahrheit ist dem Menschen zumutbar" formuliert:

> Nun steckt aber in jedem Fall [...] der Grenzfall, den wir [...] erblicken können [...]. Der Wunsch wird in uns wach, die Grenzen zu überschreiten, die uns gesetzt sind. Nicht um mich zu widerrufen, sondern um es deutlicher zu ergänzen, [...] Innerhalb der Grenzen aber haben wir den Blick gerichtet auf das Vollkommene, das Unmögliche, Unerreichbare, [...] Im Widerspiel des Unmöglichen mit dem Möglichen erweitern wir unsere Möglichkeiten.[16]

MA Jian
majian0226@hotmail.com

[16] Ingeborg Bachmann, „Die Wahrheit ist dem Menschen zumutbar," in *Werke. Vierter Band. Essays, Reden, vermischte Schriften*, hg. Christine Koschel, Inge von Weidenbaum und Clemens Münster (München: R. Piper & Co., 1993), 276.

Lynn L. Wolff
Center for German and European Studies, University of Wisconsin, Madison

To establish the twentieth-century German-language author W.G. Sebald as a "Grenzgänger," one must explore the borders that he crossed, challenged, and broke down. In considering the implications of his nationality, literary language, and the reception of his works, one also explores the borders of world literature itself. Relevant to this discussion is the claim of Sebald's "self-imposed/voluntary exile" in England, which has gained currency in recent research. This claim must, however, be challenged, for it collapses the historical perspective from which the status of "exile" needs to be considered, a perspective that Sebald's works precisely emphasize.

1. THE "GRENZGÄNGER" W.G. SEBALD

Sebald was born in 1944 as Winfried Georg, but from his time in England on he was known to his friends as "Max."[1] Although separated generationally from the tradition of postwar German authors, from an early age Sebald engaged with the questions surrounding Germany's past that these authors raised in their texts. His critical and literary texts offer a continuation of the question of *Vergangenheitsbewältigung* that was born out of the previous generation's literary productions. Sebald deeply felt the silence surrounding the Nazis' crimes and the complicity of ordinary people that dominated postwar Germany, often describing this as "a conspiracy of silence."[2] He recalls having seen in primary school newsreels with footage of the liberation of the Bergen-Belsen concentration camp and how the students were not given the chance to ask questions. The films were simply not discussed, perpetuating the silence around the atrocities of the not-too-distant past. While at the University in Freiburg in the early 1960s, Sebald's disillusionment crystallized, and he recalls having sensed an "atmosphere of falseness"[3] in higher education. During his time as a university student, the Auschwitz trials in Frankfurt highly publicized the crimes of the concentration camps, and professors were revealed as having been former Nazi party members. Sebald stated that the Auschwitz trials were "the first *public* ac-

[1] For detailed biographical accounts of Sebald's life, see Richard Sheppard, "Dexter – sinister: Some Observations on Decrypting the Mors Code in the Work of W.G. Sebald," *Journal of European Studies* 35 (2005): 419-463; and Sheppard's continuation piece "'Woods, trees, and the spaces in between': A Report on Work Published on W.G. Sebald 2005-2008," *Journal of European Studies* 39, 1 (2009): 79-128.
[2] W.G. Sebald, "W.G. Sebald," in *Writers in Conversation with Christopher Bigsby. Volume Two,* by Christopher Bigsby (Norwich, U.K.: Arthur Miller Centre for American Studies, 2001), 143.
[3] Ibid., 147.

knowledgement that there was such a thing as an unresolved German past."[4] Reproachful of Germany's *Gedächtnislosigkeit*, "lack of memory,"[5] and frustrated by the "conspiracy of silence," Sebald took a teaching assistantship in England at the age of 22, where he remained until a tragic automobile accident took his life in 2001.The delay which dominates Sebald's exposure to the Holocaust can perhaps be read as a parallel to the slow excavation and revelation of the past in his literary works. This is most prominently seen in a form of reverse chronology in several of his works.

Sebald's decision to leave Germany in the 1960s and eventually to take up permanent residence in England has prompted scholars to suggest his "self-imposed" or "voluntary" exile,[6] a designation which is both problematic and questionable. Although Sebald never explicitly referred to his living arrangement as one of exile, he expressed his awareness of the liminal status of his life and work in England, "In England nur gastweise zuhause, schwanke ich auch hier zwischen Gefühlen der Vertrautheit und der Dislokation."[7] ["Only a guest in England, I still hover between feelings of familiarity and dislocation there too."[8]] In this same speech, made on the occasion of his acceptance into the German Academy, Sebald expressed a distance towards his homeland, his feelings of being "a traitor to [his] country and a fraud" and that only in a distance from Germany, while in England, was he able to form "ideas of [his] native country."[9] Sebald was fluent in English, but his life in England nevertheless meant that he constantly dealt with issues of both linguistic and cultural translation, issues which in turn manifest themselves aesthetically and thematically in his literary works.[10] On various occasions, Sebald reflected upon his relationship to the German language. Having grown up in Southern Bavaria, Sebald considered the Southern German dialect his mother-tongue, and he recounts having made his first efforts to learn, speak, and write High German when he entered the University in Freiburg in 1963. By contrast, even after thirty years in England, Sebald still consi-

---

[4] Ibid., emphasis in original.

[5] Sigrid Löffler, "Kopfreisen in die Ferne: ein Geheimtip; in Norwich, gar nicht hinter dem Mond, lebt und schreibt W.G. Max Sebald," in *W.G. Sebald*, ed. Franz Loquai (Eggingen: Ed. Isele, 1997), 34.

[6] James Atlas, "W.G. Sebald. A Profile," *The Paris Review* 41, 151 (1999): 286; Arthur Williams, "W.G. Sebald: A Holistic Approach to Borders, Texts and Perspectives," in *German-Language Literature Today: International and Popular?*, ed. Arthur Williams, Stuart Parkes and Julian Preece (Oxford, New York: P. Lang, 2000), 103; Mark M. Anderson, "The Edge of Darkness: On W.G. Sebald," *October* 106 (2003): 103; John Zilcosky, "Sebald's Uncanny Travels. The Impossibility of Getting Lost," in *W.G. Sebald: A Critical Companion*, ed. J.J. Long and Anne Whitehead (Seattle, WA: University of Washington Press, 2004), 116; Ronald H. McKinney, "W.G. Sebald and The Questionable Business of Post-Holocaust Writing," *Philosophy Today* 49, 2 (2005): 115.

[7] W.G. Sebald, "Antrittsrede vor dem Kollegium der Deutschen Akademie," in *Campo Santo*, ed. Sven Meyer (München, Wien: Hanser, 2003), 250.

[8] W.G. Sebald, "Acceptance Speech to the Collegium of the German Academy," *Campo Santo*, ed. Sven Meyer, trans. Anthea Bell (New York: Random House, 2005), 208.

[9] Idem.

[10] See Lynn L. Wolff, "The "Solitary Mallard": On Sebald and Translation," Special Issue on W.G. Sebald, *Journal of European Studies* (forthcoming 2011).

dered English to be a foreign language, "I don't in the least feel at home in it. I use it but it sounds quite alien to me."[11]

Rather than identifying Sebald as an "exile," Sebald's works could be discussed in terms of *expatriate writing*, but nevertheless with an eye to the linguistic specificity of his success. Gerhard Fischer asserts,

> Sebald, after all, despite being an expatriate writer living in England for the better part of his life, wrote only in German [...]. His reputation rests primarily on his consummate mastery of the German language and the German literary tradition, which is quite unparalleled in contemporary writing.[12]

Fischer's conceptual program for thinking of Sebald as an expatriate writer is helpful, insofar as he sees in Sebald's works "a potentially emancipatory cultural memory that resists the push and pull of a single, hegemonic world culture."[13] The emphasis on the author's origins and his texts' linguistic material is therefore not a reactionary emphasis on national identity but rather an essential assertion of difference. I agree with Peter Madsen when he writes,

> The construction of national identity, however, is in itself a mystifying (and potentially destructive) endeavour. The seemingly natural link between literature as a linguistic art form, national language and national identity is at odds with the fact that literature travels in translation and that all nations are heterogeneous culturally speaking. From the outset the idea of world literature goes against the grain of nationalism.[14]

I would, nevertheless, argue that the specificity of Sebald's works in German—in particular the complex layering of visual and textual material, which I will outline below, as well as the various degrees of narrative mediation—cannot be denied and warrant an in-depth analysis, all in the spirit of situating his work within networks of world literature and world history.

2. Writing on the Border: Between Literary Criticism and Literature

During his first years in England, Sebald earned both his Master's and PhD in German literature, and some fifteen years later he was granted the Habilitation by the University of Hamburg. With these professional qualifications, Sebald taught courses in nineteenth- and twentieth-century German prose fiction for close to thirty years in the school of English and American Studies at the University of East Anglia

---

[11] Sebald in Bigsby, *Writers in Conversation*, 148. Furthermore, Sebald thought it unlikely that he would "become a Joseph Conrad," as Bigsby suggests, feeling it was too late for him to change his "linguistic coat."

[12] Gerhard Fischer, "Editor's Note," in *W.G. Sebald. Schreiben ex patria / Expatriate Writing*, ed. Gerhard Fischer (Amsterdam, New York: Rodopi, 2009), 12.

[13] Gerhard Fischer, "Introduction: W.G. Sebald's Expatriate Experience and His Literary Beginnings," *W.G. Sebald. Schreiben ex patria / Expatriate Writing*, ed. Gerhard Fischer (Amsterdam, New York: Rodopi, 2009), 21.

[14] Peter Madsen, "World Literature and World Thoughts: Brandes/Auerbach," *Debating World Literature*, ed. Christopher Prendergast (London; NY: Verso, 2004), 74.

in Norwich, England. As part of his professional duties, he also founded and directed the British Centre for Literary Translation in 1989, housed at the UEA, Norwich. In his last years he also taught creative writing. Sebald did not officially begin his literary career until the late 1980s. He was, however, already writing poetry as a high school student and working on a novel as a university student. Hence his literary and scholarly interests and endeavors ran side by side. Florian Radvan, one of Sebald's PhD students at the University of East Anglia, recalls that his strongest impression of Sebald was that of a "Grenzgänger," who not only crossed but blurred and dissolved borders between literary criticism and literature, English and German, words and images, fiction and reality, biography and autobiography.[15]

In an interview with Christopher Bigsby, Sebald described how he was drawn away from academic writing to writing in a "more tentative sort of way,"

> I moved from the straight monograph to essayistic exploration, dealing with my subjects in an elliptical sort of way. But even so I constantly came up against a *borderline* where I felt, well, if I could go a little bit further it might get very interesting, that is, if I were allowed to make things up.[16]

Richard Weihe notes that the tension between being a scholar of literary studies and a writer was probably the most productive source for Sebald's fictional writing and how, as an author of fiction, Sebald was free and able, "Metaphern zu verwenden, Leben und Werk im Sinne des sonst verpönten Biografismus als Einheit zu verstehen, und vor allem die Subjektivität des Schreibenden zu betonen, indem er laut und deutlich "ich" sagt."[17]

This move from literary criticism to literature is not without its risks, however. Academics who make a "career change" to writing fiction are, to put it mildly, often viewed with suspicion. As Radvan notes, "Als Hochschullehrer, der auch literarisch schrieb, wäre [Sebald] in der deutschen Akademia wohl misstrauisch beäugt, wenn nicht belächelt und wären seine Texte als Professorenprosa abgetan worden."[18] This clichéd image of an academic turned author has been used to describe Sebald, although he was working parallel on scholarly and literary projects. This skeptical, even dismissive, attitude towards professors turned authors is certainly a contributing factor to the slower reception of his works in Germany, as opposed to their positive reception outside of Germany, especially in England, the United States and France.

---

[15] Florian Radvan, "W.G. Sebald—Schriftsteller und Scholar. Erinnerungen an einen Grenzgänger zwischen Literatur und Wissenschaft," *Kritische Ausgabe* 13, 18 (2010): 58.

[16] Sebald in Bigsby, *Writers in Conversation*, 152; my emphasis.

[17] Richard Weihe, "Wittgensteins Augen. W.G. Sebalds Film-Szenario *Leben Ws*," *fair- Zeitung für Kunst und Ästhetik* 7, 4 (2009): 12.

[18] Radvan, "W.G. Sebald—Schriftsteller und Scholar," 58.

3. Transgressing the Borders of, and within, the Text: Discourse, Genre, Medium

With the borderline between literary criticism and literature in mind, we now turn to Sebald's literary texts and the way in which they demonstrate border crossing in several respects. At one and the same time imaginative fictions, biographical accounts, and autobiographical travelogues, Sebald's texts blur not only thematic but also generic boundaries. They draw upon a variety of disciplines and discourses, such as literature, literary analysis, history, architecture, and archaeology, among others. This movement across the borders of discourse, genre, and also media inscribes itself in a complex form of layering in Sebald's texts. It is the way in which Sebald explores and tests the borders between different discourses that provides new ways to reconsider the contentious and productive relationships between a number of issues and between literature and history in particular. With a vested interest in both representing the past and problematizing such representation—traditional forms of historiography in particular—a new form of literature-as-historiography, or "literary historiography," as I have termed it, emerges in Sebald's works.[19]

The problem of representation, in particular historical representation, is fundamental to Sebald's *œuvre* as a whole and is treated both explicitly and implicitly in his literary and critical works. By incorporating images, photographs in particular, in a complex manner and simultaneously reflecting on this within the literary form of his texts, Sebald thematizes the acts of seeing, remembering, and knowing, and thereby raises fundamental questions about literature's relationship to "truth" and "reality."[20] Theoretical and aesthetic questions pertinent to photography in general, and relevant to Sebald's unique text-image constellation in particular, are those of realism, authenticity, the documentation of history, and subsequently the writing of history.

In *Die Ringe des Saturn* (1995), a text that deals, among other things, with human atrocity and natural destruction, Sebald formulates an explicit critique of historical representation. The narrator in this book calls the purported truth of historiography into question, when he asserts, "schon zeigen sich in der Historiographie die unbestreitbaren Vorteile einer fiktiven Vergangenheit"[21] ["in historiography, the indisput-

---

[19] See Lynn Wolff, "Literary Historiography: W.G. Sebald's Fiction," in *W.G. Sebald: Schreiben ex patria / Expatriate Writing*, ed. Gerhard Fischer (Amsterdam; New York: Rodopi, 2009), 317-332.

[20] Various articles have treated Sebald's use of photography from multiple theoretical perspectives while almost always commenting on his particular blend of verbal and pictorial discourses. See for example: Heiner Boehncke, "Clair obscur. W.G. Sebalds Bilder," *W.G. Sebald. Text + Kritik* (2003): 43-62; Carolin Duttlinger, "Traumatic Photographs: Remembrance and the Technical Media in W.G. Sebald's *Austerlitz*," in *W.G. Sebald. A Critical Companion*, ed. J.J. Long and Anne Whitehead (Seattle, WA: University of Washington Press, 2004), 155-171; Silke Horstkotte, "Pictorial and Verbal Discourse in W. G. Sebald's *The Emigrants*," *Iowa Journal of Cultural Studies* 2 (2002): 33-50.

[21] W.G. Sebald, *Die Ringe des Saturn. Eine englische Wallfahrt* (Frankfurt/M.: Fischer Taschenbuch Verlag, 2003) [1995], 91.

able advantages of a fictitious past have become apparent"[22]. This counter-logical formulation shows that to preserve the truth of historiography, extralinguistic reality must be, by necessity, fictitious. Since this cannot be true, the narrator points to a certain degree of fictionality that is inevitable in historical accounts. The role of both imagination and invention implied here comes to the fore when the narrator describes pictorial representations of great battles in history and asserts them to be "pure Fiktionen"[23] ["without exception figments of the imagination"[24]]. The critique of historical representation, be it in historical texts or paintings, is consistent across Sebald's fiction and is thematized in essay form as well, such as in *Luftkrieg und Literatur* (1999), the revised and published form of his lectures on poetics given in Zurich in 1997. Structurally and rhetorically reminiscent of passages in *Die Ringe des Saturn*, Sebald's *Luftkrieg und Literatur* presents the reader with facts and statistics as part of the historical record of the Allied air raids on Germany at the end of World War II. Yet, any degree of certainty we may gain through this historical proof is then undermined when we are confronted with Sebald's statement: "doch was all das in Wahrheit bedeutete, das wissen wir nicht"[25] ["but we do not grasp what it all actually meant"[26]]. In critiquing historical representation, Sebald reveals and thus challenges the illusion that knowledge of the past can be easily, or directly, accessed through documents and accounts. Rather than discounting the truth value of such forms of evidence, Sebald is concerned with emphasizing the processes of mediation and interpretation that are involved in any form of historical representation.

Of further import to Sebald's critique of historical representation is the fact that official forms of historiography often overlook, and thereby silence, the "unimportant" figures of the past. Sebald puts this critical position towards historiography into practice in his literary works. Countering official historiography's erasure of individual fates, Sebald focuses on "emigrants," exiles, and, broadly stated, the victims of history. Furthermore, he endows his "factional"[27] stories with the weight usually attributed to historical accounts. *Die Ausgewanderten* (1992) and *Austerlitz* (2001) exemplify this process, for they blend "facts" and "fiction" while trying to cope with the problematic source of memory, be it individual or collective, and the repression, recovery, and representation of this memory.

Questions of authenticity and representation are at stake in this critique of historical representation and gain an increased immediacy through Sebald's particular use

---

[22] W.G. Sebald, *The Rings of Saturn*, trans. Michael Hulse (New York: New Directions, 1999) [1998], 71. This comment by the narrator is inserted at the end of a long passage in which he seamlessly quotes from Jorge Luis Borges' *Tlön, Uqbar, Orbis Tertius*.

[23] Sebald, *Die Ringe des Saturn*, 95.

[24] Sebald, *The Rings of Saturn*, 76.

[25] W.G. Sebald, *Luftkrieg und Literatur. Mit einem Essay zu Alfred Andersch* (Frankfurt am Main: Fischer Taschenbuch Verlag, 2003) [1999], 11.

[26] W.G. Sebald, *On the Natural History of Destruction*, trans. Anthea Bell (New York: Random House, 2003), 4.

[27] Peter Craven, "W.G. Sebald: Anatomy of Faction," *HEAT* 13 (1999): 212-224.

of images. The text-image relationship that is characteristic of Sebald's works is also constitutive of his poetics of engagement in the way in which it engages the reader on various levels. The images used by Sebald are predominantly, though not exclusively, photographs. Interspersed in his narratives we also find reproductions of paintings, schematic maps, pages from journals, diaries, and other books. The types of photographs that are found in Sebald's works include family snapshots and personal portraits as well as photographs of coincidental *objets trouvés* and personal possessions, ranging from the mundane to the significant. Contrasting these personal pictures are photographs of architectural structures, landscapes, and cityscapes, where individuals are strikingly absent. Sebald's complex use of images does not follow one consistent strategy, and the relationship between the text and its images is not static, but rather it shifts and changes as we read, creating multiple layers to the story and thus requiring multiple levels of analysis. That is to say, the text-image relationship must be read intratextually: the relationship of the image to the story, extratextually: the relationship of the images to an extratextual reality, and intertextually: the images and text in relation to other texts, be they literary or documentary. Sebald's use of *ekphrasis* as well as his characters' theoretical questioning of how time and space are experienced and represented provide ways to consider the medial difference between the visual and the textual and the relationship among images, imagining and imagination. Just as Sebald places historical figures alongside fictional characters to explore the ontological status of the "real," his use of photographs illustrates the multiple relationships among intra-, inter-, and extra-textual realities at play in fictional representations. Sebald's works demonstrate the potential of the literary discourse to not only re-present something ontologically prior to the text but to also present something new that comes into being only with(in) the text. While making us reconsider the border that delineates the world of creation within the text from the world of reference outside of the text, Sebald's fictional prose ultimately works against such clear distinctions.

Challenging the association of photography with authenticating an extratextual reality and the notion of photographs as a visual *aide-mémoire*, the photographs or, more broadly, the images in Sebald's text activate the imagination of both the characters as well as the readers and provide an impetus for narrative. Susan Sontag, in her book *On Photography*, has shown how photographs have been seen as the "most realistic, therefore facile, of the mimetic arts,"[28] but she also works against this illusion of photography as a direct (i.e. "accurate") objective representation of reality by reiterating the importance of angle and perspective. In short, a photograph is never neutral because there is already an interpretation implicit in the act of taking the photograph. In this way, we can understand Sebald's *Austerlitz* in particular as a text that works against a simplistic understanding of *mimesis* as imitation or direct reflection; for the images, the photographs in particular, actually prove more deceptive than revealing. For example, the closer the eponymous character examines

[28] Susan Sontag, *On Photography* (New York: Farrar, Straus and Giroux, 1977), 51.

photographs and film stills, the more obscured his vision becomes and the further away he feels from the referents. It has been argued that Sebald's narratives reveal "the mendacity or mystery [....] of visual images."[29] I would agree and push this point further by saying that Sebald's fiction lays claim to a certain kind of truth that is only possible through literature. Sebald's writing reveals the potentiality of fiction and offers a rewriting of German history and the Holocaust in particular with an emphasis on individual experience, memory and imagination.

4. Conclusion: Expanding the Borders of Knowledge through World Literature

W.G. Sebald is an author who represents a cosmopolitan consciousness that does not reject the specificity of the nation. In transcending national concerns while at the same time putting particular emphasis on some very specific concerns of German history, Sebald's works possess an inner tension. It is this tension between the global and the local that marks these works as part of world literature. While Sebald's status as a "Holocaust" author has been fiercely debated, one cannot dispute the central position this atrocity holds in his works. However, as stated above, Sebald goes beyond the particular twentieth-century European atrocity of the Holocaust, in writing of the violence of the Belgian colonial oppression in the Congo, the capitalist exploitation of the Amazon forests, and the massacres caused by Napoleon's military campaigns. Furthermore, trauma is not limited to human experience. Sebald devotes much attention to conjecturing about the pain and suffering of animals and insects and considers the destruction of nature in general. He does not privilege the human being above all other forms of life. Rather, his concern is with life in all its forms and is, in this sense, as much an ecological as well as a global vision. Although we could see the limits of Sebald's "world" on a cosmic scope, we cannot broaden our view without any bounds, for a tension remains between the global and specific concerns of individuals and distinct moments in history. By examining Sebald as an author of world literature—an author writing "literary works that circulate beyond their culture of origin"[30]—while also accounting for the specificity of his texts,[31] we can continue to work within the idea(l) of world literature, as Goethe envisaged, without dissolving it.

Lynn L. Wolff
llwolff@wisc.edu

---

[29] Russell J[ames] A[ngus] Kilbourn, "Architecture and Cinema: The Representation of Memory in W.G. Sebald's *Austerlitz*," in *W.G. Sebald: A Critical Companion*, ed. J.J. Long and Anne Whitehead (Seattle, WA: University of Washington Press, 2004), 152.

[30] David Damrosch, *What is World Literature?* (Princeton: Princeton University Press, 2003), 4.

[31] In his philology of *Weltliteratur*, Auerbach emphasizes the need to consider context, history, and culture in order to properly understand a body of literature. Erich Auerbach, "Philologie der Weltliteratur," in *Philologie der Weltliteratur. Sechs Versuche über Stil und Wirklichkeitswahrnehmung* (Frankfurt am Main: Fischer, 1992), 83-96.

Mathieu Denis
Centre canadien d'études allemandes et européennes, Université de Montréal

Ulrich Ufer
Centre canadien d'études allemandes et européennes, Université de Montréal

Boundaries have always been a part of how people have understood and made sense of their environment. The most fundamental kind of boundary comes in the form of natural geography, which imposed physical boundaries which were either impossible, or difficult, to cross before the advent of modern transportation. By contrast, the imposition of social order represents another kind of boundary. In the attempt to establish order, social organizations have always demarcated their spheres of power, influence and activity, thus implementing and setting up cultural boundaries. And on a psychological and spiritual level, boundaries between imagination and reality, between life and death and between the seen and unseen, have never ceased to intrigue and obsess humankind. Liminality, and hence the recognition of boundaries is what anthropologists call a common human experience;[1] its meaning varies according to cultural contexts. In this sense, boundaries can be a means towards the end of political sovereignty and a way of stabilizing individual identity. Boundaries can be understood as protective shields against unwelcome intrusions and intruders and as simple brute facts about the world that help to bind a specific community. From another perspective, boundaries can also be criticized and deplored as limits to human activities, or they can be perceived as obstacles which stimulate the capacity and the motivation to surmount them.

1. CONSTRUCTING AND DECONSTRUCTING BOUNDARIES IN MODERNITY

Western modernity has put great emphasis on boundary crossing, which it regarded as a promise of advancement. One of the clearest expressions of this approach was formulated long ago by Frederick J. Turner in his 1893 essay on the significance of the frontier in American history. As a meeting point between savagery and civilization, Turner regarded the frontier as the "line of most rapid and effective Americanization," a purifying process by which the European colonists were first stripped of their culture by the wilderness, but eventually became the greatest defenders of republicanism and democracy at home and in the world.[2] But before striding frontiers on the track to the West would become the symbol of American territorial expansion and its transgressive ideology, distant places offered themselves

[1] Victor Turner, *The Ritual Process. Structure and Anti-Structure* (Chicago: Aldine, 1969).
[2] Frederick J. Turner, *The Significance of the Frontier in American History* (London: Penguin, 2008) [1893].

as a screen on which to project possible solutions to present dissatisfactions at home. The imaginary Asia as a land of plenty in early modern times, for example, incited many individuals to seek fortune in the service of East India Companies.[3] Utopian literature of the sixteenth and seventeenth centuries favored far away islands as settings for the ideal society and emphasized the dangerous maritime passage that had to be undertaken to reach them. On the frontispiece of Francis Bacon's 1627 scientific program for a new science, *Nova Atlantis*, the idea that stimulation for progress must be sought beyond the horizon was allegorically expressed by the image of a ship returning with full-blown sails through the pillars of Heracles, bringing back knowledge and discoveries from distant lands. *Gulliver's Travels* by Jonathan Swift (1726) is a classic example of political satire in which the crossing of boundaries and the resulting estrangement serves to criticize a specific social order back home in the writer's native land.

The transgression of temporal borders is equally important in the culture of modernity. Overcoming traditions and reassuring that a break with the past has been made qualifies the modernist outlook just as much as its future-bound perspective. The first futuristic utopia *L'an deux mille quatre cent quarante. Rêve s'il en fût jamais*, published by Luis-Sébastien Mercier in 1771, helped to establish a view of time which would prove essential for the future-bound ideology of social change propagated by revolutionary French society in the following decades. Similarly revolutionaries of the nineteenth century, Karl Marx and others, insisted on breaks and ruptures in human history, which they regarded as the most significant historical events. In the early twentieth century the German intellectual Walter Benjamin considered the painting *Angelus Novus* by Paul Klee as emblematic of the propulsive (and destructive) forces of modernity, driving modern man unremittingly into the future and into the new.[4] The very notion of innovation as a positively connoted means to overcome limits imposed by tradition, and its close association with concepts of progress and development is no more than two centuries old.[5] The paradox is that, through the very processes of abating borders, modern Western societies were erecting new ones at the same time. Boundaries are a condition of the establishment and maintenance of social order and individual identity. The transgression or elimination of some boundaries paradoxically involves building new ones in their place.

The modern nation state of the nineteenth and twentieth centuries has defined itself by exercising sovereignty over a territorial unit and by people who shared a common mindset. The process of nation-building also involves erecting racial

---

[3] Ulrich Ufer, *Welthandelszentrum Amsterdam. Globale Dynamik und modernes Leben im 17. Jahrhundert* (Cologne: Böhlau, 2008), 87-88.

[4] Walter Benjamin, "Über den Begriff der Geschichte," in *Gesammelte Schriften Vol.* I.2 (Frankfurt am Main: Suhrkamp, 1980), 691-704.

[5] Benoît Godin, "Meddle Not With Them That Are Given to Change," Innovation as Evil. Working Paper no. 6, Project on the Intellectual History of Innovation (Montreal: INRS. 2010).

boundaries and delimitating which ethnicities are national and which are not.[6] In their most extreme formulations these racial boundaries took the form of an essentialized biological division within the human species, as has been the case in some nation-states, colonies, even in former colonies with respect to their own minorities.[7]

This discussion of boundaries can also be extended to science. The three key elements of modern science (quantification, mensuration and specialization) provide further instances of how transgressing boundaries (in this case, the limits to knowledge), resulted in the production of new ones. It is not so much that these limits withdraw with each advance of knowledge; rather that, each answer to a set of problems opens the way to a few dozens more while making new limits apparent. Building on the fundamental boundary which Cartesian philosophy had drawn between the human subject and a nature perceived as a distinct object, the rise of nomothetic science over the course of the nineteenth century implanted a strict separation between the measurable and the non-measurable aspects of the world by dividing the search for truth from search for the good, the just or the beautiful. Concentrating on the quantifiable and the measurable, taxonomies drew ever finer borders, grouping clusters and variances within sub-groups. Modern science's inherent drive to erect boundaries and to categorize the world impacted on the constitution of science itself when its actors created distinctions between different branches of knowledge that would henceforth serve a splintered academic perception of the world.[8] Disciplining the sciences, however, leads to contradictory effects in the long run when knowledge actors hide behind the fences of their disciplinary paradigms. As Thomas Kuhn noted, accepting the latter uncritically leads researchers to "puzzle solving" within thought determining and thought limiting frameworks instead of "problem solving" by finding innovative solutions outside the box.[9] Andrew Abbott has argued convincingly that those successive divisions and subdivisions did not represent any progress but rather never-ending circles around a limited number of issues and principles. His history of the social science disciplines as a continuous redrawing of the same boundaries (along fractal patterns) leads him to argue that the boundaries between the disciplines are far less significant than broadly believed.[10] Recently calls for trans-, multi-, pluri-, and interdisciplinary research have

---

[6] Paul R. Spickard, *Race and Nation: Ethnic Systems in the Modern World* (New York, Oxford: Routledge, 2005).

[7] Michèle Ducharme, "The Canadian Origins of South African Apartheid?," in *Currents – Readings in Race Relations* 3, 4 (1986): 2.

[8] Immanuel Wallerstein, *Open the Social Sciences. Report of the Gulbenkian Commission on the Restructuring of the Social Sciences* (Stanford, CA: Stanford University Press, 1996), 13-29.

[9] Thomas Kuhn, *The Structure of Scientific Revolutions* (Chicago: University of Chicago Press, 1962), 35-38.

[10] Andrew Abbott, "The Chaos of Disciplines," in *Chaos of Disciplines* (Chicago: University of Chicago Press, 2001).

multiplied and become central in national and international research programs.[11] It is expected in these times of economic crises and contested economic leadership that transcending the limits of specialization might provide innovative answers to the actual problems of society. In the wake of such discussions, the concepts of boundaries and borders themselves have become subjects of study in the social sciences.[12]

As with nation states and sciences, the economy is tearing down boundaries as much as it is erecting new ones. We are far from observing the fulfillment of the neoliberal ambition of a world bereft of borders, open to free circulation of capitals, goods, services, and persons. While modernization theory held that borders between rich and poor would be transcended in time though the forces of development, dependency theory and world system analysis have enlightened us as to how such borders constituted structural properties of the world system throughout capitalism's long history.[13] The division of labor involves borders delimitating the different steps from investment to production, and to purchase and accumulation of profit. These borders are spatial and social and assign definite tasks to specific peoples and regions, thereby also creating systemic variance with regard to participation in the creation and appropriation of surplus value.

The workings of this basic pattern can be illustrated by the earliest waves of economic globalization during the constitutive phase of the modern world system which were driven to a large extent by price differentials on the sixteenth and seventeenth century world market: Central American silver and gold, acquired and transported at the minimum cost of labor by the Spaniards gained massively in value when entering the European trade cycle and were valued even higher when entering the East Asian market, where bullion was rarer and buyers were prepared to pay double the European price.[14] Even though global silver markets integrated over time and world market prices converged towards the end of the seventeenth century,[15] the strategy of connecting different economic zones and thus exploiting the borders created by market differentials would remain a basic requirement for the dynamic of capitalism. Today, the existence, maintenance and new production of economic borders still drives globalization – in the sense of the migration of labor, production sites and capital movements – by separating and re-connecting zones of low costs of production (labor, inputs, taxation) and zones with higher living standards that allow higher profits on the consumer market.

---

[11] UNESCO, *The World Social Science Report 2010 – Knowledge Divides* (Paris: UNESCO Publishing, 2010), chapter 10.

[12] Michèle Lamont and Virág Molnár, "The Study of Boundaries in the Social Sciences," *Annual Review of Sociology* 28 (2002), 167-195.

[13] Immanuel Wallerstein, *The Modern World-System,* vol. 1-2. (New York: Academic Press, 1974, 1980).

[14] Dennis Flynn and Arturo Giraldez, "Born with a "Silver Spoon." The Origin of World Trade in 1571," *Journal of World History* 6, 2 (1995): 201–222.

[15] Matao Miyamoto and Yoshiaki Shikano, "The Emergence of the Tokugawa Monetary System in East Asian International Perspective," in *Global Connections and Monetary History, 1470-1800,* ed. Dennis Flynn, Arthur Giraldez and Richard von Glahn (Aldershot: Ashgate, 2003), 169-187.

2. BEYOND THE BOUNDARIES OF MODERNITY?

The continuous erection of new borders, boundaries and frontiers is very much part of the modern project. For many observers of current affairs, we would now have entered a new period in which the world would have become boundless thanks to the ongoing process of globalization. Some commentators such as the widely read journalist Thomas L. Friedman even discern a leveling process that does away with obstacles, frontiers and confines creating this seemingly flat world facilitating the movement of people, commodities, money and information, and resulting arguably in a new "cultural hybridity." This discreet charm of globalization and its concurrent linguistic expressions of openness and transcendence of boundaries are communicated through the images and imaginaries of international media and are reinforced by the experience of a world coming to one's home through the computer screen. The notion of a boundless world has also been consolidated by easier and more frequent travel for business people and tourists. Such representations of a "flat" and boundless world as the common lot to humankind in the late twentieth and early twenty-first centuries are being rightfully questioned. They belong to a socially positioned discourse about the world and only pertain to a few cosmopolitan elites. This social stratum could summarily be classified as coming predominantly from Western urban upper- and middle-class households with above average income and educational background. At the very top of this stratum one could find those working in international business, media and science.[16] They may represent about 0.1% of the world's population.

The manner in which the world has been made smaller through the use of electronic communication is often cited as an example of the erosion of borders. The number of Internet users has been growing by about 450% in the last decade. Yet only a mere 28.7% of the world's population has some access to the Internet. In the Middle-East, Asia and Africa these rates have increased over the same period, to reach 29.8%, 21.5% and 10.9% respectively. There are over 5 billion people living in Africa, the Middle East and Asia and among them only 20% share the experience of using the Internet including those with only limited and temporary access, and those that have some form of access but at a high cost and often outside their home.[17]

Similarly, only those with the right passport and those working for multinational companies or within other international professional infrastructures can experience this "boundless" world of global collaborations and affairs. They commute between urban global centers where they frequent the cosmopolitan quarters, eat the same food, buy the same consumer goods, communicate in a shared *lingua franca*, but overall barely engage with their local environment. Tourists are in a similar position, as tourism mostly only offers a narrow experience of otherness and the social settings

---

[16] Jonathan Friedman, "Globalization, Class and Culture in Global Systems," *Journal of World Systems Research* 6, 3 (2000): 652-655.

[17] http://www.internetworldstats.com/stats.htm

developed for tourists share very little with the world of those who provide them with services.[18] Furthermore, tourism remains an activity restricted to populations with enough time and money. The discourse about today's apparent boundless global culture ignores such limits just as much as criticism and fears of a McDonaldization of international cultures turn a blind eye to questions of social hierarchies, classes and cultural exclusions. Identifying the experience of a flat world as pertaining to a cosmopolitan elite helps to understand to what extent the world is replete with obstacles for the greater majority. Anna Tomaszewska's study of Ukrainian border crossers at Polish borders and of the difficulties they encounter in the wake of EU expansion to the East certainly enlightens us as to how the existence of national borders remains relevant even in this context of global communication. In contradiction to scenarios of open boundaries, celebrated by neoliberal globalization discourses, this border, just like so many others, involves even stronger border controls than before.

3. Border scenarios

The studies by David Simo, Ma Jian or Sarah Colvin, each in their own way, illustrate how languages and literatures show different sensitivities to the border and the boundary, both as a metaphor and as a real life phenomenon. The trilingual character of this journal, *Eurostudia,* entices etymological considerations about possible border scenarios involving the border itself, border-crossers and boarder-guards. The meanings and usages of the notions of *borders, Grenzen* and *frontières* are broadly consistent with one another. While *borders* refer primarily to physical limits the word can also be used synonymously with *boundaries* which indicate the bounds or limits of anything whether material or immaterial. The same can be said of the German *Grenze,* and the French *frontière* or *limite* whose semantic field encompasses physical and metaphorical zones of contact including geographical areas, political units, fields of knowledge, and shared values.

The exhaustive Oxford English Dictionary does not acknowledge the existence of *border-crossers* or *boundary-crossers,* and yet they are a common phenomenon. The border-crosser, though, differs in important respects from the German *Grenzgänger* whose activity is not restricted to the crossing of borders. In fact, the border passage (*Grenzübergang*) is only one aspect of the *Grenzgang.* As Sabine von Mering also suggests by her usage of the term in her article on Jewish-German relations, a *Grenzgang* may also entail a particular approach to the *Grenze,* where there is a lingering along the border and possibly an appreciation of the sensation of in-betweenness itself. The latter meaning only re-emerges in the English language through the expressions *walking the border,* or *walking the line,* which cannot be turned into a noun. In French, the meaning of *le passeur* is largely restricted to the one who

[18] Jean-Paul Dumont, "A Matter of Touristic "Indifférence"," in *American Ethnologist* 11, 1 (1984): 139-151.

merely traverses the border, a commuter. It cannot be used to depict someone interested in the study of borders or in the experience of the border scenario as such. The difficulty in grasping in translation the multi-faceted connotations of the German term *Grenzgänger* is underlined by the divergent meanings of its direct renderings in French where the metaphorical *dépasser ses limites* means more of an enterprise beyond one's capacities and where the more concrete *passage de la frontière* refers, again, solely to the act of crossing the border.

In recognition of the existence of cultural barriers, the *Grenzgänger* has been professionalized by governments, NGOs and transnational companies in the figure of the *cultural mediator* (*Kulturvermittler* or *attaché culturel*). Mediating between different cultures requires constant transitory movement. But in order to facilitate understanding through communicating cultural particularities from one side to the other, generalization can hardly be avoided. Explaining cultural differences or translating between cultures the cultural mediator must constitute cultures as entities and typify their elements from his or her own perspective when suggesting contrasts and comparisons. The cultural mediator thus easily turns into a disseminator of personal experiences and opinions – stereotypical visions are much more easily transmitted than presentations that take into account the multiple discourses and controversies over the attribution of cultural meaning. As border-transitions and mediation across borders is always followed by new limitations and by the construction of new boundaries, the impossibility of avoiding essentializing cultures in trans-border communication poses a self-contradictory threat to the profession of the cultural mediator: the very task of helping to overcome cultural barriers may paradoxically also lead to their erection.[19]

Borders involve another possible scenario: the one where the gate-keeper shouts "Stop!". Administrations of modern nation states have called this figure *boarder guard*, *Grenzbeamter*, or *agent frontalier*. However, in all three languages it is the more antiquated term that reveals this figure's original purpose. The *customs officer* or *tollkeeper*, the *Zöllner* and the *douanier* reveal the fact that throughout a career that has lasted for millennia his or her primary duty involved collecting a payment for passage. The *toll-keeper*, *Zöllner*, *douanier* is the manifestation of those powers that create and maintain borders and at the same time collect the fee necessary to cross a given border. Crossing borders and boundaries presumes the capacity for payment of one kind or another. It also presumes leaving behind a token which in a pecuniary sense can simply be money, but in a more symbolic sense can include memories, valued objects, social networks, which are all aspects of identity.

Crossing borders is expensive, either in monetary, social, individual or symbolic terms. As Pierre Bourdieu has shown with his concept of habitus and the different

---

[19] Alexandra Hausstein, "Grenzgänge, Grenzziehungen und Grenzüberschreitungen. Überlegungen zur diskursiven Macht von Kulturmittlern," ed. Asociación Mexicana de Profesores de Alemán VII/VIII (Encuentro AMPAL. Memorias, Mexico, 2008), 12-17.

forms of capitals (economic, social, cultural), there is a close interdependence between social and symbolic boundaries. Climbing up the social ladder requires the acquisition of skills and manners necessary to adapt to a certain habitus into which one has not been born. And failure to read and understand symbolic boundaries may well cause failure to overcome social boundaries too. Similar to the fee paid when crossing state borders, the (cultural) capital necessary to cross social borders may well allow the social "tourist" only a short stay if his or her capital cannot buy permanent residency in the new social stratum. The *parvenu* is likely to lack the ease and nonchalance of the traditional possessors of a specific status. She or he runs the risk of falling into the traps of overdoing it, showing off and being cast out for having crossed the limits of what is considered acceptable.[20] In other words, the toll fee required does not relieve the persons crossing social boundaries from their former identity traits: they enter neither with a clean sheet, nor are they in a position of achieving immediate social inclusion. And yet, attempts to free oneself of the stigma of previous social position also forbid the return to this initial status. Fees are paid in both directions.

Boundaries transform what passes through them. In the process any object may become an exotic curiosity. This idea of "trash to treasure" once helped early European world trade when cheap trifles were exchanged for commodities of high value, and, allegedly, land for mirror and glass.[21] Exoticism increases the value of imports and the reputation of those who bring them. In an environment favorable to innovation, the border-crossers are received with anticipated trust in their capacity to innovate by doing things differently and by taking a fresh view on established conventions. Trash can become a treasure, but the opposite is also true. Positive expectations of newcomers can easily be turned upside down: valued, appreciated and needed on one side of the border, goods, commodities and people might be deprecated on the other. Such disdain is experienced by a great deal of global migrants and refugees.

From the perspective of the xenophobic, borders are the condition of security at home in an increasingly threatening and unpredictable world; they regard borders as embattled trenches rather than permeable transit zones. On the southern fringes of the US, at the Maghreb outposts of EU immigration control, or in urban gated communities, borders are erected as protective shields, thus promoting processes that have been described as "Balkanization."[22] Discursive exclusions can play a role similar to physical boundaries. Recent public debates in England and Germany, for

[20] Pierre Bourdieu, *Distinction. A Social Critique of the Judgement of Taste* (Cambridge, MA: Harvard University Press, 1984), 95.

[21] Alexandra van Dongen (ed.), *One Man's Trash is Another Man's Treasure. The Metamorphosis of the European Utensil in the New World* (Rotterdam: Museum Boymans-van Beuningen, 1996).

[22] Jonathan Friedman, "Transnationalization, Socio-Political Disorder, and Ethnification as Expressions of Declining Global Hegemony," in *International Political Science Review / Revue internationale de science politique* 19, 3 (1998): 233-250.

example, have shown prominent politicians disparaging immigrant groups for supposedly lacking the intelligence to learn the language and culture of residence.[23] As the study by Helen Williams shows, the appearance of such discourses sometimes indicates profound changes in the political culture of a country. These physical and discursive exclusions reveal the darker side of the otherwise often joyful cosmopolitan excitement about cultural hybridity and trans-border exchanges. "The stranger," Zygmunt Bauman writes aptly, "is constantly *ante portas* - at the gate; but it is the presumed ill-will of the stranger, of a stranger conspiring to trespass, to break in and invade, that makes the gate tangible."[24] Viewed with hostility the stranger's border crossing is often perceived as an intrusion and answered with strategies of exclusion. As Georg Simmel defined the stranger in his *Exkurs über den Fremden*, the stranger is the one who comes and stays, thus contrasting the visitor or the merchant whose arrival comprises, by definition, their not too distant departure.[25] In her analysis of the Anglo-German author W.G. Sebald, Lynn Wolff presents one such case of strangeness and estrangement in the case of an author who spent his life living between borders.

Borders transform that which passes through them, but borders themselves can be mobile too. As they move, borders transform localities. Some localities and the people who live there can be quite suddenly pushed back from the centre to the periphery; others, as a result of wars and changing geographies, become the object of great tensions. This transformation is exemplified by Elżbieta Opiłowska's analysis of Polish-German border towns. The history of the present day city of Lwiw in the Ukraine also bears witness to the shifts of political borders: over the past centuries it has stood on Galician (Lew), Polish (Lwów), Austrian (Lemberg), Polish again (Lwów), Russian (Lwow) and finally Ukrainian (Lwiw) territory.

Economic borders can move even more swiftly than political borders and even though flexibility counts among the key qualifications of the modern worker,[26] the geographic reorganization of the division of labor can leave behind a majority of employees unable to move and migrate at equal pace. Such is the case when financial investment, or economic and industrial activity abandon once thriving area as, for example, the Ruhr region in central Germany. Here, the misery of losing jobs, individual status and social continuity descended upon hundreds of thousands of miners and their families during the past twenty or thirty years and did not necessitate any active border crossing or migration on their part.

---

[23] Markus Porsche-Ludwig, "Sarrazin und die Verletzung der Meinungsfreiheit," in *Zur Sache Sarrazin*, ed. Jürgen Bellers and Henry Broder (Berlin: LIT, 2011), 41.

[24] Zygmunt Bauman, *The Individualized Society* (Cambridge: Polity Press, 2001), 92.

[25] Georg Simmel, "Exkurs über den Fremden (1908)," in *Untersuchungen über die Formen der Vergesellschaftung. Georg Simmel Gesamtausgabe*, ed. Otthein Ramstedt, vol. 11 (Frankfurt am Main: Suhrkamp, 1992), 764-771.

[26] Richard Sennet, *The Corrosion of Character, The Personal Consequences Of Work In the New Capitalism.* (New York: Norton, 1998).

4. URBAN BORDER REGIMES

Borders need to be understood as socially embedded and contextualized phenomena and the best site for their study is neither the self-evident barrier nor the tollhouse, but the city as a place where economic, cultural and social border regimes are manifested in more subtle ways. In fact, the history and present situation of Germany's Ruhr region as an urban agglomeration, and of the quarter Duisburg-Marxloh in particular, provide worthwhile examples for how the border problematic of modern culture is inscribed into the city's social, cultural and economic topographies.

Stretching out along the river Ruhr between the towns of Münster, Hamm and Wuppertal to the north, east and south, and the river Rhine to the West, the Ruhr region has approximately 5.2 million citizens. With the beginning of coal mining during the early nineteenth century and the following settlement of iron and steel industries in the region, small towns like Dortmund and even villages of sometimes only a few hundred peasants, like Gelsenkirchen, turned into large towns over the span of only a few decades. Over the course of the twentieth century, they would grow to sizable cities and finally merge into the present *Metropolenregion*. Extreme demographic increase and the intensification of mining and steel industries were only possible on the basis of massive immigration. A first wave of immigrant labor arrived from the politically divided Polish territory, from Masuria and from East Prussia during the last decades of the nineteenth, and around the turn of the twentieth, century, when German industrialization gained momentum. Already by the 1890s over 25% of the Ruhr region's working population was of eastern European descent and by 1915 this figure had risen to nearly 35%.[27]

The immigrants' arrival reproduced linguistic and cultural differences within the growing cities. Far from integrating into a simple melting-pot, migrants set up societies in which they continued cultural activities from their homes and passed on a sense of identity to subsequent generations. By 1914 the "Ruhrpolen" were organized in over 1.000 societies, they printed their own newspapers and had established the third largest miners' labor union of the Ruhr area.[28] From the point of view of the region's native peasant population of the mid and late nineteenth century, migrant workers and their cultural societies as well as the whole industrial venture itself were perceived as intruders who increasingly compromised their traditional agricultural world. While most Polish societies had managed to survive increasing nationalism during the First World War by showing solidarity to the German cause, their members were exposed to enforced cultural assimilation and increasing hostility among the German labor force during the interwar years. After Germany's invasion of

[27] Figures quoted in Anna Versteegh, *De Onvermijdelijke Afkomst? De Opname van Polen in het Duits, Belgisch en Nederlands Mijnbedrijf in de Periode 1920-1930* (Hilversum: Verloren, 1994), 71.

[28] Klaus Bade, Pieter Emmer, Leo Lucassen and Jochen Oltmer (eds.), *Enzyklopädie Migration in Europa. Vom 17. Jahrhundert bis in die Gegenwart* München: Fink, 2007), 870.

Poland in 1939, migrant societies came under severe attack and were either outlawed and forced to close or had to adapt to nationalist propaganda.[29] A second wave of immigration beat the Ruhr region, when the young Federal Republic of Germany was in need of foreign labor to sustain the economy of its booming 1950s and 1960s. In this situation, border-crossers arrived from southern Europe, mainly from Italy and from Turkey, as guest workers recruited through bilateral treaties. As such they were expected to return eventually to their homelands, thus prolonging their status as strangers and complicating self-identification or acceptance by others as residents both in Germany and in the places they had left.

Cultural differences with distant geographical origins conglomerated and perpetuated in the cities of the Ruhr region. Today, the suburb Marxloh of the city of Duisburg is representative of how social, cultural, economic and other border regimes are manifested in the city. Rather than creating level and egalitarian hybridities as a result of global flows, the global processes of labor migration and economic long-term shifts should be understood as implementing local hierarchies and differentiation. Duisburg-Marxloh followed the general demographic trajectory of the Ruhr-region, growing from a small village of a few hundred peasants in the early nineteenth century into a suburb of nearly twenty thousand inhabitants today. Roughly one third of the quarter's present residents are foreigners and roughly two thirds have some form of migratory background. The number of Turkish residents is substantial and the quarter now accommodates Germany's largest Muslim community.

In a place that has been shaped by immigration over the past 120 years it would seem difficult to separate the native from the foreign. Nevertheless, cultural and, in particular, religious differences of the Muslim communities in Duisburg-Marxloh have in recent years redrawn the line between *us* and *them* and have raised the question whether the *native* should keep reign over the *foreign*. The public debate that most explicitly showed popular notions about the maintenance, alteration and re-erection of cultural borders concerned the building of the Merkez Mosque at Duisburg-Marxloh in 2008, and more particularly the height of its minaret and the question, whether a muezzin would be allowed to call to prayer.[30] From the point of view of the Muslim communities as well as of local politicians for integration, the mosque was a symbol of successful integration policies, being at the same time a sign of a growing sense of belonging and settlement on the one hand and a step towards institutional integration on the other. From the point of view of a group of residents that still identifies itself as local and claims supremacy in matters concerning the quarter's cultural identity, the mosque itself presented a manifestation of cultural intrusion. It seemed even more unacceptable that the minaret's height should exceed

[29] Ibid., 876-879.

[30] On the "Gebetsrufkonflikt" in Duisburg-Marxloh see e.g. Jörg Hüttermann, *Das Minarett. Zur politischen Kultur des Konflikts um Islamische Symbole* (München: Juventa, 2006), 180-186.

the tower of the nearby Catholic Church of Saint Peter and Paul. Out of respect for local sentiments, the Muslim community agreed on the compromise to build a smaller minaret, and to refrain from publicly calling to prayer through a muezzin.

Urban spaces are structured by multiple boundaries and Berlin offers a case in point insofar as its boundaries have resulted from a variety of willful and strategic implementations: something that Nofar Sheffi discusses in detail. In the Ruhr area, struggles over the definition of spatial boundaries around quarters with high numbers of immigrants such as Duisburg-Marxloh or Dortmund-Nordstadt have been acted out both on a pragmatic as well as on a discursive level. It is in particular through emotionalizing the urban landscape that new borders are erected. Duisburg-Marxloh has been marked by the stigma of a "no-go area" in the eyes of many inhabitants of the Ruhr area. Not only is there little incentive to take residence or to spend leisure in urban environments marked by an infrastructure of unemployment and impoverishment (run-down buildings, call centers, cell phone shops, take away eateries, gambling houses), but the quarter has so far also proved resistant to the habitual processes of gentrification which aims to attract artists to cheap studios and revelers to alternative nightlife and bars. Some of the discourses on the suburb by officials as well as by the wider public reflect the process of exclusion and stigmatization of which Marxloh has become a part. Even though crime rates in multi-ethnic Duisburg-Marxloh are not by any means higher than in other quarters of the Ruhr area with similar unemployment problems, both the local and national press have referred to the quarter as an "Angstraum" – a space of fear in which local population and even police forces feel threatened.[31] Marxloh is also often quoted in the conservative and right-wing media in which its multi-ethnic social composition is described as a "ticking time-bomb,"[32] which is then seen as representative for Germany as a whole.[33] Similar representations in media and public discourses concern the quarter around Viehofer Straße in the Ruhr city of Essen, which has also been quoted as a "gefährlicher Ort" (dangerous place).[34] By associating certain quarters and their inhabitants with emotions such as fear, aversion and contempt emotional border regimes create divisions and hierarchies in the city along lines that have already been indicated by wider concerns about security. Disturbances of the public order by crowds of unemployed youths, or street crimes by individuals and gangs easily get amalgamated in public discourse with fears over fundamentalist Islamic terrorism.[35]

Often reproached as setting up a "parallel society" and as being unwilling to integrate into a "German" society, the foreign communities of Duisburg-Marxloh

---

[31] Interview "Polizeipräsident Rolf Cebin: Kampf dem Angstraum," *Der Westen*, 29 August 2008.

[32] "Ist Duisburg-Marxloh ein "Wunder" oder eine "tickende Zeitbombe"?," *Blaue Narzisse*, 19 March 2010.

[33] "Das "Wunder von Marxloh" – mit Steuermillionen gefördert – heute ein Stützpunkt des Islamismus," *Deutschlandwoche*, 17 July 2010.

[34] "Die Angst der Polizisten in deutschen Städten," *Die Welt*, 28 July 2008.

[35] "Islamismus, Spenden aus Marxloh für die Hamas?," *Der Westen*, 15 July 2010.

ironically share many of the problems with those who draw the borders that separate strangers from locals. Unemployment rates have risen to 25% in Duisburg-Marxloh since the heavy industries began to withdraw from the Ruhr-region in the 1980s, and they equally concern Germans as well as Turkish, Polish, Bulgarian or other migrant groups. While the decline of the coal and steel industries weighs heavily on the whole region, the economic borders that separate Marxloh from more thriving parts of the Ruhr-area have become particularly visible in the context of the Ruhr region's activities as European Cultural Capital in 2010. As the centers of Ruhr cities like Dortmund, Essen, Duisburg and Bochum received relatively generous funding to make core areas presentable for visitors, this has only increased the contrast with disfavored suburbs. German retail chains and some international companies have provided the gloss of urban consumerism that brands so many city centers in look-alike fashion. While the slogan of the Ruhr city of Essen is "Die Einkaufsstadt" (the shopper's city), the European Cultural Capital has had no similar effects on Duisburg-Marxloh. Even though this is a site *par excellence*, where Europe's different cultures mix and confront one another and even though thematic links to Istanbul as the second of three European Cultural Capitals in 2010 were evident, Duisburg-Marxloh attracted very little attention by the organizers of the events.

5. Conclusion

Many discourses on the situation of today's global affairs negate the importance of borders and boundaries. Often such views have been influenced by neoliberal theories and cosmopolitan language which underline the importance, necessity and even stress the *de facto* reality of a boundless world. However, the essays of this special volume of *Eurostudia* on "Germany and Europe: Borders, and how to cross them," as well as this concluding chapter in particular, have shown that the picture is, in fact, much more complex. Modernity has its own traditions of tearing down boundaries and erecting new ones at the same time. As a Weberian ideal type, the border guard in its many guises seems to deserve more academic attention in the context of discussions of boundaries, border passages and intercultural phenomena. Also, the fact that border crossing is expensive, of which the border guard's natural function to collect the toll fee has reminded us, is only rarely addressed by the experts of global fluxes and transit cultures.

Mathieu Denis
dma@cmb.hu-berlin.de

Ulrich Ufer
ulrich.ufer@umontreal.ca